"Restaurant patrons looking for quality dining have Zagat to guide their cuisine needs. For the recruitment industry, the name is Weddle ... Peter Weddle that is."

American Staffing Association

Also By Peter Weddle

The Career Activist Republic

Work Strong: Your Personal Career Fitness System

Recognizing Richard Rabbit: A Fable About Being True to Yourself

Generalship: HR Leadership in a Time of War

Career Fitness: How to Find, Win & Keep the Job You Want in the 1990's

Postcards from Space: Being the Best in Online Recruitment
& HR Management (2001, 2005)

WEDDLE's Guide to Association Web Sites
(2002, biannually 2005-present)

WEDDLE'S Guide to Staffing Firms & Employment Agencies

WEDDLE's Directory of Employment-Related Internet Sites (annually
1999-2004, biannually 2005-2008)

Internet Resumes: Take the Net to Your Next Job

CliffsNotes: Finding a Job on the Web

CliffsNotes: Writing a Great Resume

WEDDLE's WIZNotes: Fast Facts on Job Boards
Human Resource Professionals
Engineering Professionals
Sales & Marketing Professionals
Finance & Accounting Professionals
Scientists
Managers & Executives
Women Professionals
Recent College Graduates

'Tis of Thee: A Son's Search for the Meaning of Patriotism

What People Are Saying About WEDDLE's Books & Services

As a Resource for Everyone:

"A wealth of useful, updated information"

Library Journal

"It's all excellent stuff"

CNN

"This book is a great resource. … It's like a travel guide to job boards."

Recruiter
BrassRing Systems

"Highly recommended!"

Richard Nelson Bolles
author of *What Color is Your Parachute?*

"WEDDLE's is the gorilla of knowledge and Web-sites when it comes to getting a job, managing human resources and recruiting on the Internet."

President
Stone Enterprises, Ltd

As a Resource for Recruiters & HR Professionals:

"WEDDLE's is a very useful tool that recruiters and HR professionals will find helpful."

Fortune Magazine

"When in doubt, consult WEDDLE's … an industry standard."

HRWIRE

"Your books are tremendously helpful to our recruiters. Keep up the fantastic work."

Recruiter
Harrahs

"I picked up *WEDDLE's Guide to Employment Web Sites* and want to recommend it to you … he lists a lot of relevant information that I can use to determine which sites to use."

> President
> DCI Technical Services

"I have a copy of *WEDDLE's Guide to Employment Web Sites*, which I find very useful and time saving."

> Recruiter
> CyberCable, France

As a Resource for Job Seekers & Career Activists:

"The *WEDDLE's Guide to Employment Web Sites* supplies clear, completely current information about each site's services, features and fees—helping users instantly determine which site best meets their needs. If you are looking for an objective guide to employment websites, ExecuNet recommends WEDDLE's Guide."

> ExecuNet
> The Center for Executive Careers

"I found your book in the public library. Recently, I purchased my own copy from Amazon. com. It is a terrific book for breaking down the complexity of looking for a job in the computer age. Thank you for writing this book."

> Job Seeker

"Here's one of the best Web-sites to visit and refer to regarding job-hunting. Look into it first … It'll provide you with a great competitive edge in the job market."

> Job Seeker, Washington, D.C.

"Hi, I just went to your Web-site and was blown away by all the neat material. It is presented so well and is very compelling—I could hardly resist ordering all of your books!!!"

> Career Counselor, JobWhiz

WEDDLE's

Guide

to

Employment Sites
on the Internet

2011/12

for:

Recruiters & HR Professionals
Job Seekers & Career Activists

Our 10th Edition!

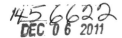
DEC 0 6 2011

ISBN: 978-1-928734-68-0

The information that appears in this Guide was obtained directly from the Web-sites themselves. Most of the data provided in the Consumer Profiles were collected in early 2011. Each site completed an extensive questionnaire about its services, features and fees and then certified the accuracy of its responses. The Internet changes quickly, however, and we work continuously to keep our information current. If you find a discrepancy in a site's profile, please notify WEDDLE's by telephone at 203.964.1888 or on the Internet at corporate@weddles.com. We will contact the site, obtain the correct information and publish it on our Web-site (www. weddles.com) in the Free Book Updates area.

Special thanks to the WEDDLE's research and production team and to our friends at VetJobs for their contribution to The Best & the Rest section of the book.

Special discounts on bulk quantities of WEDDLE's books are available for libraries, corporations, professional associations and other organizations. For details, please contact WEDDLE's at 203.964.1888.

WEDDLE's
www.weddles.com
2052 Shippan Avenue
Stamford, CT 06902

Where People Matter Most

Contents

Welcome to the 2011/12 WEDDLE's Guide!

Welcome to WEDDLE's 2011/12 Guide to Employment Sites on the Internet. This edition—our tenth—has been completely updated to deliver the information you need to survive and prosper in the challenging world of work of the 21st Century.

Today's job market stresses individuals and organizations alike. Job seekers are finding it extraordinarily difficult to find a new or better job. And, employers are struggling to find individuals with the talent they need to achieve their mission.

While there is no single solution to this problem, the Internet is a uniquely powerful resource than can assist both job seekers and employers. With over 100,000 job boards, social media sites and career portals now operating online, however, it's easy to waste your time on the wrong sites and overlook the right ones—the ones that will help you succeed.

That's why our WEDDLE's Guide has been specifically designed as a "consumer's aide." It is composed of two primary sections, each of which offers a one-of-a-kind reference for you to use.

- The first section of the book—**The Top 100**—features our picks for the best job boards, social media sites and career portals on the Web. This listing enables you to find the best sites quickly. Rather than lurching through thousands of search engine results, you can now "shop smart" and identify the right employment sites for you right away.

- The second section of the book—**The Best & the Rest**—is the single most comprehensive listing of employment sites in print. It enables you to conduct your own research and do so with precision. Instead of relying on the hit or miss experiences of friends and coworkers, you can explore the full range of sites that are likely to be helpful to you.

This format provides you with the most complete reference to the Web's employment resources available anywhere. It continues WEDDLE's tradition of publishing timely, accurate and useful information that will help you achieve the success you deserve on the Internet.

We hope you put the Guide to work for you and will tell others about it.

Peter Weddle
Stamford, Connecticut

An Important Note: The Internet, of course, is a dynamic medium and Web-sites often change between the publishing dates of our Guides. Indeed, the best sites are continuously updating their capabilities and improving their services. Whenever we become aware of a discrepancy in our published information about a site, we contact the site, obtain the correct information and then publish it on the WEDDLE's Web-site for you and others to see. So, visit www.weddles.com regularly. It and your Guide offer the best way to stay on top of the ever-changing universe of helpful employment resources on the Internet.

What is WEDDLE's?

WEDDLE's is a research, publishing, consulting and training firm specializing in organizational recruiting and human resource leadership and individual job search and career self-management.

❏ Since 1996, WEDDLE's has conducted groundbreaking surveys of:

- recruiters and job seekers, and

- Web-sites providing employment-related services.

Our research and findings have been cited in such publications as *The Wall Street Journal*, *The New York Times*, and in *Money*, *Fortune*, and *Inc.* magazines.

❏ WEDDLE's also publishes guides and other books that provide information and best practices for employers, staffing firms, job seekers, career activists, career counselors and coaches, reference librarians and academicians.

Its publications include:

- *The Career Activist Republic*

- *Work Strong: Your Personal Career Fitness System*

- *The All Pro Career Pocket Planner: The Career Fitness Regimen*

- *Recognizing Richard Rabbit: A Fable About Being True to Yourself*

- *The Success Matrix: Wisdom From the Web on Finding a Great Job*

- *Job Nation: The 100 Best Employment Sites on the Web*

- *Generalship: HR Leadership in a Time of War*

- *WEDDLE's Guide to Association Web Sites*

- *Postcards From Space: Being the Best in Online Recruitment & HR Management*

- *The Keys to Successful Recruiting and Staffing*

- *Finding Needles in a Haystack: Keywords for Finding Top Talent in Resume Databases*

- *WEDDLE's Guide to Staffing Firms & Employment Agencies*

- *WIZNotes: Fast Guides to Job Boards and Career Portals*

- *WIZNotes: Finding a Great Job on the Web*

- *WIZNotes: Writing a Great Resume*

For more information about these and other WEDDLE's publications, please visit its Web-site at Weddles.com. WEDDLE's books are available at your local bookstore, on Amazon.com and at the WEDDLE's site.

❑ WEDDLE's also provides consultation to organizations in the areas of:

- HR leadership,

- Human capital formation,

- Recruitment strategy development,

- Employment brand articulation & positioning,

- Recruitment process reengineering & optimization, and

- Web-site design, development and implementation.

❏ WEDDLE's delivers private seminars and workshops on the following subjects:

- Career self-management and success
  for HR professionals and recruiters
  for individuals in transition

- Best Practices in Internet recruiting
  for in-house corporate recruiters and managers
  for staffing firm recruiters and managers

- Optimizing the candidate experience

- Human Resource leadership.

Who is Peter Weddle?

Peter Weddle is a former recruiter and business CEO turned writer and speaker. He is the author or editor of over two dozen books and has been a columnist for *The Wall Street Journal, National Business Employment Weekly* and CNN.com. He has been cited in *The New York Times, The Washington Post, The Boston Globe, U.S. News & World Report, The Wall Street Journal, USA Today* and numerous other publications and has spoken to trade and professional associations and corporate meetings all over the world.

WEDDLE's Guides are widely recognized for their accuracy and usefulness, leading the American Staffing Association to call Weddle the "Zagat" of employment sites on the Internet.

How Does WEDDLE's Guide Work For You?

As always, your WEDDLE's Guide is a reference book that serves three important communities:

- **Those looking for talent**, including Employment Managers, in-house corporate recruiters and Human Resource practitioners, executive recruiters, staffing firm and agency recruiters, contract recruiters, and independent and consulting recruiters. If that's your job, this Guide will help you find and select the right job boards, social media sites and career portals to reach those individuals with the right skills for each of your recruiting requirements.

- **Those looking for employment opportunities**, including those actively searching for a new or better job, those setting the course for their career in the future, and those simply exploring the job market out of curiosity. Whether you're a first time job seeker or a mid-career professional, a senior executive or an hourly worker, whether you want a full time position or part time, contract, consulting or free agent work, this Guide will help you find the right job boards, social media sites and career portals to succeed at your employment objective.

- **Those who assist job seekers, career changers and individuals who seek greater fulfillment from their work**, including career counselors, coaches, and career and employment center staff professionals. If that's what you do, this Guide will help you find and select the job boards, social media sites and career portals that will best serve your clients in their job search campaigns and/ or quest for more meaningful and rewarding work.

Why do recruiters and HR professionals, job seekers and career activists, and career counselors and coaches need such a guide?

By our estimate, there are now over 100,000 employment-related Web-sites. Given that huge array of options, it's very difficult to know which sites are available and how to pick the best for a specific recruiting requirement or employment objective.

This Guide solves those problems. It introduces a wide range of the employment sites now operating online—in the United States and around the world—and provides the accurate, unbiased information that recruiters, job seekers and career counselors need to make smart choices among those sites.

How is the 2011/12 Guide Different?

This Guide continues WEDDLE's traditional commitment to accurate and useful employment information. In light of today's and tomorrow's challenging work environment, however, it is also both more focused—for fast and effective use—and more comprehensive—for thorough and precise research – than any other guide on the market.

It is composed of two sections:

The Top 100

This section lists the 100 best job boards, social media sites and career portals on the Internet today and provides detailed information about their services, features and fees for both recruiters and job seekers. There are, of course, other helpful employment destinations on the Web, but these sites are the elite.

To be considered for inclusion in The Top 100, a site must have completed an extensive questionnaire and be:

- a current or former winner of a WEDDLE's annual User's Choice Award (Please see page 55 for a description of these awards.);

    or

- a Member of the International Association of Employment Web Sites (Please see page 57 for a description of this organization.).

We use all of this information—plus the unique insight and experience Peter Weddle has accumulated during his 15+ years of observing the online employment services industry—to evaluate and select The Top 100 job boards, social media sites and career portals on the Internet today. But we don't stop there. We also provide this same information to you, so you can evaluate the sites for yourself and select the best of the best for you.

Each of The Top 100 sites is described in the Guide's full-page Consumer Profiles. These profiles look much like the easy-to-read-and-use descriptions that appear in popular travel guides. Each profile offers a detailed set of information carefully tailored to the needs of recruiters, job seekers and career counselors.

- For recruiters, this information includes each site's fees for posting a job and searching its resume database, the kinds of jobs it typically posts (i.e., full time, part time, contract, consulting), the geographic reach of its job postings, the number of people who visit the site each month, the number of resumes in its on-site database, where the site obtains those resumes, and much more.

- For job seekers and career counselors, this information includes the number and kinds of jobs that are posted on the site, the primary salary ranges and geographic locations of those jobs, whether the site has a resume or profile database, whether there is a fee to store a resume or profile in that database, whether the site takes steps to protect a person's confidentiality, and much more.

In addition, this section also provides a Cross Reference Index of the profiled sites that organizes them according to the career fields, industries and employment situations (e.g., free lance work) they cover. The Index is particularly important because Web-site names do not always accurately describe the full range of a site's capabilities and services.

The Best & the Rest

This section provides the most comprehensive directory of online employment destinations in the world. It lists over 10,000 sites and organizes them according to their occupational, geographic, industry or other specialty.

What are "online employment destinations?" They include:
- job boards,
- career portals,
- labor exchanges,
- resume databases,
- resume development and distribution sites,
- search engines that specialize in employment,
- professional and social networking sites,
- work or employment-related blogs, and
- any other site that provides employment services to individuals or employers over the Internet.

What are "employment services?" They include:
- Job postings and other employment advertisements,
- Resume and profile databases,
- Professional networking platforms,
- Career counseling information and services,
- Job search information and services, and
- Recruitment information and services.

Each site in The Best & the Rest is listed by its name and URL or Internet address.

So, whether you're looking for a job or for a talented new employee, whether you counsel those seeking a more meaningful occupation or you're working to advance your own career, this Guide can help you succeed. It provides the accurate, up-to-date and complete information you need to make smart choices among employment sites on the Internet. Said another way, WEDDLE's 2011/12 Guide to Employment Sites is a handy and reliable reference that can help you tap the extraordinary advantages of the Internet and put them to work for you.

What's In WEDDLE's Guide?

WEDDLE's 2011/12 Guide includes a number of useful resources and tools. There are, of course, **The Top 100** site profiles and **The Best & the Rest** directory of site listings. In addition, you'll find:

☑ **A Recruiter's Section** which provides an explanation of the Internet-specific recruitment terms used in the Guide and an introduction to our SmartSelect™ Process. This process provides a structured way for recruiters to make smart consumer decisions among employment service Web-sites. It's the best way we know to ensure you maximize the return you receive on your investment of time, effort and money on the Web.

☑ **A Job Seeker's & Career Counselor's Section** which provides an explanation of the Internet-specific job search terms used in the Guide and an introduction to our SmartSearch™ Process. This process provides a structured way for job seekers and career counselors to make smart consumer decisions among job boards and career portals. It will help you find those sites that are most likely to yield the best results in the pursuit of a specific employment objective.

☑ **WEDDLE's User's Choice Award Winners for 2011**. Each year, we invite recruiters and job seekers to visit the WEDDLE's Web-site (www.weddles.com) and cast their ballots for the best job boards and career portals on the Internet. The thirty (30) sites with the most votes are designated User's Choice Award winners, the pick of the toughest judges in the world—those who actually use the employment sites on the Internet.

☑ **An introduction to the International Association of Employment Web Sites (IAEWS)**. The IAEWS is the trade group for the global online employment services industry. Its members include the largest and best known job boards, social media sites and career portals in the world and a wide range of smaller, but equally as professional sites providing both general and specialized employment support. IAEWS Members deliver state-of-the-art services to both job seekers and employers, and no less important, they have pledged to adhere to the highest ethical and professional standards while doing so.

The Recruiter's & HR Professional's Section

Explanation of Terms

❏ Each site profile in The Top 100 identifies the site by its name, URL or address on the Internet, and its parent organization. Then, additional descriptive information is provided in six sections:

- **General Site Information**

- **Job Postings**

- **Resume Services**

- **Other Services**

- **Site's Self Description**

- **Contact Information**

The information that is included in each of these sections is described below.

❏ General Site Information

Date activated online: The date the site first appeared on the Internet or World Wide Web.

Importance to you: *Although not always the case, the longer a site has been in operation, the more developed its services and reliable its performance.*

Location of the site headquarters: The city and state in the United States or the city and country where the site's parent company or organization is located.

Importance to you: *A local address adds credibility to a site's claim that it reaches candidates in a specific geographic area.*

Number of people who
visit the site: The number of individuals who visit the site in a given month, with each person counted just once, regardless of how many times they came to the site. This metric is called unique visitors per month.

Importance to you: *Traffic numbers provide a reasonable estimate of the total potential candidate population you can expect to visit a site (and see the jobs you have posted there). Hence, they are similar to the audited circulation figures that recruiters use to gauge the likely yield from classified advertising. On the Internet, these numbers can also be used to compare and evaluate alternative sites.*

Time spent on site: The time visitors spend on a site measured in minutes per visit or in the number of pages of information that they view while there (page views per visitor).

Importance to you:	*This figure is an indication of a site's appeal to its visitors and thus its ability to capture their attention and draw them into the job ads posted there.*

❏ Job Postings

Post full time jobs:	Does the site post ads for full time positions?
Importance to you:	*Indicates whether the site's job posting service supports your recruiting requirement.*
Post part time/contract/ consulting jobs:	Does the site post ads for part time, contract and/or consulting positions?
Importance to you:	*Indicates whether the site's job posting service supports your recruiting requirement.*
Most prevalent types of jobs posted:	What are the predominant kinds of jobs currently being posted by recruiters?
Importance to you:	*Indicates the kinds of candidates that other recruiters are typically sourcing on the site. Their lessons-learned can be an effective guide for you.*

In some cases, abbreviations have been used to denote the kinds of jobs currently being posted on a site. These abbreviations are presented in the Table below.

Key to Career Field Abbreviations
Used in the Web Site Profiles

AD-Administrative

CM-Computer-related

CN-Communications

DP-Data Processing

EC-Electronic Commerce

EN-Engineering

FA-Finance/Accounting

HR-Human Resources

IS-Info Systems/Technology

MG-Management

OP-Operations

PG-Programming

SM-Sales/Marketing

Distribution:

What is the geographic focus of the site's job postings: regional, national, international?

Importance to you:

Indicates whether the site's reach supports the geographic specifications of your recruiting requirement.

Fee to post a job:

The cost to post a single job advertisement.

Importance to you:

To enable you to compare sites effectively, WEDDLE's lists the cost of posting a single job on the site for its standard posting period. Further, while many sites offer discount packages for multiple job postings over an extended period, it's best to "test" a site with a single posting to ensure that it can deliver the quantity and quality of candidates you need before agreeing to a long-term contract.

Posting period:

The period of time your posting will be visible on the site.

Importance to you:

The longer a position is visible on a site, the more likely it will be seen by your "dream candidate."

Link posting to your site:

Indicates whether your job posting can be connected electronically to your own site.

Importance to you:

Such connections or hyperlinks en-able you to provide additional infor-mation about your advertised oppor-tunity and thus better sell its value proposition and your employer to candidates.

❏ Resume Services

Are resumes or profiles posted on-site:

Indicates whether candidate informa-tion is stored on the site.

Importance to you:

Sites enable you to find prospective candidates by evaluating the creden-tials they have posted in a database on the site.

Number in database:

Indicates the number of resumes or profiles in the site's database.

Importance to you:

The larger the database, the higher the probability you will find candidates with exactly the skills you want.

Top occupations:

Indicates the most prevalent career fields or titles among the candidates with resumes or profiles in the site's database. (Please see the Table provided in the Job Postings section for a key to the abbreviations used in the Guide.)

Importance to you:

You will get the best results by using those sites where the database is strongest in the career fields or titles for which you are seeking candidates.

Fee to view resumes:

Indicates whether a fee must be paid to view the resumes/ profiles in the database, and if so, how much it is.

Importance to you:

Sites charge different prices for viewing and some offer job posting + resume search packages, so shop smart.

How acquired:

Indicates whether the resumes/profiles in the database are acquired directly from candidates, and/or by using software applications (called "spiders") to copy resumes from other sites, and/or from resume distribution companies that candidates pay to send out their resume via the Internet..

Importance to you:

The quality of a resume database is determined by the source of the resumes: the best—direct from candidates; the mediocre—resume distribution companies; the worst—spidered.

❏ Other Services

Is a listserv/discussion
forum offered:

This feature enables site visitors to connect with their peers online and discuss professional, trade and/or business issues with them.

Importance to you:

The quality and content of the messages that are posted in the forum or listserv enable you to identify individuals who may be a candidate for one of your openings, even though you haven't seen their resume.

Are assessment instruments
offered: Indicates whether there are skill, per-
                              sonality and other tests available on
                              the site.

Importance to you: *The data provided by these tests can
                              enhance your evaluation of a candi-
                              date's ability to (a) do a specific job
                              and (b) fit into your organization.*

Automated resume agent: Indicates whether the site automati-
                              cally notifies you whenever a new
                              candidate resume is posted on the
                              site that matches the key require-
                              ments of your job ad.

Importance to you: *This service can increase your ef-
                              ficiency and help you connect more
                              quickly with top candidates.*

Banner advertising: Indicates whether the site sells ban-
                              ner ads, which are the online equiva-
                              lent of print display ads.

Importance to you: *This service enables you to promote
                              your organization and its employment
                              brand.*

Status report on ads: Indicates whether the site provide a
                              status report on the performance of
                              your job postings and/or banner ads.

Importance to you: *Helps you shop smart by measuring the performance of a site's advertising services.*

❏ Site's Self-Description

A 50-100 word description of the site's features, services and fees, written by the site. These descriptions are edited for length, grammatical correctness and clarity, as necessary.

Importance to you: *The content and tone of the site's self description will give you a feel for its understanding of your requirements as well as its commitment to customer service.*

❏ Contact Information

Provides the name, e-mail address and telephone number of the site's preferred point of contact.

A Word on Sites That Fail to Report Information

When a site fails to provide any of the information described above, that discrepancy is noted in its Profile by the term "Not Reported."

Generally speaking, those sites that are most open about their capabilities—by providing complete and detailed information about their services, features and fees—are your best bet for maximizing your investment in online recruiting.

The SmartSelect™ Process

Let's face it, finding the right Web-site for each of your recruiting requirements is no easy task. In essence, you have two choices:

- You can follow the herd and post your jobs and search for resumes at the same sites that everyone else is using, or

- You can "shop" for recruitment sites with the same consumer savvy you use when shopping for any other important service or product.

If your choice is to be a smart consumer, the **WEDDLE's SmartSelect™** process is just what you need to get the job done!

The SmartSelect™ process is based on a very simple premise: You can be an expert in all of the best techniques for online recruiting and still not connect with high caliber candidates if you do not use those techniques on the right Web-site(s) for each of your specific recruiting requirements. Indeed, selecting the best site(s) for a given assignment is a prerequisite for effective recruiting on the Internet.

SmartSelect™ is a proven, 5-step, "recruiter friendly" process for making smart site selections. It draws on the experience and lessons-learned of successful online recruiters and the rich array of site information found in this Guide.

❑ Step 1: Determine Your Options.

Use both of the Guide's sections to identify those recruitment Web-sites that serve the occupational field and/or industry for which you are recruiting. For example, if you are recruiting for a position in Finance, the Cross Reference Index for The Top 100 and The Best & the Rest listings will pinpoint over a hundred sites worth considering.

❏ Step 2: Evaluate Your Options.

Use the Consumer Profiles and your own research to evaluate each of your site options. The profiles provide a wide range of descriptive information about each site that can be used to:

- Assess each site on its own merits, and

- Compare each site to all other sites with a common set of data.

First, evaluate each site on its own merits. We suggest that you use the following criteria from your WEDDLE's Guide:

To Post a Job Opening:

- The kind of jobs the site posts (e.g., full time, part time)

- The most prevalent types of jobs it posts (e.g., career fields, job titles)

- The geographic distribution of the jobs it posts

- If a posting can be linked to your own Web-site

To Search the Resume/Profile Database:

- The top occupations among the resumes/profiles in the database

- The location of the site's headquarters (if the site represents that it specializes a specific geographic area)

Second, take each of the sites you found acceptable on their own merits and compare them to one another. We suggest that you use the following criteria from your WEDDLE's Guide:

To Post a Job Opening:

- The number of people who visit the site

- The time they spend on the site

- The price to post a job

- The posting period

- The date the site was activated online

To Search the Resume/Profile Database:

- The number of people who visit the site

- The time they spend on the site

- The fee to search the database

- The number of resumes/profiles in the database

- How the resumes/profiles are acquired

- The date the site was activated online

Please see the Explanation of Terms on page 23 if you're unsure about what any of these criteria mean. Then, use them to select the 5-8 options that:

(a) best match your recruiting requirement and

(b) provide the best value for your organization.

.

❏ Step 3: Visit the Sites Online.

To narrow your options further, pay each of the sites a visit online. We strongly recommend that you never use a site until you have "test driven" it from a job seeker's perspective. If you don't find the experience worthwhile, chances are the candidates won't, as well. When that happens, your return on investment in a job posting or resume search will be far less than optimal and, just as bad, it's possible that your organization's image will be tarnished by its affiliation with the site.

What factors should you consider when "test driving" a job board or career portal? We suggest that you look at the following:

- <u>How easy is it to open the door?</u> Job seekers, in general, but passive job seekers, in particular, are busy people and move around the Web quickly. Therefore, it's important to check how long it takes to download the site's Home Page. Research has shown that if it takes more than 14 seconds for the site's content to present itself, job seekers are unlikely to hang around. And, as the old saying goes (with a modern twist), "Out of site, out of mind." If they aren't on the site, you clearly cannot capture their attention and recruit them there.

- <u>How easy is it to figure out what's on the site?</u> Ask yourself these questions: Is the layout of the site's Home Page intuitively obvious to the first-time visitor? Does it clearly identify the different sections or areas of the site and provide easy access to them? Does it provide intelligible and well organized tabs or links from a navigation bar so that visitors can quickly determine what's available on the site (for first-time visitors) and quickly get to the information or service they want (for repeat visitors)?

- <u>How "job seeker" friendly is the site?</u> Does the site require visitors to register before they can use any of its services? Does it provide information and insights that job seekers would find helpful? Is the site well maintained (e.g., are there grammatical errors and misspellings in the content, do pages not open or do hypertext links not work)? If the site provides a question and answer feature (which is a good sign), does it answer questions promptly? And, are the images on the site inclusive or do they show a lack of sensitivity to cultural, age or gender diversity?

❏ Step 4: Make Your Selection and Track Your Results.

Just as you would with traditional recruiting methods, the best way to recruit online is to select and use several venues or sites simultaneously. WEDDLE's recommends the following formula:

$$2GP + 3N + 1D = 1GH$$

where:

2GP represents two general purpose employment sites (sites that give you access to candidates in a wide array of career fields and locations);

3N represents three niche employment sites (one that specializes in the industry in which you're recruiting, one that specializes in the career field of your opening and one that specializes in the geographic location of the position);

1D represents a diversity employment site (to ensure you tap the full range of talent in the workforce).

Using that array of sites will optimize your yield and provide the best assurance you will find 1GH: one great hire for your organization.

In addition, be a good consumer. Keep track of each site's performance—using such metrics as the number of candidates generated, the cost-per-candidate and their quality—and refer to those data the next time and every time you "shop" for a job board.

❏ Step 5: Continually Reassess and Fine Tune Your Selections.

It's easy to become creatures of habit and return to the same site(s) over and over again when recruiting online. The Internet, however, is an extraordinarily dynamic medium, and successful online recruiting depends upon a continuous reassessment and updating of your strategy. To conduct your evaluation, use both the lessons you've learned from previous recruiting efforts (see Step 4 above), this Guide, and our Free Book Updates at www.weddles.com. Based on your assessment, fine tune your selection of recruitment Web-sites for each and every new requirement.

WEDDLE's

The Job Seeker & Career Counselor's Section

❑ Each site profile in The Top 100 identifies the site by its name, URL or address on the Internet, and its parent organization. Then, additional descriptive information is provided in six sections:

- **General Site Information**

- **Job Postings**

- **Resume Services**

- **Other Services**

- **Site's Self Description**

- **Contact Information**

The information that is included in each of these sections is described below.

❑ General Site Information

Date activated online:　　　　The date the site first appeared on the Internet or World Wide Web.

Importance to you:　　　　*Although not always the case, the longer a site has been in operation, the more developed its services and reliable its performance.*

Location of the site headquarters:　　　　The city and state in the United States or the city and country where the site's parent company or organization is located.

Importance to you:

A local address adds credibility to a site's claim that it reaches employers in a specific geographic area.

Number of people who
visit the site:

The number of individuals who visit the site in a given month, with each person counted just once, regardless of how many times they came to the site. This metric is called unique visitors per month.

Importance to you:

The number of people who visit a site each month is important to you for two reasons: (1) The figure will help you compare sites to determine which are the most popular among other job seekers. (2) It will also help you to evaluate the level of competition you will face from other job seekers when applying for openings posted on a given site.

Time spent on site:

The time visitors spend on a site measured in minutes per visit or in the number of pages of information that they view while there (page views per month.

Importance to you:

This figure is an indication of the quality of the information provid-ed by a site. The more time visi-

tors spend on the site or the more pages of information they view, the higher the site's perceived value.

❏ Job Postings

Post full time jobs:

Does the site post ads for full time positions?

<u>Importance to you</u>:

Indicates whether the site's employment opportunities will support your job search objective.

Post part time/contract/ consulting jobs:

Does the site post ads for part time, contract and/or consulting positions?

<u>Importance to you</u>:

Indicates whether the site's employment opportunities will support your job search objective.

Most prevalent types of jobs posted:

What are the predominant kinds of jobs currently being posted by recruiters?

<u>Importance to you</u>:

Helps you determine the strength of the site's job database in your particular career field or for your specific employment objective.

In some cases, abbreviations have been used to denote the kinds of jobs currently being posted on a site. These abbreviations are presented in the Table below.

Key to Career Field Abbreviations
Used in the Web Site Profiles

AD-Administrative
CM-Computer-related
CN-Communications
DP-Data Processing
EC-Electronic Commerce
EN-Engineering
FA-Finance/Accounting

HR-Human Resources
IS-Info Systems/Technology
MG-Management
OP-Operations
PG-Programming
SM-Sales/Marketing

Distribution:

What is the geographic focus of the site's job postings: regional, national, international?

Importance to you:

Indicates whether the site's employment opportunities are located either where you currently live or would like to.

Number of job postings:

What is the total number of jobs posted on the site at any given point in time?

Importance to you:

Indicates the extent of the opportunity available to you at the site so that you can determine whether it would be worth your while to visit.

Top salary levels of jobs:	What salary range (or ranges) appears most frequently among the jobs posted on the site?
<u>Importance to you</u>:	*Helps you determine whether the jobs posted on the site are at the right compensation level for you.*
Source of postings	How were the job postings on the site acquired: direct from employers, from search and staffing firms, cross-posted from other job boards, or copied from other sites (the last uses a technology called "spiders" which often results in out-of-date ads).
<u>Importance to you</u>:	*Helps you determine who will be involved in screening your credentials and the quality of an opportunity: postings from employers, search and staffing firms, and those cross-posted from other job boards are more likely to be genuine and current than those that are copied (spidered) from other sites.*

❏ Resume Services

Are resumes or profiles posted on-site:	Indicates whether you can store a resume or profile on the site.

Importance to you: *Some sites archive resumes and/ or profiles in a database that they then make available to recruiters. The database may be completely open to the public or accessible only in part (i.e., your contact information is protected until you release it).*

How long can you store: How many days, months or years can a resume or profile be left in the site's database without re-posting or updating it?

Importance to you: *If you are actively searching for a position, indicates how frequently you must return to the site to re-post your resume; if you have found a position, indicates whether you should return to the site to delete your resume from its database.*

Who can post a resume: Is posting a resume/profile on the site restricted to special categories of users (e.g., association members, those who register with the site, those in a certain career field or in a certain industry)?

Importance to you: *Indicates whether or not you are eligible to post your resume/profile in the site's database.*

Fee to post:	Must you pay a fee to store your resume or profile in the site's database?
Importance to you:	*There's nothing wrong with paying a reasonable fee to post your resume on a site, but make sure you assess the value of doing so. To evaluate the fee, use the length of time the resume will be stored on the site and the source(s) of the site's job postings to determine how much visibility you are likely to get with the kinds of recruiters you want to reach.*
Confidentiality available:	Indicates whether the site will help to protect your privacy by: (a) blocking out contact information from your resume or prohibiting employer access to the resume database (in which case, the site serves as an intermediary between you and the recruiter until you decide to reveal your identity), (b) sending you an e-mail message about appropriate openings (a job agent), or (c) some other feature.
Importance to you:	*Those sites that protect your privacy enable you to search for a new or better job whenever and wherever you want. They ensure that you remain in charge of your job search ef-*

fort and preserve your flexibility in the job market.

❏ Other Services

Is a listserv/discussion
forum offered:

This feature enables site visitors to connect with their peers online and discuss professional, trade and/or business issues with them.

<u>Importance to you:</u>

This feature provides three important benefits: (1) you can network with a wider circle of contacts than those in your local area; (2) you can expand your knowledge and visibility in your field; and (3) you can demonstrate your expertise where recruiters can see it.

Are assessment instruments
offered:

Indicates whether there are skill, personality and other tests available on the site.

<u>Importance to you:</u>

The data provided by these tests can enhance your self-knowledge and ensure that you compete for a job you can do well in an organization where you will be comfortable.

Automated job agent: A job agent is a free service that will automatically compare your specified employment objective with all of the jobs posted on the site and notify you privately whenever a match occurs.

<u>Importance to you:</u>   *You can save time and effort by using a site's job agent. While the agent is checking openings for you on the site, you can be evaluating other opportunities or networking at other sites.*

Career info provided: Indicates whether the site offers job search and career management information (e.g., interviewing tips) as well as job postings.

<u>Importance to you:</u>   *Helps you select those sites that are likely to be most beneficial to you. There are only so many hours in the day, so use sites that provide <u>both</u> appropriate job opportunities and a range of information that will help you achieve your employment objectives.*

Links to other sites: Does the site provide hypertext links or electronic connections to other sites with career and/or job search information that can be helpful to you?

Importance to you: *Helps you evaluate the potential benefit of a site to you.*

❑ Site's Self-Description

A 50-100 word description of the site's features, services and fees, written by the site. These descriptions are edited for length, grammatical correctness and clarity, as necessary.

Importance to you: *The content and tone of the site's self description will give you a feel for its understanding of your job search and career requirements as well as its commitment to customer service.*

❑ Contact Information

Provides the name, e-mail address and telephone number of the site's preferred point of contact.

A Word on Sites That Fail to Report Information

When a site fails to provide any of the information described above, that discrepancy is noted in its Profile by the term "Not Reported."

Generally speaking, those sites that are most open about their capabilities—by providing complete and detailed information about their services, features and fees—are your best bet for achieving success in your online job search.

The SmartSearch™ Process

Let's face it; finding the Web-sites that can best support your specific employment objective is no easy task. In essence, you have two choices:

- You can follow the herd and apply for jobs posted at the same sites that everyone else is using, or

- You can "shop" for employment sites with the same consumer savvy you use when looking for any other important service or product.

If your choice is to be a smart consumer, **WEDDLE's SmartSearch™** process is just what you need to get the job done!

The SmartSearch™ process is based on a very simple premise: You can be an expert in job search and in using the Internet and still not connect with your dream job if you do not look for that opportunity at the right Web-site(s). Indeed, selecting the best site(s) for your employment objective is a prerequisite for successfully using the Internet to find a new or better job.

SmartSearch™ is a proven, 5-step, "job seeker friendly" process for making smart Web-site selections. It draws on the experience and lessons-learned of successful online job seekers and the rich array of site information found in this Guide.

Step 1: Check out the Field.

Use both of the Guide's sections to identify those recruitment Web-sites that serve your occupational field, industry and/or geographic location. For example, if you are looking for a position in Finance, the Cross Reference Index for The Top 100 and The Best & the Rest listings will pinpoint over a hundred sites worth considering.

Step 2: Evaluate the Possibilities.

Use the Site Profiles and your own research to evaluate each of your site options. The profiles provide a wide range of descriptive information about each site that can be used to:

- Assess each site on its own merits, and

- Compare each site to all other site options.

One way to perform these assessments and comparisons is to focus on a sub-set of the information provided in the Consumer Profiles. We think using this information as your selection criteria can help you make quick and accurate evaluations of alternative sites and speed you to those that are most likely to work for you. It seems only fitting, therefore, that its elements, which are listed below, should form the acronym NASCAR.

NASCAR:

N **Number and kinds of jobs posted on the site (e.g., full time, part time)**
Do they match your employment objective?   Yes ___ No ___

A **Availability of a job agent**
Can you sign up a free job agent?   Yes ___ No ___

S **Salary ranges of the posted jobs**
Do they match your employment objective?   Yes ___ No ___

C **Costs to you for using the site**
Are there any fees you must pay?   Yes ___ No ___
If yes, what are they?   _____

A **Aids for job search and career management**
Does the site provide information for job search and/or career management or links to sites that do?   Yes ___ No ___

R **Resume database with confidentiality feature**
Does the site offer a database for storing a resume or profile online?   Yes ── No ──
Does the site protect the confidentiality of those storing a resume/profile in the database?   Yes ── No ──

We suggest that you use NASCAR to narrow the number of sites you are considering down to 5-8 strong possibilities.

Step 3: Visit the Sites Online.

The best way to assess your options further is to pay each of the 5-8 sites a visit online. Sites that seem all but identical on paper often have a very different look and feel on the Internet. The key is to **find those sites that provide the best experience for you:** they are easy for you to use and they provide the specific kind of support and assistance you need. Or, to put it another way, the best sites are those that provide the optimum return on your investment of time and effort when using them.

What factors should you consider when "test driving" a site? We suggest that you look at the following:

- <u>How easy is it to open the door?</u> Is the site designed for speedy access with your kind of modem and Internet service? (Unfortunately, some sites require an industrial strength computer and a very high speed Internet connection.) How can you tell? Time how long it takes to open the site's Home Page. If it takes more than 15 seconds or so, forget about it. The site has more graphics and other complex features than your system can accommodate, and that means your experience using the site is likely to be unpleasantly frustrating and inefficient.

- <u>How easy is it to figure out what's there?</u> Ask yourself these questions: Is the layout of the site's Home Page intuitively obvious and/or easy to figure out? Does it clearly identify the different sections or areas of the site and provide easy access to them? Does it provide intelligible and well organized tabs or links from a navigation bar so that you can quickly determine what's available on the site (if you're there for the first time) and quickly get to the information or service you want (if you're back for a repeat visit)?

- <u>How "job seeker" friendly is the site?</u> Does the site require you to register before you can use any of its services? Does it provide information and insights that you find helpful? Is the site well maintained (e.g., are there grammatical errors and misspellings in the content, do pages not open, or do hypertext links not work)? If the site provides a question and answer feature (which is a good sign), does it answer questions promptly? And, are the images on the site inclusive or do they show a lack of sensitivity to cultural, age or gender diversity?

Step 4: Make Your Selection and Track Your Results.

Just as you would with a traditional job search campaign, the best way to look for a job online is to select and use several venues or sites simultaneously. Each will provide you with a different channel into the job market; that's important because it's impossible to know, in advance, which organizations will be looking where on the Web.

To make sure you give yourself adequate access to the opportunities posted online and adequate visibility to the employers looking at resumes online, select and use at least five sites. WEDDLE's recommends the following formula:

$$2GP + 3N = 1GJ$$

where:

2GP represents two general purpose employment sites (sites that give you access to opportunities in a wide array of industries and locations);

3N represents three niche employment sites (one that specializes in the industry in which you want to work, one that specializes in your career field and one that specializes in the geographic location where you live or want to);

Using that array of sites will optimize your access to opportunities and provide the best assurance you will find 1GJ: one great job that's just right for you.

In addition, be a good consumer. Keep track of each site's performance—using such metrics as the number of jobs it posts in your field, the number of jobs it posts at your skill level and the caliber of the employers that post those jobs—and refer to those data the next time and every time you "shop" for a job board.

Step 5: Continually Reassess and Fine Tune Your Selections.

It's easy to become creatures of habit and return to the same site(s) over and over again when looking for a new or better job online. The Internet, however, is an extraordinarily dynamic medium, and successful online job search depends upon a continuous reassessment and updating of your site selections.

To conduct your evaluation, use both the lessons you've learned from previous job search efforts (see Step 4 above), this Guide, and our Free Book Updates at www.weddles.com. Based on your assessment, fine tune your selection of employment Web-sites every year or so. Why bother? Because in today's challenging economic environment, you just never know when you may need it.

WEDDLE's 2011 User's Choice Awards

Recruiters & Job Seekers Pick the Top Sites on the Web

Who has the best perspective on which employment sites are most helpful? We think the answer to that question is obvious … it's YOU, the recruiters and job seekers who have used the sites. You, better than anyone else, know which sites work best.

WEDDLE's User's Choice Awards give you a way to make your preferences known. It's your chance to:

- recognize the Web-sites that provide the best level of service and value to their visitors,

  and

- help others make best use of the employment resources online.

WEDDLE's User's Choice Awards are the only awards for employment sites where YOU pick the winners. Public balloting is conducted all year long at the WEDDLE's Web-site (www.weddles.com), and the 30 sites with the most votes at the end of the year are declared the Award winners. The sites selected for the 2011 User's Choice Awards are presented on the next page.

For more information about the Awards and to cast your vote for next year's winners, please visit the WEDDLE's site at www.weddles.com and click on the Online Poll button on our Home Page.

WEDDLE's 2011 User's Choice Awards

Absolutely Health Care

AfterCollege.com

AHACareerCenter.org

AllHealthcareJobs.com

AllRetailJobs.com

CareerBuilder.com

Climber.com

CollegeRecruiter.com

CoolWorks.com

Dice.com

EHSCareers.com

ExecuNet

FlexJobs.com

hCareers.com

HEALTHeCAREERS

HigherEdJobs.com

HospitalDreamJobs.com

Indeed.com

Job.com

JobCircle.com

Jobfox.com

Jobing.com

Monster

National Healthcare Career Network

Simply Hired

6FigureJobs.com

SnagAJob.com

TopUSAJobs.com

VetJobs

WSJ.com/Careers

Picked by the Toughest Judges in the World:
You & Others Who Use Online Employment Sites

The International Association of Employment Web Sites

The job board population is growing by leaps and bounds. By our count at WEDDLE's, there are now over 50,000 such sites operating in the U.S. alone, and that figure will likely double in the next three-to-five years. Similar growth is occurring in Canada, Europe, Australia and Asia.

Most of these sites are operated in accordance with generally accepted business practices. Some, however, are not. These unscrupulous job boards misrepresent the services and capabilities they provide to employers and recruiters and abuse the trust of job seekers. When you use them, therefore, they undermine your ability to succeed.

How can you protect yourself and/or the organization you represent?

Use job boards that are members of the **International Association of Employment Web Sites** (IAEWS). It's the trade association for job boards, aggregators, social media sites, technology companies, content providers, recruitment advertising agencies and other employment service sites worldwide. Every member of the IAEWS has agreed to abide by the first-ever Code of Ethics for the online employment services industry. That code ensures that you will receive accurate information about a job board's capabilities and that its services will be delivered as they are represented to you.

Who are the Members of the IAEWS? You'll find a complete membership list at the association's site: **www.EmploymentWebSites.org**. They range from some of the most famous job board and networking brands in the world to highly regarded niche sites that specialize in a career field, industry or geographic region. They include sites that are stand-alone enterprises and those that are operated by newspapers, professional publications, radio and TV stations, professional societies and associations, college and university alumni organizations and affinity groups.

So, what should you do? Shop smart when selecting a job board. Use a site you can trust. Use a site operated by an IAEWS Member:

☑ Look for the IAEWS Member icon on the site.

Member of
International Association
of Employment Web Sites

or

☑ Visit the IAEWS site and check the Member Roster.

They are The Sources of Success™.

CareerFitness.com

Today's job market is one of the most challenging in history. Tomorrow's job market will be no less so. In fact, the world of work has undergone a profound and permanent change since the Great Recession. And, it will never again be the way that it was.

This new reality means that the old fashioned ways of finding a new or better job are now ineffective. The traditional strategies for achieving career success no longer work. What you used to be able to rely on for steady employment and advancement will set you back today and deny you access to opportunities tomorrow.

What should you do?

Visit **CareerFitness.com.** It's a state-of-the-art resource center for job search and career success. Think of it as your "Careerbook" page on the Web.

Based on Peter Weddle's revolutionary book, *Work Strong: Your Personal Career Fitness System*, this site offers you an array of tools and techniques that will help you build up the strength, endurance and reach of your career. It will empower you to express and experience your unique talent in jobs that are meaningful and rewarding for you.

CareeFitness.com provides a complete toolkit for career success in today's world of work. It includes:
* A personal Career Fitness planning and status system so you can set up and keep track of everything you do for the health of your career and your success at work;

- Your very own Career Agent—an electronic image of yourself that will act as your online mentor, assistant, and cheerleader;

- Your own personal locker for storing your Career Fitness self-evaluations, your resume, your contacts and all of the other stuff you need to manage your career effectively;

- Your own personal trophy case where you can keep track of and enjoy your career victories in the world of work (even if your boss overlooks them);

- A professional networking tool so you can expand your career contacts and stay in touch with them regularly; and

- A resume builder so you can translate your career victories into a document that employers will understand and respect.

CareerFitness.com is a one-of-a-kind career self-management program specifically designed for the challenging workplace of the 21st Century. If you want to Work Strong for career success, if you want to increase the paycheck as well as the satisfaction you bring home from work, then CareerFitness. com is right for you.

WEDDLE's

The Top 100

Web-Site Profiles
for
Recruiters & Job Seekers

2011/12

The Top 100 Cross Reference Index

The sites selected for The Top 100 serve employers and recruiters, job seekers and career activists in a range of occupational fields, industries, and employment-related specialties (e.g., diversity, management). The following Cross Reference Index will help you quickly find the sites that best match your requirements or goals.

Administrative/Clerical

BrokerHunter.com
DiversityJobs.com
HEALTHeCAREERS Network
Inside Higher Ed
Job.com
MinnesotaJobs.com
Net-Temps
RetirementJobs.com
VetJobs

Associations

AHACareerCenter.org (American Hospital Association)
JAMA Career Center® (American Medical Association)
ASAE Career Headquarters (American Society of Association Executives)
BlueSteps (Association of Executive Search Consultants)
DiversityConnect.com (National Urban League)
GARP Career Center (Global Association of Risk Professionals)
HEALTHeCAREERS Network (multiple associations)
IEEE Job Site (Institute of Electrical & Electronics Engineers)
JobsInBenefits.com (International Foundation of Employee Benefit Plans)
Marketing Career Network (multiple associations)

NACElink Network (National Association of Colleges & Employers)

National Healthcare Career Network (multiple associations)

NBMBAA Employment Network (National Black MBA Association)

PedJobs (American Academy of Pediatrics)

Physics Today Jobs (American Institute of Physics)

PRSA Jobcenter (Public Relations Society of America)

SHRM HRJobs (Society for Human Resource Management)

SPIE Career Center (The International Society for Optics & Photonics)

Banking/Securities

BrokerHunter.com

eFinancialCareers.com

GARP Career Center

WallStJobs.com

Biotechnology

AgCareers.com

BioSpace

Building Management

ApartmentCareers.com

Security Jobs Network™

Communications-All Media, Creative, Editorial

Coroflot

mediabistro.com

PRSA Jobcenter

TalentZoo.com

Construction

ConstructionJobs.com

MEP Jobs

Workopolis

Customer Service

AllRetailJobs.com

BrokerHunter.com

CallCenterJobs.com

Hcareers

LatPro

MinnesotaJobs.com

RetirementJobs.com

Sales Gravy

Work In Sports

Defense

ClearedConnections

MilitaryConnection.com

MilitaryHire.com

VetJobs

Diversity

disABLEDperson.com

DiversityConnect.com

DiversityJobs.com

LatPro

RetirementJobs.com

WorkplaceDiversity.com

Education

BioSpace
Careers in Proprietary Education
HigherEdJobs
Inside Higher Ed

Engineering

AfterCollege
Aviation Employment
ClearedConnections
CollegeRecruiter.com
ConstructionJobs.com
Dice.com
IEEE Job Site
JobsInLogistics.com
JobsInManufacturing.com
LatPro
MEP Jobs
MinnesotaJobs.com
Physics Today Jobs
RetirementJobs.com
SPIE Career Center
VetJobs

Entry Level

AfterCollege
CollegeRecruiter.com
NACElink Network

Executive Search/Staffing Services & Support

BlueSteps
BountyJobs
Net-Temps

Finance & Accounting

Accounting Jobs Today

AfterCollege

BrokerHunter.com

eFinancialCareers.com

FINS from The Wall Street Journal

Hospital Jobs Online

Job.com

JobCircle.com

jobWings.com

LatPro

MinnesotaJobs.com

NBMBAA Employment Network

Net-Temps

RetirementJobs.com

6FigureJobs.com

SnagAJob.com

WallStJobs.com

General

AllCountyJobs.com

America's Job Exchange

BountyJobs

CareerBoard

CareerBuilder.com

Chicagojobs.com

disABLEDperson.com

DiversityConnect.com

FlexJobs

iHire.com

Indeed

Jobfox

Jobing.com

Job Rooster

JobsInME.com

JobsRadar

JobStreet.com Malaysia

JobTarget

MilitaryConnection.com

MilitaryHire.com

Monster.com

NACElink Network

NationJob.com

RegionalHelpWanted.com

Simply Hired

WorkplaceDiversity.com

Healthcare/Medical

Absolutely Health Care

AfterCollege

AHACareerCenter.org

AllHealthcareJobs.com

JAMA Career Center®

BioSpace

DiversityJobs.com

HEALTHeCAREERS Network

HealthJobsNationwide.com

Hospital Dream Jobs

Hospital Jobs Online

JobCircle.com

LiveCareer

National Healthcare Career Network

NursingJobs.org

PedJobs

Simply Hired

Workopolis

Hospitality

Cool Works

Hcareers

Meetingjobs

SnagAJob.com

Hourly

AllRetailJobs.com

Cool Works

JobsInManufacturing.com

SnagAJob.com

TopUSAJobs.com

Human Resources

Careers in Proprietary Education

DiversityJobs.com

EmployeeBenefitsJobs.com

ExecuNet

JobsInBenefits.com

SHRM HRJobs

Information Technology/Systems

AfterCollege

BrokerHunter.com

ClearedConnections

Dice.com

ExecuNet

FINS from The Wall Street Journal

IEEE Job Site

Job.com

JobCircle.com

mediabistro.com

MilitaryHire.com

MinnesotaJobs.com

Net-Temps

Physics Today Jobs

Simply Hired

6FigureJobs.com

SnagAJob.com

VetJobs

Workopolis

Insurance

Actuary.com

Great Insurance Jobs

Job Search/Career Advancement

BlueSteps

JobRooster

JobsRadar

LiveCareer

Logistics/Transportation

Aviation Employment

JobsInLogistics.com

JobsinTrucks.com

Management

AgCareers.com

AllHealthcareJobs.com

AllRetailJobs.com

ApartmentCareers.com

ASAE Career Headquarters

BlueSteps

BrokerHunter.com

CallCenterJobs.com

ClearedConnections

ConstructionJobs.com

Cool Works

ExecuNet

FINS from The Wall Street Journal

Hcareers

HealthJobsNationwide.com

Hospital Dream Jobs

IEEE Job Site

Inside Higher Ed

JobCircle.com

JobsInBenefits.com

JobsInLogistics.com

jobWings.com

mediabistro.com

NBMBAA Employment Network

Net-Temps

Sales Gravy

6FigureJobs.com

SnagAJob.com

VetJobs

WallStJobs.com

Work In Sports

Mathematics

Actuary.com

icrunchdata

Nonprofit

ASAE Career Headquarters

Opportunity Knocks

Operations

AgCareers.com

AllRetailJobs.com

ApartmentCareers.com

Aviation Employment

BrokerHunter.com

CallCenterJobs.com

ConstructionJobs.com

Hcareers

JobsInLogistics.com

NBMBAA Employment Network

6FigureJobs.com

SnagAJob.com

VetJobs

WallStJobs.com

Retail

AllRetailJobs.com

Net-Temps

SnagAJob.com

Sales & Marketing

AgCareers.com

AllRetailJobs.com

ASAE Career Headquarters

BrokerHunter.com

CallCenterJobs.com

Careers in Proprietary Education

CollegeRecruiter.com

ConstructionJobs.com

DiversityJobs.com

EHSCareers.com

ExecuNet

FINS from The Wall Street Journal

Great Insurance Jobs

Job.com

LatPro

Marketing Career Network

mediabistro.com

MinnesotaJobs.com

RetirementJobs.com

Sales Gravy

6FigureJobs.com

SnagAJob.com

TalentZoo.com

WallStJobs.com

Work In Sports

Workopolis

Science

AfterCollege
BioSpace
IEEE Job Site
Physics Today Jobs
SPIE Career Center

Search Engines-Employment

Indeed
Juju.com
Simply Hired
TopUSAJobs.com

Specialty-Other

AgCareers.com
America's Job Exchange
Aviation Employment
CallCenterJobs.com
ClearedConnections
Cool Works
Coroflot
disABLEDperson.com
EHSCareers.com
FlexJobs
JobsInManufacturing.com
Meetingjobs
Work In Sports

Temporary/Contract/Hourly Employment

Net-Temps
SnagAJob.com

USA-By Region/Time Zone

Eastern Time Zone

(AL, AK, DE, FL, GA, MA, MD, MI, NC, NJ, NY, OH, PA)

AllCountyJobs.com

CareerBoard

JobCircle.com

Jobing.com

JobsInME.com

RegionalHelpWanted.com

WallStJobs.com

Central TIme Zone

(IL, IA, KS, KY, LA, MN, MO, ND, NE, OK, SD, TN, TX, WI)

CareerBoard

Chicagojobs.com

Jobing.com

MinnesotaJobs.com

RegionalHelpWanted.com

Mountain Time Zone

(AZ, CO, ID, NM, UT)

CareerBoard

Jobing.com

RegionalHelpWanted.co

Western Time Zone (CA, NV, OR, WA)

CareerBoard

Jobing.com

RegionalHelpWanted.com

Canada

AllRetailJobs.com

Great Insurance Jobs

Hcareers

HEALTHeCAREERS Network

JobsInLogistics.com

JobsInManufacturing.com

jobWings.com

RegionalHelpWanted.com

Workopolis

Notes

Notes

Absolutely Health Care
www.healthjobsusa.com
CJ Ventures, Inc.

GENERAL SITE INFORMATION

Date activated online:	1999
Location of site headquarters:	Lake Worth, FL
Number of people who visit the site:	631,909 unique visitors/month
Time spent on site:	10.6 page views/visitor

JOB POSTINGS

Post full time jobs:	Yes
Post part time/contract/consulting jobs:	Yes - All
Most prevalent types of jobs posted:	Healthcare, Medical
Distribution:	National - USA

Recruiters
Fee to post a job:	$151-200/posting
Posting period:	90 days
Link posting to your site:	Yes

Job Seekers
Number of job postings:	345,000
Top salary levels of jobs:	$201-250K, $251K+/yr
Source of postings:	Employers, Staffing

RESUME SERVICES

Are resumes or profiles posted on the site:	Yes

Recruiters
Number in database:	240,000
Top occupations :	Healthcare
Fee to view resumes:	In posting fee
How acquired:	Direct from candidates

Job Seekers
How long can you store:	Indefinitely
Who can post a resume:	Those in the field
Fee to post:	None
Confidentiality available:	No

OTHER SERVICES

Is a listserv or discussion forum offered:	Yes
Are assessment instruments offered:	Yes

Recruiters
Automated resume agent:	Yes
Banner advertising:	Yes
Status report on ads:	Yes - Postings

Job Seekers
Automated job agent:	Yes
Career info provided:	Yes
Links to other sites:	Yes

SITE'S SELF DESCRIPTION

Absolutely Health Care specializes in U.S. healthcare and medical positions. We offer single job postings and programs that allow unlimited postings and resume database access. Jobs posted by our clients are also cross posted to 4,800+ affiliate sites at no extra charge. Unlimited postings and resume database access average $333 per month for annual subscribers.

Contact Information

Name:	Ken Levinson
Phone:	800-863-8314
E-Mail:	klevinson@healthjobsusa.com

Accounting Jobs Today
www.accountingjobstoday.com
Internet Brands, Inc.

GENERAL SITE INFORMATION

Date activated online:	2007
Location of site headquarters:	El Segundo, CA
Number of people who visit the site:	50,000 unique visitors/month
Time spent on site:	3.0 page views/visitor

JOB POSTINGS

Post full time jobs:	Yes
Post part time/contract/consulting jobs:	No
Most prevalent types of jobs posted:	FA
Distribution:	National - USAA

Recruiters
Fee to post a job:	$249/posting
Posting period:	30 days
Link posting to your site:	Yes

Job Seekers
Number of job postings:	3,000
Top salary levels of jobs:	Not Reported
Source of postings:	Employers

RESUME SERVICES

Are resumes or profiles posted on the site:	Yes

Recruiters
Number in database:	300,000
Top occupations :	FA
Fee to view resumes:	In posting fee
How acquired:	Direct from candidates

Job Seekers
How long can you store:	Indefinitely
Who can post a resume:	Those in the field
Fee to post:	None
Confidentiality available:	Yes

OTHER SERVICES

Is a listserv or discussion forum offered:	No
Are assessment instruments offered:	Yes

Recruiters
Automated resume agent:	Yes
Banner advertising:	Yes
Status report on ads:	Yes - Both

Job Seekers
Automated job agent:	Yes
Career info provided:	Yes
Links to other sites:	Yes

SITE'S SELF DESCRIPTION

AccountingJobsToday.com is an accounting job board and career resource dedicated to accounting and finance professionals nationwide. For employers and recruiters, we connect you with highly targeted and quality talent. Post your jobs on AccountingJobsToday.com or search our extensive and growing pool of talented job seekers via our resume database.

Contact Information

Name:	Steve Gilison
Phone:	310-280-5529
E-Mail:	advertising@accountingjobstoday.com

Actuary.com
www.actuary.com
RSG, Inc.

GENERAL SITE INFORMATION

Date activated online:	1999
Location of site headquarters:	Atlanta, GA
Number of people who visit the site:	40,000 unique visitors/month
Time spent on site:	3:30 minutes/visit

JOB POSTINGS

Post full time jobs:	Yes
Post part time/contract/consulting jobs:	Yes - All
Most prevalent types of jobs posted:	Actuarial, Insurance, Mathematics
Distribution:	International

Recruiters

Fee to post a job:	$201-250/posting
Posting period:	30 or 60 days
Link posting to your site:	Yes

Job Seekers

Number of job postings:	100
Top salary levels of jobs:	$201-250K, $251K+/yr
Source of postings:	Employers, Staffing

RESUME SERVICES

Are resumes or profiles posted on the site:	Yes

Recruiters

Number in database:	2,200
Top occupations :	Actuarial, Insurance
Fee to view resumes:	In posting fee
How acquired:	Direct from candidates

Job Seekers

How long can you store:	Indefinitely
Who can post a resume:	Anyone
Fee to post:	None
Confidentiality available:	Yes

OTHER SERVICES

Is a listserv or discussion forum offered:	Yes
Are assessment instruments offered:	Yes

Recruiters

Automated resume agent:	No
Banner advertising:	Yes
Status report on ads:	Yes - Postings

Job Seekers

Automated job agent:	Yes
Career info provided:	Yes
Links to other sites:	Yes

SITE'S SELF DESCRIPTION

Actaury.com is the leading career and professional resource for actuaries on the Internet. Actuary.com offers single job postings from $225 or job posting packs at a significant price reduction. Top name actuarial companies have posted on Actuary.com for years.

Contact Information

Name:	Jay Rollins
Phone:	770-425-8576
E-Mail:	actuary@actuary.com

AfterCollege
www.aftercollege.com
AfterCollege, Inc.

GENERAL SITE INFORMATION

Date activated online:	2000
Location of site headquarters:	San Francisco, CA
Number of people who visit the site:	600,000 unique visitors/month
Time spent on site:	15.0 page views/visitor

JOB POSTINGS

Post full time jobs:	Yes
Post part time/contract/consulting jobs:	Yes - Part time
Most prevalent types of jobs posted:	EN, IS, Business, Life Sciences, Nursing
Distribution:	National - USA

Recruiters

Fee to post a job:	$130/posting
Posting period:	30 days
Link posting to your site:	Yes

Job Seekers

Number of job postings:	177,008
Top salary levels of jobs:	$101-150K/yr
Source of postings:	Employers

RESUME SERVICES

Are resumes or profiles posted on the site:	Yes - Both

Recruiters

Number in database:	205,727
Top occupations :	EN, FA, IS, Nursing
Fee to view resumes:	None
How acquired:	Direct from individual

Job Seekers

How long can you store:	Indefinitely
Who can post a resume:	Active members
Fee to post:	None
Confidentiality available:	Yes

OTHER SERVICES

Is a listserv or discussion forum offered:	No
Are assessment instruments offered:	Yes

Recruiters

Automated resume agent:	Yes
Banner advertising:	Yes
Status report on ads:	Yes - Not Specified

Job Seekers

Automated job agent:	Yes
Career info provided:	Yes
Links to other sites:	Yes

SITE'S SELF DESCRIPTION

AfterCollege is the largest career network specializing in college recruitment, helping over 2,250,000 college students and alumni connect with employers. AfterCollege reaches students and alumni through 1,300 partner academic departments and student groups as well as through a network of 17,500+ faculty and group contacts.

Contact Information

Name:	Carrie McCullagh
Phone:	877-725-7721
E-Mail:	info@aftercollege.com

AgCareers.com
www.agcareers.com
Farms.com

GENERAL SITE INFORMATION

Date activated online:	January, 2001
Location of site headquarters:	Clinton, NC
Number of people who visit the site:	48,600 unique visitors/month
Time spent on site:	4:30 minutes/visit

JOB POSTINGS

Post full time jobs:	Yes
Post part time/contract/consulting jobs:	Yes - All
Most prevalent types of jobs posted:	Agriculture
Distribution:	International

Recruiters

Fee to post a job:	$375/posting
Posting period:	60 days
Link posting to your site:	Yes

Job Seekers

Number of job postings:	2,750
Top salary levels of jobs:	$76-100K, $101-150K/yr
Source of postings:	Employers, Staffing

RESUME SERVICES

Are resumes or profiles posted on the site:	Yes

Recruiters

Number in database:	5,000
Top occupations :	MG, OP, SM
Fee to view resumes:	$500
How acquired:	Direct from candidates

Job Seekers

How long can you store:	1 year
Who can post a resume:	Those registered
Fee to post:	None
Confidentiality available:	Yes

OTHER SERVICES

Is a listserv or discussion forum offered:	Yes
Are assessment instruments offered:	No

Recruiters

Automated resume agent:	Yes
Banner advertising:	Yes
Status report on ads:	Yes - Both

Job Seekers

Automated job agent:	Yes
Career info provided:	Yes
Links to other sites:	Yes

SITE'S SELF DESCRIPTION

AgCareers.com is the leading online job board and human resource provider for the agriculture, food, natural resources and biotechnology fields.

Contact Information

Name:	AgCareers.com
Phone:	800-929-8975
E-Mail:	agcareers@agcareers.com

AHACareerCenter.org
www.ahacareercenter.org
AHA Solutions, Inc. (American Hospital Association)

GENERAL SITE INFORMATION

Date activated online:	November, 2007
Location of site headquarters:	Chicago, IL
Number of people who visit the site:	8,031 unique visitors/month
Time spent on site:	2:57 minutes/visit

JOB POSTINGS

Post full time jobs:	Yes
Post part time/contract/consulting jobs:	Yes - Locum Tenens
Most prevalent types of jobs posted:	Healthcare
Distribution:	National - USA

Recruiters
Fee to post a job:	$250-$550/posting
Posting period:	30 days
Link posting to your site:	Yes

Job Seekers
Number of job postings:	1,600
Top salary levels of jobs:	Up to $200K+/yr
Source of postings:	Employers

RESUME SERVICES

Are resumes or profiles posted on the site:	Yes

Recruiters
Number in database:	75,000
Top occupations :	Nurses, Allied Health
Fee to view resumes:	In posting fee
How acquired:	Direct from candidate

Job Seekers
How long can you store:	Indefinitely
Who can post a resume:	Those registered
Fee to post:	None
Confidentiality available:	Yes

OTHER SERVICES

Is a listserv or discussion forum offered:	No
Are assessment instruments offered:	No

Recruiters
Automated resume agent:	Yes
Banner advertising:	No
Status report on ads:	Yes - Postings

Job Seekers
Automated job agent:	Yes
Career info provided:	Yes
Links to other sites:	Yes

SITE'S SELF DESCRIPTION

AHA's Career Center is the site for hospitals and healthcare employers seeking highly qualified applicants (from entry level to CEO), as well as job seekers looking to land the right job within healthcare. The American Hospital Association's AHACareerCenter.org is part of the National Healthcare Career Network and the fastest growing health care association job network.

Contact Information

Name:	Amy Goble
Phone:	800-242-4677
E-Mail:	careercenter@aha.org

AllCountyJobs.com
www.allcountyjobs.com
AllCountyJobs, LLC

GENERAL SITE INFORMATION

Date activated online:	1999
Location of site headquarters:	Trumbull, CT
Number of people who visit the site:	250,000 unique visitors/month
Time spent on site:	6:00 minutes/visit

JOB POSTINGS

Post full time jobs:	Yes
Post part time/contract/consulting jobs:	Yes - All
Most prevalent types of jobs posted:	Wide variety
Distribution:	Regional - CT, NY, MA, RI, NJ, VT, NH

Recruiters
Fee to post a job:	$129/posting
Posting period:	60 days
Link posting to your site:	Yes

Job Seekers
Number of job postings:	3,000
Top salary levels of jobs:	Up to $150K+/yr
Source of postings:	Employers, Staffing

RESUME SERVICES

Are resumes or profiles posted on the site:	Yes

Recruiters
Number in database:	Not Reported
Top occupations :	Wide variety
Fee to view resumes:	$10
How acquired:	Direct from candidates

Job Seekers
How long can you store:	2 years
Who can post a resume:	Those registered
Fee to post:	None
Confidentiality available:	Yes

OTHER SERVICES

Is a listserv or discussion forum offered:	No
Are assessment instruments offered:	No

Recruiters
Automated resume agent:	No
Banner advertising:	No
Status report on ads:	No

Job Seekers
Automated job agent:	No
Career info provided:	No
Links to other sites:	No

SITE'S SELF DESCRIPTION

We are a network of local online job boards. Since our start, we have always strived for one goal: connect employers with quality, targeted, local applicants. Our local job boards will let you search/post jobs from Washington, D.C. to Vermont and everywhere in between. Each site links to the others to form a network of thousands of job listings along the East Coast.

Contact Information

Name:	Information
Phone:	800-399-6651
E-Mail:	info@allcountyjobs.com

AllHealthcareJobs.com
www.allhealthcarejobs.com
Dice Holdings, Inc.

GENERAL SITE INFORMATION

Date activated online:	2005
Location of site headquarters:	New York, NY
Number of people who visit the site:	243,000 unique visitors/month
Time spent on site:	8:00 minutes/visit

JOB POSTINGS

Post full time jobs:	Yes
Post part time/contract/consulting jobs:	Yes - Part time
Most prevalent types of jobs posted:	MG, Nursing, Allied Health
Distribution:	International

Recruiters

Fee to post a job:	$295/posting
Posting period:	30 days
Link posting to your site:	Yes

Job Seekers

Number of job postings:	15,000
Top salary levels of jobs:	$101-150K, $251K+/yr
Source of postings:	Employers, Staffing

RESUME SERVICES

Are resumes or profiles posted on the site:	Yes

Recruiters

Number in database:	300,000
Top occupations :	Nursing, Allied Health
Fee to view resumes:	$1,995/year
How acquired:	Direct from candidates

Job Seekers

How long can you store:	Indefinitely
Who can post a resume:	Those in the field
Fee to post:	None
Confidentiality available:	Yes

OTHER SERVICES

Is a listserv or discussion forum offered:	No
Are assessment instruments offered:	No

Recruiters

Automated resume agent:	Yes
Banner advertising:	Yes
Status report on ads:	Yes - Postings

Job Seekers

Automated job agent:	Yes
Career info provided:	Yes
Links to other sites:	Yes

SITE'S SELF DESCRIPTION

AllHealthcareJobs.com, a Dice Holdings, Inc. service, is a leading online career site dedicated to matching healthcare professionals with the best career opportunities in their profession. Recruiters and employers can post jobs targeting specific fields within the healthcare industry including allied health, nursing, laboratory, pharmacy and medicine.

Contact Information

Name:	Tim Stene
Phone:	515-313-2069
E-Mail:	tim.stene@allhealthcarejobs.com

AllRetailJobs.com
www.allretailjobs.com
JobsInLogistics.com, Inc.

GENERAL SITE INFORMATION

Date activated online:	2001
Location of site headquarters:	North Miami Beach, FL
Number of people who visit the site:	750,000 unique visitors/month
Time spent on site:	5.0 page views/visitor

JOB POSTINGS

Post full time jobs:	Yes
Post part time/contract/consulting jobs:	Yes - All
Most prevalent types of jobs posted:	MG, SM, Customer Service
Distribution:	USA, Canada

Recruiters

Fee to post a job:	$335/posting
Posting period:	60 days
Link posting to your site:	Yes

Job Seekers

Number of job postings:	55,000
Top salary levels of jobs:	$151-200K/yr
Source of postings:	Employers, Staffing

RESUME SERVICES

Are resumes or profiles posted on the site:	Yes

Recruiters

Number in database:	1,000,000+
Top occupations :	MG, OP, SM
Fee to view resumes:	$345/month
How acquired:	Direct from candidates

Job Seekers

How long can you store:	1 year
Who can post a resume:	Anyone
Fee to post:	None
Confidentiality available:	Yes

OTHER SERVICES

Is a listserv or discussion forum offered:	No
Are assessment instruments offered:	No

Recruiters

Automated resume agent:	No
Banner advertising:	Yes
Status report on ads:	Yes - Both

Job Seekers

Automated job agent:	Yes
Career info provided:	Yes
Links to other sites:	Yes

SITE'S SELF DESCRIPTION

AllRetailJobs.com is the largest recruiting job board for the retail industry. The site specializes in target marketing campaigns that attract retail executives, regional managers, store and assistant store managers, category managers/buyers, retail logistics managers, merchandisers and department managers as well as sales and hourly associates.

Contact Information

Name:	Amy Noah
Phone:	877-562-7368
E-Mail:	amy@allretailjobs.com

America's Job Exchange
www.americasjobexchange.com
America's Job Exchange

GENERAL SITE INFORMATION

Date activated online:	June, 2007
Location of site headquarters:	Andover, MA
Number of people who visit the site:	1,250,000 unique visitors/month
Time spent on site:	4:00 minutes/visit

JOB POSTINGS

Post full time jobs:	Yes
Post part time/contract/consulting jobs:	No
Most prevalent types of jobs posted:	Wide variety
Distribution:	National - USA

Recruiters
Fee to post a job:	$129/posting
Posting period:	60 days
Link posting to your site:	Yes

Job Seekers
Number of job postings:	500,000
Top salary levels of jobs:	Up to $80K/yr
Source of postings:	Employers

RESUME SERVICES

Are resumes or profiles posted on the site:	Yes

Recruiters
Number in database:	1,000,000+
Top occupations :	Wide variety
Fee to view resumes:	$999
How acquired:	Direct from candidates

Job Seekers
How long can you store:	Indefinitely
Who can post a resume:	Those registered
Fee to post:	None
Confidentiality available:	Yes

OTHER SERVICES

Is a listserv or discussion forum offered:	Yes
Are assessment instruments offered:	Yes

Recruiters
Automated resume agent:	Yes
Banner advertising:	Yes
Status report on ads:	Yes - Both

Job Seekers
Automated job agent:	Yes
Career info provided:	Yes
Links to other sites:	Yes

SITE'S SELF DESCRIPTION

America's Job Exchange (AJE) provides search, job listings and career tools to help job seekers be successful in their job hunting and career growth. In addition, the AJE network offers specialized Web-sites for niche communities, such as veterans, seniors, disabled, minorities and many more to make the job search experience more personalized and effective.

Contact Information

Name:	Rathin Sinha
Phone:	866-923-6284
E-Mail:	customercare@americasjobexchange.com

ApartmentCareers.com
www.apartmentcareers.com
Realestatecareers, LLC

GENERAL SITE INFORMATION

Date activated online:	2000
Location of site headquarters:	Dallas, TX
Number of people who visit the site:	50,000 unique visitors/month
Time spent on site:	10.0 page views/visitor

JOB POSTINGS

Post full time jobs:	Yes
Post part time/contract/consulting jobs:	Yes - All
Most prevalent types of jobs posted:	On-site apartment staff
Distribution:	National - USA

Recruiters

Fee to post a job:	Under $100/posting
Posting period:	30 days
Link posting to your site:	Yes

Job Seekers

Number of job postings:	250+
Top salary levels of jobs:	$101-150K/yr
Source of postings:	Employers

RESUME SERVICES

Are resumes or profiles posted on the site:	Yes

Recruiters

Number in database:	20,000
Top occupations :	Property Manager
Fee to view resumes:	$250/month
How acquired:	Direct from candidates

Job Seekers

How long can you store:	Indefinitely
Who can post a resume:	Anyone
Fee to post:	None
Confidentiality available:	Yes

OTHER SERVICES

Is a listserv or discussion forum offered:	Yes
Are assessment instruments offered:	Yes

Recruiters

Automated resume agent:	Yes
Banner advertising:	Yes
Status report on ads:	Yes - Postings

Job Seekers

Automated job agent:	Yes
Career info provided:	Yes
Links to other sites:	Yes

SITE'S SELF DESCRIPTION

ApartmentCareers.com is the largest career site dedicated to advertising the staffing needs of the apartment industry. The National Apartment Association (NAA), the largest rental housing association in the U.S., selected ApartmentCareers.com to host the NAA Career Center and develop a nationwide network of association career sites to meet the needs of its 50,000 members.

Contact Information

Name:	John Cullens
Phone:	972-692-2430
E-Mail:	info@apartmentcareers.com

ASAE Career Headquarters
www.careerhq.org
American Society of Association Executives (ASAE)

GENERAL SITE INFORMATION

Date activated online:	2000
Location of site headquarters:	Washington, D.C.
Number of people who visit the site:	35,000 unique visitors/month
Time spent on site:	6.2 page views/visitor

JOB POSTINGS

Post full time jobs:	Yes
Post part time/contract/consulting jobs:	Yes - All
Most prevalent types of jobs posted:	MG, SM, Association Executive/Manager
Distribution:	National - USA

Recruiters
Fee to post a job:	$295-395/posting
Posting period:	30 days
Link posting to your site:	Yes

Job Seekers
Number of job postings:	400
Top salary levels of jobs:	$51-75K, $101-150K/yr
Source of postings:	Employers, Staffing

RESUME SERVICES

Are resumes or profiles posted on the site:	Yes

Recruiters
Number in database:	14,000
Top occupations :	MG
Fee to view resumes:	In posting fee
How acquired:	Direct from candidates

Job Seekers
How long can you store:	Indefinitely
Who can post a resume:	Anyone
Fee to post:	None
Confidentiality available:	Yes

OTHER SERVICES

Is a listserv or discussion forum offered:	No
Are assessment instruments offered:	No

Recruiters
Automated resume agent:	Yes
Banner advertising:	Yes
Status report on ads:	Yes - Postings

Job Seekers
Automated job agent:	Yes
Career info provided:	Yes
Links to other sites:	Yes

SITE'S SELF DESCRIPTION

ASAE's CareerHQ.org is the largest source of association industry jobs and resumes. It's where job seekers go to land the right job, and where employers go to find highly qualified applicants. CareerHQ.org also offers career development services, a mentoring program, and salary tables to help job seekers increase their competitive advantage.

Contact Information

Name:	Catherine Lux Fry
Phone:	202-626-2819
E-Mail:	clux@asaecenter.org

Aviation Employment
www.aviationmployment.com
Internet Brands, Inc.

GENERAL SITE INFORMATION

Date activated online:	1996
Location of site headquarters:	El Segundo, CA
Number of people who visit the site:	50,000 unique visitors/month
Time spent on site:	5:00 minutes/visit

JOB POSTINGS

Post full time jobs:	Yes
Post part time/contract/consulting jobs:	Yes - All
Most prevalent types of jobs posted:	A&P Mechanic, Engineer, Maintenance
Distribution:	International

Recruiters

Fee to post a job:	$145/posting
Posting period:	30 days
Link posting to your site:	Yes

Job Seekers

Number of job postings:	1,000
Top salary levels of jobs:	Not Reported
Source of postings:	Employers

RESUME SERVICES

Are resumes or profiles posted on the site:	Yes

Recruiters

Number in database:	155,000
Top occupations :	EN, OP, Maintenance
Fee to view resumes:	$250/month
How acquired:	Direct from candidates

Job Seekers

How long can you store:	Indefinitely
Who can post a resume:	Those registered
Fee to post:	None
Confidentiality available:	Yes

OTHER SERVICES

Is a listserv or discussion forum offered:	Yes
Are assessment instruments offered:	No

Recruiters

Automated resume agent:	Yes
Banner advertising:	Yes
Status report on ads:	Yes - Both

Job Seekers

Automated job agent:	Yes
Career info provided:	Yes
Links to other sites:	Yes

SITE'S SELF DESCRIPTION

Since 1996, AviationEmployment.com has helped millions of aviation and aerospace professionals find career opportunities. We specialize in the areas of aviation maintenance, engineering, A&P mechanic and avionics jobs. We are the #1 search result on Google for the keyword "aviation jobs." Unlike our competition, we never charge job seekers to post resumes.

Contact Information

Name:	Sales
Phone:	800-573-1848
E-Mail:	jobs@aviationemployment.com

BioSpace

www.biospace.com
onTargetjobs, Inc.

GENERAL SITE INFORMATION

Date activated online:	1985
Location of site headquarters:	Englewood, CO
Number of people who visit the site:	311,282 unique visitors/month
Time spent on site:	5:00 minutes/visit

JOB POSTINGS

Post full time jobs:	Yes
Post part time/contract/consulting jobs:	Yes - All
Most prevalent types of jobs posted:	Biotech, Pharma, Med Device, Academic
Distribution:	International

Recruiters

Fee to post a job:	$375/posting
Posting period:	60 days
Link posting to your site:	Yes

Job Seekers

Number of job postings:	3,000
Top salary levels of jobs:	$51-75K, $76-100K/yr
Source of postings:	Employers

RESUME SERVICES

Are resumes or profiles posted on the site:	Yes

Recruiters

Number in database:	280,000
Top occupations :	Clinical, Scientist
Fee to view resumes:	$6,995
How acquired:	Direct from candidates

Job Seekers

How long can you store:	1 year
Who can post a resume:	Those registered
Fee to post:	None
Confidentiality available:	Yes

OTHER SERVICES

Is a listserv or discussion forum offered:	Yes
Are assessment instruments offered:	No

Recruiters

Automated resume agent:	Yes
Banner advertising:	Yes
Status report on ads:	Yes - Both

Job Seekers

Automated job agent:	Yes
Career info provided:	Yes
Links to other sites:	Yes

SITE'S SELF DESCRIPTION

BioSpace provides employment and career resources that span the life sciences. Unlike general job boards, our leading partnerships allow us to reach niche audiences within clinical research, academia, medical device sectors, government markets and other areas. More than 75% of BioSpace.com visitors return within a week, and another 90% don't visit other industry sites.

Contact Information

Name:	Joe Kroog
Phone:	303-562-0351
E-Mail:	joe.kroog@biospace.com

BlueSteps
www.bluesteps.com
Association of Executive Search Consultants (AESC)

GENERAL SITE INFORMATION

Date activated online:	November, 2000
Location of site headquarters:	New York, NY
Number of people who visit the site:	40,000 unique visitors/month
Time spent on site:	4:00 minutes/visit

JOB POSTINGS

Post full time jobs:	No
Post part time/contract/consulting jobs:	No
Most prevalent types of jobs posted:	N/A
Distribution:	N/A

Recruiters

Fee to post a job:	N/A
Posting period:	N/A
Link posting to your site:	N/A

Job Seekers

Number of job postings:	N/A
Top salary levels of jobs:	N/A
Source of postings:	N/A

RESUME SERVICES

Are resumes or profiles posted on the site:	Yes

Recruiters

Number in database:	60,000
Top occupations :	MG, C-level
Fee to view resumes:	Members Only
How acquired:	Direct from candidates

Job Seekers

How long can you store:	Indefinitely
Who can post a resume:	Those registered
Fee to post:	$329
Confidentiality available:	Yes

OTHER SERVICES

Is a listserv or discussion forum offered:	No
Are assessment instruments offered:	No

Recruiters

Automated resume agent:	No
Banner advertising:	No
Status report on ads:	No

Job Seekers

Automated job agent:	No
Career info provided:	Yes
Links to other sites:	Yes

SITE'S SELF DESCRIPTION

As a service of the Association of Executive Search Consultants (AESC), BlueSteps gives senior executives direct visibility to over 6,000 executive recruiters at the top executive search firms worldwide. All firms are members of the AESC, the globally recognized body representing the retained executive search profession.

Contact Information

Name:	Customer Support
Phone:	800-363-1207
E-Mail:	info@bluesteps.com

BountyJobs

www.bountyjobs.com
BountyJobs, Inc.

GENERAL SITE INFORMATION

Date activated online:	November, 2006
Location of site headquarters:	New York, NY
Number of people who visit the site:	25,000 unique visitors/month
Time spent on site:	5:00 minutes/visit

JOB POSTINGS

Post full time jobs:	Yes
Post part time/contract/consulting jobs:	No
Most prevalent types of jobs posted:	Wide variety
Distribution:	International

Recruiters
Fee to post a job:	None; fee upon hiring
Posting period:	Unlimited
Link posting to your site:	No

Job Seekers
Number of job postings:	2,000+
Top salary levels of jobs:	$76-100K, $180-220K/yr
Source of postings:	Employers, Staffing

RESUME SERVICES

Are resumes or profiles posted on the site: No

Recruiters
Number in database:	N/A
Top occupations :	N/A
Fee to view resumes:	N/A
How acquired:	N/A

Job Seekers
How long can you store:	N/A
Who can post a resume:	N/A
Fee to post:	N/A
Confidentiality available:	N/A

OTHER SERVICES

Is a listserv or discussion forum offered:	No
Are assessment instruments offered:	No

Recruiters
Automated resume agent:	No
Banner advertising:	No
Status report on ads:	Yes - Postings

Job Seekers
Automated job agent:	No
Career info provided:	No
Links to other sites:	No

SITE'S SELF DESCRIPTION

BountyJobs is an online marketplace that connects employers with a national network of seasoned headhunters in seconds. Rather than being chained to the phone with headhunters all day, BountyJobs guarantees efficient collaboration with the headhunter channel through a single Web-based application. BountyJobs is the preferred contingent search solution.

Contact Information

Name:	Employers Information
Phone:	212-660-3960
E-Mail:	employers@bountyjobs.com

BrokerHunter.com
www.brokerhunter.com
BrokerHunter.com, LLC

GENERAL SITE INFORMATION

Date activated online:	2000
Location of site headquarters:	Cumming, GA
Number of people who visit the site:	170,000 unique visitors/month
Time spent on site:	5:33 minutes/visit

JOB POSTINGS

Post full time jobs:	Yes
Post part time/contract/consulting jobs:	Yes - All
Most prevalent types of jobs posted:	AD, FA, IS, OP, SM, Customer Service
Distribution:	International

Recruiters

Fee to post a job:	$495+/posting
Posting period:	60 days
Link posting to your site:	Yes

Job Seekers

Number of job postings:	8,183
Top salary levels of jobs:	Up to $251K+/yr
Source of postings:	Employers, Staffing

RESUME SERVICES

Are resumes or profiles posted on the site:	No

Recruiters

Number in database:	145,468
Top occupations :	MG, SM
Fee to view resumes:	In posting fee
How acquired:	Direct from candidates

Job Seekers

How long can you store:	Indefinitely
Who can post a resume:	Those registered
Fee to post:	None
Confidentiality available:	Yes

OTHER SERVICES

Is a listserv or discussion forum offered:	Yes
Are assessment instruments offered:	No

Recruiters

Automated resume agent:	Yes
Banner advertising:	Yes
Status report on ads:	Yes - Both

Job Seekers

Automated job agent:	Yes
Career info provided:	Yes
Links to other sites:	Yes

SITE'S SELF DESCRIPTION

BrokerHunter.com is the leading securities industry employment Web-site in the nation with over 145,000 candidates and over 8,000 job postings from hundreds of branches and firms. The company's area of expertise is in the gathering and presentation of highly tailored data related to securities industry job seekers and to financial services employers and recruiters.

Contact Information

Name:	Steve Testerman
Phone:	770-781-2629 x200
E-Mail:	sales@brokerhunter.com

CallCenterJobs.com
www.callcenterjobs.com
CallCenterJobs.com

GENERAL SITE INFORMATION

Date activated online:	1999
Location of site headquarters:	Omaha, NE
Number of people who visit the site:	143,000+ unique visitors/month
Time spent on site:	3:23 minutes/visit

JOB POSTINGS

Post full time jobs:	Yes
Post part time/contract/consulting jobs:	Yes - Part time
Most prevalent types of jobs posted:	MG, OP, SM, Customer Service
Distribution:	National - USA

Recruiters
Fee to post a job:	$175/posting
Posting period:	60 days
Link posting to your site:	Yes

Job Seekers
Number of job postings:	550
Top salary levels of jobs:	Up to $130+K/yr
Source of postings:	Employers

RESUME SERVICES

Are resumes or profiles posted on the site:	Yes

Recruiters
Number in database:	72,000
Top occupations :	MG, Customer Service
Fee to view resumes:	$225/month
How acquired:	Direct from candidates

Job Seekers
How long can you store:	2 years
Who can post a resume:	Anyone
Fee to post:	None
Confidentiality available:	Yes

OTHER SERVICES

Is a listserv or discussion forum offered:	No
Are assessment instruments offered:	Yes

Recruiters
Automated resume agent:	Yes
Banner advertising:	Yes
Status report on ads:	Yes - Both

Job Seekers
Automated job agent:	Yes
Career info provided:	Yes
Links to other sites:	Yes

SITE'S SELF DESCRIPTION

CallCenterJobs.com specializes in contact center, customer service, telesales, help desk and collections positions. We provide quality jobs and attract quality employment candidates who are not visiting the larger job boards. We also provide a directory of industry resources to provide professionals with an extensive collection of online call center resources.

Contact Information

Name:	Jim Moylan
Phone:	880-353-7529
E-Mail:	jm@callcenterjobs.com

CareerBoard
www.careerboard.com
JobServe USA

GENERAL SITE INFORMATION

Date activated online:	May, 1997
Location of site headquarters:	Beachwood, OH
Number of people who visit the site:	185,000 unique visitors/month
Time spent on site:	3.8 page views/visitor

JOB POSTINGS

Post full time jobs:	Yes
Post part time/contract/consulting jobs:	Yes - All
Most prevalent types of jobs posted:	Wide variety
Distribution:	National - USA

Recruiters

Fee to post a job:	$184/posting
Posting period:	28 days
Link posting to your site:	Yes

Job Seekers

Number of job postings:	16,000
Top salary levels of jobs:	$76-100K, $101-150K/yr
Source of postings:	Employers, Staffing

RESUME SERVICES

Are resumes or profiles posted on the site:	Yes

Recruiters

Number in database:	450,000
Top occupations :	Wide variety
Fee to view resumes:	$2/resume
How acquired:	Direct from candidates

Job Seekers

How long can you store:	2 years
Who can post a resume:	Those registered
Fee to post:	None
Confidentiality available:	Yes

OTHER SERVICES

Is a listserv or discussion forum offered:	No
Are assessment instruments offered:	Yes

Recruiters

Automated resume agent:	Yes
Banner advertising:	Yes
Status report on ads:	Yes - Both

Job Seekers

Automated job agent:	Yes
Career info provided:	Yes
Links to other sites:	Yes

SITE'S SELF DESCRIPTION

CareerBoard connects local employers with local job seekers. Our nationwide network of niche and sixty-eight geographically targeted local employment Web-sites ensures jobs are seen by the most relevant job seekers wherever they are located. Our network reaches 32 million unique visitors/month and produces quality response to postings in all categories and USA locations.

Contact Information

Name:	CareerBoard
Phone:	877-619-5627
E-Mail:	careerboard@careerboard.com

CareerBuilder.com
www.careerbuilder.com
CareerBuilder, LLC

GENERAL SITE INFORMATION
Date activated online:	1998
Location of site headquarters:	Chicago, IL
Number of people who visit the site:	25,000,000 unique visitors/month
Time spent on site:	12:00+ minutes/visit

JOB POSTINGS
Post full time jobs:	Yes
Post part time/contract/consulting jobs:	Yes - All
Most prevalent types of jobs posted:	Wide variety
Distribution:	International

Recruiters
Fee to post a job:	$400+/posting
Posting period:	30 days
Link posting to your site:	Yes

Job Seekers
Number of job postings:	1,000,000+
Top salary levels of jobs:	Not Reported
Source of postings:	Employers, Staffing

RESUME SERVICES
Are resumes or profiles posted on the site: Yes

Recruiters
Number in database:	36,000,000+
Top occupations :	Wide variety
Fee to view resumes:	Not Reported
How acquired:	Direct from candidates

Job Seekers
How long can you store:	Indefinitely
Who can post a resume:	Anyone
Fee to post:	None
Confidentiality available:	Yes

OTHER SERVICES
Is a listserv or discussion forum offered:	Yes
Are assessment instruments offered:	Yes

Recruiters
Automated resume agent:	No
Banner advertising:	Yes
Status report on ads:	Yes - Both

Job Seekers
Automated job agent:	Yes
Career info provided:	Yes
Links to other sites:	Yes

SITE'S SELF DESCRIPTION
CareerBuilder.com is the nation's largest online job site with more than 25 million unique visitors and over one million jobs. Owned by Gannett Co., Inc. (NYSE:GCI), Tribune Company, The McClatchy Company (NYSE:MNI) and Microsoft Corp. (Nasdaq: MSFT), the company offers a vast online and print network to help job seekers connect with employers.

Contact Information
Name:	Customer Service
Phone:	800-891-8880
E-Mail:	Not Reported

Careers in Proprietary Education

www.propedu.com
Careers in Proprietary Education, Inc.

GENERAL SITE INFORMATION

Date activated online:	January, 2011
Location of site headquarters:	Coconut Creek, FL
Number of people who visit the site:	1,700 unique visitors/month
Time spent on site:	4:34 minutes/visit

JOB POSTINGS

Post full time jobs:	Yes
Post part time/contract/consulting jobs:	Yes - Part time, Adjunct Faculty
Most prevalent types of jobs posted:	Campus Director, Academic Dean
Distribution:	National - USA

Recruiters

Fee to post a job:	$90/posting
Posting period:	60 days
Link posting to your site:	Yes

Job Seekers

Number of job postings:	118
Top salary levels of jobs:	Up to $125K+/yr
Source of postings:	Employers

RESUME SERVICES

Are resumes or profiles posted on the site:	Yes

Recruiters

Number in database:	200
Top occupations :	HR, SM, Higher Ed
Fee to view resumes:	$400/month
How acquired:	Direct from candidates

Job Seekers

How long can you store:	Indefinitely
Who can post a resume:	Those registered
Fee to post:	None
Confidentiality available:	Yes

OTHER SERVICES

Is a listserv or discussion forum offered:	Yes
Are assessment instruments offered:	Yes

Recruiters

Automated resume agent:	Yes
Banner advertising:	Yes
Status report on ads:	Yes - Both

Job Seekers

Automated job agent:	Yes
Career info provided:	No
Links to other sites:	Yes

SITE'S SELF DESCRIPTION

Careers in Proprietary Education is a niche site dedicated to the proprietary education industry. It links professionals with careers in proprietary education and provides for-profit and non-profit K-12 schools, colleges, universities and institutes with exceptional talent.

Contact Information

Name:	Susan Forman
Phone:	954-596-8100
E-Mail:	susan@propedu.com

Chicagojobs.com
www.chicagojobs.com
Shaker Recruitment Advertising & Communications

GENERAL SITE INFORMATION

Date activated online:	2004
Location of site headquarters:	Chicago, IL
Number of people who visit the site:	150,000 unique visitors/month
Time spent on site:	30.0 page views/visitor

JOB POSTINGS

Post full time jobs:	Yes
Post part time/contract/consulting jobs:	Yes - All
Most prevalent types of jobs posted:	Wide variety
Distribution:	Regional/USA: Chicago, IL

Recruiters

Fee to post a job:	$325/posting
Posting period:	30 days
Link posting to your site:	Yes

Job Seekers

Number of job postings:	5,000+
Top salary levels of jobs:	$31-50K, $51-75K/yr
Source of postings:	Employers

RESUME SERVICES

Are resumes or profiles posted on the site:	Yes

Recruiters

Number in database:	45,000+
Top occupations :	Wide variety
Fee to view resumes:	$675/month
How acquired:	Direct from candidates

Job Seekers

How long can you store:	Indefinitely
Who can post a resume:	Anyone
Fee to post:	None
Confidentiality available:	Yes

OTHER SERVICES

Is a listserv or discussion forum offered:	No
Are assessment instruments offered:	No

Recruiters

Automated resume agent:	Yes
Banner advertising:	Yes
Status report on ads:	Yes - Not Reported

Job Seekers

Automated job agent:	Yes
Career info provided:	Yes
Links to other sites:	Yes

SITE'S SELF DESCRIPTION

Exclusively focused on Chicagoland's 11 county area including the city, suburbs and beyond, ChicagoJobs. com's award-winning layout and enhanced services maximize exposure for both local employers and job seekers. Launched in 2004, we average 150,000 unique monthly visitors and more than 4.5 million page views each month.

Contact Information

Name:	Sales
Phone:	877-562-7244
E-Mail:	sales@chicagojobs.com

ClearedConnections
www.clearedconnections.com
Cleared People, LLC

GENERAL SITE INFORMATION

Date activated online:	November, 1999
Location of site headquarters:	Reston, VA
Number of people who visit the site:	145,000+ unique visitors/month
Time spent on site:	8:10 minutes/visit

JOB POSTINGS

Post full time jobs:	Yes
Post part time/contract/consulting jobs:	Yes - All
Most prevalent types of jobs posted:	EN, IS, MG, Government
Distribution:	International

Recruiters
Fee to post a job:	$750/5 postings
Posting period:	60 days
Link posting to your site:	Yes

Job Seekers
Number of job postings:	5,000
Top salary levels of jobs:	Up to $195K/yr
Source of postings:	Employers

RESUME SERVICES

Are resumes or profiles posted on the site:	Yes

Recruiters
Number in database:	285,000+
Top occupations :	EN
Fee to view resumes:	In posting fee
How acquired:	Direct from candidates

Job Seekers
How long can you store:	Indefinitely
Who can post a resume:	Only those in field
Fee to post:	None
Confidentiality available:	Yes

OTHER SERVICES

Is a listserv or discussion forum offered:	Yes
Are assessment instruments offered:	No

Recruiters
Automated resume agent:	Yes
Banner advertising:	Yes
Status report on ads:	Yes - Both

Job Seekers
Automated job agent:	Yes
Career info provided:	Yes
Links to other sites:	Yes

SITE'S SELF DESCRIPTION

Serving over one hundred federal contractors, ClearedConnections is an online resource for security cleared professionals. Its focus is to identify individuals with an active security clearance and facilitate an introduction to organizations with corresponding hiring requirements. ClearedConnections exclusively connects cleared personnel with cleared facilities (FCL's).

Contact Information

Name:	Robert Esti
Phone:	703-860-2246
E-Mail:	robert@clearedconnections.com

CollegeRecruiter.com
www.collegerecruiter.com
CollegeRecruiter.com

GENERAL SITE INFORMATION

Date activated online:	1996
Location of site headquarters:	Minneapolis, MN
Number of people who visit the site:	500,000 unique visitors/month
Time spent on site:	3.0 page views/visitor

JOB POSTINGS

Post full time jobs:	Yes
Post part time/contract/consulting jobs:	Yes - All
Most prevalent types of jobs posted:	EN, SM, Internships
Distribution:	National - USA

Recruiters
Fee to post a job:	$95/posting
Posting period:	30 days
Link posting to your site:	Yes

Job Seekers
Number of job postings:	700,000
Top salary levels of jobs:	$201-250K, $251K+/yr
Source of postings:	Employers, Other sites

RESUME SERVICES

Are resumes or profiles posted on the site:	No

Recruiters
Number in database:	N/A
Top occupations :	N/A
Fee to view resumes:	N/A
How acquired:	N/A

Job Seekers
How long can you store:	N/A
Who can post a resume:	N/A
Fee to post:	N/A
Confidentiality available:	N/A

OTHER SERVICES

Is a listserv or discussion forum offered:	Yes
Are assessment instruments offered:	Yes

Recruiters
Automated resume agent:	No
Banner advertising:	Yes
Status report on ads:	Yes - Postings

Job Seekers
Automated job agent:	Yes
Career info provided:	Yes
Links to other sites:	Yes

SITE'S SELF DESCRIPTION

CollegeRecruiter.com is the leading job board for college students searching for internships and recent graduates hunting for entry-level and other career opportunities. Features tens of thousands of pages of employment-related articles, blogs, videos, podcasts and other such content.

Contact Information

Name:	Steven Rothberg
Phone:	952-848-2211
E-Mail:	steven@collegerecruiter.com

ConstructionJobs.com
www.constructionjobs.com
Construction Jobs, Inc.

GENERAL SITE INFORMATION

Date activated online: 2000
Location of site headquarters: Asheville, NC
Number of people who visit the site: 165,000 unique visitors/month
Time spent on site: 2.3 page views/visitor

JOB POSTINGS

Post full time jobs: Yes
Post part time/contract/consulting jobs: Yes - All
Most prevalent types of jobs posted: EN, MG, OP, SM
Distribution: National - USA

Recruiters
Fee to post a job: $301-350/posting
Posting period: 60 days
Link posting to your site: Yes

Job Seekers
Number of job postings: 1,700
Top salary levels of jobs: $101-150K/yr
Source of postings: Employers, Staffing

RESUME SERVICES

Are resumes or profiles posted on the site: Yes

Recruiters
Number in database: 75,000
Top occupations :   EN, MG, OP, SM
Fee to view resumes: Not Reported
How acquired: Direct from candidates

Job Seekers
How long can you store: 6 months
Who can post a resume: Anyone
Fee to post: None
Confidentiality available: Yes

OTHER SERVICES

Is a listserv or discussion forum offered: No
Are assessment instruments offered: Yes

Recruiters
Automated resume agent: Yes
Banner advertising: Yes
Status report on ads: Yes - Both

Job Seekers
Automated job agent: Yes
Career info provided: Yes
Links to other sites: Yes

SITE'S SELF DESCRIPTION

ConstructionJobs.com is the nation's premier employment resource for the construction, design and building industries. Endorsed by 9 industry associations as their preferred partner for online recruiting, our award-winning job board and resume database provide a cost-effective solution that makes advertising openings and locating qualified candidates faster and easier.

Contact Information

Name: Alan Kerschen
Phone: 828-251-1344
E-Mail: info@constructionjobs.com

Cool Works
www.coolworks.com
CW, Inc.

GENERAL SITE INFORMATION

Date activated online:	November, 1995
Location of site headquarters:	Gardiner, MT
Number of people who visit the site:	108,500 unique visitors/month
Time spent on site:	4:11 minutes/visit

JOB POSTINGS

Post full time jobs:	Yes
Post part time/contract/consulting jobs:	Yes - Seasonal jobs
Most prevalent types of jobs posted:	MG, Food and beverage, Housekeeping
Distribution:	National - USA

Recruiters
Fee to post a job:	$119/posting
Posting period:	30 days
Link posting to your site:	Yes

Job Seekers
Number of job postings:	35+
Top salary levels of jobs:	Hourly, $20-100K/yr
Source of postings:	Employers

RESUME SERVICES

Are resumes or profiles posted on the site:	No

Recruiters
Number in database:	N/A
Top occupations :	N/A
Fee to view resumes:	N/A
How acquired:	N/A

Job Seekers
How long can you store:	N/A
Who can post a resume:	N/A
Fee to post:	N/A
Confidentiality available:	N/A

OTHER SERVICES

Is a listserv or discussion forum offered:	Yes
Are assessment instruments offered:	No

Recruiters
Automated resume agent:	No
Banner advertising:	Yes
Status report on ads:	No

Job Seekers
Automated job agent:	No
Career info provided:	Yes
Links to other sites:	Yes

SITE'S SELF DESCRIPTION

Cool Works® is about finding a seasonal job or career in some of the greatest places on Earth. We offer thousands of jobs in national and state parks, summer and ski resorts, camps, ranches, adventure travel companies and more. Our 5,700-member social network provides a place to compare and share work and life experiences in these unique places.

Contact Information

Name:	Bill Berg
Phone:	406-848-2380
E-Mail:	greatjobs@coolworks.com

Coroflot
www.coroflot.com
Core77, Inc.

GENERAL SITE INFORMATION

Date activated online:	1997
Location of site headquarters:	New York, NY
Number of people who visit the site:	821,000 unique visitors/month
Time spent on site:	4:32 minutes/visit

JOB POSTINGS

Post full time jobs:	Yes
Post part time/contract/consulting jobs:	Yes - Free lance, Contract
Most prevalent types of jobs posted:	Creative: Design, Direction, Strategy
Distribution:	International

Recruiters
Fee to post a job:	$265/posting
Posting period:	90 days
Link posting to your site:	Yes

Job Seekers
Number of job postings:	1,000
Top salary levels of jobs:	$50-75K, $76-$00K/yr
Source of postings:	Employers, Staffing

RESUME SERVICES

Are resumes or profiles posted on the site:	Yes

Recruiters
Number in database:	225,000+
Top occupations :	Creative
Fee to view resumes:	None
How acquired:	Direct from candidates

Job Seekers
How long can you store:	Indefinitely
Who can post a resume:	Those registered
Fee to post:	None
Confidentiality available:	No

OTHER SERVICES

Is a listserv or discussion forum offered:	No
Are assessment instruments offered:	No

Recruiters
Automated resume agent:	No
Banner advertising:	Yes
Status report on ads:	Yes - Both

Job Seekers
Automated job agent:	Yes
Career info provided:	Yes
Links to other sites:	No

SITE'S SELF DESCRIPTION

Coroflot is an employment and community site focused on the creative industries and creative professionals. Coroflot has a robust job board covering a wide range of creative disciplines while also allowing individuals to promote themselves as a design resource by creating an online profile and portfolio. The site functions as an inspiration source for all creatives.

Contact Information

Name:	Coroflot Client Support
Phone:	212-965-1998 x110
E-Mail:	support@coroflot.com

Dice.com
www.dice.com
Dice Holdings, Inc.

GENERAL SITE INFORMATION

Date activated online:	1990
Location of site headquarters:	New York, NY
Number of people who visit the site:	2,000,000 unique visitors/month
Time spent on site:	27.0 page views/visitor

JOB POSTINGS

Post full time jobs:	Yes
Post part time/contract/consulting jobs:	Yes - All
Most prevalent types of jobs posted:	Technology
Distribution:	National - USA

Recruiters

Fee to post a job:	$995 for 5 job package
Posting period:	30 days
Link posting to your site:	Yes

Job Seekers

Number of job postings:	70,000
Top salary levels of jobs:	$76-100K, $101-150K/yr
Source of postings:	Employers, Staffing

RESUME SERVICES

Are resumes or profiles posted on the site:	Yes

Recruiters

Number in database:	1,000,000+
Top occupations :	Technology
Fee to view resumes:	In posting fee
How acquired:	Direct from candidates

Job Seekers

How long can you store:	Indefinitely
Who can post a resume:	Those in the field
Fee to post:	None
Confidentiality available:	Yes

OTHER SERVICES

Is a listserv or discussion forum offered:	Yes
Are assessment instruments offered:	No

Recruiters

Automated resume agent:	Yes
Banner advertising:	Yes
Status report on ads:	Yes - Not Reported

Job Seekers

Automated job agent:	Yes
Career info provided:	Yes
Links to other sites:	Yes

SITE'S SELF DESCRIPTION

Dice, a Dice Holdings, Inc. service, is the leading career site for technology and engineering professionals. With a 20-year track record of meeting the needs of technology professionals, companies and recruiters, our specialty focus and exposure to highly skilled professional communities enable employers to reach hard-to-find, experienced and qualified candidates.

Contact Information

Name:	Dice.com Sales
Phone:	877-386-3323
E-Mail:	sales@dice.com

disABLEDperson.com
www.disabledperson.com
disABLEDperson, Inc.

GENERAL SITE INFORMATION

Date activated online: April, 2002
Location of site headquarters: Encinitas, CA
Number of people who visit the site: 5,984 unique visitors/month
Time spent on site: 4.2 page views/visitor

JOB POSTINGS

Post full time jobs: Yes
Post part time/contract/consulting jobs: No
Most prevalent types of jobs posted: Wide variety
Distribution: National - USA

Recruiters
Fee to post a job: $50/posting
Posting period: 60 days
Link posting to your site: Yes

Job Seekers
Number of job postings: 7,000
Top salary levels of jobs: Not Reported
Source of postings: Employers

RESUME SERVICES

Are resumes or profiles posted on the site: Yes

Recruiters
Number in database: 4,000
Top occupations :   Wide variety
Fee to view resumes: None
How acquired: Direct from candidates

Job Seekers
How long can you store: 85 days
Who can post a resume: Those registered
Fee to post: None
Confidentiality available: Yes

OTHER SERVICES

Is a listserv or discussion forum offered: No
Are assessment instruments offered: No

Recruiters
Automated resume agent: No
Banner advertising: Yes
Status report on ads: No

Job Seekers
Automated job agent: No
Career info provided: Yes
Links to other sites: Yes

SITE'S SELF DESCRIPTION

We are a public charity organization whose primary focus is disability employment. We want to help you, a person with a disability find employment. Our portal connects individuals with disabilities with proactive employers. So come, post your resume and look for a job. Its free! Our goal is to get as many jobs for people with disabilities as possible.

Contact Information

Name: Information
Phone: 760-420-1269
E-Mail: info@disabledperson.com

DiversityJobs.com
www.diversityjobs.com
LatPro, Inc.

GENERAL SITE INFORMATION

Date activated online:	2006
Location of site headquarters:	Plantation, FL
Number of people who visit the site:	250,000+ unique visitors/month
Time spent on site:	4:15 minutes/visit

JOB POSTINGS

Post full time jobs:	Yes
Post part time/contract/consulting jobs:	Yes - All
Most prevalent types of jobs posted:	AD, HR, SM, Healthcare
Distribution:	National - USA

Recruiters		**Job Seekers**	
Fee to post a job:	$195/posting	Number of job postings:	440,000
Posting period:	30 days	Top salary levels of jobs:	Not Reported
Link posting to your site:	Yes	Source of postings:	Employers, Other sites

RESUME SERVICES

Are resumes or profiles posted on the site:	No

Recruiters		**Job Seekers**	
Number in database:	N/A	How long can you store:	N/A
Top occupations :	N/A	Who can post a resume:	N/A
Fee to view resumes:	N/A	Fee to post:	N/A
How acquired:	N/A	Confidentiality available:	N/A

OTHER SERVICES

Is a listserv or discussion forum offered:	Yes
Are assessment instruments offered:	Yes

Recruiters		**Job Seekers**	
Automated resume agent:	Yes	Automated job agent:	Yes
Banner advertising:	Yes	Career info provided:	Yes
Status report on ads:	Yes - Both	Links to other sites:	Yes

SITE'S SELF DESCRIPTION

Developed by LatPro, Inc., DiversityJobs.com holds the #1 ranking on Google, Yahoo! and Bing for the search term "diversity jobs." Our mission is to equip African-Americans, women, Hispanics, veterans, persons with disabilities, Asian-Americans, Native Americans, members of the LGBT community and others with current jobs from employers dedicated to a diverse workforce.

Contact Information

Name:	Rob Steward
Phone:	954-727-3863
E-Mail:	sales@latpro.com

eFinancialCareers.com
www.efinancialcareers.com
Dice Holdings, Inc.

GENERAL SITE INFORMATION

Date activated online:	2000
Location of site headquarters:	New York, NY
Number of people who visit the site:	350,000 unique visitors/month
Time spent on site:	10.7 page views/visitor

JOB POSTINGS

Post full time jobs:	Yes
Post part time/contract/consulting jobs:	Yes - All
Most prevalent types of jobs posted:	Financial markets
Distribution:	International

Recruiters
Fee to post a job:	$495/posting
Posting period:	30 days
Link posting to your site:	Yes

Job Seekers
Number of job postings:	1,700
Top salary levels of jobs:	Up to $250K+/yr
Source of postings:	Employers

RESUME SERVICES

Are resumes or profiles posted on the site:	Yes

Recruiters
Number in database:	300,000
Top occupations :	Investment Banking
Fee to view resumes:	$750/month
How acquired:	Direct from candidates

Job Seekers
How long can you store:	Indefinitely
Who can post a resume:	Those in the field
Fee to post:	None
Confidentiality available:	Yes

OTHER SERVICES

Is a listserv or discussion forum offered:	No
Are assessment instruments offered:	No

Recruiters
Automated resume agent:	Yes
Banner advertising:	Yes
Status report on ads:	Yes - Not Specified

Job Seekers
Automated job agent:	Yes
Career info provided:	Yes
Links to other sites:	Yes

SITE'S SELF DESCRIPTION

eFinancialCareers, a Dice Holdings, Inc. service, is the leading global career site network in the investment banking, asset management and securities industries. eFinancialCareers provides job postings, news, salary surveys and career advice; reaches professionals in over 30 financial market sectors; and has a network of 25+ co-branded career sites in the NA industry.

Contact Information

Name:	eFinancialCareers Sales
Phone:	800-380-9040
E-Mail:	sales@efinancialcareers.com

EHSCareers.com
www.ehscareers.com
EHSCareers.com, Inc.

GENERAL SITE INFORMATION

Date activated online:	2003
Location of site headquarters:	Watkinsville, GA
Number of people who visit the site:	35,458 unique visitors/month
Time spent on site:	5.7 pageviews/visitor

JOB POSTINGS

Post full time jobs:	Yes
Post part time/contract/consulting jobs:	Yes - All
Most prevalent types of jobs posted:	Environment, Safety, Occupational Health
Distribution:	International

Recruiters
Fee to post a job:	$250/posting
Posting period:	30 days
Link posting to your site:	Yes

Job Seekers
Number of job postings:	550+
Top salary levels of jobs:	$151-200K, $201-250K/yr
Source of postings:	Employers, Staffing

RESUME SERVICES

Are resumes or profiles posted on the site:	Yes

Recruiters
Number in database:	9,000+
Top occupations :	Environmental, Safety
Fee to view resumes:	In posting fee
How acquired:	Direct from candidates

Job Seekers
How long can you store:	6 months
Who can post a resume:	Those registered
Fee to post:	None
Confidentiality available:	Yes

OTHER SERVICES

Is a listserv or discussion forum offered:	No
Are assessment instruments offered:	No

Recruiters
Automated resume agent:	Yes
Banner advertising:	Yes
Status report on ads:	Yes - Banners

Job Seekers
Automated job agent:	Yes
Career info provided:	Yes
Links to other sites:	Yes

SITE'S SELF DESCRIPTION

EHSCareers.com has been the leading job board for the environmental, occupational health and safety profession since 2003. The site is free to job seekers. Recruiters and employers pay a fee for job postings and access to job seeker profiles. EHSCareers.com is also the official job board for the National Safety Council and the National Association of EHS Managers.

Contact Information

Name:	Randy Williams
Phone:	877-213-3377
E-Mail:	randywilliams@ehscareers.com

EmployeeBenefitsJobs.com
www.employeebenefitsjobs.com
BenefitsLink.com, Inc.

GENERAL SITE INFORMATION

Date activated online:	December, 1996
Location of site headquarters:	Winter Park, FL
Number of people who visit the site:	16,000 unique visitors/month
Time spent on site:	9:00 minutes/visit

JOB POSTINGS

Post full time jobs:	Yes
Post part time/contract/consulting jobs:	Yes - All
Most prevalent types of jobs posted:	Employee benefits administration
Distribution:	National - USA

Recruiters

Fee to post a job:	$335/posting
Posting period:	60 days
Link posting to your site:	Yes

Job Seekers

Number of job postings:	225
Top salary levels of jobs:	$51-75K, $76-100K/yr
Source of postings:	Employers, Staffing

RESUME SERVICES

Are resumes or profiles posted on the site:	Yes

Recruiters

Number in database:	1,600
Top occupations :	Employee benefits
Fee to view resumes:	In posting fee
How acquired:	Direct from candidates

Job Seekers

How long can you store:	2 years
Who can post a resume:	Those in the field
Fee to post:	None
Confidentiality available:	Yes

OTHER SERVICES

Is a listserv or discussion forum offered:	Yes
Are assessment instruments offered:	No

Recruiters

Automated resume agent:	No
Banner advertising:	Yes
Status report on ads:	Yes - Both

Job Seekers

Automated job agent:	Yes
Career info provided:	Yes
Links to other sites:	Yes

SITE'S SELF DESCRIPTION

Online since 1996, EmployeeBenefitsJobs.com has high Google visibility and a loyal audience. A link to each job is published in email newsletters sent to 25,000 subscribers daily by affiliate BenefitsLink.com, the leading and first Web-site for the employee benefits community, where an advertisement for the job board appears on every page.

Contact Information

Name:	Mary Hall
Phone:	407-644-4146
E-Mail:	maryhall@benefitslink.com

ExecuNet
www.execunet.com
ExecuNet

GENERAL SITE INFORMATION

Location of site headquarters:	Norwalk, CT
Number of people who visit the site:	1,000,000 unique visitors/month
Time spent on site:	4.8 page views/visitor
Date activated online:	1995

JOB POSTINGS

Post full time jobs:	Yes
Post part time/contract/consulting jobs:	Yes - Contract
Most prevalent types of jobs posted:	HR, IS, MG, SM
Distribution:	National - USA

Recruiters
Fee to post a job:	$295/posting
Posting period:	45 days
Link posting to your site:	Yes

Job Seekers
Number of job postings:	2,600+
Top salary levels of jobs:	Up to $600K+/yr
Source of postings:	Employers, Staffing

RESUME SERVICES

Are resumes or profiles posted on the site:	Yes

Recruiters
Number in database:	26,000
Top occupations :	FA, IS, MG, SM
Fee to view resumes:	In posting fee
How acquired:	Direct from candidates

Job Seekers
How long can you store:	1 year
Who can post a resume:	Members only (fee)
Fee to post:	Included in membership
Confidentiality available:	Yes

OTHER SERVICES

Is a listserv or discussion forum offered:	Yes
Are assessment instruments offered:	Yes

Recruiters
Automated resume agent:	Yes
Banner advertising:	No
Status report on ads:	Yes - Not Reported

Job Seekers
Automated job agent:	Yes
Career info provided:	Yes
Links to other sites:	Yes

SITE'S SELF DESCRIPTION

ExecuNet is a private membership network for business leaders who believe that the right connections can produce extraordinary results in their careers and organizations. Since 1988, it has provided members access to confidential six-figure job opportunities, proprietary research and pragmatic advice.

Contact Information

Name:	Member Services
Phone:	800-637-3126
E-Mail:	member.services@execunet.comm

FINS from The Wall Street Journal
www.fins.com
Dow Jones & Company

GENERAL SITE INFORMATION

Date activated online:	2009
Location of site headquarters:	New York, NY
Number of people who visit the site:	40,000,000+ unique visitors/month
Time spent on site:	2:00 minutes/visit

JOB POSTINGS

Post full time jobs:	Yes
Post part time/contract/consulting jobs:	Yes - All
Most prevalent types of jobs posted:	FA, IS, SM
Distribution:	International

Recruiters

Fee to post a job:	$375/posting
Posting period:	30 days
Link posting to your site:	Yes

Job Seekers

Number of job postings:	11,000+
Top salary levels of jobs:	Up to $500K+/yr
Source of postings:	Employers, Staffing

RESUME SERVICES

Are resumes or profiles posted on the site:	Yes

Recruiters

Number in database:	Not Reported
Top occupations :	FA, IS, SM
Fee to view resumes:	Not Reported
How acquired:	Direct from candidates

Job Seekers

How long can you store:	Indefinitely
Who can post a resume:	Those registered
Fee to post:	None
Confidentiality available:	Yes

OTHER SERVICES

Is a listserv or discussion forum offered:	Yes
Are assessment instruments offered:	No

Recruiters

Automated resume agent:	Yes
Banner advertising:	Yes
Status report on ads:	Yes - Both

Job Seekers

Automated job agent:	Yes
Career info provided:	Yes
Links to other sites:	Yes

SITE'S SELF DESCRIPTION

FINS.com from The Wall Street Journal combines great jobs with industry-specific news and advice to help you find jobs, manage your career and get ahead. Our free, targeted sites for finance, technology and sales and marketing professionals help you stay on top of your career, whether you're actively looking for a job or working to excel in your current position.

Contact Information

Name:	Sales Inquiries
Phone:	1-877-FINS-450
E-Mail:	sales@fins.com

FlexJobs
www.flexjobs.com
FlexJobs Corporation

GENERAL SITE INFORMATION

Date activated online:	June, 2007
Location of site headquarters:	San Francisco, CA
Number of people who visit the site:	80,000 unique visitors/month
Time spent on site:	5:30 minutes/visit

JOB POSTINGS

Post full time jobs:	Yes
Post part time/contract/consulting jobs:	Yes - All
Most prevalent types of jobs posted:	Telecommuting & flexible jobs
Distribution:	International

Recruiters
Fee to post a job:	Free
Posting period:	60 days
Link posting to your site:	Yes

Job Seekers
Number of job postings:	2,000
Top salary levels of jobs:	Up to $100K+/yr
Source of postings:	Employers

RESUME SERVICES

Are resumes or profiles posted on the site:	Yes

Recruiters
Number in database:	15,000
Top occupations :	Wide variety
Fee to view resumes:	In posting fee
How acquired:	Direct from candidates

Job Seekers
How long can you store:	Indefinitely
Who can post a resume:	Those registered
Fee to post:	$49.95/year
Confidentiality available:	Yes

OTHER SERVICES

Is a listserv or discussion forum offered:	No
Are assessment instruments offered:	Yes

Recruiters
Automated resume agent:	Yes
Banner advertising:	No
Status report on ads:	No

Job Seekers
Automated job agent:	Yes
Career info provided:	No
Links to other sites:	No

SITE'S SELF DESCRIPTION

FlexJobs is an innovative job site dedicated to bringing legitimate, flexible telecommuting jobs -- and the work-life, economic, and environmental benefits they offer -- to the people who want them. FlexJobs provides job-seekers a way to find qualified, hand-screened jobs quickly, easily, and safely and is a free resource for employers to recruit top-notch candidates.

Contact Information

Name:	Sara Sutton Fell
Phone:	866-991-9222
E-Mail:	sara@flexjobs.com

GARP Career Center
http://careers.garp.com
Global Association of Risk Professionals (GARP)

GENERAL SITE INFORMATION

Date activated online:	2003
Location of site headquarters:	Jersey City, NJ
Number of people who visit the site:	10,658 unique visitors/month
Time spent on site:	3:12 minutes/visit

JOB POSTINGS

Post full time jobs:	Yes
Post part time/contract/consulting jobs:	No
Most prevalent types of jobs posted:	Banking, Investing, Financial Risk
Distribution:	International

Recruiters

Fee to post a job:	$275/posting
Posting period:	30 days
Link posting to your site:	Yes

Job Seekers

Number of job postings:	100
Top salary levels of jobs:	Up to $250K+/yr
Source of postings:	Employers

RESUME SERVICES

Are resumes or profiles posted on the site:	Yes

Recruiters

Number in database:	3,000
Top occupations :	FA, Banking, Investing
Fee to view resumes:	$375/two weeks
How acquired:	Direct from candidates

Job Seekers

How long can you store:	1 year
Who can post a resume:	Those in the field
Fee to post:	None
Confidentiality available:	Yes

OTHER SERVICES

Is a listserv or discussion forum offered:	No
Are assessment instruments offered:	No

Recruiters

Automated resume agent:	No
Banner advertising:	Yes
Status report on ads:	No

Job Seekers

Automated job agent:	Yes
Career info provided:	No
Links to other sites:	No

SITE'S SELF DESCRIPTION

The Global Association of Risk Professionals (GARP) is the leading industry association for financial risk management professionals, with over 150,000 members from 195 countries and territories. The GARP Career Center caters to the complexities of financial risk management recruiting. We serve the banking, finance, financial services, consulting and government sectors.

Contact Information

Name:	Mary Jo Roberts
Phone:	201-719-7216
E-Mail:	maryjo.roberts@garp.com

Great Insurance Jobs
www.greatinsurancejobs.com
Great Insurance Jobs, Inc.

GENERAL SITE INFORMATION

Date activated online:	2001
Location of site headquarters:	Orlando, FL
Number of people who visit the site:	115,000 unique visitors/month
Time spent on site:	3:26 minutes/visit

JOB POSTINGS

Post full time jobs:	Yes
Post part time/contract/consulting jobs:	Yes - All
Most prevalent types of jobs posted:	Insurance-related
Distribution:	USA, Canada

Recruiters
Fee to post a job:	$375/posting
Posting period:	60 days
Link posting to your site:	Yes

Job Seekers
Number of job postings:	3,000
Top salary levels of jobs:	Up to $200K+/yr
Source of postings:	Employers

RESUME SERVICES

Are resumes or profiles posted on the site:	Yes

Recruiters
Number in database:	160,000
Top occupations :	SM, Claims, UW
Fee to view resumes:	In posting fee
How acquired:	Direct from candidates

Job Seekers
How long can you store:	Indefinitely
Who can post a resume:	Those in the field
Fee to post:	None
Confidentiality available:	Yes

OTHER SERVICES

Is a listserv or discussion forum offered:	No
Are assessment instruments offered:	No

Recruiters
Automated resume agent:	Yes
Banner advertising:	Yes
Status report on ads:	Yes - Postings

Job Seekers
Automated job agent:	Yes
Career info provided:	Yes
Links to other sites:	Yes

SITE'S SELF DESCRIPTION

Great Insurance Jobs operates the insurance industry's leading career site. Functional products and services create the ultimate solution for a variety of hiring needs. Employers can reach the most qualified candidates by posting jobs or by searching our database of insurance-only professionals.

Contact Information

Name:	Heather Deyrieux
Phone:	800-818-4898 x2121
E-Mail:	heather@greatinsurancejobs.com

Hcareers
www.hcareers.com
onTargetjobs, Inc.

GENERAL SITE INFORMATION

Date activated online:	1998
Location of site headquarters:	Vancouver, British Columbia, Canada
Number of people who visit the site:	800,000 unique visitors/month
Time spent on site:	7:00 minutes/visit

JOB POSTINGS

Post full time jobs:	Yes
Post part time/contract/consulting jobs:	Yes - All
Most prevalent types of jobs posted:	MG, OP, Hotel, Restaurant
Distribution:	USA, Canada, United Kingdom

Recruiters

Fee to post a job:	$400+/posting
Posting period:	30 days
Link posting to your site:	Yes

Job Seekers

Number of job postings:	6,400
Top salary levels of jobs:	$201-250K, $251K+/yr
Source of postings:	Employers

RESUME SERVICES

Are resumes or profiles posted on the site:	Yes

Recruiters

Number in database:	160,000
Top occupations :	MG, OP, Customer Svc
Fee to view resumes:	$750/month
How acquired:	Direct from candidates

Job Seekers

How long can you store:	1 year
Who can post a resume:	Anyone
Fee to post:	None
Confidentiality available:	Yes

OTHER SERVICES

Is a listserv or discussion forum offered:	No
Are assessment instruments offered:	Yes

Recruiters

Automated resume agent:	Yes
Banner advertising:	Yes
Status report on ads:	Yes - Both

Job Seekers

Automated job agent:	Yes
Career info provided:	Yes
Links to other sites:	Yes

SITE'S SELF DESCRIPTION

Are you looking for a hotel, restaurant, food service, or any other hospitality job? Find your next hospitality career on Hcareers, the leading online job board for the hospitality industry. Hcareers attracts over 800,000 unique job seeker visitors each month – more than any other niche job board. Employers can also review over 160,000 resumes posted by job seekers.

Contact Information

Name:	Greg Tareta
Phone:	800.832.3738 x7899
E-Mail:	greg.tareta@hcareers.com

HEALTHeCAREERS Network
www.healthecareers.com
onTargetjobs, Inc.

GENERAL SITE INFORMATION

Date activated online:	1999
Location of site headquarters:	Englewood, CO
Number of people who visit the site:	515,000 unique visitors/month
Time spent on site:	5:00 minutes/visit

JOB POSTINGS

Post full time jobs:	Yes
Post part time/contract/consulting jobs:	Yes - All
Most prevalent types of jobs posted:	AD, Healthcare, Physician, Nurse
Distribution:	USA, Canada

Recruiters

Fee to post a job:	$195/posting
Posting period:	30 days
Link posting to your site:	Yes

Job Seekers

Number of job postings:	13,000
Top salary levels of jobs:	$51-75K, $76-100K+/yr
Source of postings:	Employers, Staffing

RESUME SERVICES

Are resumes or profiles posted on the site:	Yes

Recruiters

Number in database:	260,000+
Top occupations :	Physician, Nursing
Fee to view resumes:	In posting fee
How acquired:	Direct from candidates

Job Seekers

How long can you store:	Indefinitely
Who can post a resume:	Those in the field
Fee to post:	None
Confidentiality available:	Yes

OTHER SERVICES

Is a listserv or discussion forum offered:	Yes
Are assessment instruments offered:	Yes

Recruiters

Automated resume agent:	Yes
Banner advertising:	Yes
Status report on ads:	Yes - Both

Job Seekers

Automated job agent:	Yes
Career info provided:	Yes
Links to other sites:	Yes

SITE'S SELF DESCRIPTION

HEALTHeCAREERS Network is a unique recruitment tool made possible through partnerships with more than 70 healthcare associations. The Network gives employers a single point of access to recruit from participating associations and hundreds of partner Web-sites. Services also include online print campaign management and access to association career fairs.

Contact Information

Name:	Joe Steiner
Phone:	303-833-7372
E-Mail:	joe.steiner@ontargetjobs.com

HealthJobsNationwide.com
www.healthjobsnationwide.com
Healthcare Staffing Innovations, LLC

GENERAL SITE INFORMATION

Date activated online:	April, 2003
Location of site headquarters:	Woodstock, GA
Number of people who visit the site:	155,000 unique visitors/month
Time spent on site:	2:33 minutes/visit

JOB POSTINGS

Post full time jobs:	Yes
Post part time/contract/consulting jobs:	Yes - All
Most prevalent types of jobs posted:	Physician, Nurse, Therapy, Pharmacy
Distribution:	National - USA

Recruiters
Fee to post a job:	$225/posting
Posting period:	30 days
Link posting to your site:	Yes

Job Seekers
Number of job postings:	40,000+
Top salary levels of jobs:	Up to $500K+/yr
Source of postings:	Employers, Staffing

RESUME SERVICES

Are resumes or profiles posted on the site:	Yes

Recruiters
Number in database:	40,000+
Top occupations :	Healthcare
Fee to view resumes:	$600/month
How acquired:	Direct from candidates

Job Seekers
How long can you store:	Indefinitely
Who can post a resume:	Those in the field
Fee to post:	None
Confidentiality available:	Yes

OTHER SERVICES

Is a listserv or discussion forum offered:	No
Are assessment instruments offered:	No

Recruiters
Automated resume agent:	Yes
Banner advertising:	Yes
Status report on ads:	Yes - Both

Job Seekers
Automated job agent:	Yes
Career info provided:	No
Links to other sites:	Yes

SITE'S SELF DESCRIPTION

HealthJobsNationwide.com powers seven unique brands designed to serve specific segments of the healthcare industry. The seven communities we serve include physicians, advanced practice clinicians, nursing, pharmacy, therapy, technologists and health administration. While we target clinicians individually, our clients post their jobs and search resumes all in one place.

Contact Information

Name:	Dustin Martin
Phone:	888-861-5627
E-Mail:	info@healthjobsnationwide.com

HigherEdJobs
www.higheredjobs.com
Internet Employment Linkage, Inc.

GENERAL SITE INFORMATION

Date activated online:	1996
Location of site headquarters:	State College, PA
Number of people who visit the site:	780,000 unique visitors/month
Time spent on site:	7.0 page views/visitor

JOB POSTINGS

Post full time jobs:	Yes
Post part time/contract/consulting jobs:	Yes - Part time/Adjunct Faculty
Most prevalent types of jobs posted:	Higher Education (All Departments)
Distribution:	International

Recruiters

Fee to post a job:	$170/posting
Posting period:	60 days
Link posting to your site:	Yes

Job Seekers

Number of job postings:	13,000+
Top salary levels of jobs:	$200-225K/yr
Source of postings:	Employers, Staffing

RESUME SERVICES

Are resumes or profiles posted on the site:	Yes

Recruiters

Number in database:	116,000+
Top occupations :	Academic Faculty
Fee to view resumes:	$295/3 months
How acquired:	Direct from candidates

Job Seekers

How long can you store:	Indefinitely
Who can post a resume:	Those registered
Fee to post:	None
Confidentiality available:	Yes

OTHER SERVICES

Is a listserv or discussion forum offered:	No
Are assessment instruments offered:	No

Recruiters

Automated resume agent:	No
Banner advertising:	Yes
Status report on ads:	Yes - Both

Job Seekers

Automated job agent:	Yes
Career info provided:	Yes
Links to other sites:	Yes

SITE'S SELF DESCRIPTION

HigherEdJobs is the leading source for jobs and career information in academia. During 2010, more than 4,200 colleges and universities posted over 79,000 job postings to the company's Web-site. Serving higher education since 1996, HigherEdJobs now receives two million visits a month from 780,000 unique visitors representing both higher education professionals and couples.

Contact Information

Name:	John Ikenberry
Phone:	814-861-3080
E-Mail:	sales@higheredjobs.com

Hospital Dream Jobs
www.hospitaldreamjobs.com
Healthcare Communications, LLC

GENERAL SITE INFORMATION

Date activated online:	2009
Location of site headquarters:	Seattle, WA
Number of people who visit the site:	133,000 unique visitors/month
Time spent on site:	15.0 page views/visit

JOB POSTINGS

Post full time jobs:	Yes
Post part time/contract/consulting jobs:	Yes - All
Most prevalent types of jobs posted:	MG, Physicians, Nursing, Allied Health
Distribution:	National - USA

Recruiters
Fee to post a job:	$250/posting
Posting period:	90 days
Link posting to your site:	Yes

Job Seekers
Number of job postings:	65,000+
Top salary levels of jobs:	Up to $250K+/yr
Source of postings:	Employers

RESUME SERVICES

Are resumes or profiles posted on the site:	Yes

Recruiters
Number in database:	45,000
Top occupations :	Healthcare
Fee to view resumes:	In posting fee
How acquired:	Direct from candidates

Job Seekers
How long can you store:	6 months
Who can post a resume:	Those registered
Fee to post:	None
Confidentiality available:	Yes

OTHER SERVICES

Is a listserv or discussion forum offered:	Yes
Are assessment instruments offered:	No

Recruiters
Automated resume agent:	Yes
Banner advertising:	Yes
Status report on ads:	Yes - Both

Job Seekers
Automated job agent:	Yes
Career info provided:	Yes
Links to other sites:	Yes

SITE'S SELF DESCRIPTION

Hospital Dream Jobs is unique in offering 65,000+ healthcare jobs, cutting-edge technology and original in-depth healthcare resources all in one place for healthcare professionals! Our updated services in social media marketing get results through branding, blogs, Twitter, and Facebook. Our team has 20 years of experience in healthcare recruiting and Web-site technology.

Contact Information

Name:	Allison Rapaport
Phone:	800-277-8455
E-Mail:	arapaport@hospitaldreamjobs.com

Hospital Jobs Online
www.hospitaljobsonline.com
Internet Brands, Inc.

GENERAL SITE INFORMATION

Date activated online:	2001
Location of site headquarters:	El Segundo, CA
Number of people who visit the site:	110,000 unique visitors/month
Time spent on site:	2:00 minutes/visit

JOB POSTINGS

Post full time jobs:	Yes
Post part time/contract/consulting jobs:	Yes - All
Most prevalent types of jobs posted:	Nurses, Physicians, Allied Health
Distribution:	International

Recruiters

Fee to post a job:	$249/posting
Posting period:	30 days
Link posting to your site:	Yes

Job Seekers

Number of job postings:	55,000
Top salary levels of jobs:	Not Reported
Source of postings:	Employers

RESUME SERVICES

Are resumes or profiles posted on the site:	Yes

Recruiters

Number in database:	250,000
Top occupations :	Healthcare
Fee to view resumes:	$399/month
How acquired:	Direct from candidates

Job Seekers

How long can you store:	Indefinitely
Who can post a resume:	Those registered
Fee to post:	None
Confidentiality available:	Yes

OTHER SERVICES

Is a listserv or discussion forum offered:	No
Are assessment instruments offered:	No

Recruiters

Automated resume agent:	Yes
Banner advertising:	Yes
Status report on ads:	Yes - Both

Job Seekers

Automated job agent:	Yes
Career info provided:	Yes
Links to other sites:	Yes

SITE'S SELF DESCRIPTION

Hospitaljobsonline.com is the #1 hospital job board and the leader in healthcare career resources for doctors, nurses, allied health, and administration job seekers. Employers receive pre-qualified leads and resumes sent daily, access to the resume database and unlimited job postings via bulk upload.

Contact Information

Name:	Sales
Phone:	888-613-8844
E-Mail:	hjolsales@internetbrands.com

icrunchdata
www.icrunchdata.com
icrunchdata

GENERAL SITE INFORMATION

Date activated online:	2003
Location of site headquarters:	Frisco, TX
Number of people who visit the site:	165,000 unique visitors/month
Time spent on site:	6.1 page views/visitor

JOB POSTINGS

Post full time jobs:	Yes
Post part time/contract/consulting jobs:	Yes - Contract, Consulting
Most prevalent types of jobs posted:	Data, Analytics, Statistics
Distribution:	National - USA

Recruiters
Fee to post a job:	$375/posting
Posting period:	30 days
Link posting to your site:	Yes

Job Seekers
Number of job postings:	5,000
Top salary levels of jobs:	$151-200K, $201-250K/yr
Source of postings:	Employers, Other sites

RESUME SERVICES

Are resumes or profiles posted on the site:	Yes

Recruiters
Number in database:	110,000
Top occupations :	Data, Analytics
Fee to view resumes:	$495/month
How acquired:	Direct from candidates

Job Seekers
How long can you store:	Indefinitely
Who can post a resume:	Those registered
Fee to post:	None
Confidentiality available:	Yes

OTHER SERVICES

Is a listserv or discussion forum offered:	No
Are assessment instruments offered:	No

Recruiters
Automated resume agent:	Yes
Banner advertising:	Yes
Status report on ads:	Yes - Both

Job Seekers
Automated job agent:	Yes
Career info provided:	Yes
Links to other sites:	Yes

SITE'S SELF DESCRIPTION

Icrunchdata is a community of top professionals in data, analytics, and technology! Whether you are looking to hire talent or promote your brand, we can help you reach your advertising goals.

Contact Information

Name:	Todd Nevins
Phone:	214-244-5214
E-Mail:	tnevins@icrunchdata.com

IEEE Job Site

www.ieee.org/jobs
Institute of Electrical & Electronics Engineers (IEEE)

GENERAL SITE INFORMATION

Date activated online:	2001
Location of site headquarters:	New York, NY
Number of people who visit the site:	47,000 unique visitors/month
Time spent on site:	7:46 minutes/visit

JOB POSTINGS

Post full time jobs:	Yes
Post part time/contract/consulting jobs:	Yes - Part time
Most prevalent types of jobs posted:	EN, IS, MG, Scientist
Distribution:	International

Recruiters

Fee to post a job:	$250/posting
Posting period:	30 days
Link posting to your site:	Yes

Job Seekers

Number of job postings:	13,910
Top salary levels of jobs:	$101-150K/yr
Source of postings:	Employers, Staffing

RESUME SERVICES

Are resumes or profiles posted on the site:	Yes

Recruiters

Number in database:	76,814
Top occupations :	EN
Fee to view resumes:	In posting fee
How acquired:	Direct from candidates

Job Seekers

How long can you store:	Indefinitely
Who can post a resume:	Members only
Fee to post:	None
Confidentiality available:	Ye

OTHER SERVICES

Is a listserv or discussion forum offered:	No
Are assessment instruments offered:	No

Recruiters

Automated resume agent:	Yes
Banner advertising:	Yes
Status report on ads:	Yes - Banners

Job Seekers

Automated job agent:	Yes
Career info provided:	Yes
Links to other sites:	Yes

SITE'S SELF DESCRIPTION

Use the IEEE Job Site to post jobs, search resumes and pre-screen candidates, all of whom are pre-qualified, highly skilled members of the Institute of Electrical & Electronics Engineers (IEEE). Place banner ads on the site or classified and display advertising in IEEE print publications. Our unique "smart job" technology will find you the best candidates available.

Contact Information

Name:	Michael Buryk
Phone:	212-419-7571
E-Mail:	m.buryk@ieee.org

iHire.com
www.ihire.com
iHire, LLC

GENERAL SITE INFORMATION

Date activated online:	November, 1999
Location of site headquarters:	Frederick, MD
Number of people who visit the site:	1,700,000 unique visitors/month
Time spent on site:	5.1 page views/visitor

JOB POSTINGS

Post full time jobs:	Yes
Post part time/contract/consulting jobs:	Yes - All
Most prevalent types of jobs posted:	Wide variety
Distribution:	National - USA

Recruiters
Fee to post a job:	$245/posting
Posting period:	60 days
Link posting to your site:	Yes

Job Seekers
Number of job postings:	850,000
Top salary levels of jobs:	$76-100K, $101-150K/yr
Source of postings:	Employers, Staffing

RESUME SERVICES

Are resumes or profiles posted on the site:	Yes

Recruiters
Number in database:	3,250,000
Top occupations :	Wide variety
Fee to view resumes:	$300
How acquired:	Direct from candidates

Job Seekers
How long can you store:	Indefinitely
Who can post a resume:	Those in the field
Fee to post:	None
Confidentiality available:	Yes

OTHER SERVICES

Is a listserv or discussion forum offered:	No
Are assessment instruments offered:	Yes

Recruiters
Automated resume agent:	Yes
Banner advertising:	No
Status report on ads:	No

Job Seekers
Automated job agent:	Yes
Career info provided:	Yes
Links to other sites:	Yes

SITE'S SELF DESCRIPTION

iHire job seekers enjoy access to over 850,000 jobs from over 4,300 sources, as well as personalized, daily job feeds, resume and cover letter assistance, and interview and salary negotiation coaching. iHire's industry-specific focus, money-back guarantee, and resume matching technologies provide employers with a risk-free, effective alternative to conventional job boards.

Contact Information

Name:	Heather Gonzales
Phone:	877-798-4854
E-Mail:	heather.gonzales@ihire.com

Indeed
www.indeed.com
Indeed

GENERAL SITE INFORMATION

Date activated online:	2004
Location of site headquarters:	Stamford, CT
Number of people who visit the site:	40,000,000+ unique visitors/month
Time spent on site:	13:10 minutes/visit

JOB POSTINGS

Post full time jobs:	Yes
Post part time/contract/consulting jobs:	Yes - All
Most prevalent types of jobs posted:	Wide variety
Distribution:	International

Recruiters
Fee to post a job:	Pay-per-click
Posting period:	30 days
Link posting to your site:	Yes

Job Seekers
Number of job postings:	1,000,000+
Top salary levels of jobs:	Not Reported
Source of postings:	Employers, Other sites

RESUME SERVICES

Are resumes or profiles posted on the site:	Yes

Recruiters
Number in database:	N/A
Top occupations :	N/A
Fee to view resumes:	N/A
How acquired:	N/A

Job Seekers
How long can you store:	N/A
Who can post a resume:	N/A
Fee to post:	N/A
Confidentiality available:	N/A

OTHER SERVICES

Is a listserv or discussion forum offered:	Yes
Are assessment instruments offered:	Yes

Recruiters
Automated resume agent:	No
Banner advertising:	No
Status report on ads:	No

Job Seekers
Automated job agent:	Yes
Career info provided:	Yes
Links to other sites:	Yes

SITE'S SELF DESCRIPTION

Indeed is the #1 job site worldwide, with over 40 million unique visitors per month from more than 50 countries in 24 languages. Job seekers perform more than 1 billion job searches on Indeed each month. Since 2004, Indeed has given job seekers free access to millions of jobs from thousands of company Web-sites and job boards.

Contact Information

Name:	Nolan Farris
Phone:	203-564-2405
E-Mail:	nolan@indeed.com

Inside Higher Ed
www.insidehighered.com
Inside Higher Ed

GENERAL SITE INFORMATION

Date activated online:	January, 2005
Location of site headquarters:	Washington, D.C.
Number of people who visit the site:	750,000 unique visitors/month
Time spent on site:	2.0 page views/visitor

JOB POSTINGS

Post full time jobs:	Yes
Post part time/contract/consulting jobs:	Yes - Part-time, Adjunct faculty
Most prevalent types of jobs posted:	Higher Ed Faculty, Staff & Other
Distribution:	International

Recruiters

Fee to post a job:	$195/posting
Posting period:	30 days
Link posting to your site:	Yes

Job Seekers

Number of job postings:	8,000
Top salary levels of jobs:	Up to $200K+/yr
Source of postings:	Employers

RESUME SERVICES

Are resumes or profiles posted on the site:	Yes

Recruiters

Number in database:	10,000
Top occupations :	AD, MG, Faculty
Fee to view resumes:	None
How acquired:	Direct from candidates

Job Seekers

How long can you store:	Indefinitely
Who can post a resume:	Those registered
Fee to post:	None
Confidentiality available:	Yes

OTHER SERVICES

Is a listserv or discussion forum offered:	No
Are assessment instruments offered:	No

Recruiters

Automated resume agent:	Yes
Banner advertising:	Yes
Status report on ads:	Yes - Both

Job Seekers

Automated job agent:	Yes
Career info provided:	Yes
Links to other sites:	Yes

SITE'S SELF DESCRIPTION

Inside Higher Ed is the daily news Web-site for higher education professionals. Featuring breaking news, commentary, career advice, blogs, and thousands of faculty, administrative and executive job postings, more than 750,000 unique readers visit the site each month. Job content is integrated throughout the site, reaching passive candidates with related jobs.

Contact Information

Name:	Kathlene Collins
Phone:	202-659-9208 x103
E-Mail:	recruit@insidehighered.com

JAMA Career Center®
www.jamacareercenter.com
American Medical Association

GENERAL SITE INFORMATION

Date activated online:	2005
Location of site headquarters:	Chicago, IL
Number of people who visit the site:	13,714 unique visitors/month
Time spent on site:	2:55 minutes/visit

JOB POSTINGS

Post full time jobs:	Yes
Post part time/contract/consulting jobs:	Yes - Locum Tenens & other situations
Most prevalent types of jobs posted:	Physician
Distribution:	International

Recruiters
Fee to post a job:	$298.50/posting
Posting period:	30 days
Link posting to your site:	Yes

Job Seekers
Number of job postings:	5,454
Top salary levels of jobs:	Up to $999K+/yr
Source of postings:	Employers

RESUME SERVICES

Are resumes or profiles posted on the site:	Yes

Recruiters
Number in database:	5,700
Top occupations :	Physician
Fee to view resumes:	In posting fee
How acquired:	Direct from candidates

Job Seekers
How long can you store:	Indefinitely
Who can post a resume:	Those in the field
Fee to post:	None
Confidentiality available:	Yes

OTHER SERVICES

Is a listserv or discussion forum offered:	No
Are assessment instruments offered:	Yes

Recruiters
Automated resume agent:	Yes
Banner advertising:	Yes
Status report on ads:	Yes - Both

Job Seekers
Automated job agent:	Yes
Career info provided:	Yes
Links to other sites:	Yes

SITE'S SELF DESCRIPTION

JAMA Career Center® is a resource for active and passive physician job seekers. The site presents physician career opportunities, news, and resources relevant to the full spectrum of medical practice. Recruiters will find a range of posting options including multi-job packs, site wrapping, employer profiles, banner ads, and print plus online combos.

Contact Information

Name:	Classified Advertising
Phone:	800-262-2260
E-Mail:	classifieds@ama-assn.org

Job.com
www.job.com
Job.com, Inc.

GENERAL SITE INFORMATION

Date activated online:	2001
Location of site headquarters:	Fredericksburg, VA
Number of people who visit the site:	8,500,000 unique visitors/month
Time spent on site:	4:00 minutes/visit

JOB POSTINGS

Post full time jobs:	Yes
Post part time/contract/consulting jobs:	Yes - All
Most prevalent types of jobs posted:	AD, FA, IS, SM
Distribution:	National - USA

Recruiters
Fee to post a job:	Under $100/posting
Posting period:	30 days
Link posting to your site:	No

Job Seekers
Number of job postings:	500,000
Top salary levels of jobs:	Up to $251K+/yr
Source of postings:	Employers, Staffing

RESUME SERVICES

Are resumes or profiles posted on the site:	Yes

Recruiters
Number in database:	4,800,000
Top occupations :	AD, FA, IS, SM
Fee to view resumes:	Not Reported
How acquired:	Direct from candidates

Job Seekers
How long can you store:	1 year
Who can post a resume:	Members only
Fee to post:	None
Confidentiality available:	Yes

OTHER SERVICES

Is a listserv or discussion forum offered:	No
Are assessment instruments offered:	Yes

Recruiters
Automated resume agent:	Yes
Banner advertising:	Yes
Status report on ads:	Yes - Both

Job Seekers
Automated job agent:	Yes
Career info provided:	Yes
Links to other sites:	Yes

SITE'S SELF DESCRIPTION

Job.com is an online full service career portal that ranked as the 4th most visited career site in its category in January, 2009, according to comscore/Media Metrix. Job.com specializes in helping employers and recruiters hire qualified employees, while providing job seekers with a variety of career services to enhance and manage their careers.

Contact Information

Name:	Customer Service
Phone:	877-7JOBCOM
E-Mail:	hireforless@job.com

JobCircle.com

www.jobcircle.com

Human Capital Solutions, LLC

GENERAL SITE INFORMATION

Date activated online:	1998
Location of site headquarters:	West Chester, PA
Number of people who visit the site:	530,000 unique visitors/month
Time spent on site:	7.0 page views/visitor

JOB POSTINGS

Post full time jobs:	Yes
Post part time/contract/consulting jobs:	Yes - All
Most prevalent types of jobs posted:	FA, IS, MG, Healthcare
Distribution:	Regional/USA - Mid-Atlantic (PA, NJ, DE)

Recruiters

Fee to post a job:	$250/posting
Posting period:	30 days
Link posting to your site:	Yes

Job Seekers

Number of job postings:	120,000
Top salary levels of jobs:	$51-75K, $76-100K/yr
Source of postings:	Employers, Staffing

RESUME SERVICES

Are resumes or profiles posted on the site:	Yes

Recruiters

Number in database:	1,300,000
Top occupations :	FA, IS, MG, Healthcare
Fee to view resumes:	Not Reported
How acquired:	Direct from candidates

Job Seekers

How long can you store:	Indefinitely
Who can post a resume:	Anyone
Fee to post:	None
Confidentiality available:	Yes

OTHER SERVICES

Is a listserv or discussion forum offered:	No
Are assessment instruments offered:	No

Recruiters

Automated resume agent:	Yes
Banner advertising:	Yes
Status report on ads:	Yes - Postings

Job Seekers

Automated job agent:	Yes
Career info provided:	Yes
Links to other sites:	Yes

SITE'S SELF DESCRIPTION

JobCircle.com has been helping employers connect with job seekers since 1998. We're the largest independently owned job board in the Mid-Atlantic region of the United States. With hundreds of thousands of jobs and 1.2 million+ candidates, our regional site provides recruiters with a fresh, inexpensive, and effective alternative to the highly priced national job boards.

Contact Information

Name:	Joseph Stubblebine
Phone:	610-431-2001
E-Mail:	joe@jobcircle.com

Jobfox
www.jobfox.com
Jobfox

GENERAL SITE INFORMATION

Date activated online:	2005
Location of site headquarters:	McLean, VA
Number of people who visit the site:	2,000,000 unique visitors/month
Time spent on site:	20:00 minutes/visit

JOB POSTINGS

Post full time jobs:	Yes
Post part time/contract/consulting jobs:	Yes - Part time
Most prevalent types of jobs posted:	Wide variety
Distribution:	National - USA

Recruiters

Fee to post a job:	Free w/ Jobfox Boost
Posting period:	Unlimited
Link posting to your site:	Yes

Job Seekers

Number of job postings:	Not Reported
Top salary levels of jobs:	Up to $251K+/yr
Source of postings:	Employers, Other sites

RESUME SERVICES

Are resumes or profiles posted on the site:	Yes

Recruiters

Number in database:	7,000,000+
Top occupations :	Wide variety
Fee to view resumes:	Not Reported
How acquired:	Direct from candidates

Job Seekers

How long can you store:	Indefinitely
Who can post a resume:	Anyone
Fee to post:	None
Confidentiality available:	Yes

OTHER SERVICES

Is a listserv or discussion forum offered:	No
Are assessment instruments offered:	Yes

Recruiters

Automated resume agent:	Yes
Banner advertising:	No
Status report on ads:	No

Job Seekers

Automated job agent:	Yes
Career info provided:	Yes
Links to other sites:	Yes

SITE'S SELF DESCRIPTION

Jobfox is the fastest-growing career networking site that connects professionals with recruiters. Jobfox gets candidates in the "inner circle" by creating personal introductions to recruiters at companies of interest. For recruiters, Jobfox Boost(SM) automates the process of building talent pipelines, giving them a high volume, high speed social recruiting solution.

Contact Information

Name:	Dan Kimball
Phone:	703-748-0162
E-Mail:	customerservice@jobfox.com

Jobing.com
www.jobing.com
Jobing

GENERAL SITE INFORMATION

Date activated online:	2000
Location of site headquarters:	Phoenix, AZ
Number of people who visit the site:	1,500,000 unique visitors/month
Time spent on site:	10:00 minutes/visit

JOB POSTINGS

Post full time jobs:	Yes
Post part time/contract/consulting jobs:	Yes - All
Most prevalent types of jobs posted:	Wide variety
Distribution:	Regional/USA: Multiple states

Recruiters
Fee to post a job:	$299-389/posting
Posting period:	28 days
Link posting to your site:	Yes

Job Seekers
Number of job postings:	500,000+
Top salary levels of jobs:	Not Reported
Source of postings:	Employers

RESUME SERVICES

Are resumes or profiles posted on the site:	Yes

Recruiters
Number in database:	2,000,000+
Top occupations :	Wide variety
Fee to view resumes:	$600-900
How acquired:	Direct from candidates

Job Seekers
How long can you store:	Indefinitely
Who can post a resume:	Anyone
Fee to post:	None
Confidentiality available:	Yes

OTHER SERVICES

Is a listserv or discussion forum offered:	Yes
Are assessment instruments offered:	Yes

Recruiters
Automated resume agent:	Yes
Banner advertising:	Yes
Status report on ads:	Yes - Both

Job Seekers
Automated job agent:	Yes
Career info provided:	Yes
Links to other sites:	Yes

SITE'S SELF DESCRIPTION

A three-time Inc. 500 fastest-growing company, Jobing.com is the nation's largest locally-focused job board community whose mission is to connect local employers and job seekers through a variety of resources such as job postings, resume search, employment branding banners and advertising, event listings and advanced company profiles.

Contact Information

Name:	Theresa Maher
Phone:	602-571-0793
E-Mail:	theresa.maher@jobing.com

Job Rooster

www.jobrooster.com
Job Rooster

GENERAL SITE INFORMATION

Date activated online:	2009
Location of site headquarters:	San Francisco, CA
Number of people who visit the site:	25,000 unique visitors/month
Time spent on site:	5:25 minutes/visit

JOB POSTINGS

Post full time jobs:	Yes
Post part time/contract/consulting jobs:	Yes - All
Most prevalent types of jobs posted:	Wide variety
Distribution:	National - USA

Recruiters

Fee to post a job:	$75/posting
Posting period:	30 days
Link posting to your site:	Yes

Job Seekers

Number of job postings:	20,000
Top salary levels of jobs:	Up to $150K+/yr
Source of postings:	Employers

RESUME SERVICES

Are resumes or profiles posted on the site:	Yes

Recruiters

Number in database:	1,700
Top occupations :	Wide variety
Fee to view resumes:	None
How acquired:	Direct from candidates

Job Seekers

How long can you store:	Indefinitely
Who can post a resume:	Anyone
Fee to post:	None
Confidentiality available:	Yes

OTHER SERVICES

Is a listserv or discussion forum offered:	No
Are assessment instruments offered:	No

Recruiters

Automated resume agent:	No
Banner advertising:	No
Status report on ads:	No

Job Seekers

Automated job agent:	Yes
Career info provided:	Yes
Links to other sites:	No

SITE'S SELF DESCRIPTION

Jobrooster.com allows you to engage any candidate, anytime, anywhere on their mobile phone. We help job seekers in any industry or career field have access to jobs even when they are not in front of a computer. The service is primarily used by enterprise recruiters, third party staffing agencies, and recruitment advertising agencies to recruit smarter, not harder.

Contact Information

Name:	Information
Phone:	800-377-9202
E-Mail:	info@jobrooster.com

JobsInBenefits.com
www.jobsinbenefits.com
International Foundation of Employee Benefit Plans (IFEBP)

GENERAL SITE INFORMATION

Date activated online: 1998
Location of site headquarters: Milwaukee, WI
Number of people who visit the site: 80,000 unique visitors/month
Time spent on site: 4:00 minutes/visit

JOB POSTINGS

Post full time jobs: Yes
Post part time/contract/consulting jobs: Yes - All
Most prevalent types of jobs posted: HR, MG, Benefits, Compensation
Distribution: International

Recruiters
Fee to post a job:	$251-300/posting
Posting period:	60 days
Link posting to your site:	Yes

Job Seekers
Number of job postings:	150
Top salary levels of jobs:	$76-100K, $151-200K/yr
Source of postings:	Employers, Staffing

RESUME SERVICES

Are resumes or profiles posted on the site: Yes

Recruiters
Number in database:	100
Top occupations :	HR, MG, Benefits
Fee to view resumes:	None
How acquired:	Direct from candidates

Job Seekers
How long can you store:	6 months
Who can post a resume:	Those in the field
Fee to post:	IFEBP Members: None
Confidentiality available:	Yes

OTHER SERVICES

Is a listserv or discussion forum offered: Yes
Are assessment instruments offered: No

Recruiters
Automated resume agent:	No
Banner advertising:	No
Status report on ads:	Not Reported

Job Seekers
Automated job agent:	No
Career info provided:	Yes
Links to other sites:	No

SITE'S SELF DESCRIPTION

JobsInBenefits.com brings together qualified benefits/HR professionals with the companies that seek them. Because this job site is hosted by a respected association, recruiters can expect to find resumes from highly qualified benefits/HR professionals. Recruiters looking to fill multiple positions can save with the purchase of a Job Pack.

Contact Information

Name: Job Posting Service
Phone: 888-334-3327 x4
E-Mail: jobposting@ifebp.org

JobsInLogistics.com
www.jobsinlogistics.com
JobsInLogistics.com, Inc.

GENERAL SITE INFORMATION

Date activated online:	2000
Location of site headquarters:	North Miami Beach, FL
Number of people who visit the site:	300,000 unique visitors/month
Time spent on site:	7.0 page views/visitor

JOB POSTINGS

Post full time jobs:	Yes
Post part time/contract/consulting jobs:	Yes - All
Most prevalent types of jobs posted:	Logistics, Transportation, Warehousing
Distribution:	USA, Canada

Recruiters
Fee to post a job:	$335/posting
Posting period:	60 days
Link posting to your site:	Yes

Job Seekers
Number of job postings:	6,000
Top salary levels of jobs:	Up to $251K+/yr
Source of postings:	Employers, Staffing

RESUME SERVICES

Are resumes or profiles posted on the site:	Yes

Recruiters
Number in database:	550,000+
Top occupations :	EN, MG, OP, Logistics
Fee to view resumes:	$1,795/year
How acquired:	Direct from candidates

Job Seekers
How long can you store:	Indefinitely
Who can post a resume:	Anyone
Fee to post:	None
Confidentiality available:	Yes

OTHER SERVICES

Is a listserv or discussion forum offered:	No
Are assessment instruments offered:	No

Recruiters
Automated resume agent:	Yes
Banner advertising:	Yes
Status report on ads:	Yes - Both

Job Seekers
Automated job agent:	Yes
Career info provided:	Yes
Links to other sites:	Yes

SITE'S SELF DESCRIPTION

JobsInLogistics.com is North America's largest and most cost effective career and recruiting job board for the logistics, supply chain, manufacturing, transportation, distribution, purchasing, materials management and warehousing professions. JobsInLogistics.com conducts extensive target marketing to attract the top quality candidates in this niche area.

Contact Information

Name:	Amy Noah
Phone:	877-562-7678
E-Mail:	amy@jobsinlogistics.com

JobsInManufacturing.com
www.jobsinmanufacturing.com
JobsInLogistics.com, Inc.

GENERAL SITE INFORMATION

Date activated online:	2002
Location of site headquarters:	North Miami Beach, FL
Number of people who visit the site:	50,000 unique visitors/month
Time spent on site:	6.0 page views/visitor

JOB POSTINGS

Post full time jobs:	Yes
Post part time/contract/consulting jobs:	Yes - Part time
Most prevalent types of jobs posted:	EN, Manufacturing
Distribution:	USA, Canada

Recruiters

Fee to post a job:	$335/posting
Posting period:	60 days
Link posting to your site:	Yes

Job Seekers

Number of job postings:	1,500
Top salary levels of jobs:	Up to $251K+/yr
Source of postings:	Employers, Staffing

RESUME SERVICES

Are resumes or profiles posted on the site:	Yes

Recruiters

Number in database:	200,000
Top occupations :	EN, Manufacturing
Fee to view resumes:	$1,795/year
How acquired:	Direct from candidates

Job Seekers

How long can you store:	Indefinitely
Who can post a resume:	Anyone
Fee to post:	None
Confidentiality available:	Yes

OTHER SERVICES

Is a listserv or discussion forum offered:	No
Are assessment instruments offered:	No

Recruiters

Automated resume agent:	No
Banner advertising:	Yes
Status report on ads:	Yes - Both

Job Seekers

Automated job agent:	Yes
Career info provided:	Yes
Links to other sites:	Yes

SITE'S SELF DESCRIPTION

JobsInManufacturing.com is the leading job board for the manufacturing industry. By target marketing the manufacturing industry, we attract the leading professionals in plant management, production planning, materials management, engineering, quality control, purchasing, maintenance and hourly associates.

Contact Information

Name:	Amy Noah
Phone:	877-562-7678
E-Mail:	amy@jobsinlogistics.com

JobsInME.com
www.jobsinme.com
JobsInTheUS.com

GENERAL SITE INFORMATION

Date activated online:	1999
Location of site headquarters:	Westbrook, ME
Number of people who visit the site:	144,215 unique visitors/month
Time spent on site:	9:00 minutes/visit

JOB POSTINGS

Post full time jobs:	Yes
Post part time/contract/consulting jobs:	Yes - Part time, Contract, Consulting
Most prevalent types of jobs posted:	Wide variety
Distribution:	Regional - Maine

Recruiters

Fee to post a job:	Based on employer size
Posting period:	30 days
Link posting to your site:	Yes

Job Seekers

Number of job postings:	5,902
Top salary levels of jobs:	Not Reported
Source of postings:	Employers

RESUME SERVICES

Are resumes or profiles posted on the site:	Yes

Recruiters

Number in database:	32,896
Top occupations :	Wide variety
Fee to view resumes:	Based on employer size
How acquired:	Direct from candidates

Job Seekers

How long can you store:	2 years
Who can post a resume:	Those registered
Fee to post:	None
Confidentiality available:	No

OTHER SERVICES

Is a listserv or discussion forum offered:	No
Are assessment instruments offered:	No

Recruiters

Automated resume agent:	No
Banner advertising:	Yes
Status report on ads:	Yes - Both

Job Seekers

Automated job agent:	Yes
Career info provided:	Yes
Links to other sites:	Yes

SITE'S SELF DESCRIPTION

JobsInME.com's mission is to help job seekers find real, local jobs in Maine and reach their career goals. Job seekers can search jobs by location, category, duration and more. All employment opportunities are conveniently organized to facilitate job searching. Job seekers can save their custom search preferences and receive Job Alert emails on a daily/weekly basis.

Contact Information

Name:	Information
Phone:	877-374-1088
E-Mail:	info@jobsintheus.com

JobsinTrucks.com
www.jobsintrucks.com
JobsinLogistics.com

GENERAL SITE INFORMATION

Date activated online:	2004
Location of site headquarters:	North Miami Beach, FL
Number of people who visit the site:	250,000 unique visitors/month
Time spent on site:	10:00 minutes/visit

JOB POSTINGS

Post full time jobs:	Yes
Post part time/contract/consulting jobs:	Yes - All
Most prevalent types of jobs posted:	Truck Driver
Distribution:	International

Recruiters
Fee to post a job:	$245/posting
Posting period:	60 days
Link posting to your site:	Yes

Job Seekers
Number of job postings:	15,000+
Top salary levels of jobs:	Up to $100K/yr
Source of postings:	Employers

RESUME SERVICES

Are resumes or profiles posted on the site: Yes

Recruiters
Number in database:	300,000+
Top occupations :	Driver, Owner-Operator
Fee to view resumes:	$295
How acquired:	Direct from candidates

Job Seekers
How long can you store:	1 year
Who can post a resume:	In the field
Fee to post:	None
Confidentiality available:	Yes

OTHER SERVICES

Is a listserv or discussion forum offered:	No
Are assessment instruments offered:	No

Recruiters
Automated resume agent:	No
Banner advertising:	Yes
Status report on ads:	Yes - Both

Job Seekers
Automated job agent:	Yes
Career info provided:	Yes
Links to other sites:	Yes

SITE'S SELF DESCRIPTION

JobsInTrucks.com is the #1 driver job board used by employers to hire experienced drivers and owner-operators across the USA and Canada. More than 200,000 drivers visit the site each month to find jobs for Class A and Class B company driver and owner operator positions for long distance, regional and local delivery.

Contact Information

Name:	Amy Noah
Phone:	877-562-7678
E-Mail:	amy@jobsintrucks.com

JobsRadar

www.jobsradar.com
Percipio Media, LLC

GENERAL SITE INFORMATION

Date activated online:	2009
Location of site headquarters:	Cambridge, MA
Number of people who visit the site:	3,000,000 unique visitors/month
Time spent on site:	2.9 page views/visitor

JOB POSTINGS

Post full time jobs:	Yes
Post part time/contract/consulting jobs:	Yes - All
Most prevalent types of jobs posted:	Wide variety
Distribution:	National - USA

Recruiters

Fee to post a job:	None
Posting period:	90 days
Link posting to your site:	Yes

Job Seekers

Number of job postings:	1,000,000+
Top salary levels of jobs:	$51-75K, $76-100K/yr
Source of postings:	Employers, Staffing

RESUME SERVICES

Are resumes or profiles posted on the site:	Yes

Recruiters

Number in database:	9,000,000+
Top occupations :	Wide variety
Fee to view resumes:	None
How acquired:	Direct from candidates

Job Seekers

How long can you store:	Indefinitely
Who can post a resume:	Those registered
Fee to post:	None
Confidentiality available:	Yes

OTHER SERVICES

Is a listserv or discussion forum offered:	No
Are assessment instruments offered:	Yes

Recruiters

Automated resume agent:	Yes
Banner advertising:	Yes
Status report on ads:	Yes - Not Reported

Job Seekers

Automated job agent:	Yes
Career info provided:	Yes
Links to other sites:	Yes

SITE'S SELF DESCRIPTION

JobsRadar is a one-stop Web-site for job seekers and a user-friendly recruitment resource for HR groups. We not only host resumes but build and host Web-sites for registered users from which they can manage their professional online identity. In addition to job search, career directory, salary discovery, career advancement, education and scholarship tools are available.

Contact Information

Name:	Member Services
Phone:	888-671-3118
E-Mail:	info@jobsradar.com

JobTarget
www.jobtarget.com
JobTarget

GENERAL SITE INFORMATION

Date activated online:	2001
Location of site headquarters:	New London, CT
Number of people who visit the site:	2,800,000 unique visitors/month
Time spent on site:	3:12 minutes/visit

JOB POSTINGS

Post full time jobs:	Yes
Post part time/contract/consulting jobs:	Yes - All
Most prevalent types of jobs posted:	Wide variety
Distribution:	International

Recruiters

Fee to post a job:	Yes
Posting period:	30 days
Link posting to your site:	Yes

Job Seekers

Number of job postings:	460,000
Top salary levels of jobs:	$151-$200K/yr
Source of postings:	Employers, Other sites

RESUME SERVICES

Are resumes or profiles posted on the site:	Yes

Recruiters

Number in database:	1,250,000
Top occupations :	Wide variety
Fee to view resumes:	None
How acquired:	Direct from candidates

Job Seekers

How long can you store:	Indefinitely
Who can post a resume:	Anyone
Fee to post:	None
Confidentiality available:	Yes

OTHER SERVICES

Is a listserv or discussion forum offered:	No
Are assessment instruments offered:	No

Recruiters

Automated resume agent:	Yes
Banner advertising:	Yes
Status report on ads:	Yes - Postings

Job Seekers

Automated job agent:	Yes
Career info provided:	Yes
Links to other sites:	Yes

SITE'S SELF DESCRIPTION

More than one thousand organizations, including professional and trade associations, publishers, world-class companies and entrepreneurs, rely on JobTarget's best-in-class technology, generous economics and un-matched service and expertise, to power their career centers. JobTarget also helps employers advertise jobs where they will attract the most qualified talent.

Contact Information

Name:	Deborah Katz
Phone:	860-440-0635 x337
E-Mail:	d.katz@jobtarget.com

jobWings.com
www.jobwings.com
jobWings.com

GENERAL SITE INFORMATION

Date activated online:	February, 2001
Location of site headquarters:	Montreal, Quebec, Canada
Number of people who visit the site:	53,000+ unique visitors/month
Time spent on site:	1:56 minutes/visit

JOB POSTINGS

Post full time jobs:	Yes
Post part time/contract/consulting jobs:	No
Most prevalent types of jobs posted:	FA, MG
Distribution:	National - Canada

Recruiters
Fee to post a job:	$425/posting
Posting period:	30 days
Link posting to your site:	Yes

Job Seekers
Number of job postings:	90
Top salary levels of jobs:	$51-76K, $76-100K/yr
Source of postings:	Employers

RESUME SERVICES

Are resumes or profiles posted on the site:	No

Recruiters
Number in database:	N/A
Top occupations :	N/A
Fee to view resumes:	N/A
How acquired:	N/A

Job Seekers
How long can you store:	N/A
Who can post a resume:	N/A
Fee to post:	N/A
Confidentiality available:	N/A

OTHER SERVICES

Is a listserv or discussion forum offered:	No
Are assessment instruments offered:	No

Recruiters
Automated resume agent:	No
Banner advertising:	Yes
Status report on ads:	Yes - Both

Job Seekers
Automated job agent:	Yes
Career info provided:	Yes
Links to other sites:	Yes

SITE'S SELF DESCRIPTION

jobWings.com is the Internet reference for employment in the fields of finance, accounting and management for intermediate to senior level positions in Canada. Founded in February, 2001, jobWings.com quickly established itself as the leader in that field and remains so today with more than 53,000 visitors per month.

Contact Information

Name:	Information
Phone:	888-562-3464
E-Mail:	info@publipac.ca

Juju.com
www.juju.com
Juju, Inc.

GENERAL SITE INFORMATION

Date activated online:	2006
Location of site headquarters:	New York, NY
Number of people who visit the site:	2,500,000 unique visitors/month
Time spent on site:	6.7 page views/visitor

JOB POSTINGS

Post full time jobs:	Yes
Post part time/contract/consulting jobs:	Yes - All
Most prevalent types of jobs posted:	Wide variety
Distribution:	National - USA

Recruiters

Fee to post a job:	Free
Posting period:	90 days
Link posting to your site:	Yes

Job Seekers

Number of job postings:	1,000,000+
Top salary levels of jobs:	Not Reported
Source of postings:	Employers, Other sites

RESUME SERVICES

Are resumes or profiles posted on the site:	Yes

Recruiters

Number in database:	N/A
Top occupations :	N/A
Fee to view resumes:	N/A
How acquired:	N/A

Job Seekers

How long can you store:	N/A
Who can post a resume:	N/A
Fee to post:	N/A
Confidentiality available:	N/A

OTHER SERVICES

Is a listserv or discussion forum offered:	No
Are assessment instruments offered:	No

Recruiters

Automated resume agent:	No
Banner advertising:	No
Status report on ads:	No

Job Seekers

Automated job agent:	Yes
Career info provided:	No
Links to other sites:	Yes

SITE'S SELF DESCRIPTION

Juju's goal is to make job search easier. We search jobs found on thousands of employer sites and job boards around the Web and offer features that help you find the one you're looking for more efficiently. We also offer recruitment advertising that allows employers to reach millions of targeted job seekers, enhance their employment brand, and lower their cost-per-hire.

Contact Information

Name:	Brendan Cruickshank
Phone:	212-537-3898
E-Mail:	sales@juju.com

LatPro
www.latpro.com
LatPro, Inc.

GENERAL SITE INFORMATION

Date activated online:	1997
Location of site headquarters:	Plantation, FL
Number of people who visit the site:	200,000+ unique visitors/month
Time spent on site:	2:52 minutes/visit

JOB POSTINGS

Post full time jobs:	Yes
Post part time/contract/consulting jobs:	Yes - All
Most prevalent types of jobs posted:	EN, FA, SM, Customer Service
Distribution:	International - Latin America

Recruiters
Fee to post a job:	$325/posting
Posting period:	60 days
Link posting to your site:	Yes

Job Seekers
Number of job postings:	15,000
Top salary levels of jobs:	$36-50K, $51-75K/yr
Source of postings:	Employers, Staffing

RESUME SERVICES

Are resumes or profiles posted on the site: Yes

Recruiters
Number in database:	330,000
Top occupations :	EN, FA, SM
Fee to view resumes:	$385
How acquired:	Direct from candidates

Job Seekers
How long can you store:	Indefinitely
Who can post a resume:	Anyone
Fee to post:	None
Confidentiality available:	Yes

OTHER SERVICES

Is a listserv or discussion forum offered:	Yes
Are assessment instruments offered:	Yes

Recruiters
Automated resume agent:	Yes
Banner advertising:	Yes
Status report on ads:	Yes - Both

Job Seekers
Automated job agent:	Yes
Career info provided:	Yes
Links to other sites:	Yes

SITE'S SELF DESCRIPTION

Established in 1997, LatPro is the worldwide leader in providing online employment resources for Hispanic and bilingual professionals. With over 330,000 registered candidates and 90 of the Fortune 100 companies using its award-winning service, LatPro.com (available in English, Spanish and Portuguese) is the premier career destination for Latino and bilingual professionals.

Contact Information

Name:	Rob Steward
Phone:	954-727-3863
E-Mail:	sales@latpro.com

LiveCareer
www.livecareer.com
LiveCareer, Ltd.

GENERAL SITE INFORMATION

Date activated online:	January, 2005
Location of site headquarters:	New York, NY (LiveCareer North America)
Number of people who visit the site:	1,170,000 unique visitors/month
Time spent on site:	6:25 minutes/visit

JOB POSTINGS

Post full time jobs:	No
Post part time/contract/consulting jobs:	No
Most prevalent types of jobs posted:	N/A
Distribution:	N/A

Recruiters
Fee to post a job:	N/A
Posting period:	N/A
Link posting to your site:	N/A

Job Seekers
Number of job postings:	N/A
Top salary levels of jobs:	N/A
Source of postings:	N/A

RESUME SERVICES

Are resumes or profiles posted on the site:	Yes

Recruiters
Number in database:	123,500
Top occupations :	Healthcare, Biz, Trade
Fee to view resumes:	None
How acquired:	Direct from candidates

Job Seekers
How long can you store:	Indefinitely
Who can post a resume:	Anyone
Fee to post:	None
Confidentiality available:	Yes

OTHER SERVICES

Is a listserv or discussion forum offered:	No
Are assessment instruments offered:	Yes

Recruiters
Automated resume agent:	No
Banner advertising:	No
Status report on ads:	No

Job Seekers
Automated job agent:	No
Career info provided:	Yes
Links to other sites:	No

SITE'S SELF DESCRIPTION

LiveCareer is the #1 resume building site, according to Comscore. Our Online Resume Builder creates job-winning resumes and cover letters in minutes for all jobs and industries. Our career portal also has free career tests and is integrated with other career sites and companies. Over 11 million people have registered to build a resume, make a career decision or find a job.

Contact Information

Name:	Customer Service
Phone:	888-816-0576
E-Mail:	customerservice@livecareer.com

Marketing Career Network
www.mcnnetwork.org
Boxwood Technology

GENERAL SITE INFORMATION

Date activated online:	2003
Location of site headquarters:	Hunt Valley, MD
Number of people who visit the site:	25,000 unique visitors/month
Time spent on site:	9:00 minutes/visit

JOB POSTINGS

Post full time jobs:	Yes
Post part time/contract/consulting jobs:	Yes - All
Most prevalent types of jobs posted:	SM, Advertising, Public Relations
Distribution:	International

Recruiters

Fee to post a job:	$200-300/posting
Posting period:	30 days
Link posting to your site:	Yes

Job Seekers

Number of job postings:	500
Top salary levels of jobs:	$36-50K, $51-75K/yr
Source of postings:	Employers

RESUME SERVICES

Are resumes or profiles posted on the site:	Yes

Recruiters

Number in database:	41,000+
Top occupations :	SM
Fee to view resumes:	In posting fee
How acquired:	Direct from candidates

Job Seekers

How long can you store:	1 year
Who can post a resume:	Those in the field
Fee to post:	None
Confidentiality available:	Yes

OTHER SERVICES

Is a listserv or discussion forum offered:	Yes
Are assessment instruments offered:	Yes

Recruiters

Automated resume agent:	Yes
Banner advertising:	Yes
Status report on ads:	Yes - Both

Job Seekers

Automated job agent:	Yes
Career info provided:	Yes
Links to other sites:	No

SITE'S SELF DESCRIPTION

The Marketing Career Network (MCN) is an online recruitment resource that aligns employers with professional marketing membership organizations. It brings together audiences in every marketing discipline and connects them through a single job board network.

Contact Information

Name:	Mary Kay Carey
Phone:	410-891-2402
E-Mail:	info@mcnnetwork.org

mediabistro.com
www.mediabistro.com
mediabistro.com

GENERAL SITE INFORMATION

Date activated online:	1997
Location of site headquarters:	New York, NY
Number of people who visit the site:	3,084,995 unique visitors/month
Time spent on site:	2:11 minutes/visit

JOB POSTINGS

Post full time jobs:	Yes
Post part time/contract/consulting jobs:	Yes - Part time
Most prevalent types of jobs posted:	IS, MG, SM, Editorial, Media
Distribution:	International

Recruiters
Fee to post a job:	$251-300/posting
Posting period:	30 days
Link posting to your site:	Yes

Job Seekers
Number of job postings:	1,300
Top salary levels of jobs:	$76-100K, $151-200K/yr
Source of postings:	Employers, Staffing

RESUME SERVICES

Are resumes or profiles posted on the site:	No

Recruiters
Number in database:	N/A
Top occupations :	N/A
Fee to view resumes:	N/A
How acquired:	N/A

Job Seekers
How long can you store:	N/A
Who can post a resume:	N/A
Fee to post:	N/A
Confidentiality available:	N/A

OTHER SERVICES

Is a listserv or discussion forum offered:	Yes
Are assessment instruments offered:	No

Recruiters
Automated resume agent:	No
Banner advertising:	Yes
Status report on ads:	Yes - Banners

Job Seekers
Automated job agent:	Yes
Career info provided:	Yes
Links to other sites:	No

SITE'S SELF DESCRIPTION

Mediabistro is the number one destination to reach job seekers in the media industry. Our members/users hear about us through word-of-mouth and at our invitation-only cocktail parties (we don't advertise), so our candidates are savvy, and our traffic is targeted. Post your job online and reach out to over 400,000 registered creative and business-side professionals.

Contact Information

Name:	Customer Service
Phone:	212-389-2000
E-Mail:	jobcare@mediabistro.com

Meetingjobs
www.meetingjobs.com
Meetingjobs, LLC

GENERAL SITE INFORMATION

Date activated online:	1997
Location of site headquarters:	Southern Pines, NC
Number of people who visit the site:	16,200 unique visitors/month
Time spent on site:	2.2 page views/visitor

JOB POSTINGS

Post full time jobs:	No
Post part time/contract/consulting jobs:	Yes - All
Most prevalent types of jobs posted:	Meeting, Convention, Special events
Distribution:	International

Recruiters
Fee to post a job:	$275/posting
Posting period:	30 days
Link posting to your site:	Yes

Job Seekers
Number of job postings:	40
Top salary levels of jobs:	Up to $220K/yr
Source of postings:	Employers

RESUME SERVICES

Are resumes or profiles posted on the site:	Yes

Recruiters
Number in database:	24,000
Top occupations :	OP, SM
Fee to view resumes:	In posting fee
How acquired:	Direct from candidates

Job Seekers
How long can you store:	Indefinitely
Who can post a resume:	Those in the field
Fee to post:	None
Confidentiality available:	Yes

OTHER SERVICES

Is a listserv or discussion forum offered:	Yes
Are assessment instruments offered:	No

Recruiters
Automated resume agent:	Yes
Banner advertising:	Yes
Status report on ads:	Yes - Both

Job Seekers
Automated job agent:	Yes
Career info provided:	Yes
Links to other sites:	Yes

SITE'S SELF DESCRIPTION

Meetingjobs, a career job board and Web-site serving the meetings, special events, conference, tradeshow and hospitality industries. The industry's first and most widely used employment site, offering 22,000+ candidates, multiple search options for the hiring official and an up-to-date job board.

Contact Information

Name:	Dawn Penfold
Phone:	212-689-7686
E-Mail:	dawn@meetingjobs.com

MEP Jobs
www.mepjobs.com
Industry People Group

GENERAL SITE INFORMATION

Date activated online:	1996
Location of site headquarters:	Des Moines, IA
Number of people who visit the site:	50,000 unique visitors/month
Time spent on site:	5:00 minutes/visit

JOB POSTINGS

Post full time jobs:	Yes
Post part time/contract/consulting jobs:	Yes - All
Most prevalent types of jobs posted:	EN, HVAC, Construction
Distribution:	National - USA

Recruiters

Fee to post a job:	$395/posting
Posting period:	30 days
Link posting to your site:	Yes

Job Seekers

Number of job postings:	20,000
Top salary levels of jobs:	$76-100K, $151-200K/yr
Source of postings:	Employers, Staffing

RESUME SERVICES

Are resumes or profiles posted on the site:	Yes

Recruiters

Number in database:	25,000
Top occupations :	EN, Trades
Fee to view resumes:	Not Reported
How acquired:	Direct from candidates

Job Seekers

How long can you store:	1 year
Who can post a resume:	Anyone
Fee to post:	None
Confidentiality available:	Yes

OTHER SERVICES

Is a listserv or discussion forum offered:	No
Are assessment instruments offered:	No

Recruiters

Automated resume agent:	Yes
Banner advertising:	Yes
Status report on ads:	Yes - Not Reported

Job Seekers

Automated job agent:	Yes
Career info provided:	Yes
Links to other sites:	Yes

SITE'S SELF DESCRIPTION

MEP Jobs is the leading career site for the mechanical, electrical and plumbing industries. Each day, thousands of HVAC, facilities, electrical and plumbing professionals and employers find each other on MEP Jobs.

Contact Information

Name:	Doug Mitchell
Phone:	888-482-2562
E-Mail:	dmitchell@mepjobs.com

MilitaryConnection.com
www.militaryconnection.com
MilitaryConnection.com

GENERAL SITE INFORMATION

Date activated online:	2006
Location of site headquarters:	Simi Valley, CA
Number of people who visit the site:	250,000 unique visitors/month
Time spent on site:	25:00 minutes/visit

JOB POSTINGS

Post full time jobs:	Yes
Post part time/contract/consulting jobs:	Yes - All
Most prevalent types of jobs posted:	Wide variety
Distribution:	International

Recruiters

Fee to post a job:	$175/posting
Posting period:	60 days
Link posting to your site:	Yes

Job Seekers

Number of job postings:	10,000
Top salary levels of jobs:	Up to $251K+/yr
Source of postings:	Employers

RESUME SERVICES

Are resumes or profiles posted on the site:	Yes

Recruiters

Number in database:	15,000
Top occupations :	Wide variety
Fee to view resumes:	In posting fee
How acquired:	Direct from candidates

Job Seekers

How long can you store:	1 year
Who can post a resume:	Those registered
Fee to post:	None
Confidentiality available:	Yes

OTHER SERVICES

Is a listserv or discussion forum offered:	Yes
Are assessment instruments offered:	Yes

Recruiters

Automated resume agent:	No
Banner advertising:	Yes
Status report on ads:	Yes - Both

Job Seekers

Automated job agent:	No
Career info provided:	Yes
Links to other sites:	Yes

SITE'S SELF DESCRIPTION

We are called the Go To Site for jobs, resources, articles and more for military veterans and their families. We offer clients the opportunity to repeat their message in additional and creative ways. We are excellent at reaching passive job seekers too. Users average 25 minutes on site according to Alexa, drawn by the most up-to-date resources and databases for transition.

Contact Information

Name:	Debbie Gregory
Phone:	800-817-3777
E-Mail:	debbieg@militaryconnection.com

MilitaryHire.com
www.militaryhire.com
The Mentor Group, Inc.

GENERAL SITE INFORMATION

Date activated online:	1999
Location of site headquarters:	The Villages, FL
Number of people who visit the site:	12,000 unique visitors/month
Time spent on site:	1.7 page views/visitor

JOB POSTINGS

Post full time jobs:	Yes
Post part time/contract/consulting jobs:	Yes - All
Most prevalent types of jobs posted:	IS, Defense, Security Clearance
Distribution:	International

Recruiters
Fee to post a job:	$101-150/posting
Posting period:	30 days
Link posting to your site:	Yes

Job Seekers
Number of job postings:	22,430
Top salary levels of jobs:	$76-100K, $151-200K/yr
Source of postings:	Employers, Other sites

RESUME SERVICES

Are resumes or profiles posted on the site:	Yes

Recruiters
Number in database:	460,467
Top occupations :	IS, Defense
Fee to view resumes:	In posting fee
How acquired:	Direct from candidates

Job Seekers
How long can you store:	1 year
Who can post a resume:	Those in the field
Fee to post:	None
Confidentiality available:	Yes

OTHER SERVICES

Is a listserv or discussion forum offered:	Yes
Are assessment instruments offered:	Yes

Recruiters
Automated resume agent:	Yes
Banner advertising:	Yes
Status report on ads:	Yes - Postings

Job Seekers
Automated job agent:	Yes
Career info provided:	Yes
Links to other sites:	Yes

SITE'S SELF DESCRIPTION

MilitaryHire.com is the leading Internet job board for military personnel. As of 2011, we represent nearly 500,000 military candidates. MilitaryHire.com was developed by veterans, for veterans! We specialize in the military experienced candidate. The departing military candidate has the skills that are crucial in today's competitive business environments.

Contact Information

Name:	Michael Weiss
Phone:	800-585-3690
E-Mail:	mweiss@militaryhire.com

MinnesotaJobs.com
www.minnesotajobs.com
Trumor, Inc.

GENERAL SITE INFORMATION

Date activated online:	1995
Location of site headquarters:	East Bethel, MN
Number of people who visit the site:	100,000+ unique visitors/month
Time spent on site:	6:00+ minutes/visit

JOB POSTINGS

Post full time jobs:	Yes
Post part time/contract/consulting jobs:	Yes - All
Most prevalent types of jobs posted:	EN, FA, IS, Customer Service
Distribution:	Regional/USA: MN

Recruiters

Fee to post a job:	$151-200/posting
Posting period:	30 days
Link posting to your site:	Yes

Job Seekers

Number of job postings:	2,200
Top salary levels of jobs:	$76-100K, $151-200K/yr
Source of postings:	Employers

RESUME SERVICES

Are resumes or profiles posted on the site:	Yes

Recruiters

Number in database:	42,000
Top occupations :	AD, EN, SM
Fee to view resumes:	In posting fee
How acquired:	Direct from candidates

Job Seekers

How long can you store:	6 months
Who can post a resume:	Those registered
Fee to post:	None
Confidentiality available:	Yes

OTHER SERVICES

Is a listserv or discussion forum offered:	Yes
Are assessment instruments offered:	Yes

Recruiters

Automated resume agent:	Yes
Banner advertising:	Yes
Status report on ads:	Yes - Both

Job Seekers

Automated job agent:	Yes
Career info provided:	Yes
Links to other sites:	Yes

SITE'S SELF DESCRIPTION

MinnesotaJobs.com is the leading online recruitment resource for Minnesota. In addition to our popular Web site, celebrating 16 years of helping people, MinnesotaJobs.com has embraced social media outlets to help employers reach highly qualified, achievement oriented future employees.

Contact Information

Name:	Penny Freymiller
Phone:	763-784-9393
E-Mail:	penny@minnesotajobs.com

Monster.com
www.monster.com
Monster Worldwide, Inc.

GENERAL SITE INFORMATION

Date activated online:	1994
Location of site headquarters:	New York, NY
Number of people who visit the site:	46,000,000 unique visitors/month
Time spent on site:	18.0 page views/visitor

JOB POSTINGS

Post full time jobs:	Yes
Post part time/contract/consulting jobs:	Yes - All
Most prevalent types of jobs posted:	Wide variety
Distribution:	International

Recruiters
Fee to post a job:	$210-395/posting
Posting period:	60 days
Link posting to your site:	Yes

Job Seekers
Number of job postings:	1,210,000+
Top salary levels of jobs:	Not Reported
Source of postings:	Employers

RESUME SERVICES

Are resumes or profiles posted on the site:	Yes

Recruiters
Number in database:	60,000,000+
Top occupations :	Wide variety
Fee to view resumes:	Multiple solutions
How acquired:	Direct from candidates

Job Seekers
How long can you store:	2 years
Who can post a resume:	Anyone
Fee to post:	None
Confidentiality available:	Yes

OTHER SERVICES

Is a listserv or discussion forum offered:	Yes
Are assessment instruments offered:	Yes

Recruiters
Automated resume agent:	Yes
Banner advertising:	Yes
Status report on ads:	Yes - Both

Job Seekers
Automated job agent:	Yes
Career info provided:	Yes
Links to other sites:	Yes

SITE'S SELF DESCRIPTION

Monster.com®, the leading job matching engine, is dedicated to matching talent to opportunity with unrivaled precision. Monster offers employers a full array of online products and services for building and growing a talented workforce and matches seekers to meaningful careers, inspiring them to improve their lives through the world of work.

Contact Information

Name:	Monster Customer Central
Phone:	800-MONSTER
E-Mail:	moreinfo@monster.com

NACElink Network
www.nacelink.com
The National Association of Colleges & Employers (NACE)

GENERAL SITE INFORMATION

Date activated online:	September, 2002
Location of site headquarters:	Bethlehem, PA
Number of people who visit the site:	2,310,000 unique visitors/month
Time spent on site:	68.7 page views/visitor

JOB POSTINGS

Post full time jobs:	Yes
Post part time/contract/consulting jobs:	Yes - All
Most prevalent types of jobs posted:	Wide variety
Distribution:	National - USA (college students/alumni)

Recruiters
Fee to post a job:	None at college sites
Posting period:	30 days
Link posting to your site:	Yes

Job Seekers
Number of job postings:	704,000 (network-wide)
Top salary levels of jobs:	$35-50K, $51-75K/yr
Source of postings:	Employers

RESUME SERVICES

Are resumes or profiles posted on the site:	Yes

Recruiters
Number in database:	Varies by college
Top occupations :	Wide variety
Fee to view resumes:	Varies by college
How acquired:	Direct from candidates

Job Seekers
How long can you store:	Indefinitely
Who can post a resume:	Students/alumni
Fee to post:	None
Confidentiality available:	Yes

OTHER SERVICES

Is a listserv or discussion forum offered:	No
Are assessment instruments offered:	No

Recruiters
Automated resume agent:	No
Banner advertising:	No
Status report on ads:	No

Job Seekers
Automated job agent:	Yes
Career info provided:	No
Links to other sites:	Yes

SITE'S SELF DESCRIPTION

The NACElink Network is a national recruiting network and suite of Web-based recruiting and career services automation tools serving colleges, employers and student/alumni job candidates. The NACElink Network is committed not only to excellence in its products and services but also to focusing on the career center as the provider of jobs and connections to employers.

Contact Information

Name:	Sales
Phone:	703-351-0200
E-Mail:	sales@nacelink.com

National Healthcare Career Network
www.nhcnnetwork.org
Boxwood Technology

GENERAL SITE INFORMATION

Date activated online:	October, 2007
Location of site headquarters:	Hunt Valley, MD
Number of people who visit the site:	25,116 unique visitors/month
Time spent on site:	9:06 minutes/visit

JOB POSTINGS

Post full time jobs:	Yes
Post part time/contract/consulting jobs:	Yes - All
Most prevalent types of jobs posted:	Nurse, Physician, Allied Health
Distribution:	National - USA

Recruiters
Fee to post a job:	$250-550/posting
Posting period:	30 days
Link posting to your site:	Yes

Job Seekers
Number of job postings:	2,000+
Top salary levels of jobs:	$76-100K, $101-150K/yr
Source of postings:	Employers

RESUME SERVICES

Are resumes or profiles posted on the site: Yes

Recruiters
Number in database:	52,000+
Top occupations :	Healthcare
Fee to view resumes:	In posting fee
How acquired:	Direct from candidates

Job Seekers
How long can you store:	1 year
Who can post a resume:	Those registered
Fee to post:	None
Confidentiality available:	Yes

OTHER SERVICES

Is a listserv or discussion forum offered:	Yes
Are assessment instruments offered:	Yes

Recruiters
Automated resume agent:	Yes
Banner advertising:	Yes
Status report on ads:	Yes - Both

Job Seekers
Automated job agent:	Yes
Career info provided:	Yes
Links to other sites:	Yes

SITE'S SELF DESCRIPTION

The National Healthcare Career Network is the fastest growing healthcare association job board network available. The Network links job boards of more than 200 leading healthcare associations, which are the preferred resource for healthcare talent. We can serve employers in filling positions ranging from volunteers and hourly staff to physicians and executive management.

Contact Information

Name:	Information
Phone:	888-271-6426
E-Mail:	info@hncnnetwork.org

NationJob.com
www.nationjob.com
NationJob Network, Inc.

GENERAL SITE INFORMATION

Date activated online:	1995
Location of site headquarters:	Des Moines, IA
Number of people who visit the site:	400,000 unique visitors/month
Time spent on site:	6:30 minutes/visit

JOB POSTINGS

Post full time jobs:	Yes
Post part time/contract/consulting jobs:	Yes - All
Most prevalent types of jobs posted:	Wide variety
Distribution:	International

Recruiters

Fee to post a job:	$250/posting
Posting period:	30 days
Link posting to your site:	Yes

Job Seekers

Number of job postings:	60-65,000
Top salary levels of jobs:	$51-75K, $76-100K+/yr
Source of postings:	Employers

RESUME SERVICES

Are resumes or profiles posted on the site:	Yes

Recruiters

Number in database:	750,000+
Top occupations :	Wide variety
Fee to view resumes:	In posting fee
How acquired:	Direct from candidates

Job Seekers

How long can you store:	Indefinitely
Who can post a resume:	Anyone
Fee to post:	None
Confidentiality available:	Yes

OTHER SERVICES

Is a listserv or discussion forum offered:	No
Are assessment instruments offered:	Yes

Recruiters

Automated resume agent:	No
Banner advertising:	Yes
Status report on ads:	Yes - Not Reported

Job Seekers

Automated job agent:	Yes
Career info provided:	Yes
Links to other sites:	Yes

SITE'S SELF DESCRIPTION

NationJob.com is the leading provider of community based recruitment. Our core business is our Community Job Network, a partnership between NationJob.com and membership-based organizations offering members significant discounts and creating a custom job site for member employers.

Contact Information

Name:	Barb Avery
Phone:	888-256-0920
E-Mail:	bavery@nationjob.com

NBMBAA Employment Network
www.nbmbaa.org
National Black MBA Association (NBMBAA)

GENERAL SITE INFORMATION

Date activated online:	1996
Location of site headquarters:	Chicago, IL
Number of people who visit the site:	65,000 unique visitors/month
Time spent on site:	7.0 page views/visitor

JOB POSTINGS

Post full time jobs:	Yes
Post part time/contract/consulting jobs:	Yes - All
Most prevalent types of jobs posted:	FA, MG, OP
Distribution:	National - USA

Recruiters

Fee to post a job:	$250/posting
Posting period:	60 days
Link posting to your site:	Yes

Job Seekers

Number of job postings:	2,000
Top salary levels of jobs:	Up to $250K/yr
Source of postings:	Employers

RESUME SERVICES

Are resumes or profiles posted on the site:	Yes

Recruiters

Number in database:	35,000
Top occupations :	FA, MG, OP
Fee to view resumes:	$1,500/month
How acquired:	Direct from candidates

Job Seekers

How long can you store:	5 years
Who can post a resume:	Those registered
Fee to post:	None
Confidentiality available:	Yes

OTHER SERVICES

Is a listserv or discussion forum offered:	No
Are assessment instruments offered:	No

Recruiters

Automated resume agent:	Yes
Banner advertising:	No
Status report on ads:	Yes - Postings

Job Seekers

Automated job agent:	Yes
Career info provided:	Yes
Links to other sites:	Yes

SITE'S SELF DESCRIPTION

The National Black MBA Association has and will continue to celebrate the triumphs of the "Black Business Professional" year round. The NBMBAA Employment Network links employers with NBMBAA members, diverse MBA holders and other job seekers.

Contact Information

Name:	Sales
Phone:	973-992-7311
E-Mail:	nbmbaa-sales@workplacediversity.com

Net-Temps
www.net-temps.com
Net-Temps, Inc.

GENERAL SITE INFORMATION

Date activated online:	1996
Location of site headquarters:	North Chelmsford, MA
Number of people who visit the site:	813,552 unique visitors/month
Time spent on site:	4.8 page views/visitor

JOB POSTINGS

Post full time jobs:	Yes
Post part time/contract/consulting jobs:	Yes - All
Most prevalent types of jobs posted:	AD, FA, IS, MG, Retail
Distribution:	USA, Canada

Recruiters
Fee to post a job:	$99/posting
Posting period:	30 days
Link posting to your site:	Yes

Job Seekers
Number of job postings:	30,695
Top salary levels of jobs:	$50-95K/yr
Source of postings:	Staffing

RESUME SERVICES

Are resumes or profiles posted on the site:	Yes

Recruiters
Number in database:	2,976,000
Top occupations :	AD, FA, IS, MG
Fee to view resumes:	$295/month/3000 views
How acquired:	Direct from candidates

Job Seekers
How long can you store:	Indefinitely
Who can post a resume:	Those registered
Fee to post:	None
Confidentiality available:	Yes

OTHER SERVICES

Is a listserv or discussion forum offered:	Yes
Are assessment instruments offered:	Yes

Recruiters
Automated resume agent:	Yes
Banner advertising:	Yes
Status report on ads:	Yes - Postings

Job Seekers
Automated job agent:	Yes
Career info provided:	Yes
Links to other sites:	Yes

SITE'S SELF DESCRIPTION

Net-Temps is an online job board for temp, temp-to-perm, and direct-hire employment exclusively through staffing companies. Our Job Distribution Network of over 20,000 employment-related Web-sites is one of the most cost-effective approaches to talent acquisition on the Internet. Net-Temps is a top-ranked job board and has over 15 years experience in operation.

Contact Information

Name:	Jean Vosler
Phone:	978-251-7272
E-Mail:	jean@net-temps.com

NursingJobs.org
www.nursingjobs.org
Internet Brands, Inc.

GENERAL SITE INFORMATION

Date activated online:	2006
Location of site headquarters:	El Segundo, CA
Number of people who visit the site:	200,000 unique visitors/month
Time spent on site:	4:00 minutes/visit

JOB POSTINGS

Post full time jobs:	Yes
Post part time/contract/consulting jobs:	Yes - All
Most prevalent types of jobs posted:	Nurses
Distribution:	International

Recruiters
Fee to post a job:	$249/posting
Posting period:	30 days
Link posting to your site:	Yes

Job Seekers
Number of job postings:	1,000
Top salary levels of jobs:	Not Reported
Source of postings:	Employers

RESUME SERVICES

Are resumes or profiles posted on the site:	Yes

Recruiters
Number in database:	250,000
Top occupations :	Nursing
Fee to view resumes:	$399/month
How acquired:	Direct from candidates

Job Seekers
How long can you store:	Indefinitely
Who can post a resume:	Those registered
Fee to post:	None
Confidentiality available:	Yes

OTHER SERVICES

Is a listserv or discussion forum offered:	Yes
Are assessment instruments offered:	No

Recruiters
Automated resume agent:	Yes
Banner advertising:	Yes
Status report on ads:	Yes - Both

Job Seekers
Automated job agent:	Yes
Career info provided:	Yes
Links to other sites:	Yes

SITE'S SELF DESCRIPTION

With its #1 position on Google and Yahoo! for such terms as "nursing jobs," NursingJobs.org is the Internet's leading site dedicated solely to nurses seeking employment. Advertising to this audience is an ideal way to promote your products, services or organization. We have multiple ad positions available and would welcome the opportunity to work with you.

Contact Information

Name:	Sales
Phone:	888-613-8844
E-Mail:	sales@nursingjobs.org

Opportunity Knocks
www.opportunityknocks.org
Opportunity Knocks

GENERAL SITE INFORMATION

Date activated online:	1999
Location of site headquarters:	Atlanta, GA
Number of people who visit the site:	288,000 unique visitors/month
Time spent on site:	7:00 minutes/visit

JOB POSTINGS

Post full time jobs:	Yes
Post part time/contract/consulting jobs:	Yes - Part time, Contract, Consulting
Most prevalent types of jobs posted:	Nonprofit
Distribution:	National - USA

Recruiters

Fee to post a job:	$100/posting
Posting period:	30 days
Link posting to your site:	Yes

Job Seekers

Number of job postings:	750
Top salary levels of jobs:	$76-100K/yr
Source of postings:	Employers, Staffing

RESUME SERVICES

Are resumes or profiles posted on the site:	Yes

Recruiters

Number in database:	210,000
Top occupations :	Nonprofit
Fee to view resumes:	$109/week
How acquired:	Direct from candidates

Job Seekers

How long can you store:	Indefinitely
Who can post a resume:	Anyone
Fee to post:	None
Confidentiality available:	Yes

OTHER SERVICES

Is a listserv or discussion forum offered:	Yes
Are assessment instruments offered:	Yes

Recruiters

Automated resume agent:	Yes
Banner advertising:	Yes
Status report on ads:	Yes - Not Reported

Job Seekers

Automated job agent:	Yes
Career info provided:	Yes
Links to other sites:	Yes

SITE'S SELF DESCRIPTION

Opportunity Knocks is the national online job site focused exclusively on the nonprofit community. We are the premier destination to find nonprofit jobs and access valuable resources for developing successful careers in the nonprofit community. For employers, we are the best way to find qualified candidates and receive valuable information that organizations need.

Contact Information

Name:	Joe Folan
Phone:	678-916-3013
E-Mail:	jfolan@opportunityknocks.org

PedJobs

www.pedjobs.org
American Academy of Pediatrics

GENERAL SITE INFORMATION

Date activated online:	June, 2001
Location of site headquarters:	Elk Grove Village, IL
Number of people who visit the site:	32,000 unique visitors/month
Time spent on site:	3.2 page views/visitor

JOB POSTINGS

Post full time jobs:	Yes
Post part time/contract/consulting jobs:	Yes - Locum Tenens
Most prevalent types of jobs posted:	Pediatricians, Pediatric nurses
Distribution:	International

Recruiters

Fee to post a job:	$390/posting
Posting period:	30 days
Link posting to your site:	Yes

Job Seekers

Number of job postings:	410
Top salary levels of jobs:	Not Reported
Source of postings:	Employers

RESUME SERVICES

Are resumes or profiles posted on the site:	Yes

Recruiters

Number in database:	716
Top occupations :	Pediatrician, Nurse
Fee to view resumes:	In posting fee
How acquired:	Direct from candidates

Job Seekers

How long can you store:	1 year
Who can post a resume:	Those registered
Fee to post:	None
Confidentiality available:	Yes

OTHER SERVICES

Is a listserv or discussion forum offered:	No
Are assessment instruments offered:	Yes

Recruiters

Automated resume agent:	Yes
Banner advertising:	Yes
Status report on ads:	Yes - Both

Job Seekers

Automated job agent:	Yes
Career info provided:	Yes
Links to other sites:	Yes

SITE'S SELF DESCRIPTION

PedJobs is the official American Academy of Pediatrics resource for pediatric careers. It is the only resource dedicated exclusively to the field of pediatrics and its subspecialties. It is a member of the National Healthcare Career Network (NHCN). PedJobs delivers more pediatric professionals as candidates – and more qualified ones – than any other site in the world.

Contact Information

Name:	Mary Lynn Bower
Phone:	847-434-7902
E-Mail:	mbower@aap.org

Physics Today Jobs
www.physicstoday.org/jobs
American Institute of Physics (AIP)

GENERAL SITE INFORMATION

Date activated online:	1993
Location of site headquarters:	College Park, MD
Number of people who visit the site:	85,000 unique visitors/month
Time spent on site:	3.8 page views/visitor

JOB POSTINGS

Post full time jobs:	Yes
Post part time/contract/consulting jobs:	Yes - All
Most prevalent types of jobs posted:	EN, Science, Computing
Distribution:	International

Recruiters
Fee to post a job:	$495/posting
Posting period:	30 days
Link posting to your site:	Yes

Job Seekers
Number of job postings:	250
Top salary levels of jobs:	Not Reported
Source of postings:	Employers

RESUME SERVICES

Are resumes or profiles posted on the site:	Yes

Recruiters
Number in database:	8,000
Top occupations :	Researcher, Teaching
Fee to view resumes:	In posting fee
How acquired:	Direct from candidates

Job Seekers
How long can you store:	1 year
Who can post a resume:	Those in the field
Fee to post:	None
Confidentiality available:	Yes

OTHER SERVICES

Is a listserv or discussion forum offered:	No
Are assessment instruments offered:	No

Recruiters
Automated resume agent:	Yes
Banner advertising:	Yes
Status report on ads:	Yes - Both

Job Seekers
Automated job agent:	Yes
Career info provided:	Yes
Links to other sites:	Yes

SITE'S SELF DESCRIPTION

Physics Today Jobs is part of the AIP Career Network. Network partners include the American Association of Physicists in Medicine, American Association of Physics Teachers, American Physical Society, AVS Science and Technology, IEEE Computer Society, and the Society of Physics Students and Sigma Pi Sigma.

Contact Information

Name:	Bonnie Feldman
Phone:	301-209-3190
E-Mail:	ptjobs@aip.org

PRSA Jobcenter
www.prsa.org/jobcenter
The Public Relations Society of America (PRSA)

GENERAL SITE INFORMATION

Date activated online:	April, 2008
Location of site headquarters:	New York, NY
Number of people who visit the site:	22,580 unique visitors/month
Time spent on site:	2:51 minutes/visit

JOB POSTINGS

Post full time jobs:	Yes
Post part time/contract/consulting jobs:	Yes - All
Most prevalent types of jobs posted:	Public Relations, Corp Communications
Distribution:	National - USA

Recruiters

Fee to post a job:	$250-350/posting
Posting period:	30 days
Link posting to your site:	Yes

Job Seekers

Number of job postings:	2,200
Top salary levels of jobs:	$151-200K/yr
Source of postings:	Employers, Staffing

RESUME SERVICES

Are resumes or profiles posted on the site:	Yes

Recruiters

Number in database:	17,100+
Top occupations :	PR, Communications
Fee to view resumes:	In posting fee
How acquired:	Direct from candidates

Job Seekers

How long can you store:	Indefinitely
Who can post a resume:	Anyone
Fee to post:	None
Confidentiality available:	Yes

OTHER SERVICES

Is a listserv or discussion forum offered:	Yes
Are assessment instruments offered:	Yes

Recruiters

Automated resume agent:	Yes
Banner advertising:	Yes
Status report on ads:	Yes - Both

Job Seekers

Automated job agent:	Yes
Career info provided:	Yes
Links to other sites:	Yes

SITE'S SELF DESCRIPTION

The PRSA Public Relations and Communications Jobcenter is the most targeted community of public relations and communications jobs. Post a job of any length for a discounted flat fee. Whether you are posting PR jobs, community relations, corporate communications, or similar positons, PRSA Jobcenter connects you with more than 77,000 potential employees.

Contact Information

Name:	Richard Spector
Phone:	212-460-1406
E-Mail:	richard.spector@prsa.org

RegionalHelpWanted.com
www.regionalhelpwanted.com
onTargetjobs, Inc.

GENERAL SITE INFORMATION

Date activated online:	1999
Location of site headquarters:	Denver, CO
Number of people who visit the site:	1,330,000 unique visitors/month
Time spent on site:	8:00 minutes/visit

JOB POSTINGS

Post full time jobs:	Yes
Post part time/contract/consulting jobs:	Yes - All
Most prevalent types of jobs posted:	Wide variety
Distribution:	Local markets in USA, Canada

Recruiters
Fee to post a job:	$125-375/posting
Posting period:	30 days
Link posting to your site:	Yes

Job Seekers
Number of job postings:	50,000+
Top salary levels of jobs:	$20-30K, $31-50K/yr
Source of postings:	Employers

RESUME SERVICES

Are resumes or profiles posted on the site: Yes

Recruiters
Number in database:	180,000+
Top occupations :	Wide variety
Fee to view resumes:	In posting fee
How acquired:	Direct from candidates

Job Seekers
How long can you store:	Indefinitely
Who can post a resume:	Anyone
Fee to post:	None
Confidentiality available:	Yes

OTHER SERVICES

Is a listserv or discussion forum offered:	No
Are assessment instruments offered:	No

Recruiters
Automated resume agent:	Yes
Banner advertising:	Yes
Status report on ads:	Yes - Both

Job Seekers
Automated job agent:	Yes
Career info provided:	Yes
Links to other sites:	Yes

SITE'S SELF DESCRIPTION

RegionalHelpWanted.com partners with local broadcast radio stations to design, build and maintain recruitment Web-sites throughout the United States and Canada. RegionalHelpWanted operates over 400 regional sites.

Contact Information

Name:	Tony Garcia
Phone:	303-847-4260
E-Mail:	tony.garcia@regionalhelpwanted.com

RetirementJobs.com
www.retirementjobs.com
RetirementJobs.com, Inc.

GENERAL SITE INFORMATION

Date activated online:	2006
Location of site headquarters:	Watham, MA
Number of people who visit the site:	250,000 unique visitors/month
Time spent on site:	3:51 minutes/visit

JOB POSTINGS

Post full time jobs:	Yes
Post part time/contract/consulting jobs:	Yes - Part time
Most prevalent types of jobs posted:	SM, Customer Service
Distribution:	National - USA

Recruiters

Fee to post a job:	Under $100/posting
Posting period:	30 days
Link posting to your site:	Yes

Job Seekers

Number of job postings:	25,000
Top salary levels of jobs:	$36-50K, $51-75K/yr
Source of postings:	Employers, Staffing

RESUME SERVICES

Are resumes or profiles posted on the site:	Yes

Recruiters

Number in database:	500,000
Top occupations :	AD, EN, FA
Fee to view resumes:	In posting fee
How acquired:	Direct from candidates

Job Seekers

How long can you store:	1 year
Who can post a resume:	Those registered
Fee to post:	None
Confidentiality available:	Yes

OTHER SERVICES

Is a listserv or discussion forum offered:	No
Are assessment instruments offered:	No

Recruiters

Automated resume agent:	Yes
Banner advertising:	Yes
Status report on ads:	Yes - Both

Job Seekers

Automated job agent:	Yes
Career info provided:	Yes
Links to other sites:	Yes

SITE'S SELF DESCRIPTION

RetirementJobs.com is a career portal for Baby Boomers. Its mission is to deliver opportunity, inspiration, community and counsel to people over age 50 seeking work that matches their lifestyle needs. The site is free for job seekers. It makes money by charging placement fees to employers and advertisers.

Contact Information

Name:	Pete Mullen
Phone:	781-890-5050
E-Mail:	support@retirementjobs.com

Sales Gravy
www.salesgravy.com
3 Palms Publishing Group, LLC

GENERAL SITE INFORMATION

Date activated online:	November, 2006
Location of site headquarters:	Thomson, GA
Number of people who visit the site:	337,210 unique visitors/month
Time spent on site:	10.5 page views/visitor

JOB POSTINGS

Post full time jobs:	Yes
Post part time/contract/consulting jobs:	No
Most prevalent types of jobs posted:	MG, SM, Customer Service
Distribution:	International

Recruiters
Fee to post a job:	$399/unlimited posting
Posting period:	30 days
Link posting to your site:	Yes

Job Seekers
Number of job postings:	90,000
Top salary levels of jobs:	$76-100K, $101-150K/yr
Source of postings:	Employers, Staffing

RESUME SERVICES

Are resumes or profiles posted on the site:	Yes

Recruiters
Number in database:	225,000
Top occupations :	MG, SM
Fee to view resumes:	$499/month
How acquired:	Direct from candidates

Job Seekers
How long can you store:	180 days
Who can post a resume:	Anyone
Fee to post:	None
Confidentiality available:	Yes

OTHER SERVICES

Is a listserv or discussion forum offered:	Yes
Are assessment instruments offered:	Yes

Recruiters
Automated resume agent:	Yes
Banner advertising:	Yes
Status report on ads:	Yes - Both

Job Seekers
Automated job agent:	Yes
Career info provided:	Yes
Links to other sites:	Yes

SITE'S SELF DESCRIPTION

Sales Gravy is the most visited sales employment Web-site on the planet. Our singular mission is advancing sales as a profession, and we believe that sales professionals are the elite athletes of the business world. On Sales Gravy, we offer thousands of pages of free training and personal development content and host an active community of sales professionals.

Contact Information

Name:	Get Help
Phone:	706-664-0810
E-Mail:	gethelp@salesgravy.com

Security Jobs Network™
www.securityjobs.net
Security Jobs Network, Inc.

GENERAL SITE INFORMATION

Date activated online:	1998
Location of site headquarters:	Warrenton, VA
Number of people who visit the site:	21,500 unique visitors/month
Time spent on site:	7:00 minutes/visit

JOB POSTINGS

Post full time jobs:	Yes
Post part time/contract/consulting jobs:	No
Most prevalent types of jobs posted:	Individual & Corporate Security
Distribution:	International

Recruiters		**Job Seekers**	
Fee to post a job:	None	Number of job postings:	400
Posting period:	30 days	Top salary levels of jobs:	Up to $550K/yr
Link posting to your site:	Yes	Source of postings:	Employers, Staffing

RESUME SERVICES

Are resumes or profiles posted on the site:	No

Recruiters		**Job Seekers**	
Number in database:	N/A	How long can you store:	N/A
Top occupations :	N/A	Who can post a resume:	N/A
Fee to view resumes:	N/A	Fee to post:	N/A
How acquired:	N/A	Confidentiality available:	N/A

OTHER SERVICES

Is a listserv or discussion forum offered:	No
Are assessment instruments offered:	No

Recruiters		**Job Seekers**	
Automated resume agent:	No	Automated job agent:	No
Banner advertising:	No	Career info provided:	No
Status report on ads:	No	Links to other sites:	Yes

SITE'S SELF DESCRIPTION

Security Jobs Network™ is a subscription-based service providing up-to-date information based on comprehensive research and the collection of current executive, professional-level security and asset protection opportunities, including corporate security and loss prevention; public, private, civil or criminal investigation; executive protection and other similar positions.

Contact Information

Name:	Inquiry
Phone:	866-767-5627
E-Mail:	inquiry@securityjobs.net

SHRM HRJobs
www.shrm.org/jobs
Society for Human Resource Management (SHRM)

GENERAL SITE INFORMATION

Date activated online:	1999
Location of site headquarters:	Alexandria, VA
Number of people who visit the site:	116,300 unique visitors/month
Time spent on site:	15:00 minutes/visit

JOB POSTINGS

Post full time jobs:	Yes
Post part time/contract/consulting jobs:	Yes - All
Most prevalent types of jobs posted:	HR
Distribution:	International

Recruiters
Fee to post a job:	$154/posting
Posting period:	30 days
Link posting to your site:	Yes

Job Seekers
Number of job postings:	600
Top salary levels of jobs:	$201-250K, $251K+/yr
Source of postings:	Employers, Staffing

RESUME SERVICES

Are resumes or profiles posted on the site:	Yes

Recruiters
Number in database:	26,000
Top occupations :	HR
Fee to view resumes:	$649 w/ a job posting
How acquired:	Direct from candidates

Job Seekers
How long can you store:	Indefinitely
Who can post a resume:	Those in the field
Fee to post:	None
Confidentiality available:	Yes

OTHER SERVICES

Is a listserv or discussion forum offered:	No
Are assessment instruments offered:	No

Recruiters
Automated resume agent:	No
Banner advertising:	No
Status report on ads:	No

Job Seekers
Automated job agent:	Yes
Career info provided:	Yes
Links to other sites:	No

SITE'S SELF DESCRIPTION

The Society for Human Resource Management (SHRM) is the world's largest professional association devoted to human resource management. Our mission is to serve the needs of HR professionals by providing the most current and comprehensive resources, and to advance the profession by promoting HR's essential strategic role.

Contact Information

Name:	Omar Scott
Phone:	703-535-6166
E-Mail:	omar.scott@shrm.org

Simply Hired
www.simplyhired.com
Simply Hired, Inc.

GENERAL SITE INFORMATION

Date activated online:	2005
Location of site headquarters:	Mountain View, CA
Number of people who visit the site:	14,000,000 unique visitors/month
Time spent on site:	4:00 minutes/visit

JOB POSTINGS

Post full time jobs:	Yes
Post part time/contract/consulting jobs:	Yes - All
Most prevalent types of jobs posted:	Healthcare, Technology
Distribution:	International

Recruiters

Fee to post a job:	Pay-per-click
Posting period:	Indefinite
Link posting to your site:	Yes

Job Seekers

Number of job postings:	7,000,000
Top salary levels of jobs:	Not Reported
Source of postings:	Other sites

RESUME SERVICES

Are resumes or profiles posted on the site:	No

Recruiters

Number in database:	N/A
Top occupations :	N/A
Fee to view resumes:	N/A
How acquired:	N/A

Job Seekers

How long can you store:	N/A
Who can post a resume:	N/A
Fee to post:	N/A
Confidentiality available:	N/A

OTHER SERVICES

Is a listserv or discussion forum offered:	Yes
Are assessment instruments offered:	Yes

Recruiters

Automated resume agent:	No
Banner advertising:	Yes
Status report on ads:	Yes - Both

Job Seekers

Automated job agent:	Yes
Career info provided:	Yes
Links to other sites:	Yes

SITE'S SELF DESCRIPTION

With more than seven million job listings worldwide, Simply Hired is the world's largest job search engine and recruitment advertising network. The company powers jobs on over 10,000 network partner sites, and operates global sites in 22 countries and 11 languages on six continents.

Contact Information

Name:	Matt Baum - Sales
Phone:	650.930.1000
E-Mail:	info@simplyhired.com

6FigureJobs.com
http://www.6figurejobs.com
Workstream, Inc.

GENERAL SITE INFORMATION

Date activated online:	1996
Location of site headquarters:	Stamford, CT
Number of people who visit the site:	156,404 unique visitors/month
Time spent on site:	3:31 minutes/visit

JOB POSTINGS

Post full time jobs:	Yes
Post part time/contract/consulting jobs:	Yes - All
Most prevalent types of jobs posted:	FA, IS, MG, SM
Distribution:	International

Recruiters
Fee to post a job:	$575+/posting
Posting period:	30 days
Link posting to your site:	Yes

Job Seekers
Number of job postings:	2,700+
Top salary levels of jobs:	Up to $350K+/yr
Source of postings:	Employers, Staffing

RESUME SERVICES

Are resumes or profiles posted on the site: Yes

Recruiters
Number in database:	700,000+
Top occupations :	FA, IS, MG, OP, SM
Fee to view resumes:	In posting fee
How acquired:	Direct from candidates

Job Seekers
How long can you store:	Indefinitely
Who can post a resume:	Those registered
Fee to post:	None
Confidentiality available:	Yes

OTHER SERVICES

Is a listserv or discussion forum offered:	Yes
Are assessment instruments offered:	Yes

Recruiters
Automated resume agent:	Yes
Banner advertising:	Yes
Status report on ads:	Yes - Both

Job Seekers
Automated job agent:	Yes
Career info provided:	Yes
Links to other sites:	Yes

SITE'S SELF DESCRIPTION

Find and hire today's best executive and senior-level talent. 6FigureJobs.com offers the largest active and passive recruitment database of "pre-screened" executives and senior-level professionals. 6FigureJobs is unique for its focus on only employment opportunities that pay over $100,000 per annum.

Contact Information

Name:	Anne Hunt Cheevers
Phone:	800-605-5154 x301
E-Mail:	anne.cheevers@6figurejobs.com

SnagAJob.com
www.snagajob.com
SnagAJob.com, Inc.

GENERAL SITE INFORMATION

Date activated online:	2000
Location of site headquarters:	Glen Allen, VA
Number of people who visit the site:	6,000,000 unique visitors/month
Time spent on site:	6:40 minutes/visit

JOB POSTINGS

Post full time jobs:	Yes
Post part time/contract/consulting jobs:	Yes - Part time
Most prevalent types of jobs posted:	SM, Food Service, Retail
Distribution:	National - USA

Recruiters
Fee to post a job:	$89/posting
Posting period:	30 days
Link posting to your site:	Yes

Job Seekers
Number of job postings:	200,000+
Top salary levels of jobs:	Hourly
Source of postings:	Employers, Staffing

RESUME SERVICES

Are resumes or profiles posted on the site:	Yes

Recruiters
Number in database:	27,000,000
Top occupations :	FA, IS, MG, OP, SM
Fee to view resumes:	In posting fee
How acquired:	Direct from candidates

Job Seekers
How long can you store:	Indefinitely
Who can post a resume:	Those registered
Fee to post:	None
Confidentiality available:	Yes

OTHER SERVICES

Is a listserv or discussion forum offered:	Yes
Are assessment instruments offered:	Yes

Recruiters
Automated resume agent:	Yes
Banner advertising:	Yes
Status report on ads:	Yes - Both

Job Seekers
Automated job agent:	Yes
Career info provided:	Yes
Links to other sites:	Yes

SITE'S SELF DESCRIPTION

SnagAJob.com, the nation's largest job search site and online community, has helped connect hourly workers with quality full-time and part-time jobs in a wide range of industries since 2000. Headquartered in Richmond, VA, SnagAJob.com also provides both job seekers and employers with valued insights and a cutting-edge interface that are unique to hourly employment.

Contact Information

Name:	Customer Service
Phone:	804-236-9934
E-Mail:	info@snagajob.com

SPIE Career Center
www.spie.org/careercenter
SPIE - The International Society for Optics and Photonics

GENERAL SITE INFORMATION

Date activated online:	2001
Location of site headquarters:	Bellingham, WA
Number of people who visit the site:	6,500 unique visitors/month
Time spent on site:	3:30 minutes/visit

JOB POSTINGS

Post full time jobs:	Yes
Post part time/contract/consulting jobs:	Yes - All
Most prevalent types of jobs posted:	EN
Distribution:	International

Recruiters
Fee to post a job:	$375+/posting
Posting period:	30 days
Link posting to your site:	Yes

Job Seekers
Number of job postings:	660
Top salary levels of jobs:	$101-150K, $151-200K/yr
Source of postings:	Employers, Staffing

RESUME SERVICES

Are resumes or profiles posted on the site:	Yes

Recruiters
Number in database:	365
Top occupations :	EN
Fee to view resumes:	In posting fee
How acquired:	Direct from candidates

Job Seekers
How long can you store:	1 year
Who can post a resume:	Those in the field
Fee to post:	None
Confidentiality available:	Yes

OTHER SERVICES

Is a listserv or discussion forum offered:	No
Are assessment instruments offered:	No

Recruiters
Automated resume agent:	Yes
Banner advertising:	Yes
Status report on ads:	Yes - Both

Job Seekers
Automated job agent:	Yes
Career info provided:	Yes
Links to other sites:	Yes

SITE'S SELF DESCRIPTION

Your source for optics and photonics jobs and talent. Recruit your next hire or find your next job on the SPIE Career Center. Job seekers can search job listings, set up email alerts, and view the 'Advice+Tools' section. Employers may post jobs and gain access to a resume database, create a Resume Alert, and participate in job fairs held at SPIE conferences.

Contact Information

Name:	Sara Leibert
Phone:	360-715-3705
E-Mail:	jobsales@spie.org

TalentZoo.com
www.talentzoo.com
TalentZoo, Inc.

GENERAL SITE INFORMATION

Date activated online:	2001
Location of site headquarters:	Atlanta, GA
Number of people who visit the site:	250,000 unique visitors/month
Time spent on site:	5:40 minutes/visit

JOB POSTINGS

Post full time jobs:	Yes
Post part time/contract/consulting jobs:	Yes - All
Most prevalent types of jobs posted:	Advertising, New Media, Creative
Distribution:	National - USA

Recruiters
Fee to post a job:	$199/posting
Posting period:	30 days
Link posting to your site:	Yes

Job Seekers
Number of job postings:	500
Top salary levels of jobs:	Up to $200K/yr
Source of postings:	Employers, Staffing

RESUME SERVICES

Are resumes or profiles posted on the site:	Yes

Recruiters
Number in database:	200,000
Top occupations :	SM, Advertising
Fee to view resumes:	$499
How acquired:	Direct from candidates

Job Seekers
How long can you store:	Indefinitely
Who can post a resume:	Those registered
Fee to post:	None
Confidentiality available:	Yes

OTHER SERVICES

Is a listserv or discussion forum offered:	No
Are assessment instruments offered:	No

Recruiters
Automated resume agent:	Yes
Banner advertising:	Yes
Status report on ads:	Yes - Both

Job Seekers
Automated job agent:	Yes
Career info provided:	Yes
Links to other sites:	No

SITE'S SELF DESCRIPTION

TalentZoo.com is a nationwide career site focused on the communications industry. We offer a job board, resume access, news and trends and unique content authored by industry leaders for our users. The site was named by Forbes as "Best of the Web."

Contact Information

Name:	Amy Hoover
Phone:	404-607-1955
E-Mail:	support@talentzoo.com

TopUSAJobs.com
www.topusajobs.com
TopUSAJobs.com, Inc.

GENERAL SITE INFORMATION

Date activated online:	2003
Location of site headquarters:	North Miami Beach, FL
Number of people who visit the site:	4,000,000+ unique visitors/month
Time spent on site:	5.0 page views/visitor

JOB POSTINGS

Post full time jobs:	Yes
Post part time/contract/consulting jobs:	Yes - All
Most prevalent types of jobs posted:	Wide variety
Distribution:	National - USA

Recruiters

Fee to post a job:	Pay-per-click
Posting period:	Open-ended
Link posting to your site:	Yes

Job Seekers

Number of job postings:	1,500,000+
Top salary levels of jobs:	Hourly to $250K+/yr
Source of postings:	Employers, Staffing

RESUME SERVICES

Are resumes or profiles posted on the site:	No

Recruiters

Number in database:	N/A
Top occupations :	N/A
Fee to view resumes:	N/A
How acquired:	N/A

Job Seekers

How long can you store:	N/A
Who can post a resume:	N/A
Fee to post:	N/A
Confidentiality available:	N/A

OTHER SERVICES

Is a listserv or discussion forum offered:	No
Are assessment instruments offered:	No

Recruiters

Automated resume agent:	No
Banner advertising:	Yes
Status report on ads:	Yes - Postings

Job Seekers

Automated job agent:	No
Career info provided:	Yes
Links to other sites:	Yes

SITE'S SELF DESCRIPTION

TopUSAJobs.com, the first pay-per-click job search engine, is a leading provider of targeted candidate traffic to hundreds of job boards, companies and staffing agencies. Since 2003, TopUSAJobs has given job seekers free access to millions of jobs nationwide with our easy-to-use search functionalities.

Contact Information

Name:	Shelly Mudd
Phone:	866-712-5627
E-Mail:	shelly@topusajobs.com

VetJobs
www.vetjobs.com
VetJobs.com, Inc.

GENERAL SITE INFORMATION

Date activated online:	November, 1999
Location of site headquarters:	Roswell, GA
Number of people who visit the site:	110,000 unique visitors/month
Time spent on site:	21.0 page views/visitor

JOB POSTINGS

Post full time jobs:	Yes
Post part time/contract/consulting jobs:	Yes - All
Most prevalent types of jobs posted:	AD, EN, IS, MG, OP, Defense
Distribution:	International

Recruiters
Fee to post a job:	$195/posting
Posting period:	60 days
Link posting to your site:	Yes

Job Seekers
Number of job postings:	37,000
Top salary levels of jobs:	$75-100K, $201-250K/yr
Source of postings:	Employers, Staffing

RESUME SERVICES

Are resumes or profiles posted on the site:	Yes

Recruiters
Number in database:	120,000
Top occupations :	AD, EN, IS, MG, OP
Fee to view resumes:	$2,000/year
How acquired:	Direct from candidates

Job Seekers
How long can you store:	Indefinitely
Who can post a resume:	Those in the field
Fee to post:	None
Confidentiality available:	Yes

OTHER SERVICES

Is a listserv or discussion forum offered:	No
Are assessment instruments offered:	Yes

Recruiters
Automated resume agent:	No
Banner advertising:	Yes
Status report on ads:	Yes - Both

Job Seekers
Automated job agent:	No
Career info provided:	Yes
Links to other sites:	Yes

SITE'S SELF DESCRIPTION

Veterans of Foreign Wars sponsored VetJobs is the leading military-related job board on the Internet. The jobs database is available to anyone who visits the site, but to post a resume a candidate must have been associated with the military family. Thousands of veterans worldwide have found jobs with the hundreds of employers who use VetJobs to reach the veteran market.

Contact Information

Name:	Ted Daywalt
Phone:	770-993-5117
E-Mail:	tdaywalt@vetjobs.com

WallStJobs.com
www.wallstjobs.com
WallStJobs.com, Inc.

GENERAL SITE INFORMATION

Date activated online:	1999
Location of site headquarters:	Garden City, NY
Number of people who visit the site:	64,238 unique visitors/month
Time spent on site:	12:40 minutes/visit

JOB POSTINGS

Post full time jobs:	Yes
Post part time/contract/consulting jobs:	Yes - All
Most prevalent types of jobs posted:	FA, MG, OP, SM
Distribution:	National - USA

Recruiters
Fee to post a job:	$250/posting
Posting period:	30 days
Link posting to your site:	Yes

Job Seekers
Number of job postings:	1,565
Top salary levels of jobs:	$76-100K, 101-150K/yr
Source of postings:	Employers

RESUME SERVICES

Are resumes or profiles posted on the site:	Yes

Recruiters
Number in database:	295,801
Top occupations :	FA, MG, OP, SM
Fee to view resumes:	Not Reported
How acquired:	Direct from candidates

Job Seekers
How long can you store:	Indefinitely
Who can post a resume:	Those in the field
Fee to post:	None
Confidentiality available:	Yes

OTHER SERVICES

Is a listserv or discussion forum offered:	No
Are assessment instruments offered:	No

Recruiters
Automated resume agent:	Yes
Banner advertising:	Yes
Status report on ads:	Yes - Both

Job Seekers
Automated job agent:	Yes
Career info provided:	Yes
Links to other sites:	Yes

SITE'S SELF DESCRIPTION

Launched in 1999, WallStJobs.com has become one of the most well-recognized and well-respected recruitment resources for the financial services industry. We know the industry because we are staffed by financial services professionals as well as recruiters with prior experience at personnel agencies serving the financial services community.

Contact Information

Name:	Robert Graber
Phone:	516-873-8100
E-Mail:	rgraber@wallstjobs.com

Work In Sports
www.workinsports.com
Work In Sports, LLC

GENERAL SITE INFORMATION

Date activated online:	2000
Location of site headquarters:	Scottsdale, AZ
Number of people who visit the site:	250,000 unique visitors/month
Time spent on site:	3:00 minutes/visit

JOB POSTINGS

Post full time jobs:	Yes
Post part time/contract/consulting jobs:	Yes - Part time
Most prevalent types of jobs posted:	MG, SM, Customer Service, Sports-related
Distribution:	National - USA

Recruiters

Fee to post a job:	Free
Posting period:	Indefinite
Link posting to your site:	Yes

Job Seekers

Number of job postings:	3,100
Top salary levels of jobs:	$76-100K, $101-150K/yr
Source of postings:	Employers, Other sites

RESUME SERVICES

Are resumes or profiles posted on the site:	Yes

Recruiters

Number in database:	40,000
Top occupations :	MG, SM
Fee to view resumes:	None
How acquired:	Direct from candidates

Job Seekers

How long can you store:	Indefinitely
Who can post a resume:	Those registered
Fee to post:	None
Confidentiality available:	Yes

OTHER SERVICES

Is a listserv or discussion forum offered:	No
Are assessment instruments offered:	No

Recruiters

Automated resume agent:	No
Banner advertising:	No
Status report on ads:	No

Job Seekers

Automated job agent:	Yes
Career info provided:	Yes
Links to other sites:	Yes

SITE'S SELF DESCRIPTION

Work In Sports is the complete sports employment resource, working with pro teams, leagues, facilities, NCAA athletic departments and other organizations in the sports industry. Employers can post unlimited jobs and internships and search the resume database of qualified applicants at no charge.

Contact Information

Name:	John Mellor
Phone:	480-905-8077
E-Mail:	jmellor@workinsports.com

Workopolis
www.workopolis.com
Toronto Star Newspapers, Ltd. and Square Victoria Digital Properties Inc.

GENERAL SITE INFORMATION

Date activated online:	2000
Location of site headquarters:	Toronto, Ontario, Canada
Number of people who visit the site:	1,600,000 unique visitors/month
Time spent on site:	6:30 minutes/visit

JOB POSTINGS

Post full time jobs:	Yes
Post part time/contract/consulting jobs:	Yes - All
Most prevalent types of jobs posted:	IS, SM, Health, Trades
Distribution:	National - Canada

Recruiters

Fee to post a job:	$700/posting
Posting period:	30 days
Link posting to your site:	Yes

Job Seekers

Number of job postings:	30,000+
Top salary levels of jobs:	Not Reported
Source of postings:	Employers, Staffing

RESUME SERVICES

Are resumes or profiles posted on the site:	Yes

Recruiters

Number in database:	2,000,000
Top occupations :	AD, IS, SM
Fee to view resumes:	$1,250/month
How acquired:	Direct from candidates

Job Seekers

How long can you store:	Indefinitely
Who can post a resume:	Those registered
Fee to post:	None
Confidentiality available:	Yes

OTHER SERVICES

Is a listserv or discussion forum offered:	No
Are assessment instruments offered:	Yes

Recruiters

Automated resume agent:	Yes
Banner advertising:	Yes
Status report on ads:	Yes - Both

Job Seekers

Automated job agent:	Yes
Career info provided:	Yes
Links to other sites:	Yes

SITE'S SELF DESCRIPTION

Workopolis.com is the Canadian leader in the Internet recruitment and career transition solutions field, helping employers and candidates connect with each other online. Along with offering employers the tools to post jobs online and search a database of millions of candidate resumes, Workopolis also offers ground-breaking employer branding tools.

Contact Information

Name:	Jason Karsh
Phone:	416 957-8385
E-Mail:	support@workopolis.com

WorkplaceDiversity.com
www.workplacediversity.com
WorkplaceDiversity.com, LLC

GENERAL SITE INFORMATION

Date activated online:	1999
Location of site headquarters:	Livingston, NJ
Number of people who visit the site:	153,000 unique visitors/month
Time spent on site:	8.5 page views/visitor

JOB POSTINGS

Post full time jobs:	Yes
Post part time/contract/consulting jobs:	Yes - All
Most prevalent types of jobs posted:	Professional
Distribution:	National - USA

Recruiters
Fee to post a job:	$151-200/posting
Posting period:	60 days
Link posting to your site:	Yes

Job Seekers
Number of job postings:	9,000
Top salary levels of jobs:	$101-150K, $151-200K/yr
Source of postings:	Employers

RESUME SERVICES

Are resumes or profiles posted on the site:	Yes

Recruiters
Number in database:	184,000
Top occupations :	Wide variety
Fee to view resumes:	Not Reported
How acquired:	Direct from candidates

Job Seekers
How long can you store:	Indefinitely
Who can post a resume:	Anyone
Fee to post:	None
Confidentiality available:	Yes

OTHER SERVICES

Is a listserv or discussion forum offered:	No
Are assessment instruments offered:	Yes

Recruiters
Automated resume agent:	Yes
Banner advertising:	Yes
Status report on ads:	Yes - Both

Job Seekers
Automated job agent:	Yes
Career info provided:	Yes
Links to other sites:	Yes

SITE'S SELF DESCRIPTION

WorkplaceDiversity.com, the source for diversity talent®, is the preeminent job search web site for corporate recruiters who are seeking experienced diverse talent. Our goal is to create a connection between companies that support diversity and experienced, distinct candidates by providing one location for recruiters to post open positions.

Contact Information

Name:	Mike Monsport
Phone:	972-992-7311
E-Mail:	sales@workplacediversity.com

Notes

Notes

WEDDLE's

The Best & the Rest

2011/12

A Directory of 10,000+ Employment Sites

Sites in bold are Peter's picks plus members of the International Association of Employment Web Sites. They are among the best employment sites on the Web.

The Best & the Rest Site Categories

The Best & the Rest is a directory of over 10,000 employment sites organized into career field, industry and geographic location categories. The categories are presented below. Within each category, sites are listed alphabetically by their name, which may or may not be their URL or Internet address.

Sites are continuously upgrading their content, so addresses for specific site subsections (e.g., the job board on an association site) may change from that listed in the directory. If you find that a site's address does not work – that is, the site does not open or you get an error message – use a technique called "peeling." It involves sequentially eliminating each of the extensions between the forward slashes in the site's address until the address works. Begin with the last extension in the address and eliminate one extension at a time until the site opens. Then, look for links on the open page to find the specific area of the site you seek.

For example, the directory might list the following address for a site you want to visit: www.the-name-of-the-site.com/adposts/jobs/newposts.html. If you were to use that address and it did not open to a page on the site, "peel" away the first extension – newposts.htm – and try again with the remaining address: www.the-name-of-the-site.com/adpost/jobs. Repeat that process until the address works and the site opens.

Keeping Our Information Up-to-Date

WEDDLE's makes every effort to keep the information it publishes current and up-to-date. The Internet, however, is always changing, and WEDDLE's is always seeking updates and corrections to its listings. If you find a discrepancy, please notify us at 203.964.1888 or on the Internet at corporate@weddles.com. We appreciate your assistance and pay careful attention to what you tell us.

Whenever we become aware of a change or discrepancy, we contact the appropriate site, obtain the correct information and then publish it on our Web-site for you and others to see. So, log onto **www.weddles.com** regularly and click on the link entitled Free Book Updates on our toolbar. It's the best way to stay on top of the ever-changing universe of helpful employment resources on the Internet.

Site Categories & Index (continued)

Site Categories

— A —

Administrative/Clerical/Secretarial (see also Classifieds)

Advertising/Public Relations

Agriculture

Archeology/Anthropology

Architecture

Arts

Association-Professional & Trade/Affinity Group

Astronomy

Automotive

Aviation

— B —

Banking

Bilingual/Multilingual Professionals

Biology/Biotechnology

Blogs – Job Seekers

Blogs – Recruiters

Building Industry-Construction & Management

Business

— C —

Call Center

Career Counseling/Job Search Services

Chemistry

Child & Elder Care

Site Categories & Index (continued)

Classifieds-Newspaper

College/Internships/Entry Level/Graduate School Graduates

Computer (see also High Tech/Technology and Information Technology/
Information Systems)

Computer-Aided Design, Manufacturing & Engineering

Construction (see also Engineering)

Consultants

Contract Employment/Part Time Employment (see also Search Firms)

Cosmetology

Culinary/Food Preparation (see also Hospitality)

— D —

Data Processing

Defense (see also Military Personnel Transitioning into the Private
Sector)

Dental

Diversity

— E —

Economists

Education/Academia

Employee Referral

Energy & Utilities

Engineering

Entertainment/Acting

Environmental

Equipment Leasing

Exchanges-Labor

Executive/Management

Site Categories & Index (continued)

— F —

Fashion

Feminism

Fiber Optics

Finance & Accounting (see also Banking, Insurance)

Funeral Industry

— G —

Gaming

General

Graphic Arts/Electronic & Traditional

— H —

Healthcare/Medical

High Tech/Technical/Technology

Hospitality (see also Culinary/Food Preparation)

Hourly (see also Classifieds-Newspaper)

Human Resources

— I —

Industrial/Manufacturing

Information Technology/Information Systems

Insurance

International

Investment/Brokerage

Site Categories & Index (continued)

— J —

Job Fairs Online
Journalism & Media (see also Graphic Arts)

— L —

Law/Legal
Law Enforcement & Fire Departments
Library & Information Science
Linguistics
Logistics & Maintenance

— M —

Military Personnel Transitioning into the Private Sector
Mining
Modeling
Music

— N —

Non-Profit
Networking

— O —

Outdoors/Recreation/Sports

Site Categories & Index (continued)

— P —

Packaging-Food & Drug

Pharmaceutical

Physics

Printing & Bookbinding

Public Sector/Government

Publishing

Purchasing

— Q —

Quality/Quality Control

— R —

Real Estate

Recruiters Resources

Recruitment Advertising-Non-Newspaper Print & Online

Regional-US

Religion

Retail

— S —

Sales & Marketing

Science/Scientists

Search Engines

Search Firms/Staffing Agencies/Recruiters

Security-Building & Business

Senior Workers/Mature Workers/"Retired" Workers

Social Service

Statistical & Math

— T —

Telecommunications

Telecommuting

Trade Organizations

Training

Transportation -Land & Maritime

— V —

Volunteer Positions

— Y —

Young Adult/Teen Positions

-A-

Administrative/Clerical/Secretarial (See also Classifieds)

Admin Careers	www.admincareers.com
AdminJob.ca [Canada]	www.adminjob.ca
AdminJobs.ie [Ireland]	www.adminjobs.ie
Association of Executive and Administration Professionals	www.theaeap.com
4Secretarial Jobs	www.4secretarialjobs.com
Front Recruitment [United Kingdom]	www.frontrecruitment.co.uk
Get File Clerk Jobs	www.getfileclerkjobs.com
GxPJobs.com [United Kingdom]	www.gxpjobs.com
iHireMedicalSecretaries.com	www.ihiremedicalsecretaries.com
iHireSecretarial.com	www.ihiresecretarial.com
International Association of Administrative Professionals Job Board	http://jobs.iaap-hq.org
Jobs4Clerical	www.jobs4clerical.com
LondonOfficeJobs.co.uk [United Kingdom]	www.londonofficejobs.co.uk
LondonSecretarialJobs.co.uk [United Kingdom]	www.londonsecretarialjobs.co.uk
Office Recruit [United Kingdom]	www.officerecruit.com
ReceptionistJobStore.com	www.receptionistjobstore.com
Secrecruit.co.uk [United Kingdom]	www.secrecruit.co.uk
SecretarialCareers.co.uk [United Kingdom]	www.secretarialcareers.co.uk
SecretarialJobsBoard.co.uk [United Kingdom]	www.secretarialjobsboard.co.uk
Secretary Help Wanted	www.secretaryhelpwanted.com
SecretaryJobStore	www.secretaryjobstore.com
Secsinthecity [United Kingdom]	www.secsinthecity.com
VirtualAssistants.com	www.virtualassistants.com

Advertising/Public Relations

Ad Age	www.adage.com

Ad Agency Jobs	www.adagencyjobs.net
Adholes.com	http://adholes.com
Ad Week	www.adweek.com
The American Advertising Federation	www.aaf.org/jobs
Association of National Advertisers Job Opportunities	www.ana.net/careers/content/careers
Capital Communicator	www.capitalcommunicator.com
Communicators & Marketers Jobline	http://cmjobline.org
Council of Public Relations Firms	www.prfirms.org
CreativeJobsCentral.com	www.creativejobscentral.com
Direct Marketing Association	www.the-dma.org/careercenter
eMarketing & Commerce's Job Connection	www.jobs.emarketingandcommerce.com
iHire Advertising	www.ihireadvertising.com
International Association of Business Communicators	www.iabc.org
The Internet Advertising Bureau Job Board	www.iab.net/jobs
MarketingHire.com	www.marketinghire.com
MassMediaJobs.com	www.massmediajobs.com
Mediabistro	www.mediabistro.com
Media Job Market	www.mediajobmarket.com
Media Jobs	www.mediajobs.com
MediaRecruiter.com	www.mediarecruiter.com
NationJob Network-Advertising & Media Jobs Page	www.nationjob.com/media
Opportunities in Public Affairs	www.opajobs.com
PaidContent.org	http://jobs.paidcontent.org
Promotion Marketing Association Job Bank	www.pmalink.org
Public Relations Society of America Job Center	www.prsa.org
PRWeek Jobs [United Kingdom]	www.prweekjobs.co.uk
SimplyPRJobs.co.uk [United Kingdom]	www.simplyprjobs.co.uk
TalentZoo.com	www.talentzoo.com
Television Bureau of Advertising	www.tvb.org/nav/build_frameset.aspx

| Women Executives in Public Relations | www.wepr.org |
| Work in PR | www.workinpr.com |

Agriculture

AgCareers.com	www.agcareers.com
Agriculture Industry Now	www.agricultureindustrynow.com
AgricultureJobs.com	www.agriculturejobs.com
AgriSeek.com	www.agriseek.com
AgriSupport Online	www.agrisupportonline.com
American Society of Agricultural and Biological Engineers	www.asabe.org
American Society of Agronomy	www.agronomy.org
American Society of Animal Science	www.asas.org
American Society of Horticultural Science HortOpportunities	www.ashs.org
California Agricultural Technical Institute ATI-Net	www.atinet.org/jobs.asp
Dairy Network Career Center	www.dairynetwork.com
FarmRanchJobs.com	www.farmranchjobs.com
Farms.com	www.farms.com/
Jobs in Horticulture	www.hortjobs.com
PMA Foundation Job Bank	www.pmafit.com
Texas A&M Poultry Science Department	http://gallus.tamu.edu/careerops.htm
The Outdoor Job	www.theoutdoorjob.com
Weed Science Society of America WeedJobs: Positions in Weed Science	www.wssa.net/WSSA/Students/index.htm

Archeology/Anthropology

| American Anthropology Association | www.aaanet.org/profdev/careercenter.cfm |
| Society for American Archeology Careers, Opportunities & Jobs | www.saa.org/careers/index.html |

Architecture

AEC Job Bank	www.aecjobbank.com
AEJob.com	www.aejob.com
American Institute of Architects Online	www.aia.org
Archinect	www.archinect.com
ArchitectJobs.com	www.architectjobs.com
ArchitectJobsOnline	www.architectjobsonline.com
ArchitectureJobs.co.uk	www.architecturejobs.co.uk
ArchitectJobsOnline	www.architectjobsonline.com
Arkitectum.com	www.arkitectum.com
CreativeJobsCentral.com	www.creativejobscentral.com
Environmental Construction Engineering Architectural Jobs Online	www.eceajobs.com
ReferWork-Jobs.com	www.referwork-jobs.com
Society of Naval Architects and Marine Engineers	www.sname.org
World Architecture News	www.worldarchitecturenews.com

Arts

ArtInfo	www.artinfo.com
ArtJob	www.artjob.org
Art Libraries Society of North America JobNet	www.arlisna.org/jobnet.html
ArtNetwork	http://artmarketing.com
The Art Newspaper	www.theartnewspaper.com
ArtSearch	www.artsearch.us
The Arts Deadline List	http://artdeadlineslist.com
Artshub.com.au [Australia]	www.artshub.com.au
ArtsJobsOnline.com [United Kingdom]	www.artsjobsonline.com
Arts Opportunities	www.artsopportunities.org
Creative Shake	www.creativeshake.com
Dance USA	www.danceusa.org

HireCulture	www.hireculture.org
iHireCommercialArt	www.ihirecommercialart.com
New York Foundation for the Arts	www.nyfa.org

Association-Professional & Trade/Affinity Group

AcademyHealth	www.academyhealth.org
Academy of Family Physicians	www.fpjobsonline.org
Academy of Managed Care Pharmacy	www.amcp.org
Academy of Medical-Surgical Nurses	www.medsurgnurse.org
The Advanced Computing Systems Association	www.usenix.org
Adventure Travel Trade Association	www.adventuretravel.biz
Allegheny County Medical Society	www.acms.org
Alliance of Merger and Acquisition Advisors	www.amaaonline.com
American Academy of Dermatology	www.aad.org
American Academy of Otolaryngology-Head & Neck Surgery	www.entnet.org/Community/public/careers.cfm
American Academy of Ambulatory Care Nursing	www.aaacn.org
American Academy of Cardiovascular and Pulmonary Rehabilitation	www.aacvpr.org
American Academy of Nurse Practitioners	www.aanp.org
American Academy of Pharmaceutical Physicians & Investigators	www.appinet.org
American Academy of Physician Assistants	www.aapa.org
American Academy of Professional Coders	www.aapc.com
American Accounting Association	http://aaahq.org/placements/default.cfm
The American Advertising Federation	www.aaf.org/jobs/index.html
American Agricultural Economic Association Employment Service	https://aaea.execinc.com/classifieds
American Anthropology Association	www.aaanet.org/profdev/careercenter.cfm
American Association of Brewing Chemists	www.asbcnet.org

American Association for Budget and Program Analysis	www.aabpa.org/main/careerdev.htm#jobs
American Association of Cardiovascular and Pulmonary Rehabilitation	www.aacvpr.org
American Association of Cereal Chemists	www.aaccnet.org/membership/careerplacement.asp
American Association for Clinical Chemistry	www.aacc.org
American Association of Critical Care Nurses	www.aacn.org
American Association of Finance & Accounting	www.aafa.com/careers.htm
American Association of Gynecologic Laparoscopists	www.aagl.org
American Association of Law Libraries Job Placement Hotline	www.aallnet.org/hotline/hotline.asp
American Association of Medical Assistants	www.aama-ntl.org
American Association of Neurological Surgeons	www.aans.org
American Association of Neuromuscular & Electrodiagnostic Medicine	www.aanem.org
American Association of Occupational Health Nurses	www.aaohn.org
American Association of Oral & Maxillofacial Surgeons	www.aaoms.org
American Association of Pharmaceutical Sales Professionals	www.pharmaceuticalsales.org
American Association of Pharmaceutical Scientists	www.aaps.org
American Association of Physics Teachers	www.aapt.org
American Association of Respiratory Care	www.aarc.org
American Astronomical Society Job Register	www.aas.org/career
American Bankers Association	http://aba.careerbank.com
American Bankruptcy Institute Career Center	www.abiworld.org
American Chemical Society	http://portal.acs.org
American College of Allergy, Asthma & Immunology	www.acaai.org

American College of Cardiology	www.acc.org
American College of Chest Physicians	www.chestnet.org
American College of Clinical Pharmacology	www.accp1.org
American College of Clinical Pharmacy	www.accp.com
American College of Emergency Physicians	www.acep.org
American College of Foot and Ankle Surgeons	www.acfas.org
American College of Healthcare Executives Employment Service	www.ache.org
American College of Nurse Midwives	www.acnw.org
American College of Obstetricians and Gynecologists	www.acog.org
American College of Occupational and Environmental Medicine	www.acoem.org
American College of Physicians	www.acponline.org/career_connection
American College of Physician Executives	www.acpe.org
American College of Preventive Medicine	www.acpm.org
American College of Rheumatology	www.rheumatology.org
American College of Surgeons	www.facs.org
American Counseling Association	www.counseling.org
American Dental Hygienists' Association	www.adha.org/careerinfo/index.html
American Design Drafting Association	www.adda.org
American Dietetic Association	www.eatright.org
American Economic Association	www.aeaweb.org/joe
American Educational Research Association Job Openings	www.jobtarget.com/home/index.cfm?site_id=557
American Evaluation Association	www.eval.org/Programs/careercenter.asp
American Forest & Paper Association	www.afandpa.org
American Foundation for the Blind	www.afb.org
American Gastroenterological Association	www.healthecareers.com/site_templates/AGA/ index.asp?aff=AGA&SPLD=AGA
American Geriatrics Society	www.americangeriatrics.org
American Healthcare Radiology Administrators	www.ahraonline.org
American Hotel and Lodging Association	www.ahla.com

American Industrial Hygiene Association	www.aiha.org
American Institute of Architects Online	www.aia.org
American Institute of Biological Sciences	www.aibs.org
American Institute of Certified Public Accountants Career Center	www.cpa2biz.com/AST/AICPA_CPA2BIZ_ Browse/Additional_Resources/CareerCenter.jsp
American Institute of Chemical Engineers Career Services	www.aiche.org/careers
The American Institute of Chemists	www.theaic.org
American Institute of Graphic Arts	www.aiga.org
American Library Association Library Education and Employment Menu Page	www.ala.org/ala/education/educationcareers.cfm
American Marketing Association Career Center	www.marketingpower.com/Careers/Pages/ JobBoard.aspx
American Medical Association JAMA Career Center	www.ama-assn.org
American Medical Technologists	www.amtl.com
American Meteorological Society Employment Announcements	www.ametsoc.org
American Nurses Association	www.nursingworld.org
American Occupational Therapy Association	www.aota.org
American Pharmaceutical Association	www.aphanet.org
American Psychiatric Association	www.psych.org
American Psychiatric Nurses Association	www.apna.org
American Physical Society	www.aps.org/careers/index.cfm
American Physical Therapy Association	www.apta.org
American Psychological Association	www.apa.org/careers/psyccareers
American Psychological Society Observer Job Listings	www.psychologicalscience.org/jobs
American Registry of Diagnostic Medical Sonographers	www.ardms.org
American Registry of Radiologic Technologists	www.arrt.org
American Society of Agricultural and Biological Engineers	www.asabe.org

American Society of Agronomy	www.agronomy.org
American Society of Animal Science	www.fass.org/job.asp
American Society of Association Executives CareerHQ	www.careerhq.org
American Society for Cell Biology	www.ascb.org
American Society for Clinical Laboratory Science	www.ascls.org
American Society for Clinical Pathology	www.ascp.org
American Society of Clinical Pharmacology and Therapeutics	www.ascpt.org
American Society of Gene Therapy	www.asgt.org
American Society of General Surgeons	www.theasgs.org
American Society of Horticultural Science HortOpportunities	www.ashs.org/careers.html
American Society for Information Science & Technology	www.asis.org
American Society of Interior Designers Job Bank	www.asid.org/career_center/job_opp/job.asp
American Society of Journalists & Authors	www.freelancewritersearch.com
American Society for Law Enforcement Training	www.aslet.org
American Society of Mechanical Engineers Career Center	www.asme.org/jobs
American Society for Microbiology	www.asm.org
American Society of PeriAnesthesia Nurses	www.aspan.org
American Society of Pharmacognosy	www.phcog.org
American Society of Plant Biologists	www.aspb.org
American Society of Professional Estimators	www.aspenational.com
American Society of Radiologic Technologists	www.asrt.org
American Society for Training & Development Job Bank	http://jobs.astd.org
American Society of Travel Agents	www.asta.org
American Society of Women Accountants Employment Opportunities	www.aswact.org
American Speech-Language Hearing Association Online Career Center	www.asha.org/about/career

American Statistical Association Statistics Career Center	www.amstat.org/careers
American Veterinary Medical Association Career Center	http://jobs.avma.org
American Water Works Association Career Center (Water Jobs)	www.awwa.org
Apartment Association of Greater Dallas	www.aagdallas.org
Apartment Association of Tarrant County	www.aatcnet.org/subsite/CareerCenter/ careercenterindex.htm
Arizona Hospital and Healthcare Association AZHealthJobs	www.azhha.org
Art Libraries Society of North America JobNet	http://arlisna.org/jobs.html
Association for Applied Human Pharmacology [Germany]	www.agah-web.de
Association of Career Professionals International	www.acpinternational.org
Association of Certified Fraud Examiners Career Center	www.acfe.com/career/career.asp
Association of Clinical Research Professionals Career Center	www.acrpnet.org
Association for Computing Machinery Career Resource Center	http://acm.org
Association for Educational Communications and Technology Job Center	www.aect.org
Association for Environmental and Outdoor Education	www.aeoe.org
Association of Executive Search Consultants	www.bluesteps.com
Association of ex-Lotus Employees	www.axle.org
Association of Finance Professionals Career Services	www.afponline.org/pub/cs/career_services.html
Association of Graduate Careers Advisory Service [United Kingdom]	www.agcas.org.uk
Association for Healthcare Documentation Integrity	www.ahdionline.org

The Association for Institutional Research	www.airweb.org
Association of Internet Professionals National Job Board	www.internetprofessionals.org
AssociationJobBoards.com	www.associationjobboards.com
Association of Latino Professionals in Finance & Accounting Job Postings	www.alpfa.org
Association of Management Consulting Firms	www.amcf.org
Association of National Advertisers Job Opportunities	www.ana.net/careers/content/careers
Association of Perioperative Registered Nurses Online Career Center	www.aorn.org/CareerCenter/
Association of Research Libraries	www.arl.org
Association of Staff Physician Recruiters	www.aspr.org
Association for Strategic Planning	www.strategyplus.org
Association of Teachers of Technical Writing	http://cms.english.ttu.edu/ATTW
Association of University Teachers [United Kingdom]	www.AUT4Jobs.com
Association for Women in Computing	www.awc-hq.org
Association of Women's Health, Obstetric & Neonatal Nurses	www.awhonn.org
Bank Administration Institute	www.bai.org
Bank Marketing Association	www.bmanet.org
Bay Bio	www.baybio.org
Biomedical Engineering Society	www.bmes.org
Biotechnology Association of Alabama	www.bioalabama.com
Biotechnology Association of Maine	www.mainebiotech.org
Biotechnology Council of New Jersey	www.newjerseybiotech.org
Black Data Processing Association Online	www.bdpa.org
Board of Pharmaceutical Specialties	www.bpsweb.org
Business Marketing Association	www.marketing.org
California Academy of Family Physicians	www.fpjobsonline.org
California Agricultural Technical Institute ATI-Net AgJobs	www.atinet.org/jobs.asp

California Dental Hygienists' Association   www.cdha.org/employment/index.html
     Employment Opportunities

California Mortgage Brokers Association   www.cambweb.org
     Career Center

California Separation Science Society   www.casss.org

Canadian Society of Biochemistry/Molecular/   www.medicine.mcgill.ca/expmed/emjl/expmed_
     Cellular Biologists Job Listing   whoislinking.htm

Capital Markets Credit Analysts Society   www.cmcas.org
     Resume Service

Chicago Medical Society   www.cmsdocs.org

College of American Pathologists   www.cap.org

College and University Personnel Association   www.cupahr.org/jobline
     JobLine

Colorado Academy of Family Physicians   www.fpjobsonline.org

Colorado Health and Hospital Association   www.cha.com

Computing Research Association Job   www.cra.org/ads
     Announcements

Controlled Release Society   www.controlledrelease.org

Council for Advancement & Support of   www.case.org/jobs
     Education Jobs Online

Council of Public Relations Firms   www.prfirms.org

Dermatology Nurses' Association   www.dnanurse.org

Design Management Institute Job Bank   www.dmi.org/dmi/html/jobbank/jobbank_d.jsp

Digital Printing and Imaging Association   www.sgia.org/employment
     Employment Exchange (with the
     Screenprinting & Graphic
     Imaging Association International)

DirectEmployers Association   www.directemployers.org

Direct Marketing Association   www.the-dma.org/careercenter

Drilling Research Institute Classifieds   www.drillers.com/Visitor/Drilling_JobSearch.aspx

Drug Information Association Employment   www.diahome.org/DIAHome/Resources/
     Opportunities   FindJob.aspx

Editorial Freelancers Association   www.the-efa.org

Emergency Medicine Residents Association	www.emra.org
Employers Resource Association	www.hrxperts.org
Financial Executives Institute Career Center	www.financialexecutives.org
Financial Management Association International Placement Services	www.fma.org/Placement
Financial Managers Society Career Center	www.fmsinc.org/cms/?pid=1025
Financial Women International Careers	www.fwi.org
FindMortgageJobs.com	www.findmortgagejobs.com
Florida Academy of Family Physicians	www.fpjobsonline.org
Global Association of Risk Professionals Career Center	www.garp.com/careercenter/index.asp
Georgia Academy of Family Physicians	www.fpjobsonline.org
Georgia Association of Personnel Services	http://70.85.148.53:5574/JobBoard/tabid/53/Default.aspx
Georgia Pharmacy Association	www.gpha.org
Graphic Artists Guild JobLine	www.graphicartistsguild.org
Harris County Medical Society	www.hcms.org
Healthcare Businesswomen's Association	www.hbanet.org
Healthcare Information and Management Systems	www.himss.org
Healthcare Financial Management Association	www.hfma.org
Hispanic American Police Command Officers Association	www.hapcoa.org
History of Science Society	www.hssonline.org
HIV Medicine Association	www.hivma.org
HTML Writers Guild HWG-Jobs	www.hwg.org/lists/hwg-jobs
Human Resource Association of the National Capital Area Job Bank Listing	http://hra-nca.org/job_list.asp
Human Resource Independent Consultants (HRIC) On-Line Job Leads	www.hric.org
Human Resource Management Association of Mid Michigan Job Postings	www.hrmamm.com/jobpostings/index.php
Illinois Academy of Family Physicians	www.fpjobsonline.org

Illinois Recruiters Association	www.illinoisrecruiter.ning.com
Infectious Diseases Society of America	www.idsa.org
Institute of Electrical & Electronics Engineers Job Site	www.ieee.org/web/careers/home/index.html
Institute of Food Science & Technology	www.ifst.org
Institute of Internal Auditors Online Audit Career Center	www.theiia.org/careers
Institute of Management Accountants Career Center	www.imanet.org/development_career.asp
Institute of Management and Administration's Supersite	www.ioma.com
Institute of Real Estate Management Jobs Bulletin	www.irem.org
Institute for Supply Management Career Center	www.ism.ws/CareerCenter/index.cfm
The Instrumentation, Systems and Automation Society Online ISA Jobs	www.isa.org/isa_es
International Association of Administrative Professionals Job Board	http://jobs.iaap-hq.org
International Association of Business Communicators Career Centre	www.iabc.com
International Association of Conference Centers Online (North America)	www.iacconline.org
International Association for Commercial and Contract Management	www.iaccm.com
International Association for HR Information Management Job Central	http://hrim.hrdpt.com
International Code Council	www.iccsafe.org
International Customer Service Association Job Board	www.icsatoday.org
International Foundation of Employee Benefit Plans Job Postings	www.ifebp.org
International Health Economics Association	www.healtheconomics.org
Independent Human Resource Consultants	www.ihrca.com

Association	
International Society for Molecular	www.ismpminet.org/career
Plant-Microbe Interactions	
International Society for Performance	www.ispi.org
Improvement Job Bank	
International Society for Pharmaceutical	www.ispe.org
Engineering	
Iowa Biotechnology Association	www.iowabiotech.org
Latinos in Information Sciences and	www.a-lista.org
Technology Association	
Marine Executive Association	www.marineea.org
Maryland Association of CPAs Job Connect	www.macpa.org/content/classifieds/public/
	search.aspx
Mathematical Association of America	www.mathclassifieds.com
Massachusetts Biotechnology Council	www.massbio.org
Massachusetts Environmental Education Society	www.massmees.org
Massachusetts Healthcare Human Resources	www.mhhra.org
Association	
MdBio, Inc. (Maryland Bioscience)	http://techcouncilmd.com/mdbio
Media Communications Association International	www.mca-i.org
Job Hotline	
Media Human Resources Association	http://jobs/shrm.org
Medical-Dental-Hospital Business Association	www.mdhba.org
Medical Group Management Association	www.mgma.com
Medical Marketing Association	www.mmanet.org
Metroplex Association of Personnel Consultants	www.recruitingfirms.com
MichBIO	www.michbio.org
The Minerals, Metals, Materials Society JOM	www.tms.org
Missouri Academy of Family Physicians	www.fpjobsonline.org
Missouri Pharmacy Association	www.morx.com
Music Library Association Job Placement	www.musiclibraryassoc.org/employmentanded/
	joblist/index.shtml

National Alliance of State Broadcasters Associations CareerPage	www.careerpage.org
National Apartment Association	www.naahq.org
National Association of Black Accountants, Inc. Career Center	http://nabacareercenter.nabainc.org
National Association of Boards of Pharmacy	www.nabp.net
National Association for College Admission Counseling Career Opportunities	www.nacac.com/classifieds.cfm
National Association of Colleges & Employers (NACE)	www.nacelink.com
National Association for Female Executives	www.nafe.com
National Association of Hispanic Nurses Houston Chapter	www.nahnhouston.org
National Association of Hispanic Publications Online Career Center	www.nahp.org
National Association of Orthopaedic Nurses	www.orthonurse.org
National Association of Pharmaceutical Sales Representatives	www.napsronline.org
National Association for Printing Leadership	www.napl.org
National Association of Printing Ink Manufacturers	www.napim.org
National Association of Sales Professionals Career Center	www.nasp.com
National Association of School Psychologists	www.nasponline.org
National Association of Securities Professionals Current Openings	www.nasphq.org/career.html
National Association of Securities Professionals (Atlanta) Current Openings	www.naspatlanta.org/career.html
National Association of Securities Professionals Underground Railroad	www.nasp-ny.org
National Association of Social Workers Joblink	www.socialworkers.org/joblinks/default.asp
National Black Police Association	www.blackpolice.org

National Community Pharmacists Association	www.ncpanet.org
Pharmacy Matching Service	
National Confectioners' Association	www.candyusa.com
National Contract Management Association	www.ncmahq.org
National Defense Industrial Association	http://ndia.monster.com
National Environmental Health Association	www.neha.org
National Federation of Paralegal Associations	www.paralegals.org
Career Center	
National Field Selling Association	www.nfsa.com
National Fire Prevention Association Online	www.nfpa.org
Career Center	
National Funeral Directors Association	www.nfda.org
National Insurance Recruiters Association	www.nirassn.com
Online Job Database	
National Latino Peace Officers Association	www.nlpoa.org
National League for Nursing	www.nln.org
National Organization of Black Law	www.noblenational.org
Enforcement Executives	
National Organization of Black Chemists	www.engin.umich.edu/societies/nobcche
and Chemical Engineers	
National Parking Association	http://careers.npapark.org
National Rural Recruitment & Retention Network	www.3rnet.org
National Society of Black Engineers	http://national.nsbe.org
National Society of Black Physicists	www.nsbp.org
National Society of Collegiate Scholars	www.nscs.org
Career Connection	
National Society of Hispanic MBAs Career	www.nshmba.org
Center	
National Society of Professional Engineers	www.nspe.org/Employment/index.html
Employment	
National Sporting Goods Association	www.nsga.org
National Venture Capital Association	www.nvca.org
National Weather Association Job Corner	www.nwas.org

National Women's Studies Association	www.nwsa.org
National Writers Union Job Hotline	www.nwu.org
Nationwide Process Servers Association	www.processserversassociation.com
Network of Commercial Real Estate Women Job Bank	www.crewnetwork.org
New Jersey Metro Employment Management Association	www.njmetroema.org
New Jersey Human Resource Planning Group	www.njhrpg.org
The New York Biotechnology Association	www.nyba.org
New York Society of Association Executives Career Center	www.nysaenet.org
New York Society of Security Analysts Career Resources	www.nyssa.org/AM/Template. cfm?Section=career_development
New York State Academy of Family Physicians	www.fpjobsonline.org
Newspaper Association of America Newspaper CareerBank	www.naa.org/classified/index.html
North American Association for Environmental Education	www.naaee.org
North American Spine Society	www.spine.org
Northeast Human Resource Association	www.nehra.org
Oklahoma State Medical Association	www.osmaonline.org
Orleans Parish Medical Society	www.opms.org
Oregon Bioscience Association	www.oregon-bioscience.com
Pennsylvania Academy of Family Physicians	www.fpjobsonline.org
Petroleum Services Association of Canada Employment	www.psac.ca
PhysicsToday.org	www.physicstoday.org
Project Management Institute Career Headquarters	www.pmi.org
Promotion Marketing Association Job Bank	www.pmalink.org/jobbank/default.asp
Radiological Society of North America	www.rsna.org
Radiology Business Management Association	www.rbma.org
Real Estate Lenders Association	www.rela.org

Risk & Insurance Management Society Careers	www.rims.org/resources/careercenter
Sales & Marketing Executives International Career Center	www.smei.org
Screenprinting & Graphic Imaging Association International	www.sgia.org/employment
Securities Industry Association Career Resource Center	www.sifma.com/services/career_center/ career_center.html
Sheet Metal and Air Conditioning Contractor's Association	www.smacna.org
Society for American Archeology Careers, Opportunities & Jobs	www.saa.org/careers/index.html
Society of Automotive Engineers Job Board	www.sae.org/careers/recrutad.htm
Society of Competitive Intelligence Professionals Job Marketplace	www.scip.org/CareerCenter
Society of Diagnostic Medical Sonographers	www.sdms.org
Society of Gastroenterology Nurses & Associates	www.sgna.org
Society of Hispanic Professional Engineers Career Services	www.shpe.org
Society of Hospital Medicine Career Center	www.hospitalmedicine.org
Society for Human Resource Management HRJobs	http://jobs/shrm.org
Society for Industrial & Organizational Psychology JobNet	www.siop.org/JobNet
Society of Mexican American Engineers and Scientists	www.maes-natl.org
Society of Naval Architects and Marine Engineers	www.sname.org
Society of Nuclear Medicine	www.snm.org
Society of Petrologists & Well Log Analysts Job Opportunities	www.spwla.org
Society of Risk Analysis Opportunities	www.sra.org/opportunities.php
Society of Satellite Professionals International Career Center	www.sspi.broadbandcareers.com/Default.asp
Society of Women Engineers Career Services	http://careers.swe.org

**SPIE Web-International Society for Optical
        Engineering**   www.spieworks.com

Strategic Account Management Association   www.strategicaccounts.org
        Career Resources

Student Conservation Association   www.thesca.org

Teachers of English to Speakers of   www.tesol.org
        Other Languages Job Finder

Technical Association of the Pulp & Paper   www.tappi.org/careercenter/careercenter.asp
        Industry Career Center

Telecommunication Industry Association Online www.tiaonline.org

Texas Academy of Family Physicians   www.fpjobsonline.org

Texas Apartment Association   www.taa.org/member/industry/careerCenter

Texas Healthcare & Bioscience Institute   www.thbi.org

Texas Medical Association   www.texmed.org

Utah Life Sciences Association   www.utahlifescience.com

Virginia Biotechnology Association   www.vabio.org

Washington Biotechnology & Biomedical   www.wabio.com
        Association

Washington Multi-Family Housing Association http://careers.wmfha.org

Weed Science Society of America WeedJobs: www.wssa.net/WSSA/Students/index.htm
        Positions in Weed Science

Wisconsin Academy of Family Physicians   www.fpjobsonline.org

Wisconsin Biotechnology Association   www.wisconsinbiotech.org

Wisconsin Medical Society   www.wisconsinmedicalsociety.org

Women in Technology   www.womenintechnology.org

Women in Technology International (WITI) 4Hire www.witi4hire.com

Women Executives in Public Relations   www.wepr.org

The Chronicle of Higher Education   http://chronicle.com/jobs

Space-Careers.com   www.space-careers.com

SpaceJobs.com   www.spacejobs.com

Astronomy

American Astronomical Society Job Register	www.aas.org/career
Board of Physics & Astronomy	www7.nationalacademies.org
HigherCareers.com	www.highercareers.com
The Chronicle of Higher Education	http://chronicle.com/jobs
Physics & Astronomy Online	www.physlink.com
Space-Careers.com	www.space-careers.com
SpaceJobs.com	www.spacejobs.com

Automotive

Autocareers	www.autocareers.com
Auto Head Hunter	www.autoheadhunter.net
Auto Industry Central	www.autoindustrycentral.com
AutoJobs.com	www.autodealerjobs.com
Auto Jobs	www.autodealerjobs.com
Automotive Aftermarket Jobs	www.customtrucks.net
Automotive Careers Today	www.autocareerstoday.net
Automotive JobBank	www.automotivejobbank.com
AutomotiveJobs.com	www.automotivejobs.com
AutomotiveJobsOnline.com	www.automotivejobsonline.com
Best Auto Jobs	www.bestautojobs.com
CarDealerJobs.com	www.cardealerjobs.com
CareerRPM.com	www.careerrpm.com
Dealer Classified	www.dealerclassified.com
Great Auto Jobs	www.greatautojobs.com
InAutomotive.com [United Kingdom]	www.inautomotive.com
Motor Careers	www.motorcareers.com
Motor Sports Employment	www.motorsportsemployment.com
NeedTechs.com	www.needtechs.com
Racing Jobs	www.racingjobs.com
ShowroomToday.com	www.showroomtoday.com

Aviation

Aeroindustryjobs	www.aeroindustryjobs.com
AeroSpaceNews.com	www.aerospacenews.com
AircraftEngineers.com [United Kingdom]	www.aircraftengineers.com
AirJobsDaily.com	www.airjobsdigest.com
AirlineJobFinder.com	www.airlinejobfinder.com
AirlinePilotJobs.com	www.airlinepilotjobs.com
All Port Jobs	www.allportjobs.com
AVCrew.com	www.avcrew.com
AVjobs.com	www.avjobs.com
Avianation.com	www.avianation.com
AviationCareers	www.aviationcareers.net
Aviation Employment.com	www.aviationemployment.com
Aviation Employment Board	www.aviationemploymentboard.net
Aviation Employment NOW	www.aenworld.com
Aviation Employment Placement Service	www.aeps.com
AviationJobSearch.com	www.aviationjobsearch.com
Aviation Jobs Central	www.aviationjobscentral.com
Aviation Jobs Online	www.aviationjobsonline.com
Aviation Tire	www.aviationtire.com
Aviation Today	www.aviationtoday.com
Aviation Week	www.aviationweek.com
Aviation World Services	www.aviationworldservices.com
Best Aviation	www.bestaviation.net
Blue Collar Jobs	www.bluecollarjobs.com
Careers in Aviation	www.aec.net
Climbto350.com	www.climbto350.com
Federal Aviation Administration Resumes	www.faa.gov
Find A Pilot	www.findapilot.com
Flightdeck Recruitment	www.flightdeckrecruitment.com
Flight Global	www.flightglobal.com
FliteJobs.com	www.flitejobs.com
Fly Contract	www.flycontract.com

Get Pilot Jobs	www.getpilotjobs.com
Just Helicopters	www.justhelicopters.com
Landings	www.landings.com
NationJob Network-Aviation	www.nationjob.com/aviation
Pilot Career Center	www.pilotcareercenter.com
Pilot Jobs	www.pilotjobs.com
Space Careers	www.space-careers.com
Worldwide 747 Pilots & Operators Job Portal	www.747pilotjobs.org

-B-

Banking

Alliance of Merger and Acquisition Advisors	www.amaaonline.com
American Banker Online Career Zone	www.americanbanker.com/Careerzone.html
American Bankers Association	http://aba.careerbank.com
American Bankruptcy Institute Career Center	www.abiworld.org
Bank Administration Institute	www.bai.org
Bank Gigs	www.bankgigs.com
Bank Jobs	www.bankjobs.com
Bank Marketing Association	www.bmanet.org
BankingBoard.com	www.bankingboard.com
Banking Careers	www.bankingcareers.com
Banking & Financial Services Career Network	www.searchbankingjobs.com
Banking Job Site	www.bankingjobsite.com
Banking Job Store	www.bankingjobstore.com
CareerBank.com	www.careerbank.com
CreditCardJobs.net	www.creditcardjobs.net
Credit Union Board	www.creditunionboard.net
eFinancialCareers.com	www.efinancialcareers.com
FinancialJobBank	www.financialjobbank.com

Financial Job Network	www.fjn.com
FINANCIALjobs.com	www.financialjobs.com
Financial Women International Careers	www.fwi.org
The Finance Beat	http://business.searchbeat.com/finance.htm
FindMortgageJobs.com	www.findmortgagejobs.com
Florida Banking Jobs Online	www.bankjobsflorida.com
GetBankTellerJobs	www.getbanktellerjobs.net
GTNews [United Kingdom]	www.gtnews.com
iHireBanking.com	www.ihirebanking.com
Jobs4Banking.com	www.jobs4banking.com
JobsinCredit [United Kingdom]	www.jobsincredit.com
Loan Closer Jobs	www.loancloserjobs.com
LoanOfficerJobs.com	www.loanofficerjobs.com
Loan Originator Jobs	www.loanoriginatorjobs.com
LoanProcessorJobs.com	www.loanprocessorjobs.com
LoanServicingJobs.com	www.loanservicingjobs.com
MortgageBoard	www.mortgageboard.com
Mortgage Job Store	www.mortgagejobstore.com
Real Estate Finance Jobs	www.realestatefinancejobs.com
Real Estate Lenders Association	www.rela.org
Society of Risk Analysis Opportunities	www.sra.org/opportunities.php
TitleBoard.net	www.titleboard.net
TopBankingJobs	www.topbankingjobs.com
True Careers	www.truecareers.com
UnderwritingJobs.com	www.underwritingjobs.com

Bilingual/Multilingual Professionals

Asianet	www.asianetglobal.com
Asian-Jobs.com	www.asian-jobs.com
BilingualCareer.com	www.bilingualcareer.com
BilingualJobBaord	www.bilingualjobboard.com
Bilingual-Jobs	www.bilingual-jobs.com

CHALLENGEUSA	www.challengeusa.com
Eflweb	www.eflweb.com
Euroleaders	www.euroleaders.com
ExposureJobs [Europe]	www.exposurejobs.com
GetBilingualJobs	www.getbilingualjobs.net
Hispanic Chamber of Commerce	www.ushcc.com
Hispanic-Jobs.com	www.hispanic-jobs.com
iHispano	www.ihispano.com
Language123	http://language123.com
LatPro	www.latpro.com
National Society of Hispanic MBAs Career Center	www.nshmba.org
SaludosWeb	www.saludos.com
Society of Hispanic Professional Engineers Career Services	www.shpe.org
Top Language Jobs [Europe]	www.toplanguagejobs.co.uk
Two Lingos	www.twolingos.com
Zhaopin.com	www.zhaopin.com

Biology/Biotechnology

American Chemical Society	http://portal.acs.org
American Institute of Biological Sciences	www.aibs.org
American Society of Agricultural and Biological Engineers	www.asabe.org
American Society for Cell Biology	www.ascb.org
American Society of Gene Therapy	www.asgt.org
American Society for Gravitational and Space Biology	http://asgsb.org/index.php
American Society of Limnology and Oceanography	http://aslo.org
American Society for Microbiology	www.asm.org
American Society of Plant Biologists	www.aspb.org

Bay Bio	www.baybio.org
Bermuda Biological Station for Research, Inc.	www.bios.edu
Biocareer.com	www.biocareer.com
BioCareers.co.za [South Africa]	www.biocareers.co.za
BioExchange.com	www.bioexchange.com
Biofind	www.biofind.com
BioFlorida	www.bioflorida.com
BioJobNet.com	www.biojobnet.com
BiologyJobs.com	www.biologyjobs.com
Biomedical Engineering Society	www.bmes.org
Bio Research Online	www.bioresearchonline.com
BioSource Technical Service	www.biosource-tech.com
BioSpace Career Center	www.biospace.com
BioTech Job Site	www.biotechjobsite.com
BiotechSales/Chemistry Career Search	www.biotechsaleschemistry.com
Biotechnology Association of Alabama	www.bioalabama.com
Biotechnology Association of Maine	www.mainebiotech.org
Biotechnology Calendar, Inc.	www.biotech-calendar.com
Biotechnology Council of New Jersey	www.newjerseybiotech.org
Biotechnology Industry Organization	www.bio.org
BioView	www.bioview.co.il/HTMLs/Home.aspx
Canadian Society of Biochemistry/Molecular/ Cellular Biologists Job Listing	www.medicine.mcgill.ca/expmed/emjl/ expmed_whoislinking.htm
CanMed [Canada]	www.canmed.com
Cell Press Online	www.cell.com/cellpress
ChemJobs.net	www.chemjobs.net
ChemPharma	www.chempharma.net
Connecticut's BioScience Cluster	www.curenet.org
Drug Information Association Employment Opportunities	www.diahome.org/DIAHome/Resources/ FindJob.aspx
GxPJobs.com [United Kingdom]	www.gxpjobs.com
HireBio.com	www.hirebio.com
HireLifeScience	www.hirelifescience.com

Iowa Biotechnology Association	www.iowabiotech.org
Jobscience Network	http://jobs.jobscience.com
The London Biology Network [United Kingdom]	www.biolondon.org.uk
Massachusetts Biotechnology Council	www.massbio.org
MdBio, Inc. (Maryland Bioscience)	http://techcouncilmd.com/mdbio
Medzilla	www.medzilla.com
MichBIO	www.michbio.org
Nature	www.nature.com
The New York Biotechnology Association	www.nyba.org
North Carolina Biotechnology Center	www.ncbiotech.org
North Carolina Genomics & Bioinformatics	www.ncgbc.org
Oregon Bioscience Association	www.oregon-bioscience.com
Organic-Chemistry	www.organic-chemistry.org
PharmacyWeek	www.pharmacyweek.com
PharmaOpportunities	www.pharmaopportunites.com
RPhrecruiter.com	www.rphrecruiter.com
Rx Career Center	www.rxcareercenter.com
Science Careers	http://sciencecareers.sciencemag.org
Sciencejobs.com	www.newscientistjobs.com
The Science Jobs	www.thesciencejobs.com
SCIENCE Online	www.scienceonline.org
Scijobs.com	www.sciencecareers.sciencemag.org
SciWeb Biotechnology Career Center	www.biocareers.com
Texas Healthcare & Bioscience Institute	www.thbi.org
Utah Life Sciences Association	www.utahlifescience.com
Virginia Biotechnology Association	www.vabio.org
Washington Biotechnology & Biomedical Association	www.wabio.com
Wisconsin Biotechnology Association	www.wisconsinbiotech.org

Blogs-Job Search/Careers

Baily WorkPlay	www.baileyworkplay.com

BlogEmploi [France]	www.cadresonline.com/coaching/blog/index_blog_emploi.php
BoldCareer.com	www.boldcareer.com
Boston.com	www.boston.com/jobs
Career Advice & Resources Blog	www.resumelines.com/blog
Career Assessment Goddess	http://blog.careergoddess.com
Career Chaos	www.coachmeg.typepad.com/career_chaos/
CareerHub	http://careerhub.typepad.com/main
Career and Job Hunting Blog	www.quintcareers.com/career_blog
CollegeRecruiter.com Insights By Candidates Blog	www.collegerecruiter.com/insightblog
Dave Opton's Blog at ExecuNet	www.execunet.com
DearAnyone.com	www.dearanyone.com/work
Dr. Bamster's Blog	http://drbamstersblog.squarespace.com
Dream Big	http://letsdreambig.blogspot.com
Employment Digest	www.employmentdigest.net
Find A New Job	http://findnewjob.blogspot.com
From the Inside Out	http://iyjnjen.blogspot.com
Get That Job	http://getthatjob.blogspot.com
GetTheJob's Job Seeker Blog	www.getthejob.com
Guerrilla Job Hunting	http://guerrillajobhunting.typepad.com/guerrilla_job_hunting
Heather's Blog at Microsoft	http://blogs.msdn.com/b/heatherleigh
HireBlog	http://hireblog.blogspot.com
IWorkWithFools.com	www.iworkwithfools.com
Job Search Opportunity Tips & Advice	http://job-search-opportunity.blogspot.com/
Jobs Blog/Technical Careers at Microsoft	http://blogs.msdn.com/b/jobsblog
Jobs, Job Seekers, Employers & Recruiters	http://employment.typepad.com
Knock 'em Dead Blog	http://bknock-em-dead.blogspot.com
Life@Work	http://dbcs.typepad.com
The Monster Blog	http://monster.typepad.com/monsterblog
My Blog By Jan Melnik	http://myblog.janmelnik.com

The Occupational Adventure	http://curtrosengren.typepad.com occupationaladventure
Peter Weddle's WorkStrong Blog	www.weddles.com/workstrong
Retail Anonymous	http://retailanonymous.blogspot.com
Secrets of the Job Hunt	http://secretsofthejobhunt.blogspot.com/
SecurityClearanceJobsBlog.com	www.securityclearancejobsblog.com
TechLawAdvisor.com Job Postings	http://techlawadvisor.com/jobs
The Virtual Handshake	www.thevirtualhandshake.com/blog
WildJobSafari	www.wildjobsafari.blogspot.com
WorkBloom	http://workbloom.com/default.aspx
Workers Work	www.workerswork.com
Wurk	www.wurk.net
Yaps4u.net	www.yaps4u.net

Blogs-Recruiters

Advanced Online Recruiting Techniques	http://recruiting-online.spaces.live.com
Amitai Givertz's Recruitomatic Blog	http://recruitomatic.wordpress.com
The Asia Pacific Headhunter	http://searchniche.blogs.com
Bells and Whistles	www.rcirs.com/blog
Blog Indeed	http://blog.indeed.com
Cheezhead.com	www.cheezhead.com
CyberSleuthing Blog (Shally Steckerl)	www.ere.net/blogs/CyberSleuthing
Digability by Jim Stroud	http://digability.blogspot.com
Hiring Technical People	http://jrothman.com/blog/htp/
JobBoarders.com	www.jobboarders.com
Jobster	http://jobster.blogs.com
MarketingHeadhunter.com	www.marketingheadhunter.com
Mini Microsoft	http://minimsft.blogspot.com
MN Headhunter	www.mnheadhunter.com
PassingNotes.com	www.passingnotes.com
Peter Weddle's WorkStrong Blog	www.weddles.com/workstrong
Recruiting.com	www.recruiting.com

RecruitingAnimal.com	www.recruitinganimal.com
RecruitingBlogs.com	www.recruitingblogs.com
Seth Godin's Blog	http://sethgodin.typepad.com
SimplyHired Blog	http://blog.simplyhired.com
Talentism	http://jjhunter.typepad.com
TechCrunch	www.techcrunch.com

Building Contruction/Management (see also Construction)

AllHousingJobs.co.uk [United Kingdom]	www.allhousingjobs.co.uk
Apartment Association of Greater Dallas	www.aagdallas.org
Apartment Association of Tarrant County	www.aatcnet.org/subsite/CareerCenter/ careercenterindex.htm
ApartmentCareerHQ.org	www.apartmentcareerHQ.org
ApartmentCareers.com	www.apartmentcareers.com
ApartmentJobs.com	www.apartmentjobs.com
Apartment Jobz	www.apartmentjobz.com
Building Industry Exchange	www.building.org
BuilderJobs	www.builderjobs.com
Construction4Professionals.co.uk [United Kingdom]	www.construction4professionals.co.uk
EstimatorJobs.com	www.estimatorjobs.com
HelmetstoHardhats.com	www.helmetstohardhats.com
HVACagent.com	www.hvacagent.com
iHireBuildingTrades.com	www.ihirebuildingtrades.com
International Code Council	www.iccsafe.org/Pages/default.aspx
JobsinConstruction [United Kingdom]	www.jobsinconstruction.co.uk
JobsinSurveying [United Kingdom]	www.jobsinsurveying.co.uk
JustEngineers.net [Australia]	www.justengineers.net
MaintenanceEmployment.com	www.maintenanceemployment.com
National Apartment Association	www.naahq.org/Pages/welcome.aspx
NewHomeSalesJobs.com	www.newhomesalesjobs.com

ProjectManagerJobs.com	www.projectmanagerjobs.com
Senior Housing Jobs	www.seniorhousingjobs.com
SuperintendentJobs.com	www.superintendentjobs.com
Texas Apartment Association	www.taa.org/sitemap
QCEmployMe.com	http://regionalhelpwanted.com/ quad-cities-il-ia-jobs
Sheet Metal and Air Conditioning Contractor's Association	www.smacna.org
TopBuildingJobs.com	www.topbuildingjobs.com
UtilityJobSearch.com [United Kingdom]	www.utilityjobsearch.com
Washington Multi-Family Housing Association	http://careers.wmfha.org

Business

Alliance of Merger and Acquisition Advisors	www.amaaonline.com
American Bankruptcy Institute Career Center	www.abiworld.org//AM/Template. cfm?Section=Home
American Society for Quality	www.asq.org/career
APICS	www.apics.org/default.htm
Association of Executive and Administration Professionals	www.theaeap.com
Association of MBAs	www.mbaworld.com
Association for Strategic Planning	www.strategyplus.org
Barron's Online	http://online.barrons.com/home-page
Big Charts	http://bigcharts.marketwatch.com
Billboard	www.billboard.com
Biz Journals	www.bizjournals.com/jobs
Bloomberg.com	www.bloomberg.com
BPOJobSite.com [India]	www.bpojobsite.com
Business Finance	http://businessfinancemag.com
Business Marketing Association	www.marketing.org/i4a/pages/index. cfm?pageid=1
Capital Hill Blue	http://chblue.com

CareerJournal.com	http://online.wsj.com/home-page/careers
CareerMarketplace.com	www.careermarketplace.com
Career Network	www.careernetwork.com/section/Home/5
Careers In Business	http://careers-in-business.jobsinthemoney.com
CNBC/Career Center	www.cnbc.com
CNNMoney.com	http://money.cnn.com/
CondeNet	www.condenastdigital.com/index.html
Corporate Finance Net	www.corpfinet.com
Corporate Watch	www.corpwatch.org
CreditCardJobs.net	www.creditcardjobs.net
Crain's Chicago	www.chicagobusiness.com
Customer Service Management	www.csm-us.co/mhc3.asp
Customer Service University	www.customerserviceuniversity.com
Degree Hunter	http://degreehunter.net
Dow Jones	www.dowjones.com
e-Marketer	www.e-marketer.com
Entrepreneur	www.entrepreneur.com/magazine/entrepreneur/index.html
ForeignMBA.com	www.foreignmba.com
Fortune	http://money.cnn.com/magazines/fortune/
Global Careers	www.globalcareers.com
Harvard Business Review	www.hbsp.Harvard.edu
Hollywood Reporter	www.hollywoodreporter.com/hr/index.jsp
HomeOfficeJob.com	www.homeoffice.com
Hoover's Online	www.hoovers.com
iHireSecurity.com	www.ihiresecurity.com
Inc.	www.inc.com
Industry Week	www.industryweek.com
International Association of Business Communicators	www.iabc.com
International Association for Commercial and Contract Management	www.iaccm.com

International Customer Service Association Job Board	www.icsatoday.org
Internet News	www.internetnews.com
Jane's Information Group	www.janes.com
JobsinRisk.com [United Kingdom]	www.jobsinrisk.com
Journal of Commerce	www.joc.com
Kiplinger	www.kiplinger.com
latinMBA.com	www.latinmba.com
MBA Careers	www.mbacareers.com
MBA-Exchange.com	www.mba-exchange.com/candidates/ mba_jobs.php
MBA Free Agents	www.mbafreeagents.com
MBAGlobalNet	www.mbaglobalnet.com
MBAJobs.net	www.mbajobs.net
MBAmatch.com [United Kingdom]	www.mbamatch.com
MBA Style Magazine	www.mbastyle.com
MBATalentWire.com	www.mbatalentwire.com
MeetingJobs.com	www.meetingjobs.com
MinorityMBAs	www.minoritymbas.com
Multiunitjobs.com	www.multiunitjobs.com
National Society of Hispanic MBAs Career Center	www.nshmba.org
New York Black MBA	www.nyblackmba.org
P-Jobs	www.pjobs.org
Pro2Net	http://accounting.smartpros.com
Product Development & Management Association	www.pdma.org
ReceptionistJobStore.com	www.receptionistjobstore.com
Red Herring	www.redherring.com
Securities Industry Association Career Resource Center	www.sifma.com/services/career_center/ career_center.html
Smart Money	www.smartmoney.com

Society of Competitive Intelligence Professionals Job Marketplace	www.scip.org/CareerCenter
Strategy+Business	www.strategy-business.com
The Street	www.thestreet.com
TANG	https://nyustern.campusgroups.com/home
Top Startups	www.topstartups.com
VAR Business	www.crn.com/cwb/careers
Vault	www.vault.com/wps/portal/usa
WetFeet.com	www.wetfeet.com

-C-

Call Center

AnswerStat	www.answerstat.com
Cactussearch.co.uk [United Kingdom]	www.cactussearch.co.uk
CallCenterCareers.com	www.callcentercareers.com/index.jsp
CallCenterClassifieds	www.callcenterclassifieds.com
CallCenterJob.ca [Canada]	www.callcenterjob.ca
CallCenterJobs.com	www.callcenterjobs.com
CallCenterOps.com	www.callcenterops.com
CallCenterProfi.de [Germany]	www.callcenterprofi.de/index.php;sid= 5df09c06c9fdf1810ce006b8f9beab9f
Get Call Center Jobs	www.getcallcenterjobs.com
JobsinContactCentres [United Kingdom]	www.jobsincontactcentres.com
Teleplaza	www.teleplaza.com/jp.html

Career Counseling/Job Search Services

America's Career InfoNet	www.acinet.org
American Evaluation Association	www.eval.org/programs/careercenter.asp
AskNaukri.com [India]	http://asknaukri.com

Association of Career Professionals International	www.iacpm.org
Association of Graduate Careers Advisory Service [United Kingdom]	www.agcas.org.uk
Association of Executive Search Consultants	www.bluesteps.com
BrainBench	www.brainbench.com
Bright.com	www.bright.com
Canadian Association of Career Educators & Employers	www.cacee.com
CanadianCareers.com	www.canadiancareers.com
CareerDNA	www.careerdna.netstatic/home
CareerFitness.com	www.careerfitness.com
CareerHarmony.com	www.careerharmony.com
Career Management International	www.cmi-lmi.com
CareerVoyages.gov	www.careervoyages.gov
CareersUSA.com	www.careersusa.com
Computing Technology Industry Association Career Compass	http://tcc.comptia.org
CVTips.com	www.cvtips.com
DDI	www.ddiworld.com
Eggsprout	www.eggsprout.com
eLance	www.elance.com
The Engineering Specific Career Advisory Problem-Solving Environment	https://engineering.purdue.edu/Engr
ePredix	www.previsor.com
Executive Agent	www.myresumeagent.com
ExecutiveResumes.com	www.executiveresumes.com
Exxceed	www.exxceed.com
FaceCV [Italy]	www.facecv.it
FreeLancingProjects.com	www.freelancingprojects.com
Get Me A Job	www.getmeajob.com
GetMoreJobOffers.com [United Kingdom]	www.getmorejoboffers.com
GlassDoor.com	www.glassdoor.com/index.htm
GotResumes.com	www.gotresumes.com

Gray Hair Management LLC	www.grayhairmanagement.com
Guru.com	www.guru.com
Hoovers Online	www.hoovers.com
JibberJobber.com	www.jibberjobber.com/login.php
JobBait.com	www.jobbait.com
JobConnect.org	www.jobconnections.org
Jobfiler.com	www.jobfiler.com
Job Hunter's Bible	www.jobhuntersbible.com
JobSearchNews.com	http://jobsearchnews.com
JobseekersAdvice.com [United Kingdom]	www.jobseekersadvice.com
JobStar	http://jobstar.org/index.php
JobVoting.com [Germany]	www.jobvoting.com
JobsRadar	www.jobsradar.com
Kaplan Career Services	www.kaplan.com/pages/default.aspx
Kelzen.com [Austria]	www.kelzen.com/en
Kununu.com [Austria]	www.kununu.com
The Limited	www.thelimited.com
LiveCareer	www.livecareer.com
MyWebCareer	www.mywebcareer.com
National Association of Colleges & Employers	www.jobweb.com
National Association for College Admission Counseling Career Opportunities	www.nacac.com/classifieds.cfm
National Association of Colleges & Employers (NACE)	www.nacelink.com
National Board for Certified Counselors	www.nbcc.org
National Career Development Association	www.ncda.org
ThePhoenixLink.com	www.thephoenixlink.com
PitchYourTalent [Southeast Asia]	www.pitchyourtalent.com
Pursut.com	www.pursut.com
Ready Minds	www.readyminds.com
Real-Home-Employment	www.real-home-employment.com
RentaCoder.com	www.vworker.com/RentACoder/DotNet/ default.aspx

ResumeBlaster	www.resumeblaster.com
ResumeBomber	www.resumebomber.com
ResumeBucket	www.resumebucket.com
ResumeXPRESS	www.resumexpress.com
Resume Network	www.resume-network.com
The Resume Place, Inc.	www.resume-place.com
ResumeRabbit.com	www.resumerabbit.com
Resumes on the Web	www.resweb.com
Resume Workz	www.resumeworkz.com
The Riley Guide	www.rileyguide.com
Rypple.com	www.rypple.com
Salary.com	www.salary.com
Seidbet Associates	www.seidbet.com
SingleMindedWomen.com	http://singlemindedwomen.com
Skill Scape	www.skillscape.com
SoloGig	www.sologig.com
Tweetajob	www.tweetajob.com
TweetMyJobs.com	www.tweetmyjob.com
Vault	www.vault.com/wps/portal/usa
Vizibility	www.vizibility.com
WEDDLE's Newsletters, Guides & Directories	www.weddles.com
Wetfeet.com	www.wetfeet.com
WorkBloom.com	www.workbloom.com
WorkMinistry.com	www.workministry.com
Yourcha.de [Germany]	www.yourcha.com/de/employee/home/s
ZoomInfo.com	www.zoominfo.com

Chemistry

American Chemical Society	http://portal.acs.org/portal/acs/corg/content
American Chemical Society Rubber Division	www.rubber.org
American Association of Brewing Chemists	www.asbcnet.org/placement/jobs.htm

American Association of Cereal Chemists	www.aaccnet.org/membership careerplacement.asp
American Association for Clinical Chemistry	www.aacc.org/Pages/default.aspx
American Institute of Chemical Engineers Career Services	www.aiche.org/careers
The American Institute of Chemists	www.theaic.org/DesktopDefault.aspx
BiotechSales/Chemistry Career Search	www.biotechsaleschemistry.com
Chememploy	www.chemweek.com/chemploy
Chemical Industry Central	www.chemicalindustrycentral.com
Chemical Week	www.chemweek.com
Chemist Jobs	www.chemistjobs.com
Chemistry & Industry	www.soci.org/Chemistry-and-Industry/ CnI-Data/2010/11
ChemJobs.net	www.chemjobs.net/chemjobs.html
ChemPeople.com [United Kingdom]	www.chempeople.com
ChemPharma	www.chempharma.net
Chem Web	www.chemweb.com
HireLifeScience	www.hirelifescience.com
ihireChemists.com	www.ihirechemists.com
Intratech	www.intratech1.com
Jobscience Network	http://jobs.jobscience.com
Jobs in Chemistry	www/jobsinchemistry.com
Nature	www.nature.com
New Scientist Jobs	www.newscientistjobs.com
Organic Chemistry Jobs Worldwide [Belgium]	www.organicworldwide.net/jobs
PlasticsJobsForum.com	www.plasticsjobsforum.com
Poly Sort	www.polysort.com
Science Careers	http://sciencecareers.sciencemag.org/
Scijobs.org	http://sciencecareers.sciencemag.org/
ScienceJobs.org	www.sciencejobs.org

Child & Elder Care

AuPair In Europe	www.planetaupair.com/aupaireng.htm
CareGuide	www.careguide.net
4Nannies.com	www.4nannies.com
Nannyjob.co.uk [United Kingdom]	www.nannyjob.co.uk
NurseryWorldJobs.co.uk [United Kingdom]	www.nurseryworldjobs.co.uk
SitterByZip	www.sitterbyzip.com

Classifieds-Newspaper

International

Jobb24.se [Sweden]	www.jobb24.se
TheLondonPaper.com [United Kingdom]	www.thelondonpaper.com
Mobiljob [France]	www.topannonces.fr/petites-annonces--offres-d-emploi-interim.html
TimesJobs.com [India]	www.timesjobs.com
Vlan [Belgium]	www.vlan.be
TheWest.com.au [Australia]	http://au.news.yahoo.com/thewest/

National

The Wall Street Journal	http://online.wsj.com/home-page
USA Today	www.usatoday.com

Alabama

Birmingham News	www.bhamnews.com
Huntsville Times	www.htimes.com
Mobile Register Online	www.mobileregister.com
Montgomery Advertiser	www.montgomeryadvertiser.com
The Tuscaloosa News	www.tuscaloosanews.com

Alaska

Anchorage Daily News	www.adn.com
Fairbanks Daily News	http://fairbanks.abracat.com
Frontiersman	www.frontiersman.com
Juneau Empire	www.juneauempire.com
Nome Nugget	www.nomenugget.com

Arizona

Arizona Daily Sun (Flagstaff)	www.azdailysun.com
The Daily Courier (Prescott)	www.dcourier.com
East Valley Tribune (Mesa)	www.eastvalleytribune.com
Geebo	www.geebo.com
Phoenix News Times	www.phoenixnewtimes.com
Today's News-Herald (Lake Havasu City)	www.havasunews.com

Arkansas

Benton Courier	www.bentoncourier.com
Jonesboro Sun	www.jonesborosun.com
The Sentinel-Record (Hot Springs)	www.hotsr.com

California

BayAreaClassifieds.com	www.bayareaclassifieds.com
Geebo	www.geebo.com
Inland Valley Daily Bulletin	www.dailybulletin.com
Los Angeles Daily News	www.dailynews.com
Los Angeles Times	www.latimes.com
Mercury News (San Jose)	www.bayarea.com
Orange County Register	www.ocregister.com
Pasadena Star-News	www.pasadenastarnews.com
The Press Enterprise	www.pe.com
Press Telegram of Long Beach	www.presstelegram.com

Redlands Daily Facts	www.redlandsdailyfacts.com
Sacramento Bee	www.sacbee.com
San Bernadino Sun	www.sbsun.com
San Francisco Chronicle	www.sfgate.com
San Gabriel Valley Tribune	www.sgvtribune.com
Whittier Daily News	www.whittierdailynews.com

Colorado

Aspen Daily News	www.aspendailynews.com
Colorado Springs Independent	www.csindy.com
The Daily Sentinel (Grand Junction)	www.gjsentinel.com
Denver Post	www.denverpost.com
Durango Herald	www.durangoherald.com
Rocky Mountain News	www.rockymountainnews.com/jobs

Connecticut

The Advocate (Stamford)	www.stamfordadvocate.com
Danbury News-Times	www.newstimes.com
TheDay.com (New London)	www.theday.com
Hartford Courant	www.courant.com
New Haven Register	www.newhavenregister.com
Waterbury Republican American	www.rep-am.com

Delaware

Dover Post	www.doverpost.com
The News Journal (Wilmington)	www.delawareonline.com

District of Columbia

Geebo	www.geebo.com
JobFetch.com	www.jobfetch.com
The Washington Post	www.washingtonpost.com

Washington Times   www.washingtontimes.com

Florida

Florida Times Union (Jacksonville)   http://jacksonville.com

Geebo   www.geebo.com

Miami Herald   www.miami.com

Orlando Sentinel   www.orlandosentinel.com

Pensacola News Journal   www.pnj.com

St. Petersburg Times   www.sptimes.com

Georgia

The Albany Herald   www.albanyherald.net/classbrowse.htm

Atlanta Journal and Constitution   www.ajc.com

Augusta Chronicle   http://chronicle.augusta.com

Macon Telegraph   www.macon.com

Savannah Morning News   www.savannahnow.com

Hawaii

Hawaii Tribune-Herald (Hilo)   www.hawaiitribune-herald.com/index.html

Honolulu Advertiser   www.honoluluadvertiser.com

Honolulu Star-Bulletin   www.starbulletin.com

Maui News   www.mauinews.com

West Hawaii Today (Kailua)   www.westhawaiitoday.com

Idaho

Cedar Rapids Gazette   www.gazetteonline.com

The Daily Nonpareil (Council Bluffs)   http://southwestiowanews.com/council_
                                                      bluffs/front/

Des Moines Register   www.desmoinesregister.com

Quad City Times (Davenport)   http://qctimes.com

Sioux City Journal   www.siouxcityjournal.com

Illinois

Chicago Tribune	www.chicagotribune.com
The Daily Register (Canton)	www.cantondailyledger.com
Geebo	www.geebo.com
Herald & Review (Decatur)	www.herald-review.com
The News-Gazette (Champaign)	www.news-gazette.com
Register-News (Mount Vernon)	http://register-news.com
The State Journal Register (Springfield)	www.sj-r.com
The Herald-Times (Bloomington)	www.heraldtimesonline.com
Indianapolis Star News	www.indystar.com

Indiana

The News-Sentinel (Fort Wayne)	www.fortwayne.com
Post-Tribune (Gary)	www.post-trib.com/index.html
South Bend Tribune	www.sbinfo.com

Kansas

Daily Union (Junction City)	www.thedailyunion.net
Kansas City Kansan	www.kansascitykansan.com
Salina Journal	www.saljournal.com
The Topeka Capital Journal	www.cjonline.com
Wichita Eagle	www.kansas.com

Kentucky

The Courier-Journal (Louisville)	www.courier-journal.com
The Daily News (Bowling Green)	www.bgdailynews.com
Grayson County News-Gazette (Leitchfield)	www.gcnewsgazette.com
Lexington Herald Leader	www.kentucky.com
Sentinel News (Shelbyville)	www.sentinelnews.com

Louisiana

The Advocate (Baton Rouge)	www.advocate.com
The Times (Shreveport)	www.shreveporttimes.com
The Times-Picayune (New Orleans)	www.nola.com

Maine

Bangor Daily News	www.bangornews.com
Kennebec Journal (Augusta)	http://kennebecjournal.mainetoday.com
Lewiston Sun Journal	www.sunjournal.com
Portland Press Herald	www.portland.com
The Times Record (Brunswick)	www.timesrecord.com

Maryland

Baltimore Sun	www.baltimoresun.com
The Capital (Annapolis)	www.hometownannapolis.com
The Herald-Mail (Hagerstown)	www.herald-mail.com
JobFetch.com	www.jobfetch.com
The Star Democrat (Easton)	www.stardem.com

Massachusetts

The Boston Globe	www.boston.com/bostonglobe
The Eagle-Tribune (Lawrence)	www.eagletribune.com
Geebo	www.geebo.com
The Sun (Lowell)	www.lowellsun.com
The Salem News	www.salemnews.com
Union-News & Sunday Republican (Springfield)	www.masslive.com

Michigan

Ann Arbor News	www.mlive.com/annarbornews
Detroit Free Press	www.freep.com
Flint Journal	www.mlive.com/flintjournal

| Grand Rapids Press | www.mlive.com/grpress |
| Lansing State Journal | www.lansingstatejournal.com |

Minnesota

Duluth News-Tribune	www.duluthnewstribune.com
Elk River Star News	www.erstarnews.com
The Journal (New Ulm)	www.oweb.com
Minneapolis Star Tribune	www.startribune.com
Saint Paul Pioneer Press	www.twincities.com

Mississippi

The Clarion Ledger (Jackson)	www.clarionledger.com
Meridian Star	www.meridianstar.com
The Natchez Democrat	www.natchezdemocrat.com
The Sun Herald (Biloxi)	www.sunherald.com
The Vicksburg Post	www.vicksburgpost.com

Missouri

The Examiner (Independence)	www.examiner.net
Hannibal Courier-Post	www.hannibal.net
Jefferson City News Tribune	www.newstribune.com
Joplin Globe	www.joplinglobe.com
Springfield News-Leader	www.news-leader.com

Montana

Billings Gazette	http://billingsgazette.com
Bozeman Daily Chronicle	www.bozemandailychronicle.com
Helena Independent Record	www.helenair.com
Missoulian	www.missoulian.com
The Montana Standard (Butte)	www.mtstandard.com

Nebraska

Columbus Telegram	www.columbustelegram.com
Lincoln Journal Star	www.journalstar.com
North Platte Telegraph	www.nptelegraph.com
Omaha World-Herald	www.omaha.com
Scotts Bluff Star-Herald	www.starherald.com

Nevada

Elko Daily Free Press	http://elkodaily.com
Las Vegas Review-Journal	www.lvrj.com
Las Vegas Sun	www.lasvegassun.com
Nevada Appeal (Carson City)	www.nevadaappeal.com
Reno Gazette Journal	www.rgj.com

New Hampshire

Concord Monitor	www.concordmonitor.com
Keene Sentinel	www.keenesentinel.com
Portsmouth Herald	www.seacoastonline.com
The Telegraph (Nashua)	www.nashuatelegraph.com
The Union Leader (Manchester)	www.theunionleader.com

New Jersey

Asbury Park Press	www.app.com
Courier-Post (Cherry Hill)	www.courierpostonline.com
The Montclair Times	www.northjersey.com/towns/Montclair.html
The Star Ledger (Newark)	www.nj.com
The Trentonian	www.trentonian.com

New Mexico

Albuquerque Journal	www.abqjournal.com
The Gallup Independent	www.gallupindependent.com

Los Alamos Monitor	www.lamonitor.com
Santa Fe New Mexican	www.santafenewmexican.com
The Silver City Daily Press	www.scdailypress.com/ee/ silvercitydailypress/index.php

New York

Albany Democrat Herald	http://democratherald.com
Geebo	www.geebo.com
Ithaca Times	www.zwire.com/site/news. cfm?brd=1395&nr=1&nostat=1
New York Post	www.nypost.com
The New York Times	www.nytimes.com
Syracuse New Times	www.newtimes.com

North Carolina

Charlotte Observer	www.charlotteobserver.com/943
Greensboro News-Record	www.news-record.com
News & Observer (Raleigh)	www.newsobserver.com
StarNewsOnline.com	www.starnewsonline.com
Winston-Salem Journal	www2.journalnow.com/home

North Dakota

Bismarck Tribune	www.bismarcktribune.com
Grand Forks Herald	www.grandforks.com
The Jamestown Sun	www.jamestownsun.com
Minot Daily News	www.minotdailynews.com

Ohio

Cincinnati Enquirer	www.enquirer.com
The Cleveland Nation	www.clnation.com
Columbus Dispatch	www.dispatch.com/live/content/index.html
Dayton Daily News	www.daytondailynews.com

Springfield News Sun   www.springfieldnewssun.com

Oklahoma

Altus Times   www.altustimes.com
Lawton Constitution   www.lawton-constitution.com
The Oklahoman (Oklahoma City)   www.newsok.com
OKC.gov   www.okc.gov
Ponca City News   www.poncacitynews.com
Tulsa World   www.tulsaworld.com

Oregon

East Oregonian (Pendleton)   http://eastoregonian.com/index.asp
The Oregonian (Portland)   www.oregonian.com
The Register-Guard (Eugene)   www.registerguard.com/web/news/index.csp
Springfield News   www.hometownnews.com
Statesman Journal (Salem)   www.statesmanjournal.com

Pennsylvania

CityPaperJobs.net   www.citypaper.net/jobs/index.php
Erie Daily Times-News   www.goerie.com
Geebo   www.geebo.com
The Philadelphia Inquirer   www.philly.com
Pittsburg Post-Gazette   www.post-gazette.com
Scranton Times Tribune   http://thetimes-tribune.com
The Times Leader (Wilkes-Barre)   www.timesleader.com

Rhode Island

The Narragansett Times (Wakefield) www.narragansetttimes.com
The Pawtucket Times   www.pawtuckettimes.com
Providence Journal   www.projo.com/projojobs
Sakonnet Times (Portsmouth)   www.eastbayri.com

South Carolina

Camden Chronicle Independent | www.chronicle-independent.com/site/
news.cfm?brd=1382

Free Times (Columbia) | www.free-times.com

The Greenville News | www.greenvilleonline.com

The Post and Courier (Charleston) | www.postandcourier.com

The Sun Times (Myrtle Beach) | www.thesunnews.com/myrtlebeachonline

South Dakota

Argus Leader (Sioux Falls) | www.argusleader.com

Brookings Daily Register | www.brookingsregister.com

The Capital Journal (Pierre) | www.capjournal.com

The Freeman Courier | www.freemansd.com

Huron Plainsman | www.plainsman.com

Tennessee

Chattanooga Times Free Press | www.timesfreepress.com/home

Daily Post-Athenian | www.dpa.xtn.net

Knoxville News Sentinel | www.knoxnews.com

Memphis Flyer | www.memphisflyer.com

The Tennessean (Nashville) | www.tennessean.com

Texas

Austin American-Statesman | www.austin360.com

Dallas Morning News | www.dallasnews.com

El Paso Times | www.elpasotimes.com

Geebo | www.geebo.com

Houston Chronicle | www.chron.com

San Antonio Express News | www.mysanantonio.com

Utah

The Daily Herald (Provo)	www.heraldextra.com
Herald Journal (Logan)	www.hjnews.com
Salt Lake Tribune	www.sltrib.com
Standard-Examiner (Ogden)	www.standard.net

Vermont

Addison County Independent (Middlebury)	www.addisonindependent.com
Burlington Free Press	www.burlingtonfreepress.com
Deerfield Valley News (West Dover)	www.dvalnews.com
Stowe Reporter	www.stowetoday.com
Valley News (White River Junction)	www.vnews.com

Virginia

The Daily Progress (Charlottesville)	www2.dailyprogress.com
Danville Register Bee	www2.godanriver.com
JobFetch.com	www.jobfetch.com
The News-Advance (Lynchburg)	www2.newsadvance.com
Richmond Times-Dispatch	www2.timesdispatch.com
Virginian-Pilot (Norfolk)	http://pilotonline.com

Washington

The Columbian (Vancouver)	www.columbian.com
Geebo	www.geebo.com
The News Tribune (Tacoma)	www.thenewstribune.com
The Olympian (Olympia)	www.theolympian.com
Seattle Post-Intelligencer	www.seattlepi.com
The Spokesman-Review (Spokane)	www.spokane.net

West Virginia

Charlestown Daily Mail	www.dailymail.com

Clarksburg Exponent Telegram	www.cpubco.com
The Dominion Post (Morgantown)	www.dominionpost.com
Times West Virginian (Fairmont)	http://timeswv.com
Wheeling News-Register	www.news-register.com

Wisconsin

Green Bay Press Gazette	www.greenbaypressgazette.com
The Journal Times (Racine)	www.journaltimes.com
La Crosse Tribune	www.lacrossetribune.com
Milwaukee Journal Sentinel	www.jsonline.com
Wisconsin State Journal (Madison)	http://host.madison.com

Wyoming

Douglas Budget	www.douglas-budget.com
Wyoming Tribune-Eagle	www.wyomingnews.com

College/Internships/Entry Level/Graduate School

Entry-Level

Aboutjobs.com	www.aboutjobs.com
Activate.co.uk [United Kingdom]	www.activate.co.uk
AfterCollege.com	www.aftercollege.com
AtCollegeJobs	www.atcollegejobs.com
Barefootstudent.com	www.barefootstudent.com/directory/search/ students
THE BLACK COLLEGIAN Online	www.blackcollegian.com
Campus Career Center	www.campuscareercenter.com
Campus Grotto	www.campusgrotto.com
CampusRN.com	www.campusrn.com
Canadian Association of Career Educators & Employers	www.cacee.com

Career Conferences	www.careerconferences.com
CareerEdge [Canada]	www.careeredge.ca
Career Explorer	https://access.bridges.com/auth/login.do?target
	Uri=%2Fportal%2FlandingPage.do
Careerfair.com	www.careerfair.com
College Central Network	www.collegecentral.com
CollegeGrad.com	www.collegegrad.com
CollegeHelpers.com	www.collegehelpers.com
College Job Bank	www.collegejobbank.com
College Job Board	www.collegejobboard.com/cjb/index.cfm
College News Online	www.collegenews.com/college_careers
College PowerPrep	www.powerprep.com
CollegeRecruiter.com	www.collegerecruiter.com
Colleges	www.colleges.com
Current Jobs for Graduates	www.graduatejobs.com
EntryLevelJobs.net	www.entryleveljobs.net
Experience	www.experience.com
FuseJobs.co.uk [United Kingdom]	www.fusejobs.co.uk
Get.hobsons.co.uk [United Kingdom]	www.get.hobsons.co.uk
Thegraduate.co.uk [United Kingdom]	www.thegraduate.co.uk
Graduating Engineer & Computer Careers Online	www.graduatingengineer.com
TheJobBox.com	www.thejobbox.com/tjb/index.cfm?page=main
job-hunt.org	www.job-hunt.org
JobPostings.net	www.jobpostings.net
JobScribble.com	www.jobscribble.com
JustClick.co.uk [United Kingdom]	www.justclick.co.uk
Mapping Your Future	http://mappingyourfuture.org/
MBAGlobalNet	www.mbaglobalnet.com
MBAmatch.com [United Kingdom]	www.mbamatch.com
MBA Style Magazine	www.mbastyle.com
Milkround.com [United Kingdom]	www.milkround.com
Monster Campus	http://college.monster.com

National Association of Colleges & Employers	www.nacelink.com
National Society of Collegiate Scholars Career Connection	www.nscs.org
National Society of Hispanic MBAs Career Center	www.nshmba.org
New England Higher Education Recruitment Consortium	www.newenglandherc.org/home/index.cfm?site_id=660
New York Black MBA	www.nyblackmba.org
OverseasJobs.com	www.overseasjobs.com
Peterson's	www.petersons.com
Princeton Review Online	www.princetonreview.com
Prospects.ac.uk [United Kingdom]	www.prospects.ac.uk
SallieMae/TrueCareers	www.truecareers.com
SnagAJob	www.snagajob.com
Student Affairs	www.studentaffairs.com
Student Central	www.studentcentral.com
UniJobs.at [Austria]	www.unijobs.at
Vault.com [Europe]	www.vault.com/wps/portal/usa

Internships

InternJobs.com	www.internjobs.com
Internship Programs	www.internshipprograms.com
Internships	www.internships.com
Internships4You	www.internships4you.com
Internweb	www.internweb.com
Paid Internships	www.paidinternships.com

Summer Jobs

Barefootstudent.com	www.barefootstudent.com/directory/search/students
CollegeJobs.co.uk [United Kingdom]	www.collegejobs.co.uk

CoolWorks — www.coolworks.com

ResortJobs.com — www.resortjobs.com

Student Awards — www.studentawards.com

StudentJobs.gov — www.usajobs.gov/studentjobs

Study Abroad — www.studyabroad.com

SummerJobs.com — www.summerjobs.com

Super College — www.supercollege.com

Teens 4 Hire — www.teens4hire.org

TenStepsforStudents.org — www.tenstepsforstudents.org

University Directories — www.universitydirectories.com/
career-partners.asp

University Links — www.ulinks.com

Youth@Work — www.youthatwork.org

College/University Affiliated

California State University - Chico — www.csuchico.edu/careers

Career Development Center at Rensselaer
Polytechnic Institute — www.rpi.edu/dept/cdc

Case Western Reserve University — www.cwru.edu

The Catholic University of America Career
Services Office — http://careers.cua.edu

Clemson University — www.clemson.edu

Columbia University [Master of Science in
Construction Administration] — www.theconstructionjob.com

Drake University — www.drake.edu

Drexel University — www.drexel.edu

Duke University Job Resources — http://career.studentaffairs.duke.edu

Emory University Rollins School of Public Health — www.sph.emory.edu/cms/current_students/
career_services/index.html

Foothill-De Anza Community College — www.fhda.edu/jobs

Georgia State University Career Services — www.gsu.edu/career

Georgia Tech Career Services Office — www.career.gatech.edu

Loyola College — www.loyola.edu/thecareercenter/index.html

Nova Southeastern University	www.nova.edu
Oakland University	www.oakland.edu/careerservices
Profiles Database	www.profilesdatabase.com
Purdue University Management Placement Office	www.krannert.purdue.edu/departments/gcs
San Francisco State University Instructional Technologies	www.itec.sfsu.edu
University of Arkansas	www.uark.edu/home
U.C. Berkeley Work-Study Programs	http://workstudy.berkeley.edu
University of Virginia Career Planning & Placement	www.hrs.virginia.edu
University of Wisconsin-Madison School of Business Career Center	www.bus.wisc.educ/areer
Washington and Lee University	www.wlu.edu/x6.xml
Worcester Polytechnic Institute	www.wpi.edu

Computer (See High Tech/Technical/Technology and Information Technology/Information Systems

Computer-Aided Design, Manufacturing & Engineering

American Design Drafting Association	www.adda.org
Auto CAD Job Network	www.acjn.com
Computer-Aided Three-Dimensional Interactive Application Job Network	www.catjn.com
e-Architect	www.e-architect.com
GetCADJobs.com	www.getcadjobs.com
Just CAD Jobs	www.justCADjobs.com
ManufacturingJobs.com	www.manufacturingjobs.com
Manufacturing.Net	www.manufacturing.net
PLMjobs	www.plmjobs.com

UG Job Network (Unigraphics)   www.ugjn.com

Construction (See also Engineering)

A/E/C JobBank   www.aecjobbank.com
AGC Iowa Careers   www.agciajobs.com
Air Conditioning-Heating-Refrigeration News   www.achrnews.com
AirConditioningJobs.com   www.airconditioningjobs.com
Akhtaboot [Jordan]   www.akhtaboot.com
Aljazeerajobs.com [Middle East]   www.aljazeerajobs.com
All Port Jobs   www.allportjobs.com
American Society of Professional Estimators   www.aspenational.org
ASHRAEjobs.com (Heating, Refrigeration,   www.ashraejobs.com
  Air Conditioning)

Bayt.com [United Arab Emirates]   www.bayt.com
Bconstructive [United Kingdom]   www.bconstructive.co.uk
Blue Collar Jobs   www.bluecollarjobs.com
Build Find   www.buildfind.com
BuilderJobs   www.builderjobs.com
Builder Online   www.builder.hw.net
Building.com   www.building.com
Building Services [United Kingdom]   www.buildingservicesjobs.co.uk
Building Trades Jobs   www.tradesjobs.com
Careerjunctionme.com [Middle East]   www.careerjunctionme.com
Careers In Construction   www.careersinconstruction.com
CarpenterJobs.com   www.carpenterjobs.com
CarpenterJobsite.com   www.carpenterjobsite.com
Construction/Careers   www.construction.com
ConstructionEducation.com   www.constructioneducation.com
Construction Executive Online   www.constructionexecutive.com
Construction4Professionals.co.uk   www.construction4professionals.co.uk
  [United Kingdom]
Construction Gigs   www.constructiongigs.com

Construction Industry Central	www.constructionindustrycentral.com
TheConstructionJob [Columbia University]	www.theconstructionjob.com
ConstructionJobForce	www.constructionjobforce.com
Construction Job Search [United Kingdom]	www.constructionjobsearch.co.uk
ConstructionJobs.com	www.constructionjobs.com/index_eng.cfm
ConstructionJobsNow [United Kingdom]	www.constructionjobsnow.co.uk
ConstructionWorkforce.net	www.constructionwork.com
ConstructionWorkforce.net	www.constructionworkforce.net
Constructor [United Kingdom]	www.constructor.co.uk
Electricalagent	www.electricalagent.com
Electrical Employment	www.cossin.com/page3.html
Engineering News Record	http://enrconstruction.com
Environmental Construction Engineering Architectural Jobs Online	www.eceajobs.com
Estimator Jobs	www.estimatorjobs.com
GeneralConstructionJobs.com	www.generalconstructionjobs.com
GetElectricianJobs.com	www.getelectricianjobs.com
go4constructionJobs	www.go4constructionjobs.com
Grist.org	http://jobs.grist.org
HelmetstoHardhats.com	www.helmetstohardhats.com
HomeBuilderJobs.com	www.bigbuildercareers.com
HVACagent.com	www.hvacagent.com
HVAC Industry	www.hvac-industry.com
HVAC Mall	www.hvacmall.com
The HVAC Source	www.thehvacsource.com
ihireBuildingTrades.com	www.ihirebuildingtrades.com
ihireConstruction.com	www.ihireconstruction.com
Just Construction [United Kingdom]	www.justconstruction.net
JustEngineers.net [Australia]	www.justengineers.net
JobsinConstruction [United Kingdom]	www.jobsinconstruction.co.uk
JobsinSurveying [United Kingdom]	www.jobsinsurveying.co.uk
Jobsite.co.uk [United Kingdom]	www.jobsite.co.uk
Maintenance Engineer	www.maintenanceemployment.com

Materials Jobs	www.welding-engineer.com
Maxim Recruitment [United Kingdom]	www.maximrecruitment.co.uk
MEPjobs.com [mechanical, electrical, plumbing]	www.mepjobs.com/%28S%28wkttyv31uqwii2nnc qhtqbml%29%29/default.aspx
Metal Working Portal	http://metal-working.tradeworlds.com
MonsterGulf.com [Middle East]	www.monstergulf.com
MyConstructionJobs.net	www.myconstructionjobs.net
National Association of Women in Construction	www.nawic.org/nawic/Default.asp
NaukriGulf.com [Middle East]	www.naukrigulf.com
Offsite Jobs [United Kingdom]	www.offsitejobs.co.uk
Plumbingagent	www.plumbingagent.com
Plumbing Careers	www.plumbingcareers.com
PlumbingGigs.com	www.plumbinggigs.com
PlumbingHelper.com	www.plumbinghelper.com
PLUMBjob.com	www.plumbjobs.com
ProjectManagerJobs.com	www.projectmanagerjobs.com
QCEmployMe.com	http://regionalhelpwanted.com/ quad-cities-il-ia-jobs
RecruitConstruction [United Kingdom]	www.recruitconstruction.com
ReferWork-Jobs.com	www.referwork-jobs.com
RefrigeJobs.com	www.refrigejobs.com
Right of Way	www.rightofway.com
SkilledWorkers.com [Canada]	www.skilledworkers.com
SuperintendentJobs.com	www.superintendentjobs.com
TopBuildingJobs.com	www.topbuildingjobs.com
TradesJobs.com	www.tradesjobs.com
Trade Jobs Online	www.tradejobsonline.com
UtilityJobSearch.com [United Kingdom]	www.utilityjobsearch.com
Utility Jobs Online	www.utilityjobsonline.com
Welding Jobs	www.weldingjobs.com

Consultants

Aejob.com	www.aejob.com
AndersenAlumni.net	www.andersenalumni.net
Association of Management Consulting Firms	www.amcf.org
Career Lab	www.careerlab.com
CEWeekly.com	www.ceweekly.com
Computerwork.com	www.computerwork.com
ConsultLink.com	www.consultlink.com
ConsultantsBoard.com [United Kingdom]	www.consultantsboard.com
Consulting Career Quest	www.consultingcareerquest.com
Consulting Magazine	www.consultingmag.com
GenerationMom.com	www.generationmom.com
GlenRecruitment.co.uk [United Kingdom]	www.glenrecruitment.co.uk
HotGigs.com	www.hotgigs.com
The Independent Consultants Network	www.inconet.com
JobNews.at [Austria]	www.jobnews.at
Medical Consultants Network	www.mcn.com
SoloGig.com	www.sologig.com
Top-Consultant.com	www.top-consultant.com/UK/ career/appointments.asp
TrainingConsortium.com	www.trainingconsortium.com

Contract Employment/Part Time Employment (See also Search Firms)

AllFreeLanceWork.com	www.allfreelancework.com
Ants	www.ants.com
AutomationTechies.com	www.automationtechies.com
Camp Jobs	www.campjobs.com
Camp Staff	www.campstaff.com
CanadaParttime.com [Canada]	www.canadaparttime.com/content/flash
ContractCareers.com	www.contractcareers.com

Contract Employment Weekly Jobs Online	www.ceweekly.com
Contractjob.com	www.contractjob.com
Contract Job Hunter	www.cjhunter.com
contractjobs.com	www.contractjobs.com
ContractJobsite.com	www.contractjobsite.com
ContractedWork	www.contractedwork.com
ContractingCareers	www.contractingcareers.com
Contracts247 [United Kingdom]	www.contracts247.co.uk
Creative Freelancers	www.freelancers.com
DangerZoneJobs	www.dangerzonejobs.com
DoaAProject.com	www.doaproject.com
eLance	www.elance.com
eMoonlighter	www.moonlighter.com
ExperienceNet.com	www.experiencenet.com
Flexjobs.com	www.flexjobs.com
Fly Contract	www.flycontract.com
Freelancer	www.freelancer.com
Game Contractor	www.gamecontractor.com
Go Freelance	www.gofreelance.com
Guru.com	www.guru.com
HireMeNow.com	www.hiremenow.com
Homeworkers	www.homeworkers.org
HotGigs.com	www.hotgigs.com
iFreelance	www.ifreelance.com
Jobble	www.jobble.net
JobsinLogistics.com	www.jobsinlogistics.com
Labor Ready	www.laborready.com
LifeguardingJobs.com	www.lifeguardingjobs.com
Mediabistro	www.mediabistro.com
Net-Temps	www.net-temps.com
ProductionBase.co.uk [United Kingdom]	www.productionbase.co.uk
Project4Hire.com	www.project4hire.com
Ready People	www.readypeople.eu

RoadTechs.com	www.roadtechs.com
Software Contractors Guild	www.scguild.com
Sheet Metal and Air Conditioning Contractor's Association	www.smacna.org
SnagAJob	www.snagajob.com
Sologig	www.sologig.com
Subcontract.com	www.subcontract.com
Summer Jobs	www.summerjobs.com
Talent Connections	www.talentconnections.net
TelecommutingJobs	www.tjobs.com
Temps Online.co.uk [United Kingdom]	www.tempsonline.co.uk
Training Consortium	www.trainingconsortium.net
Travel Per Diem Contract	www.travelperdiemcontract.com
U Bid Contract Contracting Portal	www.ubidcontract.com

Cosmetology

BeautyJobs	www.beautyjobs.com
BehindtheChair.com	www.behindthechair.com
SalonEmployment.com	www.salonemployment.com
Salon Gigs	www.salongigs.com
SalonJobStore	www.salonjobstore.com
Salon Jobs	www.salonjobs.com
SalonPost.com	www.salonpost.com
Spa and Salon Jobs	www.spaandsalonjobs.com

Culinary/Food Preparation (See also Hospitality)

American Association of Brewing Chemists	www.scisoc.org
American Association of Cereal Chemists	www.scisoc.org
American Culinary Federation	www.acfchefs.org
Bakery-Net	www.bakerynet.com

BookaChef.co.uk [United Kingdom]	www.bookachef.co.uk
Careers in Food	www.careersinfood.com
Caterer.com [United Kingdom]	www.caterer.com
Chef Jobs [United Kingdom]	www.chefjobs.co.uk
Chef Jobs Network	http://chefjobsnetwork.com
Chef2Chef.com	www.chef2chef.com
Chefs Employment	www.chefsemployment.com
Escoffier Online	http://escoffier.com
FineDiningJobs.com	www.finediningjobs.com
Focus-management [United Kingdom]	www.focusmanagement.co.uk
Food And Drink Jobs.com	www.foodanddrinkjobs.com
Food Industry Jobs	www.foodindustryjobs.com
Hcareers	www.hcareers.com
iHireChefs.com	www.ihirechefs.com
JobsinCatering [United Kingdom]	www.jobsincatering.com
JobsinHotels [United Kingdom]	www.jobsinhotels.com
Jobstore [United Kingdom]	www.jobstore.co.uk
National Confectioners' Association	www.candyusa.com
National Restaurant Association	www.restaurant.org/careers
Restaurant Jobs [United Kingdom]	www.restaurantjobs.co.uk
RollingPinJobs.com	www.rollingpinjobs.com
SommelierJobs.com	www.sommelierjobs.com
Star Chefs	www.starchefs.com
WineJobsOnline [New Zealand]	www.winejobsonline.con
Wine & Hospitality Jobs	www.wineandhospitalityjobs.com
YachtChefs.com	www.yachtchefs.com

-D-

Data Processing

Black Data Processing Association Online	www.bdpa.org
DataNewsJobs.com [Belgium]	http://datanews.rnews.be/datanews/nl/jobs/

Dice	www.dice.com
Jobvertise	www.jobvertise.com

Defense (see also Military Personnel Transitioning into the Private Sector)

AeroIndustryJobs.com	www.aeroindustryjobs.com
Aviation Week	www.aviationweek.com
ClearanceJobs.com	www.clearancejobs.com
ClearedJobs.net	www.clearedjobs.net
ClearedConnections.com	www.clearedconnections.com
DangerZoneJobs	www.dangerzonejobs.com
The Defense Talent Network	www.defensetalent.com
Dice	www.dice.com
GovJobs.com	www.govjobs.com
IntelJobs.com	www.inteljobs.com
Intelligence.gov	www.intelligence.gov
IntelligenceCareers.com	www.intelligencecareers.com
Military.com	www.military.com
Military Connection	www.militaryconnection.com
Military Connections	www.militaryconnections.com
MilitaryHire.com	www.militaryhire.com
SecurityClearanceJobsBlog	www.securityclearancejobsblog.com
SecurityClearedJobs.com [United Kingdom]	www.securityclearedjobs.com
Security Job Zone	www.securityjobzone.com
SpaceJobs.com	www.spacejobs.com
USA Jobs	www.usajobs.com
USDefenseJobs.com	www.usdefensejobs.com
VetJobs	www.vetjobs.com

Dental

American Dental Hygienists' Association	www.adha.org/careerinfo
California Dental Hygienists' Association	http://cdha.org/employment
DentalJobs.com	www.dentaljobs.com
DentalPost.com	www.dentalpost.com
Foothill College Biological & Health Sciences	www.foothill.fhda.edu/bio/jobs.php
iHireDental.com	www.ihiredental.com
Jobscience Network	http://jobs.jobscience.com
MedHunters Dental Hygiene	www.medhunters.com
Medical-Dental-Hospital Business Association	www.mdhba.org
OverseasDentist.com	www.overseasdentist.com
SmileJobs.com	www.smilejobs.com

Diversity

Diversity-General

Affirmative Action Register	www.insightintodiversity.com
Anchorage Diversity	www.anchoragediversity.com
Career Moves	www.jvs-boston.org
CommunityConnectJobs.com	www.communityconnectjobs.com
Corporate Diversity Search	www.corpdiversitysearch.com
Diversity.com	www.diversity.com
DiversityAlliedHealth.com	www.diversityalliedhealth.com
Diversity Careers	www.diversitycareers.com
Diversity Careers [Canada]	www.diversitycareers.ca
Diversity Central	www.diversityhotwire.com
DiversityConnect	www.diversityconnect.com
Diversity Employment	www.diversityemployment.com
Diversity Events	www.diversityevents.com
DiversityInc.com	www.diversityinc.com
DiversityJobFairs.com	www.diversityjobfairs.com
Diversity Job Network	www.diversityjobnetwork.com

DiversityJobs.com — http://diversityjobs.com

DiversityLink — www.diversitylink.com

Diversity Search — www.diversitysearch.com

DiversityWorking — www.diversityworking.com

DiversityZone.com — www.diversityzone.com

EmployDiversity — www.employdiversity.com

Equal Opportunity Publications, Inc. — www.eop.com

HireDiversity.com — www.hirediversity.com

IMDiversity.com — www.imdiversity.com

Insight Into Diversity — www.insightintodiversity.com

Jobs4Diversity.com — www.jobs4diversity.com

LeadingDiversity.com — http://leadingdiversity.ning.com

MinnesotaDiversity.com — www.minnesotadiversity.com

The Multicultural Advantage — www.multicuturaladvantage.com

National Diversity Newspaper Job Bank — www.newsjobs.net

Society for Human Resource Management Diversity Page — www.shrm.org/hrdisciplines/Diversity/Pages/default.aspx/

WorkplaceDiversity.com — www.workplacediversity.com

Age

Age Positive Jobs [United Kingdom] — www.agepositivejobs.com

Canada's Fifty-Plus — www.fifty-plus.net

Encore — www.encore.org

Forty Plus — www.fortyplus.org

GeezerJobs.com — www.geezerjobs.com

National Commission on Aging — www.ncoa.org

PrimeCB.com — www.primecb.com

RetiredBrains — www.retiredbrains.com/default.aspx

RetirementJobs.com — www.retirementjobs.com

Workforce50 — www.workforce50.com

Bilingual Persons

Asianet	www.asianetglobal.com
Asian-Jobs.com	www.asian-jobs.com
BilingualCareer.com	www.bilingualcareer.com
Bilingual-Jobs	www.bilingual-jobs.com
CHALLENGEUSA	www.challengeusa.com
Eflweb	www.eflweb.com
Euroleaders	www.euroleaders.com
Hispanic Chamber of Commerce	www.ushcc.com
iHispano	www.ihispano.com
Hispanic-Jobs.com	www.hispanic-jobs.com
LatPro	www.latpro.com
National Society of Hispanic MBAs Career Center	www.nshmba.org
SaludosWeb	www.saludos.com
Society of Hispanic Professional Engineers Career Services	www.shpe.org
Top Language Jobs [Europe]	www.toplanguagejobs.co.uk

Ethnicity

Afro-Americ@	www.afro.com
Alianza (Latino)	www.alianza.org
A Mighty River	www.amightyriver.com
Asianet	www.asianetglobal.com
AsianAve.com	www.asianave.com
Association of Latino Professionals in Finance & Accounting Job Postings	www.alpfa.org
Black Career Women Online	www.bcw.org
THE BLACK COLLEGIAN Online	www.blackcollegian.com
Black Data Processing Association Online	www.bpda.org
Black Enterprise Magazine Career Center	www.blackenterprise.com
Blackgeeks	www.blackgeeks.com

BlackPlanet.com	www.blackplanet.com
Black Voices	www.blackvoices.com
Black World	www.blackworld.com
Chicago Chinese Computing Professional Assn	www.cccpa.org
El Nuevo Herald	www.elnuevoherald.com
Ethnicity	www.ethnicity.com
Ethnicjobsite.co.uk [United Kingdom]	www.ethnicjobsite.co.uk
GoldSea	www.goldsea.com/Text
HierosGamos	www.hg.org
Hispanic American Police Command Officers Association	www.hapcoa.org
Hispanic Business.com	www.hispanicbusiness.com/Redirect/ Welcome.asp
Hispanic Chamber of Commerce	www.ushcc.com
Hispanic-Jobs.com	www.hispanic-jobs.com
Hispanic Online	www.hispaniconline.com
iHispano.com	www.ihispano.com
JournalismNext.com	www.journalismnext.com
latinMBA.com	www.latinmba.com
LatinoHire.com	www.latinohire.com
Latinos in Information Sciences and Technology Association	www.a-lista.org
LatPro	www.latpro.com
MiGente.com	www.migente.com
Minorities Job Bank	www.imdiversity.com
MinorityAffairs.com	www.minorityaffairs.com
MinorityITJobs.com	www.minorityitjobs.com
Minority Jobs	www.minorityjobs.net
MinorityJobsite.com	www.minorityjobsite.com
Minority Career Network	www.minoritycareernet.com
Minority MBAs	www.minoritymbas.com
MinorityNurse.com	www.minoritynurse.com
Minority Professional Network	www.minorityprofessionalnetwork.com

NAACP Job Fair	www.naacpjobfair.com
National Association of Hispanic Nurses Houston Chapter	www.nahnhouston.org
National Association of African Americans in Human Resources	www.naaahr.us/default.aspx
National Association of Black Accountants, Inc. Career Center	http://nabacareercenter.nabainc.org
National Association of Hispanic Publications Online Career Center	www.nahp.org
National Black MBA Association, Inc.	www.nbmbaa.org
National Black MBA Association New York Chapter	www.nyblackmba.org
National Latino Peace Officers Association	www.nlpoa.org
National Organization of Black Law Enforcement Executives	www.noblenational.org
National Organization of Black Chemists and Chemical Engineers	www.engin.umich.edu/societies/nobcche
National Society of Black Engineers	http://national.nsbe.org
National Society of Black Physicists	www.nsbp.org
National Society of Hispanic MBAs Career Center	www.nshmba.org
National Urban League	www.nul.org
NativeAmericanJobs.com	www.nativeamericanjobs.com
NetNoir	www.netnoir.com
PharmaDiversity	www.pharmadiversity.com
Saludos Web Site	www.saludos.com
Society of Hispanic Professional Engineers Career Services	www.shpe.org
Society of Mexican American Engineers and Scientists	www.maes-natl.org
Worksfm.com [United Kingdom]	www.worksfm.com

Gender

The Ada Project	http://women.cs.cmu.edu/ada/
AdvancingWomen	www.advancingwomen.com
American Society of Women Accountants Employment Opportunities	www.aswact.org
Association for Women in Communications	www.womcom.org
Association for Women in Computing	www.awc-hq.org
Career Women	www.careerwomen.com
DCWebWomen	www.dcwebwomen.org
Electra	http://electra.com
Feminist Majority Foundation Career Center	www.feminist.org/911/jobs/joblisting.aspp
Financial Women International Careers	www.fwi.org
Healthcare Businesswomen's Association	www.hbanet.org/home.aspx
JobsandMoms.com	www.jobsandmoms.com
National Association of Women in Construction	www.nawic.org/nawic/Default.asp
National Female Executives	www.nafe.com
Sistahspace	http://groups.yahoo.com/group/SistahSpace
Society of Women Engineers Career Services	http://careers.swe.org
Webgrrls International	www.webgrrls.com
Women Connect.com	www.womenconnect.com
Women In Communications Washington, D.C. Chapter	www.awic-dc.org
Women in Federal Law Enforcement	www.wifle.org
WomenforHire.com	www.womenforhire.com
Women in Technology	www.womenintechnology.org
Women in Technology International (WITI) 4Hire	www.witi4hire.com
Women Work! The National Network for Women's Employment	www.womenwork.org
Women's Executive Network	www.thewen.com
Women's Finance Exchange	www.wfedallas.org
WomensJobList.com	www.womensjoblist.com
WomenSportsJobs.com	www.womensportjobs.com
Women's Sport Services	www.wiscnetwork.com

Women's Wear Daily	www.wwd.com
Womens-work	www.womans-work.com
Women Executives in Public Relations	www.wepr.org
Worksfm.com [United Kingdom]	www.worksfm.com

National Origin

Iconjob [India]	www.iconjob.com
Job-Quest.net [United Kingdom]	www.job-quest.net
VISA Jobs	www.h1visajobs.com

Physical Disability

AbilityEdge [Canada]	http://overview.careeredge.ca/index.asp?FirstTime=True&context=0&FromContext=2&language=1
AbilityJobs.com	www.abilityjobs.com
Disability Job Board	www.disabilityjobboard.com
Disability Job Site	www.disabilityjobsite.com
disABLEDperson.com	www.disabledperson.com
Disabled-World	www.disabled-world.com
GettingHired.com	www.gettinghired.com
Job Ability	www.jobability.com
JobAccess.org	www.jobaccess.org
Job Accommodation Network	http://askjan.org/
NBDC	www.business-disability.com/index.aspx
New Mobility	www.newmobility.com
Return 2 Work	www.return2work.org

Religion

Christian Jobs Online	www.christianjobs.com
Jewish Vocational Service Jobs Page	www.jvs-boston.org/index.php?option=com_content&task=view&id=104

Sexual Orientation

Pride Source   www.pridesource.com

Veterans

Army Career & Alumni Program   www.acap.army.mil

Blue-to-Gray   www.corporategray.com

Center for Employment Management   www.cfainstitute.org/pages/index.aspx

ClearanceJobs.com   www.clearancejobs.com

ClearedJobs.net   www.clearedjobs.net

Corporate Gray Online   www.corporategrayonline.com

The Defense Talent Network   www.defensetalent.com

Green-to-Gray   www.corporategray.com

HelmetstoHardhats.com   www.helmetstohardhats.com

Hire Quality   www.hire-quality.com

HireVetsFirst.gov   www.dol.gov/vets

Jobs4Vets.com   www.jobs4vets.com

Landmark Destiny Group   www2.recruitmilitary.com

Military.com   www.military.com

Military Careers   www.todaysmilitary.com/careers

Military Connection   www.militaryconnection.com

Military Connections   www.militaryconnections.com

MilitaryHire.com   www.militaryhire.com

MilitaryExits   www.militaryexits.com

Military JobZone   www.militaryjobzone.com

Military Spouse Corporate Career Network   www.msccn.org

Military Spouse Job Search   http://jobsearch.spouse.military.com

MilitaryStars.com   www.militarystars.com

My Future   www.myfuture.com

Operation Transition   https://www.dmdc.osd.mil/appj/dwp/index.jsp

RecruitAirForce.com   https://www2.recruitmilitary.com/

RecruitMarines.com   https://www2.recruitmilitary.com/

RecruitMilitary.com   https://www2.recruitmilitary.com/

RecruitNavy.com	https://www2.recruitmilitary.com/
Reserve Officers Association	www.roa.org/site/PageServer
Stripes.com	www.stripes.com
Transition Assistance Online	www.taonline.com
Veterans Today	www.veteranstoday.com
VetJobs	www.vetjobs.com

-E-

Economists

American Agricultural Economics Association	www.aaes.org
American Economic Association	www.aeaweb.org/joe
EconCareers	www.econcareers.com
Econ-Jobs.com	www.econ-jobs.com
Economist.com	www.economist.com
Inomics	www.inomics.com
International Health Economics Association	www.healtheconomics.org

Education/Academia

About.com	www.about.com/careers
Academic Careers Online	www.academiccareers.com
Academic Employment Network	www.academploy.com
AcademicKeys	www.academickeys.com
Academic Physician & Scientist	www.acphysci.com
Academic Position Network	www.apnjobs.com
Academic360	www.academic360.com
Affirmative Action Register	www.insightintodiversity.com
American Association of Physics Teachers	www.aapt.org

American Bankruptcy Institute Career Center	www.abiworld.org//AM/Template.cfm?Section=Home
American Educational Research Association Job Openings	www.jobtarget.com/home/index.cfm?site_id=557
American Psychological Society Observer Job Listings	www.psychologicalscience.org/jobs
ArtJob Online	www.artjob.org/cgi-local/displayPage.pl?page=index.html
Association for Environmental and Outdoor Education	www.aeoe.org
Association of Graduate Careers Advisory Service [United Kingdom]	www.agcas.org.uk
The Association for Institutional Research	www.airweb.org
Association of Teachers of Technical Writing	http://english.ttu.edu/ATTW
Association of University Teachers [United Kingdom]	www.AUT4Jobs.com
ATeacherJobSearch.com	www.ateacherjobsearch.com
BizSchoolJobs	www.bizschooljobs.com
Campus Review	www.campusreview.com.au
Canadian Society of Biochemistry and Molecular and Cellular Biologists	www.medicine.mcgill.ca/expmed/emjl/expmed_whoislinking.htm
Careers in Proprietary Education	www.propedu.com
ChristianUniversityJobs.com	www.christianuniversityjobs.com
ccJobsOnline.com	www.ccjobsonline.com
The Chronicle of Higher Education	http://chronicle.com/jobs
College and University Personnel Association JobLine	www.cupahr.org/jobline
Community Learning Network	www.cln.org
Computing Research Association Job Announcements	www.cra.org/ads
Council for Advancement & Support of Education Jobs Online	www.case.org/x26241.xml
Dave's ESL Café	www.eslcafe.com

The Directory Recruitment Service [Australia]	www.thedirectory.aone.net.au/page8.htm
EdJoin	www.edjoin.org
Education America Network	www.educationamerica.net
Education Bug	www.educationbug.org
EducationJobs.com	www.educationjobs.com
Education Week on the Web	www.edweek.org/ew/index.html
Education World Jobs	www.educationworld.com/jobs
EFLWEB: English as a Second or Foreign Language	www.eflweb.com
e-Math	www.ams.org/home/page
The ESL Café's Job Center	www.eslcafe.com/jobs
ESL Worldwide	www.eslworldwide.com
Eteach.com [United Kingdom]	www.eteach.com
FacultyJob.com	www.facultyjob.com
FEcareers.co.uk [United Kingdom]	www.fecareers.co.uk
FEjobs.com [United Kingdom]	www.fejobs.com
Foothill-De Anza Community College District	www.fhda.edu/jobs
GeoWebServices-RocketHire	www.geowebservices.com
GreatInfo.com	http://greatinfo.com
Grist.org	http://jobs.grist.org
Higher Careers.com	www.highercareers.com
HigherEdJobs.com	www.higheredjobs.com
The Higher Education Recruitment Consortium	www.hercjobs.org
HireEd.com	www.hireed.com
History of Science Society	www.hssonline.org
HotEducationJobs	www.hoteducationjobs.com
Hudson Institute	www.hudson.org
Humanities and Social Sciences Online	www.h-net.org
Independent School Management	http://isminc.com
Inside Higher Ed	www.insidehighered.com
Jaeger's Ince-Math	www.ams.org/home/page/employment
JOE: Job Opportunities for Economists	www.aeaweb.org/joe
JobsinEducation [United Kingdom]	www.jobsineducation.com

Jobs in Linguistics	http://linguistlist.org/jobs/
Jobs.ac.uk [United Kingdom]	www.jobs.ac.uk
K-12 Jobs	www.k12jobs.com
Library Job Postings	www.libraryjobpostings.org
Massachusetts Environmental Education Society	www.massmees.org
Math-Jobs	www.math-jobs.com
The Minerals, Metals, Materials Society JOM	www.tms.org/TMSHome.aspx
MinorityNurse.com	www.minoritynurse.com
Music Library Association Job Placement	www.musiclibraryassoc.org/employmentanded/joblist/index.shtml
NationJob Network-Education Job Openings	www.nationjob.com/education
National Association for College Admission Counseling Career Opportunities	www.nacac.com/classifieds.cfm
National Council of Teachers of Math Jobs	www.nctm.org
National Information Services and Systems [United Kingdom]	www.hero.ac.uk/uk/home/index.cfm
National Teacher Recruitment	www.recruitingteachers.com
National Women's Studies Association	www.nwsa.org
New England Higher Education Recruitment Consortium	www.newenglandherc.org/home/index.cfm?site_id=660
The New Jersey Higher Education Recruitment Consortium	www.njepadeherc.org/home/index.cfm?site_id=685
North American Association for Environmental Education	www.naaee.org
Now Hiring Teachers	www.nowhiringteachers.com
PhDjobs.com	www.phdjobs.com
Phds.org	www.phds.org
PhysicsToday.org	www.physicstoday.org
PLATO	www.skillsnet.com
RISE: Resources for Indispensable Schools and Educators	www.risenetwork.org
Scholarly Jobs	www.scholarlyjobs.com
School-Jobs	www.school-jobs.net

SchoolSpring.com	www.schoolspring.com
School Staff	www.schoolstaff.com
Scoted Jobs [Scotland]	www.scotedjobs.com
Superintendent Jobs	www.superintendentjobs.com
Teach for America	www.teachforamerica.org
Teach Network [United Kingdom]	www.teachnetwork.co.uk
Teacher Jobs	www.teacherjobs.com
Teachers of English to Speakers of Other Languages Job Finder	www.tesol.org/s_tesol/index.asp
Teachers-Teachers	www.teachers-teachers.com
TeachingJobs.com	www.teachingjobs.com
TedJob: Top Higher-Education Jobs	www.tedjob.com
Top School Jobs	www.topschooljobs.org
Tefl-jobs.co.uk [United Kingdom]	www.tefl-jobs.co.uk
University of Illinois at Urbana-Champaign Grad School of Library & Information Science Placement Online-Library Job Service	www.lis.illinois.edu/careers
University of Wisconsin School of Education	http://careers.education.wisc.edu
University Job Bank	www.universityjobs.com
UniversityJobs.com	www.universityjobs.com

Employee Referral

G2Bux	http://g2bux.ourtoolbar.com
H3.com	www.h3.com
Interview Exchange ReferredHire	www.interviewexchange.com
Jobster	www.jobster.com
JobThread.com	www.jobthread.com
JobTonic.com [United Kingdom]	www.jobtonic.com
Jobvite	http://recruiting.jobvite.com
KarmaOne	www.karmaone.com

Energy & Utilities

Akhtaboot [Jordan]	www.akhtaboot.com
Aljazeerajobs.com [Middle East]	www.aljazeerajobs.com
Bayt.com [United Arab Emirates]	www.bayt.com
Careerjunctionme.com [Middle East]	www.careerjunctionme.com
Careers in Wind	www.careersinwind.com
Drilling Research Institute Classifieds	www.drillers.com/pages/view/jobs
Earthworks-Jobs.com [United Kingdom]	www.earthworks-jobs.com
Energy Careers	www.energycareers.com
Energy Central Jobs	www.energycentraljobs.com
EnergyJobsNetwork	www.energyjobsnetwork.com
Energy Jobs Portal	www.energyjobsportal.com
Electric Net	www.electricnet.com
Get Utility Jobs	www.getutilityjobs.com
Green Energy Jobs	www.greenenergyjobs.com
GreenEnergyJobsOnline.com	www.greenenergyjobsonline.com
iHireUtilities	www.ihireutilities.com
Jobs in Biofuels	www.jobsinbiofuels.com
Jobs in Solar Power	www.jobsinsolarpower.com
Jobs in Wind Power	www.jobsinwindpower.com
NaukriGulf.com [Middle East]	www.naukrigulf.com
NukeWorker.com	www.nukeworker.com
Oil & Gas Jobs	www.earthworks-jobs.com
OilandGasJobSearch	www.oilandgasjobsearch.com
Oil Career	www.oilcareer.com
OilCareers.com	www.oilcareers.com
Oil Exec	www.oilexec.com
Oil Industry Jobs	www.oilsurvey.com
Oil Job	www.oiljob.com
Oil-Offshore Marine	www.oil-offshore-marine.com
PennEnergyJobs.com	www.pennenergyjobs.com
Petroleum & Mining Job Portal	www.pmjobs.net
Power Magazine	www.powermag.com

Power Online	www.poweronline.com
Power Plant Pro	www.powerplantpro.com
Professional Energy Jobs	www.professionalenergyjobs.com
RenewableEnergyJobs.com [United Kingdom]	www.renewableenergyjobs.com
RenewableEnergyWorld.com	www.renewableenergyworld.com
RigZone	www.rigzone.com
SecurityClearedJobs.com [United Kingdom]	www.securityclearedjobs.com
SustainableBusiness.com	www.sustainablebusiness.com
Think Network	www.globalenergyjobs.com
Utility Jobs Online	www.utilityjobsonline.com
World Oils	www.worldoils.com
WorldwideWorker	www.worldwideworker.com

Engineering

Engineering-General

AEJob.com	www.aejob.com
A1A Jobs	www.a1ajobs.com
All4Engineers.de [Germany]	www.all4engineers.com
AmericanJobs.com	www.americanjobs.com
Balfour Betty Rail UK [United Kingdom]	www.bbrailjobs.com
Bayt.com [United Arab Emirates]	www.bayt.com
Beechwood Recruit [United Kingdom]	www.beechwoodrecruit.com
Career Marketplace Network	www.careermarketplace.com
Degree Hunter	http://degreehunter.net
Dice	www.dice.com
Discover Jobs	www.discover-jobs.com
The Engineer [United Kingdom]	www.theengineer.co.uk
Engineer.net	www.engineer.net
EngineerBoard [United Kingdom]	www.engineerboard.co.uk
EngineerJobs.com	www.engineerjobs.com
Engineering Central	www.engcen.com/jobbank.htm

Engineering Classifieds	www.engineeringclassifieds.com/Main/ Default.asp
Engineering Giant	www.engineergiant.com
Engineering Institute of Canada	www.eic-ici.ca
EngineeringJobs.com	www.engineeringjobs.com
EngineeringJobs.co.uk [United Kingdom]	www.engineeringjobs.co.uk
EngineeringJobsNow [United Kingdom]	www.engineeringjobsnow.co.uk
Engineering News Record	http://enrconstruction.com
Engineer Web	www.engineerweb.com
The Engineering Specific Career Advisory Problem-Solving Environment	https://engineering.purdue.edu/Engr
The Engineering Technology Site [United Kingdom]	www.engineers4engineers.co.uk
4EngineeringJobs	www.4engineeringjobs.com
iHireEngineering.com	www.ihireengineering.com
In Automotive [United Kingdom]	www.inautomotive.com
interEC.net	www.interec.net
Jim Finder [United Kingdom]	www.jimfinder.com
Job Net	www.jobnet.org
Job Search for Engineers	www.interec.net
Jobs 4 Engineers	www.ajob4engineers.com
Jobs4Engineering.com	www.jobs4eng.com
JobsinConstruction [United Kingdom]	www.jobsinconstruction.co.uk
JobsinSurveying [United Kingdom]	www.jobsinsurveying.co.uk
JustEngineers.net [Australia]	www.justengineers.net
National Society of Professional Engineers Employment	www.nspe.org/Employment/index.html
PennEnergyJobs.com	www.pennenergyjobs.com
PlanetRecruit [United Kingdom]	www.planetrecruit.com
QualityEngineerJobs.com	www.qualityengineerjobs.com
Rail Job Search [United Kingdom]	www.railjobsearch.com/index.html
ReferWork-Jobs.com	www.referwork-jobs.com
SecurityClearedJobs.com [United Kingdom]	www.securityclearedjobs.com

Tech Employment   www.techemployment.com

ThaiEngineeringJobs.com [Thailand]   www.thaiengineerjobs.com/en/index.asp

Think Network   www.thinkjobs.com

Utility Job Search [United Kingdom]   www.utilityjobsearch.com

Worldwide Worker   www.worldwideworker.com

Aeronautical/Aviation

Aeroindustryjobs   www.aeroindustryjobs.com

Aeronautical Engineering Jobs [United Kingdom] www.aeronauticalengineeringjobs.co.uk

Aerospace Jobs   http://hometown.aol.com/aerojobs

AeroSpaceNews.com   www.aerospacenews.com

AircraftEngineers.com [United Kingdom]   www.aircraftengineers.com

Agricultural

American Society of Agricultural and Biological   www.asabe.org
      Engineers

Chemical

American Chemical Society   http://portal.acs.org/portal/acs/corg/content

American Institute of Chemical Engineers   www.aiche.org/careers
      Career Services

Chemical Engineer   www.chemicalengineer.com

ChemJobs.net   www.chemjobs.net/chemjobs.html

Jobs in Chemistry   www/jobsinchemistry.com

National Organization for Black Chemists and   www.engin.umich.edu/societies/nobcche
      Chemical Engineers

Civil

American Society of Civil Engineers   www.asce.org

Civil Engineering Central   www.civilengineeringcentral.com

Civil Engineering Jobs   www.civilengineeringjobs.com

CIVILjobs.com	www.civiljobs.com
iCivil Engineer	www.icivilengineer.com/jobs

Construction

A/E/C Job Bank	www.aecjobbank.com
CED Magazine	www.cedmagazine.com
PlumbingCareers.com	www.plumbingcareers.com
PLUMBjob.com	www.plumbjobs.com
Structural Engineer Job Source	www.structuralengineerjobsource.com
Utility Jobs Online	www.utilityjobsonline.com

Diversity

National Society of Black Engineers	http://national.nsbe.org
Society of Hispanic Professional Engineers Career Services	www.shpe.org
Society of Mexican American Engineers and Scientists	www.maes-natl.org
Society of Women Engineers Career Services	http://careers.swe.org

Electrical/Electronics

EDN Access	www.edn.com
eeProductCenter	http://cmpmedia.globalspec.com
EE Times	www.eetimes.com
Electric Net	www.electricnet.com
Electrical Engineer	www.electricalengineer.com
ElectroMagneticCareers.com	www.electromagneticcareers.com
Electronic News Online	www.edn.com
Institute of Electrical & Electronics Engineers Job Site	www.ieee.org/education_careers/index.html
National Electrical Contractors Association	www.necanet.org
RF Globalnet	www.rfglobalnet.com
Test & Measurement World	www.tmworld.com

UG Job Network (Unigraphics CAD/CAM/CAE) www.ugjn.com
Yaps4u.net www.yaps4u.net

Environmental

Earthworks-Jobs.com [United Kingdom] www.earthworks-jobs.com
Environmental Construction Engineering www.eceajobs.com
      Architectural Jobs Online
GeoWebServices-RocketHire www.geowebservices.com
Grist.org http://jobs.grist.org

Industrial/Manufacturing

AutomationTechies.com www.automationtechies.com
iHireManufacturingEngineers.com www.ihiremanufacturingengineers.com
Industrial Engineer www.industrialengineer.com
NukeWorker.com www.nukeworker.com
Plastics Jobs Forum.com www.plasticsjobsforum.com
Power Magazine www.powermag.com

Mechanical

American Society of Mechanical Engineers www.asme.org/jobs
    Career Center
Jobs for Mechanical Engineers www.mechanicalengineer.com
Mechanical Engineers Magazine Online www.memagazine.orgg

Mining/Petroleum

Drilling Research Institute Classifieds www.drillers.com/pages/view/jobs
Ethanol-Jobs.com www.ethanol-jobs.com
Job Oil www.joboil.com
The Minerals, Metals, Materials Society JOM www.tms.org/TMSHome.aspx
Oil & Gas Jobs www.earthworks-jobs.com/comm.htm
Oil Career www.oilcareer.com

Oil Industry Jobs	www.oilsurvey.com
Oil Job	www.oiljob.com
RigZone.com	www.rigzone.com

Software

Career Center @ Semiconductor Online	www.semiconductoronline.com
Computer-Aided Three-Dimensional Interactive Application Job Network	www.catjn.com
Semi Web	www.semiweb.com

Systems

The Instrumentation, Systems and Automation Society Online ISA Jobs	www.isa.org/isa_es
Society for Information Display	www.sid.org/jobmart/jobmart.htmll

Transportation

Right Of Way	www.rightofway.com
RoadTechs.com	www.roadtechs.com
Society of Automotive Engineers Job Board	www.sae.org/careers/recruitad.htm
Society of Naval Architects and Marine Engineers	www.sname.org/SNAME/SNAME/Homeg

Other Specialty

Biodiesel-Jobs	www.biodiesel-jobs.com
Biomedical Engineering Society	www.bmes.org/aws/BMES/pt/sp/home_page
CFD Online (Computational Fluid Dynamics)	www.cfd-online.com
Contract Employment Weekly	www.ceweekly.com
Graduating Engineer & Computer Careers Online	www.graduatingengineer.com
Human Factors Careers	www.hfcareers.com

International Society for Pharmaceutical Engineering	www.ispe.org
JustCADJobs.com	www.justcadjobs.com
MaterialsEngineerJobs.com	www.materialsengineeerjobs.com
National Association of Grad & Prof Students	www.nagps.org
National Association of Radio and Telecommunications Engineers	www.narte.org
QA Engineer Jobs	www.qaengineerjobs.com
QualityEngineerJobs.com	www.qualityengineerjobs.com
ScientistWorld.com [United Kingdom]	www.scientistworld.com
Space Jobs	www.spacejobs.com
SPIE Web-International Society for Optical Engineering	http://spie.org/app/buyersguide/index.aspx
Wireless Design Online	www.wirelessdesignonline.com

Entertainment/Acting

Airwaves Media Web	www.airwaves.com
Airwaves Media Web	www.airwaves.com
Answers4Dancers.com	www.answers4dancers.com
ArtJob Online	www.artjob.org
Backstage.com	www.backstage.combso/index.jsp
BestRad!oJobs	www.bestradiojobs.com
Casting-America	www.castingsociety.com
Casting Daily	www.castingnet.com
CreativeJobsCentral.com	www.creativejobscentral.com
CrewNet	www.crewnet.com
CruiseShipJobs.com	www.cruiseshipjobs.com
Dance USA	www.danceusa.org
Designer Max	www.designermax.com
Entertainment Careers	www.entertainmentcareers.net
EntertainmentJobs.com	www.entertainmentjobs.com
Employment Network	www.employnow.com

Filmbiz.com	www.filmbiz.com
4 Entertainment Jobs	www.4entertainmentjobs.com
Grapevine Jobs [United Kingdom]	www.grapevinejobs.com/home.asp
Hollywood Web	www.hollywoodweb.com
JobMonkey.com	www.jobmonkey.com
Mass Media Jobs	www.massmediajobs.com
Media Communications Association International Job Hotline	www.mca-i.org
National Association of Broadcasters	www.nab.org
New England Film	www.newenglandfilm.com/jobs.htm
Opportunities Online [United Kingdom]	www.opps.co.uk
PlanetSharkProductions.com	www.planetsharkproductions.com
Playbill On-Line	www.playbill.com
ProductionBase.co.uk [United Kingdom]	www.productionbase.co.uk
Radio Online	http://menu.radio-online.com/cgi-bin/ rolmenu.exe/menu
Showbizjobs.com	www.showbizjobs.com
Show Biz Data	www.showbizdata.com
Society of Broadcast Engineers	www.sbe.org
Theatre Jobs	www.theatrejobs.com
TVjobs.com	www.tvjobs.com
TV and Radio Jobs	www.tvandradiojobs.com
VarietyCareers.com	http://thebiz.variety.com/home/index.cfm? site_id=7307
Voice of Dance	www.voiceofdance.com/v1/index.cfm

Environmental

AEJob.com	www.aejob.com
American College of Occupational and Environmental Medicine	www.acoem.org
American Water Works Association Career Center (Water Jobs)	www.awwa.org

APSnet-Plant Pathology Online	www.apsnet.org
Association for Environmental and Outdoor Education	www.aeoe.org
AutomationTechies.com	www.automationtechies.com
Biodiesel-Jobs	www.biodiesel-jobs.com
Bright Green Talent	www.brightgreentalent.com
Earthworks-Jobs.com [United Kingdom]	www.earthworks-jobs.com
Eco.org	www.eco.org
EE-Link: The Environmental Education Web Server	http://eelink.net/pages/EE+Jobs+Database
EHScareers.com	www.ehscareers.com
EnviroNetwork	www.environetwork.org/default.aspx
EnvironmentalCareer Center	www.environmentalcareer.com
Environmental Career Opportunities	www.ecojobs.com
Environmental Careers Bulletin Online	www.ecbonline.com
Environmental Careers Organization	www.eco.org
Environmental Careers World	www.environmentaljobs.com
Environmental Construction Engineering Architectural Jobs Online	www.eceajobs.com
Environmental Data Interactive Exchange Job Centre [United Kingdom]	www.edie.net
Environmental Employment Pages	www.datacorinc.com/employment.php
Environmental Engineer	www.environmentalengineer.com
Environmental-Expert.com	www.environmental-expert.com
Environmental Jobs	www.environmentaljobs.com
Environmental Jobs & Careers	www.ejobs.org
Environmental Nes	www.enn.com
EnviroWorld	www.enviroworld.com
Ethanol-Jobs.com	www.ethanol-jobs.com
GeoWebServices-RocketHire	www.geowebservices.com
GIS Jobs Clearinghouse	www.gjc.org
Great Green Careers	www.greatgreencareers.com
GreenBiz.com	http://jobs.greenbiz.com//

Green Dream Jobs	www.sustainablebusiness.com
Green Energy Jobs	www.greenenergyjobs.com
GreenEnergyJobsOnline.com	www.greenenergyjobsonline.com
GreenJobs.com	www.greenjobs.com
Green Jobs Online [United Kingdom]	www.greenjobsonline.co.uk
Job.com	www.job.com
Jobs In Waste [United Kingdom]	www.jobsinwaste.co.uk
Massachusetts Environmental Education Society	www.massmees.org
National Environmental Health Association	www.neha.org
Nevada Mining	www.nevadamining.org
New Scientist Jobs	www.newscientistjobs.com
North American Association for Environmental Education	www.naaee.org
Organic-Chemistry	www.organic-chemistry.org
Pollution Online	www.pollutiononline.com
Power Online	www.poweronline.com
Public Works	www.publicworks.com
Pulp & Paper Online	www.pulpandpaperonline.com
PureGreenJobs.com	www.puregreenjobs.com
RenewableEnergyJobs	www.renewableenergyjobs.net
RenewableEnergyWorld.com	www.renewableenergyworld.com
The Science Jobs	www.thesciencejobs.com
Solar Jobs [United Kingdom]	www.solarjobs.com
Solid Waste	www.solidwaste.com
Student Conservation Association	www.thesca.org
SustainableBusiness.com	www.sustainablebusiness.com
Universities Water Information Network	www.ucowr.siu.edu
Water Online	www.wateronline.com

Equipment Leasing

Equipment Leasing and Finance Association	www.elfaonline.org
Jobvertise	www.jobvertise.com

Leasing News	www.leasingnews.org/Classified/Jwanted/ Jwanted.htm

Exchanges-Recruiter/Employment/Job Seeker

America's Job Exchange	www.americasjobexchange.com
@Recruiter.com	www.atrecruiter.com
Avoxa.com	www.avoxa.fr/v2/htm
Dealsplit.com	www.dealsplit.com
eLance	www.elance.com
FreelancingProjects.com	www.freelancingprojects.com
Guru.com	www.guru.com
HotGigs	www.hotgigs.com
JobCentral.com	www.jobcentral.com
RentaCoder.com	www.vworker.com/RentACoder/DotNet/ default.aspx
Sologig.com	www.sologig.com

Executive/Management

Executive-General

AllExecutiveJobs.com [United Kingdom]	www.allexecutivejobs.com
TheBigChair.com.au [Australia]	http://thebigchair.com.au
B7 Appointments [United Kingdom]	www.business7.co.uk/b7-appointments
Association of Executive Search Consultants	www.bluesteps.com
CareerJournal.com	http://online.wsj.com/public/page/ news-career-jobs.html
CFO.com	www.cfo.com
CFO Jobsite	www.cfojobsite.com
CIO	http://itjobs.cio.com/a/all-jobs/list?source= top_nav/
Consultants Board [United Kingdom]	www.consultantsboard.com

Consultants United [United Kingdom]	www.consultantsunited.com
CVTrumpet.co.uk [United Kingdom]	www.cvtrumpet.co.uk
eChannelLinecareers.com [Canada]	www.echannellinecareers.com
Exec2Exec.com [United Kingdom]	www.exec2exec.com
ExecuNet	www.execunet.com
execSearches.com	www.execsearches.com
TheExecutiveClub.com [United Kingdom]	www.theexecutiveclub.com
Executive-i.com [United Kingdom]	www.executive-i.com
ExecutiveOpenings.com [United Kingdom]	www.executiveopenings.com
Executive Placement Services	www.execplacement.com
Executive Registry	www.executiveregistry.com
Executive Taskforce [New Zealand]	http://executivetaskforce.org/
Executives Online [United Kingdom]	www.executivesonline.co.uk
ExecutivesontheWeb.com [United Kingdom]	www.executivesontheweb.com
ExecutivesOnly.com	www.executivesonly.com
Experteer.co.uk [United Kingdom]	www.experteer.co.uk
FazJob.net [Germany]	http://fazjob.net
50kandup.com	http://jobs.50kandup.com/home/index.cfm? site_id=2167
GoldJobs [United Kingdom]	www.goldjobs.com/overview/default.asp
Grist.org	http://jobs.grist.org
High Tech Partners [United Kingdom]	www.hightechpartners.com
NetShare	www.netshare.com
New Life Network [United Kingdom]	www.newlifenetwork.co.uk
PlatinumJobs.com [United Kingdom]	www.platinumjobs.com/overview/default.asp
RiteSite.com	www.ritesite.com/Login/index.cfm
Score	www.scn.org/civic/score-online
Seek Executive [Australia]	http://executive.seek.com.au
Top-Consultant.com [United Kingdom]	www.top-consultant.com/UK/career/ appointments.asp

Management-General

The American Management Association Management Jobs	http://management-jobs.amanet.org
CardBrowser.com	www.cardbrowser.com
CareerFile	www.careerfile.com
Corporate Alumni	www.selectminds.com
Eclectic [Netherlands]	www.eclectic.eu
Futurestep	www.futurestep.com
Institute of Management & Administration's Supersite	www.ioma.com
International Economic Development Council	www.iedconline.org
Jobs.ac.uk [United Kingdom]	www.jobs.ac.uk
Jobs4Managers.com	www.jobs4managers.com
TheLadders.com	www.theladders.com
MBA Careers	www.mbacareers.com
MBA Global Net	www.mbaglobalnet.com
Monster Management	www.monster.com
Multiunitjobs.com	www.multiunitjobs.com
National Black MBA Association	www.nbmbaa.org
Net Expat	www.netexpat.com
PMjob.ca [Canada]	www.pmjob.ca
6FigureJobs	www.6figurejobs.com
Stern Alumni Outreach Career	www.stern.nyu.edu
TopJobs.ch [Switzerland]	www.topjobs.ch
Zhaopin.com [China]	www.zhaopin.com

Career Field-Specific

CM Today	www.cmcrossroads.com
Compliance Jobs	www.compliancejobs.com
Construction Executive Online	www.constructionexecutive.com
Financial Executives Institute Career Center	www.financialexecutives.org
Ft.com-Financial Times [United Kingdom]	www.ft.com

Hispanic American Police Command Officers Association	www.hapcoa.org
National Organization of Black Law Enforcement Executives	www.noblenational.org
NursingExecutives.com	www.nursingexecutives.com

Industry-Specific

American Bankers Association	http://aba.careerbank.com
American College of Healthcare Executives	http://ache.org
American College of Physician Executives	www.acpe.org
American Society of Association Executives CareerHQ	www.careerhq.org
boardnetUSA	www.boardnetusa.org/public/home.asp
The Brass Key	www.thepoliceexecutive.com
CFO Publishing	http://cfonet.com
HospitalityExecutive.com	www.hospitalityexecutive.com
Medical Group Management Association	www.mgma.com
New York Society of Association Executives Career Center	www.nysaenet.org/NYSAENET/NYSAENET/Home
Women Executives in Public Relations	www.wepr.org
GxPJobs.com [United Kingdom]	www.gxpjobs.com

-F-

Fashion

Be The 1	www.bethe1.com/en
DrapersOnline [United Kingdom]	www.drapersonline.com
Fashion Career Center	www.fashioncareercenter.com
Fashion Group International	www.fgi.org
Fashion Net	www.fashion.net/jobs
CreativeJobsCentral.com	www.creativejobscentral.com

RagTradeJobs.com [Australia]   www.ragtradejobs.com

Feminism

FeministCampus.org   www.feministcampus.org
Feminist Majority Foundation Online   www.feminist.org

Fiber Optics

The Fiber Optic Association   www.thefoa.org/foanewsletter.
     html#anchor651744

Fiber Optic Marketplace   www.fiberoptic.com
Fiber Optics Online   www.fiberopticsonline.com

Finance & Accounting (See also Banking, Insurance)

Accounting-General

AccountancyAgeJobs.com [United Kingdom]   www.accountancyagejobs.com
AccountancyJobsBoard [United Kingdom]   www.accountancyjobsboard.co.uk
Accountant Careers   www.accountantcareers.com
Accountant Gigs   www.accountantgigs.com
AccountantJobs.com   www.accountantjobs.com
Accountant Jobs Chicago   www.accountantjobschicago.com
AccountManager.com   www.accountmanager.com
Accounting.com   www.accounting.com
Accounting & Finance Jobs   www.accountingjobs.com
Accounting Classifieds   www.accountingclassifieds.com/Main/Default.asp
Accounting Jobs in New York   www.accounting-jobs-in-new-york.com
Accounting Jobs Online   www.accountingjobsonline.com
Accounting Jobs Today   www.accountingjobstoday.com
AccountingNet   www.accountingnet.com

Accounting Now	www.accountingnow.com
Accounting Professional	www.accountingprofessional.com
Ambition [Australia]	www.ambition.com.au
American Accounting Association Web Placement Service	http://aaahq.org/placements/default.cfm
American Society of Women Accountants	www.aswact.org
AndersenAlumni.net	www.andersenalumni.net
Antsjobs.ie [Ireland]	www.antsjobs.ie
Awesome Accountants	www.awesomeaccountants.comh/aa.asp
Bean Brains	www.beanbrains.com
CA Magazine	www.camagazine.com
CASource [Canada]	www.casource.com
Certified Management Accountants of Canada	www.cma-canada.org
iHire Accounting	www.ihireaccounting.com
JobsFinancial [United Kingdom]	www.jobsfinancial.com
Jobs4Accounting	www.jobs4accounting.com
MyAccountancyJobs [United Kingdom]	www.myaccountancyjobs.com
MyAccountingJobs.net	www.myaccountingjobs.net
National Association of Black Accountants, Inc. Career Center	http://nabacareercenter.nabainc.org/index.cfm?
National Society of Accountants	www.nsacct.org/index.asp
Search Accounting Jobs	www.searchaccountingjobs.com
ThaiFinanceJobs.com [Thailand]	www.thaifinancejobs.com/en/index.asp
TotallyFinancial.com.au [Australia]	www.totallyfinancial.com/australia

Accountants-Certified Public Accountants

American Association of Hispanic Certified Public Accountants	www.aahcpa.org
American Institute of Certified Public Accountants Career Center	www.cpa2biz.com
CPA Jobs	www.cpajobs.com
CPANet	www.cpanet.com
Illinois CPA Society Career Center	www.icpas.org/hc-career-center.aspx?id=2178

Institute of Management Accountants Career Center	www.imanet.org/development_career.asp
Inside Careers Guide to Chartered Accountancy [United Kingdom]	www.insidecareers.co.uk
Institute of Chartered Accountants of Alberta [Canada]	www.albertacas.ca/Home.aspxhttp://www.albertacas.ca/Home.aspx
Maryland Association of CPAs Job Connect	www.macpa.org/content/classifieds/public/search.aspx
New Jersey Society of CPAs	www.njscpa.org
New York State Society of CPAs	www.nysscpa.org/classified/main.cfm
Tennessee Society of CPA's	www.tscpa.com

Audit

AccountantAuditor.net	www.accountantauditor.net
Audit Jobs Chicago	www.auditjobschicago.com
Audit Net	www.auditnet.org
AuditProfessional.com	www.auditprofessional.com
AuditorJobs.com	www.auditorjobs.com
Institute of Internal Auditors Online Audit Career Center	www.theiia.org/careers
InternalAuditJobs.net [United Kingdom]	www.internalauditjobs.net

Brokerage/Investment

Advocis	www.advocis.ca
Annuitiesnet.com	www.annuitiesnet.com/v2
Association for Investment Management and Research	www.cfainstitute.org
Bond Buyer	www.bondbuyer.com
BrokerHunter.com	www.brokerhunter.com
International Association for Registered Financial Planners	http://careers.iarfc.org
Investment Management and Trust Exchange	www.antaeans.com

National Venture Capital Association	www.nvca.org
New York Society of Security Analysts Career Resources	www.nyssa.org/AM/Template. cfm?Section=career_development
Securities Industry Association Career Resource Center	www.sifma.com/services/career_center/ career_center.html
Society of Actuaries	www.soa.org
Society of Risk Analysis Opportunities	www.sra.org/opportunities.php
WallStJobs.com	www.wallstjobs.com

Finance-General

American Association of Finance & Accounting	www.aafa.com/careers.html
American Bankruptcy Institute Career Center	www.abiworld.org
Association of Finance Professionals Career Services	www.afponline.org/pub/cs/career_services.html
Association of Latino Professionals in Finance & Accounting Job Postings	www.alpfa.org
Bloomberg.com	www.bloomberg.com
Business Finance Magazine	http://businessfinancemag.com
Business-Money Magazine	www.business-money.com
CareerBank.com	www.careerbank.com
CareerJournal.com	http://online.wsj.com/public/page/ news-career-jobs.html
CareerJournal.com Europe	http://online.wsj.com/public/page/ news-career-jobs.html
Careers in Finance	www.careers-in-finance.com
CFO.com	www.cfo.com
CFOEurope.com	www.cfoeurope.com
CFO and CPA Jobs	www.cfoandcpajobs.com
CFO Publishing	http://cfonet.com
eFinancial Careers	www.efinancialcareers.com
eFinancialCareers.fr [France]	www.efinancialcareers.fr
The Finance Beat	www.search-beat.com/finance.htm
Finance and Commerce	www.finance-commerce.com

Finance Job Network	www.financialjobnet.com
Finance Job Store	www.financejobstore.com
FinanceJobs.net	www.financejobs.net
Financial Executives Institute Career Center	www.financialexecutives.org
Financial Executive Networking Group	www.thefeng.org
Financial Job Bank	www.financialjobbank.com
Financial Job Network	www.fjn.com
FinancialJobs.com	www.financialjobs.com
Financial Management Association International Placement Services	www.fma.org/Placement
Financial Managers Society Career Center	www.fmsinc.org/default.aspx
Financial Positions	www.financialpositions.com/Main/Default.asp
Financial Women International Careers	www.fwi.org
FINS from The Wall Street Journal	www.fins.com
Fortune	http://money.cnn.com/magazines/fortune/
Ft.com -Financial Times [United Kingdom]	www.ft.com
GAAP Web [United Kingdom]	www.gaapweb.com
iHire Finance	www.ihirefinance.com
JobWings.com	www.jobwings.com
JobsFinancial.com [United Kingdom]	www.jobsfinancial.com
jobsinthemoney.com	www.jobsinthemoney.com
TheLadders.com	www.theladders.com
NationJob Network: Financial Jobs Page	www.nationjob.com/financial
PfJobs [United Kingdom]	www.pfjobs.co.uk
QUANTster.com [United Kingdom]	www.quantster.com
Smart Pros FinanceJobs.com	http://accounting.smartpros.com/x10522.xml

Financial Analysis

Actuary.com	www.actuary.com
Alliance of Merger and Acquisition Advisors	www.amaaonline.com
American Association for Budget and Program Analysis	www.aabpa.org/main/careerdev.htm#jobs
Capital Markets Credit Analysts Society	www.cmcas.org

Resume Service

CFA Institute	www.cfainstitute.org
Global Association of Risk Professionals Career Center	www.garp.com/careercenter/index.asp
Hedge Fund Intelligence LLC [United Kingdom]	www.hedgefundintelligence.com
JobsinRisk.com [United Kingdom]	www.jobsinrisk.com
QuantFinanceJobs.com	www.quantfinancejobs.com
QUANTster.com	www.quantster.com
Risk & Insurance Management Society Careers	www.rims.org/resources/careercenter/Pages/default.aspx
Risk Management Web	www.riskmanagementweb.com
Toronto Society of Financial Analysts [Canada]	www.tsfa.ca
UnderwritingJobs.com	www.uwjobs.com

Finance-Banking

American Bankers Association	http://aba.careerbank.com
BankingBoard.com	www.bankingboard.com
BankJobs	www.bankjobs.com
CreditJobs.com	http://creditjobs.com/index.asp
CreditUnionBoard.com	www.creditunionboard.net
Escrowboard.com	www.escrowboard.net
FindMortgageJobs.com	www.findmortgagejobs.com
JobsinCredit [United Kingdom]	www.jobsincredit.com
MortgageBoard.com	www.mortgageboard.com
Mortgage Job Store	www.mortgagejobstore.com
National Banking Network	www.banking-financejobs.com
Titleboard.net	www.titleboard.net

Finance-Controller

Cash Management Career Center	www.amgi.com
Controller Jobs	www.controllerjobs.com

Finance-Other

Fund Raising Jobs	www.fundraisingjobs.com
Healthcare Financial Management Association	www.hfma.org
IFSjobs.com	www.ifsjobs.com
JobsinCredit [United Kingdom]	www.jobsincredit.com
JobsinRisk.com [United Kingdom]	www.jobsinrisk.com
MBA Careers	www.mbacareers.com
MBA-Exchange.com	www.mba-exchange.com
MBA Free Agents	www.mbafreeagents.com
MBAGlobalNet	www.mbaglobalnet.com
MBAJobs.net	www.mbajobs.net/
MBAmatch.com [England]	www.mbamatch.com
MBA Style Magazine	www.mbastyle.com
MBATalentWire.com	www.mbatalentwire.com
National Black MBA Association, Inc.	www.nbmbaa.org
National Society of Hispanic MBAs Career Center	www.nshmba.org
Real Estate Finance Jobs	www.realestatefinancejobs.com
Smart Money	www.smartmoney.com

Tax

CareersinAudit [Europe]	www.careersinaudit.com/home/home.aspx
Planet Audit [United Kingdom]	www.planetaudit.net
eTaxjobs.com	www.etaxjobs.com
Tax Jobs	www.taxjobs.com
Tax Jobs Chicago	www.taxjobschicago.com
Tax-Talent.com	www.tax-talent.com

Free Lance/Free Agents

AF Work	www.allfreelancework.com
AllFreeLance.com	www.allfreelance.com

American Society of Journalists & Authors	www.freelancewritersearch.com
Editorial Freelancers Association	www.the-efa.org
eLance	www.elance.com
FreeLanceMom.com	www.freelancemom.com
FreeLanceWriting.com	www.freelancewriting.com
FreeLancers Network [United Kingdom]	www.freelancers.net
FreeLancingProjects.com	www.freelancingprojects.com
Go Freelance	www.gofreelance.com
Guru.com	www.guru.com
HotGigs.com	www.hotgigs.com
iFreelance.com	www.ifreelance.com
Real-Home-Employment	www.real-home-employment.com
RentaCoder.com	www.vworker.com
SoloGig	www.sologig.com
Training Consortium	www.trainingconsortium.net
Telecommuting Jobs	www.tjobs.com

Funeral Industry/Services

Abbott and Hast Classifieds	www.abbottandhast.com/classads.html
FuneralNet	www.funeralnet.com
FuneralWire.com	www.funeralwire.com
National Funeral Directors Association	www.nfda.org

-G-

Gaming

BlueFoxJobs.com	www.bluefoxjobs.com
Casino Careers Online	www.casinocareers.com
CroupierLink.com	www.croupierlink.com
Game Jobs	www.gamejobs.com

General

50kandup.com	http://jobs.50kandup.com
555-1212	www.555-1212.com
About Jobs	www.aboutjobs.com
Abracat	www.abracat.com
ActiJob	www.act1staff.com
Adicio	www.adicio.com
Adquest 3D	www.adquest3d.com
AECPII	www.aecpii.com
Alianza (Latino)	www.alianza.org
AllStarJobs	www.allstarjobs.com
AmericanJobs.com	www.americanjobs.com
American Preferred Jobs	www.preferredjobs.com
AmpleJobs	www.amplejobs.com
Ants.com	www.ants.com
Any Who	www.anywho.com
Asianet	www.asianetglobal.com
Association Job Source	www.jobsourcenetwork.com
AssociationJobBoards.com	www.associationjobboards.com
Authoria	www.authoria.com
Available Jobs	www.availablejobs.com
BaseJobs.com [Canada]	www.basejobs.com
Bayt.com [United Arab Emirates]	www.bayt.com
BDOJobs.com	www.bdojobs.com
Best Jobs USA	www.bestjobsusa.com
Best Local Jobs	www.bestlocaljobs.com
Big Dog Hub	www.bigdoghub.com
Biz Journals	www.bizjournals.com/jobs
Black Career Women Online	www.bcw.org
THE BLACK COLLEGIAN Online	www.blackcollegian.com
BlowSearch	www.blowsearch.com
Blue Collar Jobs	www.bluecollarjobs.com
Boldface Jobs	www.boldfacejobs.com

Boston Globe	www.boston.com/bostonglobe
Branch Staff Online	www.branchstaffonline.com
Business Week Online	www.businessweek.com/managing/career
Career.com	www.career.com
CareerBoard	www.careerboard.com
CareerBuilder.com	www.careerbuilder.com
CareerLink.com	http://america.careerlink.com
Career Center	www.careercenters.com
The Career Connection	www.career-connection.com
CareerExposure	www.careerexposure.com
Careerfile.com	www.careerfile.com
Career Giant	www.careergiant.com
CareerLife Connection	www.careerlifeconnection.com
Career Magazine	www.careermag.com
Careermetasearch.com	www.careermetasearch.com
Career Network	www.career-network.com
Career Quest	http://careerquestusa.com
Career Resource Center	www.careers.org
CareerShop	www.autohiresoftware.com
Careers.org	www.careers.org
Career Span	http://careerspan.com/hc3.asp
Career Talk	www.careertalkguys.com
Career Xchange	www.careerxchange.com
CareerMVP.com	www.careermvp.com
CBCJobs.com	www.cbcjobs.com
Chain Store Guide	www.chainstoreguide.com
Chattanooga Publishing	www.chatpub.com
Chowk	www.chowk.com
City Search.com	www.citysearch.com
Classifieds 2000	www.classifieds2000.com
Classified Solutions Group	www.classifiedsolutionsgroup.com
Climber	www.climber.com
Community Associations Institute	www.caionline.org/Pages/Default.aspx

Contract Employment Connection	www.ntes.com
Contract-Jobs.com	www.contract-jobs.com
craigslist	www.craigslist.org
Creative Hotlist	www.creativehotlist.com
Customer Service Management	www.csm-us.co
Daily Digest	www.le-digest.com
Database America	www.infousa.com
Delphi Forums	http://delphi.com
DirectEmployers Association	www.directemployers.org
Direct Marketing Association	www.the-dma.org/careercenter
Diversity Careers	www.diversitycareers.com
Diversity Employment	www.diversityemployment.com
DiversityLink	www.diversitylink.com
Diversity Search	www.diversitysearch.com
eBullpen.com	www.ebullpen.com
e-learning Jobs	www.e-learningjobs.com
ePage Internet Classifieds	http://epage.com/
eCom Recruitment	www.ecomrecruitment.com
eJobResource.com	www.ejobresource.com
Employers Online	www.employersonline.com
Employmax	www.employmax.com
Employment	www.employment.com
Employment-inc.com	www.employment-inc.com
Employment 911	www.employment911.com
EmploymentGuide.com	www.employmentguide.com
EmploymentSource	www.employmentsource.net
Employment Spot	www.employmentspot.com
Employment Weekly	www.employment-weekly.com
eNeighborhoods	www.eneighborhoods.com
The EPages Classifieds	www.ep.com
Ephron Taylor	http://ephren.typepad.com/
First Market Research	http://firstmarket.com
FlipDog.com	www.flipdog.com

4Jobs	www.4jobs.com
Fresh Jobs	www.freshjobs.comemp/Home
Friday-Ad [United Kingdom]	www.friday-ad.co.uk
Fun Jobs	www.funjobs.com
Future Access Employment Guide	www.futureaccess.com
Garage.com	www.garage.com
Get A Job	www.getajob.com
GettheJob	www.getthejob.com
Go Jobs	www.gojobs.com
Google.com	www.google.com
Got A Job	www.gotajob.com
HelpWanted	www.helpwanted.com
Help-Wanted.net	www.help-wanted.net
Hire Web	www.hireweb.comHW2CP.aspx
Hiring Network	www.hiringnetwork.com/common/tips.asp
How2FindAJob.com	www.how2findajob.com
Hot Resumes	www.hotresumes.com
Hennepin County Job Openings	www.co.hennepin.mn.us
HispanicBusiness.com	www.hispanicbusiness.com
100 Hot	www.100hot.com
Human-Intelligence.com	www.human-intelligence.com
iHireJobNetwork	www.iHireJobNetwork.com
Ideal Jobs.com	www.idealjobs.com
InfoSpace.com	www.infospace.com/ispace/ws/index
Insta Match	www.instamatch.com
International Career Employment Center	www.internationaljobs.org
International Customer Service Association Job Board	www.icsatoday.org
Internet Career Connection	www.iccweb.com
Internet Traffic Report	www.internettrafficreport.com
Iowa Smart Idea	www.smartcareermove.com
Job.com	www.job.com
Job Ads1	www.jobads1.com

JobaLot	www.jobalot.com
Job Animal	www.jobanimal.com
JobBank	www.jobbank.com
JobBank USA	www.jobbankusa.com
Job Catalog	www.jobcatalog.com
JobCenterUSA.com	www.jobcenterusa.com
JobCentral	www.jobcentral.com
JobCrank.com	www.jobcrank.com
JobDango	www.jobdango.com
JobDig	www.jobdig.com
JobDiscover.com	www.jobdiscover.com
Job Exchange	www.jobexchange.com
JobFind.com	www.bostonherald.com/jobfind
JobFox.com	www.jobfox.com
Job Fly	www.jobfly.com
Job Front	www.jobfront.com
Job-Hunt	www.job-hunt.org
Job Hunt	www.jobhunt.com
Jobing.com	www.jobing.com
JobisJob	www.jobisjob.com
Job Launch	www.joblaunch.com
Job Lynx	www.muchbetterjobs.com
Job Master	www.rvp.com/jh
JobNewsRadio.com	www.jobnewsradio.com
JobOpenings	www.jobopenings.net
Job Point Connection	www.jobpoint.com
Job Safari	www.jobsafari.com
Job SAT	www.jobsat.com
Job-Search-Engine	www.job-search-engine.com
JobSeekUSA.com	www.jobseekusa.com
Job Sleuth	www.jobsleuth.com
Job Sniper	www.jobsniper.com
JobSpin.com	www.jobspin.com

Job Star	http://jobstar.org/index.php
JobTarget	www.jobtarget.com
Jobvertise	www.jobvertise.com
Jobs.com	www.jobs.com
Jobs Inc.	www.jobsinc.com
Jobs+	www.jobsplus.org
Jobs America	www.us.plusjobs.com
Jobs at Corporations	www.searchbeat.com/jobs2.htm
JobsDB [Hong Kong]	www.jobsdb.com
JobsDirectUSA	www.jobsdirectusa.com
JobsGroup.net	www.jobsgroup.net
Jobs Online	www.jobsonline.net
Jobs on the Web	www.jobsontheweb.com
LatPro	www.latpro.com
Liszt	www.topica.com
LocalCareers	www.localcareers.com
LocalJobNetwork	www.localjobnetwork.com
Local Jobs	www.localjobs.com
LocalOpenings.com	www.localopenings.com
Lycos City Guide	http://lycos.oodle.com/cities
Mail.com	http://corp.mail.com
MegaJobSites	www.megajobsites.com
Meta Crawler	www.metacrawler.com/
Minorities Job Bank	www.imdiversity.com
Minority Career Network	www.minoritycareernet.com
Monitor	www.monitordaily.com
Monster.com	www.monster.com
My Job Search	www.myjobsearch.com
MySpace	www.myspace.com/careers
NationCareer	www.nationcareer.com
National Diversity Newspaper Job Bank	www.newsjobs.net
NationJob Network	www.nationjob.com
NationJobSearch.com	www.nationjob.com

Nationwide Consultants	www.nationwideconsultants.com
Neighbor Works Net	www.nw.org/network/home.asp
NetNoir	www.netnoir.com
Net-Temps	www.net-temps.com
NewYorkJobs.com	www.newyorkjobs.com
NicheClassifieds.com	www.nicheclassifieds.com
NicheJobs.com	www.nichejobs.com
NotchUp.com	www.notchup.com/c/home
NowHiring.com	www.nowhiring.com
1to1media.com	www.1to1media.com
Online-Jobs	www.online-jobs.com
Only-Jobs	www.only-jobs.com
PageBites.com	www.pagebites.com
People Bank	www.peoplebank.com
Personnel Department	www.careermachine.com
PlanetRecruit [United Kingdom]	www.planetrecruit.com
PlugStar.com	www.plugstar.com
PreferredJobs	www.preferredjobs.com
Pro Hire.com	http://jobs.prohire.com
QuietHire	www.quiethire.com
Quintessential Careers	http://quintcareers.com/index.html
RecruiterConnection	www.recruiterconnection.com
Recruiters Online	www.recruitersonline.com
Recruiting Shark	www.recruitingshark.com
ReferTalent.com	www.refertalent.com
RegionalHelpWanted.com	www.regionalhelpwanted.com
Rep Resources	www.represources.com
Resume Blaster	www.resumeblaster.com
ResumeXPRESS	www.resumexpress.com
ResumeRabbit.com	www.resumerabbit.com
Resumes on the Web	www.resweb.com
Resumes2work.com	www.resumes2work.com
Resunet	www.resunet.com

RetiredBrains	www.retiredbrains.com
Revolution.net	www.revolution.net
Saludos Web Site	www.saludos.com
Searchease	www.searchease.com
Second Life Jobfinder	www.SLJobFinder.com
See Me Resumes	www.seemeresumes.com
Select Minds	www.selectminds.com
Skill Hunter	www.skillhunter.com
Smuz.com	www.smuz.com
Start Up Jobs	www.startupjobs.com
Start Up Zone	www.startupzone.com
Starting Point	www.stpt.com
State Jobs	http://statejobs.com
The Sunday Paper	www.sundaypaper.com
SwapJobs.com	www.swapjobs.com
Talentology	www.peoplefilter.com
Talent Technology	www.peoplefilter.com
TargetedJobSites.com	www.jobhill.com
Telecommuting Jobs	www.tjobs.com
Teleplaza	www.teleplaza.com
TeleportJobs.com	www.teleportjobs.com
TopJobUSA	www.topjobusa.com
Thingama Job	www.thingamajob.com
TopUSAJobs	www.topusajobs.com
Totaljobs.com	www.totaljobs.com
TNTJobz.net	www.tntjobz.net
Tripod	www.tripod.lycos.com
Union Jobs Clearinghouse	www.unionjobs.com
United States Department of Labor	www.dol.gov
UpSeek	www.upseek.com
US Jobs	www.usjobs.com
USJobNet.com	www.usjobnet.com
Vault	www.vault.com/wps/portal/usa

Vertical Net	www.bravosolution.com/cms/us
Virtual Recruiting Network	www.dmpmail.com
The Wall Street Journal Careers Page	http://online.wsj.com/public/page/news-career-jobs.html
Web Crawler	www.webcrawler.com
Web Reference	www.webreference.com
Wetfeet	www.wetfeet.com
Wiserworker.com	www.wiserworker.com
Womenswire	www.womenswire.net
Work at Home Digest	www.workathomedigest.com
WorkLife.com	www.worklife.com
Work-Web	www.work-web.com
Working.ca [Canada]	www.working.ca
Workopolis [Canada]	www.workopolis.com
The World Wide Web Employment Office	www.employmentoffice.net
WorldWorkz.com	www.worldworkz.com
Yahoo! HotJobs	www.hotjobs.yahoo.com
Yep.com	www.yep.com

Graphic Arts/Electronic & Traditional (See also Journalism & Media)

ACM Siggraph	www.siggraph.org
3DSite	www.3dsite.com
Adrecruiter	www.adrecruiter.com
American Institute of Graphic Arts	www.aiga.org
Animation Industry Database	www.aidb.com
Animation World Network	www.awn.com
Capital Communicator	www.capitalcommunicator.com
CG Society/society of Digital Artists [Australia]	www.gcsociety.org
Communication Arts Magazine	www.commarts.com
Communications Round Table	www.roundtable.org

Computer Graphics + Animation + Visual Effects Job Board	www.cggigs.com
Contracted Work	www.contractedwork.com
Copy Editor Newsletter	http://jobs.copyeditor.com/home/index.cfm?site_id=502
Coroflot	www.coroflot.com
CreativeHeads.net	www.creativeheads.net
CreativeShake.com	www.creativeshake.com
DesignJobs.co.uk [United Kingdom]	www.designjobs.co.uk
Design Sphere Online Job Hunt	www.dsphere.net
Desktop Publishing	http://desktoppublishing.com
DigitalMediaJobs.com [United Kingdom]	www.digitalmediajobs.com
FolioMag.com	www.foliomag.com
Freelance BBS	www.freelancebbs.com
GamesIndustry.biz	www.gamesindustry.biz
Get a FreeLancer	www.freelancer.com
Graphic Artists Guild JobLine	www.graphicartistsguild.org
Graphic Design Freelance Jobs	www.graphicdesignfreelancejobs.com
iFreelance	www.ifreelance.com
Interior Design Jobs	https://interiordesignjobs.sellisp.com/Default.asp
Media Lab	www.media.mit.edu
Media Street.com	www.mediastreet.com
Mip Map	www.mipmap.com
National Association of Printing Ink Manufacturers	www.napim.org
Noble Desktop	www.nobledesktop.com
PaidContent.org	http://jobs.paidcontent.org
Print Jobs	www.printjobs.com
PrintWorkers.com	www.printworkers.com
Printing Careers	www.printingcareers.com
Screenprinting & Graphic Imaging Association International	www.sgia.org/employment
Silicon Alley Insider	http://jobs.businessinsider.com/

VFXWorld   www.vfxworld.com

-H-

Healthcare/Medical

Healthcare-General

Absolutely Health Care   www.healthjobsusa.com

Allegheny County Medical Society   www.acms.org

AllHealthcareJobs.com   www.allhealthcarejobs.com

America's Health Care Source   www.healthcaresource.com

American Medical Association   http://jamacareernet.ama-assn.org
      JAMACareerNet

ANEScareer.com   www.anescareer.com

CARDIOcareer.com   www.cardiocareer.com

Centers for Disease Control   www.cdc.gov

Chicago Medical Society   www.cmsdocs.org

Discover Jobs   www.discover-jobs.com

EMcareer.com   www.emcareer.com

ENT-career.com   www.ent-career.com

FocusonHealthcare.com   www.focusonhealthcare.com

FPCareer.com   www.fpcareer.com

GASTROcareer.com   www.gastrocareer.com

Georgia Department of Human Resources   www.dhrjobs.com

GovMedCareers.com   www.govmedcareers.com

GreenLeg.com   www.greenleg.com

GxPJobs.com [United Kingdom]   www.gxpjobs.com

Harris County Medical Society   www.hcms.org/Template.aspx?id=4

HealthAndWellnessJobs.com   www.healthandwellnessjobs.com

Healthcare Businesswomen's Association   www.hbanet.org/home.aspx

HealthcareCareerWeb.com   www.healthcarecareerweb.com

Health Care Jobs Online   www.hcjobsonline.com

Health Care Match	www.healthcarematch.com
Health Care Hiring	www.healthcarehiring.com
HealthCare Job Store	www.healthcarejobstore.com
Healthcare/Monster	http://monster.com
HealthCareRecruitment.com	www.healthcarerecruitment.com
Health Care Seeker	www.healthcareseeker.com
HealthcareSource	www.healthcaresource.com
Healthcare Traveler Jobs	www.healthcaretravelerjobs.com
HealthCareerWeb.com	www.healthcareerweb.com
HEALTHeCAREERS	http://assoc.healthecareers.com
Health Direction	www.healthdirection.com
HealthJobsNationwide.com	www.healthjobsnationwide.com
HealthJobsUK.com [United Kingdom]	www.healthjobsuk.com/select_sector
HealthJobsUSA.com	www.healthjobsusa.com
Health Network USA	www.unitedsearch.com
Health Seek.com	www.healthseek.com
HealthOpps	http://healthcare.careerbuilder.co
HireBio.com	www.hirebio.com
HireRX.com	www.hirerx.com
HireMedical.com	www.hiremedical.com
HireMedics.com	www.hiremedics.com
HireNursing.com	www.hirenursing.com
HireCentral.com	www.hirecentral.com
HOSPITALISTcareer.com	www.hospitalistcareer.com
IMcareer.com	www.imcareer.com
JobFox.com	www.jobfox.com
Jobscience Network	http://jobs.jobscience.com
Job Span	www.jobspan.com
Jobs4Healthcare.com	www.jobs4healthcare.com
Jobs4Medical.com	www.jobs4medical.com
JobsinHealth [United Kingdom]	www.jobsinhealth.co.uk
Jobs in Healthcare	www.jobsinhealthcare.com
JobsinNHS [United Kingdom]	www.jobsinnhs.co.uk

Med Careers	www.medcareers.com
Med Connect	www.medconnect.com
Medhunters	www.medhunters.com
MedLaunch	www.medlaunch.com
MedMarket	www.medical-admart.com
MedicSolve.com [United Kingdom]	www.medicsolve.com
Medical AdMart	www.medical-admart.com
Medical Design Online	www.medicaldesignonline.com
MedicalJobList.com	www.medicaljoblist.com
Medical Matrix	www.medmatrix.org
Medical Words	www.md123.com
MedicalWorkers.com	www.medicalworkers.com
Medicenter.com	www.medicenter.com
Medi-Smart	www.medi-smart.com/renal4.htm
MEDopportunities.com	www.medopportunities.com
MEDSTER.com	www.medster.com
MedHunting.com	www.medhunting.com
MedWorking.com	www.medworking.com
Medzilla	www.medzilla.com
Modern Healthcare	www.modernhealthcare.com
MyHealthJobs.com	www.myhealthjobs.com
The National Assembly	www.nassembly.org
National Association for Health Care Recruitment	www.nahcr.com
National Healthcare Career Network	www.nhcnnetwork.com
National Rural Recruitment & Retention Network	www.3rnet.org
NEPHcareer.com	www.nephcareer.com
NEUROcareer.com	www.neurocareer.com
New England Journal of Medicine	http://content.nejm.org
TheNursingJobsite.com [United Kingdom]	www.thenursingjobsite.com
OBGYNcareer.com	www.obgyncareer.com
Oklahoma State Medical Association	www.osmaonline.org
ONCOLOGYcareer.com	www.oncologycareer.com

OnlyLTCjobs.com	www.onlyltcjobs.com
Orleans Parish Medical Society	www.opms.org
PeopleMenders.com	www.peoplemenders.com
Pflegekarriere.de [Germany]	www.pflegekarriere.de
PharmaTalentPool.com [United Kingdom]	www.pharmatalentpool.com
PhysicianCareerJobs.com	www.physiciancareerjobs.com
RealMedical.com	www.realmedical.com
Texas Medical Association	www.texmed.org
Wisconsin Medical Society	www.wisconsinmedicalsociety.org

Acute Care/Critical Care/Intensive Care

American Association of Critical Care Nurses	www.aacn.org
JobICU.com	www.jobicu.com
Jobscience Network	http://jobs.jobscience.com

Addiction/Substance Abuse

Addiction Medicine Jobs	www.addictionmedicinejobs.com
Substance Abuse Jobs	www.substanceabusejobs.com

Administration/Management

American College of Healthcare Executives	http://ache.org
American College of Physician Executives	www.acpe.org
Association of Staff Physician Recruiters	www.aspr.org
College of Healthcare Information Management Executives	www.cio-chime.org
Grist.org	http://jobs.grist.org
Healthcare Financial Management Association	www.hfma.org
Healthcare Information and Management Systems	www.himss.org/ASP/index.asp
Healthline Management	www.hmistl.com
Massachusetts Healthcare Human Resources Association	www.mhhra.org

Medical Case Management Jobs	www.casemanagementjobs.com
Medical-Dental-Hospital Business Association	www.mdhba.org
Medical Group Management Association	www.mgma.com
Medical Transcription Jobs	www.mtjobs.com
NursingExecutives.com	www.nursingexecutives.com
Radiology Business Management Association	www.rbma.org
Senior Housing Jobs	www.seniorhousingjobs.com

Allied Health

Allied Health Jobs	www.alliedhealthjobs.com
Allied Health Opportunities Directory	www.gvpub.com
DiversityAlliedHealth.com	www.diversityalliedhealth.com

Anesthesiology

American Society of PeriAnesthesia Nurses	www.aspan.org
ANEScareer.com	www.anescareer.com
CRNAjobs.com	www.crnajobs.com
Gas Jobs	www.gasjobs.com
IConnect2Anesthesiology.com	www.iconnect2anesthesiology.com

Cardiology

American College of Cardiology	www.acc.org
American Association of Cardiovascular and Pulmonary Rehabilitation	www.aacvpr.org
CARDIOcareer.com	www.cardiocareer.com
Cardiologist Jobs	www.cardiologistjobs.com
Cardioworking.com	www.cardioworking.com
Jobscience Network	http://jobs.jobscience.com

Equipment-Healthcare

American Medical Technologists	www.amtl.com

Device Space	www.devicespace.com
Healthcare Information and Management Systems	www.himss.org/ASP/index.asp
iHireMedTechs.com	www.ihiremedtechs.com
MDL Career Center	http://careercenter.devicelink.com
MedicalDeviceStar	www.medicaldevicestar.com
PharmaOpportunities	www.pharmaopportunites.com

Hospital

AHACareerCenter.org (American Hospital Association)	www.ahacareercenter.org
Arizona Hospital and Healthcare Association AZHealthJobs	www.azhha.org
CareerHospital.com	www.careerhospital.com
Colorado Health and Hospital Association	www.cha.com
Connecticut Hospital Association	www.chime.org
Hospital Dream Jobs	www.hospitaldreamjobs.com
Hospital Jobs Online	www.hospitaljobsonline.com
HospitalSoup.com	www.hospitalsoup.com
Hospital Web	www.hospitallink.com
JobHospital.com	www.jobhospital.com
Medical-Dental-Hospital Business Association	www.mdhba.org
Society of Hospital Medicine Career Center	www.hospitalmedicine.org

International

CanMed [Canada]	www.canmed.com
DERWeb [United Kingdom]	www.derweb.co.uk
EMBL Job Vacancies [Germany]	www.embl.de
HUM-MOLGEN [Germany]	www.hum-molgen.org/positions
Medjobsuk.com [United Kingdom]	www.medjobsuk.com
Opportunities Online [United Kingdom]	www.opps.co.uk

Midwife

American College of Nurse Midwives   www.acnw.org

MidwifeJobs   http://assoc.healthecareers.com

NMC4Jobs.com [United Kingdom]   www.nmc4jobs.com

Professional Information from the American   www.midwife.org
       College of Nurse-Midwives

Nurses/Nursing

AAcademy of Medical-Surgical Nurses   www.medsurgnurse.org

AllNurses.com   http://allnurses.com

American Academy of Ambulatory Care Nursing   www.aaacn.org

American Academy of Nurse Practitioners   www.aanp.org/AANPCMS2

American Association of Critical Care Nurses   www.aacn.org

American Association of Occupational Health   www.aaohn.org
       Nurses

American College of Nurse Midwives   www.acnw.org

American Nurses Association   www.nursingworld.org

American Psychiatric Nurses Association   www.apna.org

American Society of PeriAnesthesia Nurses   www.aspan.org

ANNAlink   http://anna.inurse.com

Association of Perioperative Registered Nurses   www.aorn.org/CareerCenter
       Online Career Center

Association of Women's Health, Obstetric &   www.awhonn.org
       Neonatal Nurses

Best Nurse Jobs   www.bestnursejobs.com

Camp Nurse Jobs   www.campnursejobs.com

CampusRN.com   www.campusrn.com

CRNA Jobs   www.crnajobs.com

Dermatology Nurses' Association   www.dnanurse.org

GraduateNurse.com   www.graduatenurse.com

Guaranteed Employment Advertising &   www.nurse-recruiter.com
       Resume Service

HappyCareer.com	www.happycareer.com
HealthJobsUSA.com	www.healthjobsusa.com
HireNursing.com	www.hirenursing.com
Hot Nurse Jobs	www.hotnursejobs.com
iHireNursing.com	www.ihirenursing.com
Jobscience Network	http://jobs.jobscience.com
Locum Tenens	www.locumtenens.com
MinorityNurse.com	www.minoritynurse.com
National Association of Hispanic Nurses Houston Chapter	www.nahnhouston.org
National Association of Orthopaedic Nurses	
National League for Nursing	www.orthonurse.org
National Rural Recruitment & Retention Network	www.nln.org
Nurse.com	www.3rnet.org
Nurse Director Jobs	www.nurse.com
NurseJobShop.com	www.directorofnursingjobs.com
NurseJobs.com	www.nursejobshop.com
Nurse Manager Jobs	www.nursejobs.com
Nurse-Recruiter.com	http://nursemanagerjobs.org
NurseTown.com	www.nurse-recruiter.com
NurseUniverse.com	www.nursetown.com
NurseZone.com	www.nurseuniverse.com
Nurseserve [United Kingdom]	www.nursezone.com
Nurses for a Healthier Tomorrow	www.nurserve.co.uk
NursingCareersToday.com	www.nursesource.org
Nursing Center	www.nursingcareerstoday.com
NursingExecutives.com	www.nursingcenter.com
NursingJobs.com	www.nursingexecutives.com
Nursing-Jobs.us	www.nursingjobs.com
NursingMatters.com	www.nursing-jobs.us
NursingNetUK [United Kingdom]	www.rn.com
Psychiatric Nurse Jobs	www.nursingnetuk.com
RN.com	http://psychiatric.nurse.jobs.topusajobs.com
RNNetwork	www.rn.com

RNSearch.com	www.rnnetwork.com
Society of Gastroenterology Nurses &	www.rnsearch.com
Associates	www.sgna.org
TravelNurseSource.com	
TravelNursing.com	www.travelnursesource.com
TravelNursingUSA.com	www.travelnursing.com
	www.travelnursingusa.com

OBGYN

AdvancedPracticeJobs.com	www.healthjobsnationwide.com
American Association of Gynecologic	www.aagl.org
Laparoscopists	
American College of Obstetricians	www.acog.org
and Gynecologists	
OBGYNCareer.com	www.obgyncareer.com
Obstetric Jobs	www.obstetricjobs.com

Pediatrics

Pediatric Jobs	www.pediatricjobs.com
PedJobs	www.pedjobs.com

Pharmacist/Pharmacy (See also Pharmaceutical)

American Association of Pharmaceutical	www.aapspharmaceutica.com/index.asp
Scientists	
American Chemical Society	http://portal.acs.org/portal/acs/corg/content
American Pharmaceutical Association	www.pharmacist.com
Association for Applied Human Pharmacology	www.agah.info
[Germany]	
ChemJobs.net	www.chemjobs.net/chemjobs.html
Elite Pharmacy Jobs	www.elitepharmacyjobs.com
HireRX.com	www.hirerx.com
iHirePharmacy.com	www.ihirepharmacy.com

International Society for Pharmaceutical Engineering	www.ispe.org
Pharmacareers.co.uk [United Kingdom]	www.pharmacareers.co.uk
Pharmaceutical Rep Jobs	http://pharmaceuticalrepjobs.org
PharmacyWeek	www.pharmacyweek.com
PharmaOpportunities	www.pharmaopportunites.com
PharmaTalentPool [United Kingdom]	www.pharmatalentpool.com
Pharmiweb.com [United Kingdom]	www.pharmiweb.com
RPhRecruiter	www.rphrecruiter.com
RxCareerCenter	www.rxcareercenter.com
RxWebportal	www.rxwebportal.com

Physical Therapy/Occupational Therapy

American Academy of Cardiovascular and Pulmonary Rehabilitation	www.aacvpr.org
American Association of Occupational Health Nurses	www.aaohn.org
American College of Occupational and Environmental Medicine	www.acoem.org
American Occupational Therapy Association	www.aota.org
American Physical Therapy Association	www.apta.org
American Society of Clinical Pharmacology and Therapeutics	www.ascpt.org
JobsforPTs.com	www.jobsforphysicaltherapists.com
JobsOT.com	www.jobsot.com
PhysicalTherapist.com	www.physicaltherapist.com
Physical Therapist Jobs	www.physicaltherapistjobs.com
PT Central	www.ptcentral.com
PTjobs.com	www.ptjobs.com
Rehab License Network	www.rehablicense.com
Rehab Options	www.rehaboptions.com
RehabWorld	www.rehabworld.com
TherapyJobs.com	www.therapyjobs.com

UKTherapist.co.uk [United Kingdom]   www.uktherapist.co.uk

Physicians/Physician Assistants

Academic Physician & Scientist	www.acphysci.com
American Academy of Family Physicians	www.fpjobsonline.org
American Academy of Physician Assistants	www.aapa.org
American College of Chest Physicians	www.chestnet.org/accp
American College of Emergency Physicians	www.acep.org
American College of Physicians	www.acponline.org/career_connection
American College of Physician Executives	www.acpe.org
American Medical Association JAMA CareerCenter	http://jamacareernet.ama-assn.org
California Academy of Family Physicians	www.fpjobsonline.org
Colorado Academy of Family Physicians	www.fpjobsonline.org
Doc Job	www.boston.com/jobs/news/archive/job_doc
Doc on the Web	www.webdoc.com
DoctorWork.com	www.doctorwork.com
Ed Physician	www.edphysician.com
Florida Academy of Family Physicians	www.fpjobsonline.org
Georgia Academy of Family Physicians	www.fpjobsonline.org
iHirePhysicians.com	www.ihirephysicians.com
Illinois Academy of Family Physicians	www.fpjobsonline.org
Locum Tenens	www.locumtenens.com
MD Job Site	www.mdjobsite.com
MD Search	www.mdsearch.com
MEDopportunities.com	www.medopportunities.com
Missouri Academy of Family Physicians	www.fpjobsonline.org
National Rural Recruitment & Retention Network	www.3rnet.org
New England Journal of Medicine Career Center	http://content.nejm.org
New York State Academy of Family Physicians	www.fpjobsonline.org
Pennsylvania Academy of Family Physicians	www.fpjobsonline.org
Physician Crossroads	www.physiciancrossroads.com
Physician Work	www.physicianwork.com

Physician's Employment	www.physemp.com
Practice Link	www.practicelink.com
Profiles Database	www.profilesdatabase.com
Texas Academy of Family Physicians	www.fpjobsonline.org
UO Magazine	www.uoworks.com
Web MD	www.webmd.com
Wisconsin Academy of Family Physicians	www.fpjobsonline.org

Psychology/Psychiatry/Mental Health

American Counseling Association	www.counseling.org
American Psychiatric Association	www.psych.org
American Psychiatric Nurses Association	www.apna.org
American Psychological Association PsycCareers	www.apa.org/careers/psyccareers
American Psychological Society	www.psychologicalscience.org/jobs
iHireMentalHealth.com	www.ihirementalhealth.com
iHireTherapy.com	www.ihiretherapy.com
Mental Health Jobs	http://mentalhealthjobsin.com
Mental Health Net	www.mentalhelp.net
National Association of School Psychologists	www.nasponline.org
Psychiatric Nurse Jobs	http://psychiatric.nurse.jobs.topusajobs.com
Psychiatrist Jobs	www.psychiatrists.com
Psychologist Jobs	www.psychologistjobs.com
RehabWorld	www.rehabworld.com
Social Psychology Network	www.socialpsychology.org
SocialService.com	www.socialservice.com

Radiology/Radiologic Technicians

American Healthcare Radiology Administrators	www.ahraonline.org
American Registry of Diagnostic Medical Sonographers	www.ardms.org
American Registry of Radiologic Technologists	www.arrt.org

American Society of Radiologic Technologists	www.asrt.org
AuntMinnie.com	www.auntminnie.com
iHireRadiology.com	www.ihireradiology.com
NukeWorker.com	www.nukeworker.com
Radiological Society of North America	www.rsna.org
Radiology Business Management Association	www.rbma.org
RadWorking.com	www.radworking.com
RTJobs.com	www.allhealthcarejobs.com
Society of Diagnostic Medical Sonographers	www.sdms.org
Society of Nuclear Medicine	www.snm.org

Research

American Society for Clinical Laboratory Science	www.ascls.org
American Society for Clinical Pathology	www.ascp.org
American Society of Clinical Pharmacology and Therapeutics	www.ascpt.org
Association for Applied Human Pharmacology [Germany]	www.agah.info
Association of Clinical Research Professionals Career Center	www.acrpnet.org
Biotechemployment.com	www.biotechemployment.com
Biotechnology Industry Organization	www.bio.org
Canadian Society of Biochemistry and Molecular and Cellular Biologists Experimental Medicine Job Listing	www.medicine.mcgill.ca
History of Science Society	www.hssonline.org
American Medical Association JAMA CareerCenter	http://jamacareernet.ama-assn.org
Jobs4dd.com	www.jobs4dd.com
Texas Healthcare & Bioscience Institute	www.thbi.org

Specialties-Other

American Academy of Dermatology	www.aad.org
American Academy of Professional Coders	www.aapc.com
American Association of Cardiovascular and Pulmonary Rehabilitation	www.aacvpr.org
American Association of Medical Assistants	www.aama-ntl.org
American Association of Neuromuscular & Electrodiagnostic Medicine	www.aanem.org
American Association of Respiratory Care	www.aarc.org
American College of Occupational and Environmental Medicine	www.acoem.org
American Dietetic Association	www.eatright.org
American Industrial Hygiene Association	www.aiha.org
American College of Allergy, Asthma & Immunology	www.acaai.org
American College of Preventive Medicine	www.acpm.org
American College of Rheumatology	www.rheumatology.org
American Gastroenterological Association	http://assoc.healthecareers.com
American Geriatrics Society	www.americangeriatrics.org
American Society of Ichthyologists and Herpetologists	www.asih.org
American Society for Microbiology	www.asm.org
AnswerStat	www.answerstat.com
Association for Healthcare Documentation	www.ahdionline.org Integrity
CancerJobs.net [United Kingdom]	www.cancerjobs.net
College of American Pathologists	www.cap.org
EHScareers.com	www.ehscareers.com
EMcareer.com	www.emcareer.com
Emedcareers	www.emedcareers.com
Emergency Medicine Residents Association	www.emra.org
ENT-career.com	www.ent-career.com
FieldMedics.com	www.fieldmedics.com
FPcareer.com	www.fpcareer.com

GASTROcareer.com	www.gastrocareer.com
HIV Medicine Association	www.hivma.org
HOSPITALISTcareer.com	www.hospitalistcareer.com
ihireMedicalSecretaries.com	www.ihiremedicalsecretaries.com
ihireNutrition.com	www.ihirenutrition.com
IMcareer.com	www.imcareer.com
Infectious Diseases Society of America	www.idsa.org
International Health Economics Association	www.healtheconomics.org
Jobscience Network	http://jobs.jobscience.com
jobsSLP.com	www.jobsslp.com
Medical Consultants Network	www.mcn.com
MedicalSalesJobs.com	www.mymedicalsalesjobs.com
MedicalSecretaryJobs.com	www.medicalsecretary.com
National Environmental Health Association	www.neha.org
NEPHcareer.com	www.nephcareer.com
NEUROcareer.com	www.neurocareer.com
North American Spine Society	www.spine.org/Pages/Default.aspx
ONCOLOGYcareer.com	www.oncologycareer.com
Renal World	www.nephron.org/renalworld
Senior Housing Jobs	www.seniorhousingjobs.com
Travel Per Diem Contract	www.travelperdiemcontract.com

Students/Recent Graduates

American Medical Association (Resident and Fellow Section)	www.ama-assn.org/ama/pub/category/194.html
CampusRN.com	www.campusrn.com
Career Espresso	www.sph.emory.edu/CAREER/index.php
The College of Education & Human Development at the University of Minnesota	http://cehd.umn.edu/ETCS
Degree Hunter	www.degreehunter.com
Profiles Database	www.profilesdatabase.com

Surgery/Surgeons/Surgical Nurses

Academy of Medical-Surgical Nurses	www.medsurgnurse.org
American Association of Neurological Surgeons	www.aans.org
American College of Foot and Ankle Surgeons	www.acfas.org
American College of Surgeons	www.facs.org
American Society of General Surgeons	www.theasgs.org
American Association of Oral & Maxillofacial Surgeons	www.aoms.org
SurgicalAssistants.com	www.surgicalassistants.com

High Tech/Technical/Technology

The Ada Project	http://women.cs.cmu.edu/ada/
AmericanJobs.com	www.americanjobs.com
Association for Educational Communications and Technology Job Center	www.aect.org
ButternutJobs.com [United Kingdom]	www.butternutjobs.com
Career Net	www.careernet.com
Contract Employment Weekly	www.ceweekly.com
CyberMediaDice.com [India]	www.cybermediadice.com
High Technology Careers	www.hightechcareers.com/hc3.asp
HireAbility.com	www.hireability.com
IrishDev.com [Ireland]	www.irishdev.com
Job Authority	www.jobauthority.com
Job Searching - Technical	http://jobsearchtech.about.com
JobsInSearch.com	www.jobsinsearch.com
Just Tech Jobs	www.justtechjobs.com
JustTechnicalJobs [United Kingdom]	www.jobsgroup.net
TheLadders.com	www.theladders.com
Latinos in Information Sciences and Technology Association	www.a-lista.org
LookTech.com	www.looktech.com
MEMSNet	www.memsnet.org

New Dimensions in Technology, Inc.	www.ndt.com
New Mexico High Tech Job Forum	www.nmtechjobs.com
RecruTech.ca [Canada]	www.recrutech.ca
SalesRecruits.com	http://cardbrowser.com
ScientistWorld.com [United Kingdom]	www.scientistworld.com
Society for Technical Communications	www.stc.org
TechJobsScotland	www.techjobscotland.com
Technical Recruiters	www.technicalrecruiters.com
TechResults	www.techresults-nv.com
Tiny Tech Jobs	www.tinytechjobs.com
US Tech Jobs	www.ustechjobs.com
Virtual Job Fair	http://careerexpo.jobing.com

Hospitality (See also Culinary/Food Preparation)

Hospitality-General

AllHospitality.co.uk [United Kingdom]	www.hospitalityonline.co.uk
AnyWorkAnywhere.com [United Kingdom]	www.anyworkanywhere.com
Avero	www.averoinc.com/
Barzone [United Kingdom]	www.barzone.co.uk
BlueFoxJobs.com	www.bluefoxjobs.com
Cool Works	www.coolworks.com
Hcareers	www.hcareers.com
Hospitality Link	www.hospitalitylink.com
Hospitality Net Virtual Job Exchange [Netherlands]	www.hospitalitynet.org/index.html
Hospitality Online	www.hospitalityonline.com
HospitalityRecruitment.co.uk [United Kingdom]	www.hospitalityrecruitment.co.uk
Hotel Jobs [United Kingdom]	www.hoteljobs.co.uk
Hotel Travel Jobs	www.hoteltraveljobs.com
HOTELScareers.com	www.catererglobal.com
iHireHospitality.com	www.ihirehospitality.com

iHireHospitalityServices.com www.ihirehospitalityservices.com
JobLoft.com [Canada] www.jobloft.com
JobLux [United Kingdom] www.joblux.co.uk
Job Monkey www.jobmonkey.com
JobsinHotels [United Kingdom] www.jobsinhotels.com
MeetingJobs.com www.meetingjobs.com
The Publican [United Kingdom] www.thepublican.com
Resort Work [United Kingdom] www.resortwork.co.uk
SeasonalEmployment.com www.seasonalemployment.com
247recruit.com [United Kingdom] www.247recruit.com

Food Preparation

BookaChef.co.uk [United Kingdom] www.bookachef.co.uk
Careers in Food www.careersinfood.com
Caterer.com [United Kingdom] www.caterer.com
CatererGlobal.com [United Kingdom] www.catererglobal.com
FineDiningJobs.com www.finediningjobs.com
Food and Drink Jobs www.foodanddrinkjobs.com
FoodIndustryJobs.com www.foodindustryjobs.com
National Restaurant Association www.restaurant.org/careers
Restaurant Job Site www.restaurantjobsite.com
SommelierJobs.com www.sommelierjobs.com
StarChefs www.starchefs.com
Wine & Hospitality Jobs www.wineandhospitalityjobs.com

Hotel

American Hotel and Lodging Association www.ahla.com
CatererGlobal www.catererglobal.com
Hotel Jobs www.hoteljobs.com
Hotel Jobs Network www.hoteljobsnetwork.com
Hotel Restaurant Jobs www.hotelrestaurantjobs.com
LuxuryHotelJobs.com www.luxuryhoteljobs.com

Management

Executive Placement Services	www.execplacement.com
Hcareers	www.hcareers.com
HospitalityExecutive.com	www.hospitalityexecutive.com

Resorts

Cooljobs	http://cooljobs.com
CoolWorks.com	www.coolworks.com
HospitalityAdventures.com	www.hospitalityadventures.com
Resortjobs.co.uk [United Kingdom]	www.resortjobs.co.uk
Resort Work [United Kingdom]	www.resortwork.co.uk
SpaOpportunities [United Kingdom]	www.spaopportunities.com

Travel

American Society of Travel Agents	www.astanet.org
TravelJobSearch.com [United Kingdom]	www.traveljobsearch.com

Other Specialty

Casino Careers Online	www.casinocareers.com
International Association of Conference Centers Online	www.iacconline.org
Lifeguardingjobs.com	www.lifeguardingjobs.com
MeetingJobs.com	www.meetingjobs.com
Museum Jobs	www.museumjobs.com
ScottishHospitalityJobs.com [Scotland]	www.scottishhospitalityjobs.com
Showbizjobs.com	www.showbizjobs.com
SkiingtheNet	www.skiingthenet.com

Hourly Workers (See also Classifieds-Newspaper)

CmonJob.fr	www.cmonjob.fr

EmploymentGuide.com	www.employmentguide.com
GrooveJob.com	www.groovejob.com
ParisJob.com	www.parisjob.com
SnagaJob	www.snagajob.com
YouApplyHere.com	www.youapplyhere.com

Human Resources (See also Recruiters' Resources)

Human Resources-General

American Management Association International	www.amanet.org
ERE.net	www.ere.net
HR Connections	www.hrjobs.com
HRjob.ca [Canada]	www.humanresourcesjobs.ca
HR Job Net	www.hrjobnet.com
HR-Jobs	www.hr-jobs.net
HR Staffers	www.hrstaffers.com
HR World	www.hrworld.com
HRIM Mall	www.hrimmall.com
HRM Jobs	www.hrmjobs.com
Human Resources.org	www.humanresources.org
iHireHR.com	www.ihirehr.com
JobBoarders.com	www.jobboarders.com
Jobs4HR.com	www.jobs4hr.com
TheLadders.com	www.theladders.com
NationJob Network: Human Resources Job Page	www.nationjob.com/hr
NewHRJobs.com	www.newhrjobs.com
PersonnelTodayJobs.com [United Kingdom]	www.personneltoday.com
Recruitmentcareeers.co.uk [United Kingdom]	www.recruitmentcareers.co.uk
SimplyHRJobs [United Kingdom]	www.simplyhrjobs.co.uk
Society for Human Resource Management HRJobs	http://jobs.com/

Workforce.com   www.workforce.com

Assessment/Evaluation/Selection

American Evaluation Association   www.eval.org/programs/careercenter.asp

Compensation & Benefits

BenefitsLink   www.benefitslink.com

International Foundation of Employee   www.jobsinbenefits.com
**   Benefit Plans Job Postings**

Salary.com   www.salary.com

WorkersCompensation.com   www.workerscompensation.com

World at Work Job Links (American   www.worldatwork.org
    Compensation Association)

Consulting

Human Resource Independent Consultants   www.hric.org
    (HRIC) On-Line Job Leads

Diversity

Career Center for Workforce Diversity   www.eop.com

DiversityCareers.com   www.diversitycareers.com

Diversity Connect   www.diversityconnect.com

DiversityInc.com   www.diversityinc.com

DiversityJobs.com   www.diversityjobs.com

DiversityWorking.com   www.diversityworking.com

IMDiversity.com   www.imdiversity.com

WorkplaceDiversity.com   www.workplacediversity.com

Industry Specific

Cable and Telecommunications Human   www.cthra.com
    Resources Association

College and University Personnel Association JobLine	www.cupahr.org/jobline
HRS Jobs	www.hrsjobs.com
Massachusetts Healthcare Human Resources Association	www.mhhra.org
Media Human Resource Association	http://jobs.com/
National Association of Colleges & Employers (NACE)	www.nacelink.com

Information Systems

HRISjobs.com	www.hrisjobs.com
International Association for Human Resource Information Management Job Central	http://ihr.hrdpt.com

Recruiting

Academy of Healthcare Recruiters	www.academyofhealthcarerecruiters.com
Alliance of Medical Recruiters	www.physicianrecruiters.com
American Staffing Association	www.staffingtoday.net
Arizona Technical Recruiters Association	www.atraaz.org/pages/recruiterjobopenings.html
Association of Executive Search Consultants	www.aesc.org/eweb
Association of Financial Search Consultants	www.afsc-jobs.com
Association of Staff Physician Recruiters	www.aspr.org
California Staffing Professionals	www.catss.org
Canadian Technical Recruiters Network	www.ctrn.org
Colorado Technical Recruiters Network	www.ctrn.org
Delaware Valley Technical Recruiters Network	www.dvtrn.org
ERE.net	www.ere.net
Houston High Tech Recruiters Network	www.hhtrn.org
Illinois Recruiters Association	http://illinoisrecruiter.ning.com
International Association of Corporate and Professional Recruitment	www.iacpr.org
Minnesota Technical Recruiters Network	www.mntrn.com

National Association of Executive Recruiters	www.naer.org
National Association for Health Care Recruitment	www.nahcr.com
National Association of Legal Search Consultants	www.nalsc.org
National Association of Personnel Services	www.napsweb.org
National Association of Physician Recruiters	www.napr.org
National Insurance Recruiters Association Online Job Database	www.nirassn.com
New Jersey Metro Employment Management Association	www.njmetroema.org
New Jersey Staffing Association	www.njsa.com
New Jersey Technical Recruiters Alliance	www.njtra.org
Northeast Human Resource Association	www.nehra.com
Northwest Recruiters Association	www.nwrecruit.org/nwra
OnrecJobs.com [United Kingdom]	www.onrecjobs.com
Personnel Management Association of Western New England	http://hrmawne.shrm.org
Recruiters Network	www.recruitersnetwork.com
RecruitingJobs.com	www.recruitingjobs.com
The Regional Technical Recruiter's Association	www.rtra.com
Southeast Employment Network Inc.	www.nonprofitdata.com
Technical Recruiters Network	www.trnchicago.org
Texas Association of Staffing	www.texasstaffing.org
WEDDLE's Research & Publications	www.weddles.com

Regional

Central Iowa Chapter, SHRM	http://ci.shrm.org
Chesapeake Human Resources Association	www.chra.com
Dallas Human Resource Management Association	www.dallashr.org
Houston Human Resource Management Association	www.hrhouston.org

Howard County Human Resources Society	www.hocohrs.org
HRMA Resource Bank	www.hrma.org
Human Resource Association of Broward County	www.hrabc.org
Human Resource Association of Central Indiana	www.hraci.org
Human Resource Association of Greater Kansas City	http://hrma-kc.org
Human Resource Association of Greater Oak Brook	www.hraoakbrook.org
Human Resource Association of the National Capital Area Job Bank Listing	http://hra-nca.org/job_list.asp
Human Resource Association of New York	www.nyshrm.org
Human Resource Management Association of Mid Michigan Job Postings	http://hrmamm.com/jobpostings/index.php
Human Resources Online [Russia]	www.hro.ru
Illinois Association of Personnel Services	www.searchfirm.com
JobsinSearch [United Kingdom]	www.jobsinsearch.com
Navigator Online	www.lwhra.org
New Jersey Human Resource Planning Group	www.njhrpg.org
Northeast Human Resource Association	www.nehra.com
Ohio State Council (SHRM)	www.ohioshrm.org
Personnel Management Association of Western New England	http://hrmawne.shrm.org
The Portland Human Resource Management Assn	www.pbcs.jp
Sacramento Area Human Resources Association	www.sahra.org
SHRM Atlanta	www.shrmatlanta.org
SHRM Jacksonville	www.shrmjax.org
Tri-State Human Resource Management Assn	http://wss3.tristatehr.org/default.aspx
Tulsa Area Human Resources Association	www.tahra.org

Training & Development

American Society for Training & Development Job Bank	http://jobs.astd.org

Instructional Systems Technology Jobs	http://education.indiana.edu/ist/students/jobs/
International Society for Performance	joblink.html
Improvement Job Bank	www.ispi.org
Training Consortium	www.trainingconsortium.net
Training Forum	www.trainingforum.com
Trainingjob.com	www.trainingjob.com
TrainingProviderJobs.co.uk [United Kingdom]	www.trainingproviderjobs.co.uk

Other Specialty

New Jersey Human Resource Planning Group	www.njhrpg.org
OD Network On-line	www.odnetwork.org

-I-

Industrial/Manufacturing

American Chemical Society Rubber Division	www.rubber.org
American Forest & Paper Association	www.afandpa.org
Association of Industrial Metalizers, Coaters &	www.aimcal.org
Laminators	
Auto Glass Magazine	www.glass.org
AutomationTechies.com	www.automationtechies.com
Blue Collar Jobs	www.bluecollarjobs.com
Bluewire Technologies	www.bluewire-technologies.com
CastingJobs.com	www.castingjobs.com
CoatingsCareers.com	www.coatingscareers.com
COBRA	www.technologysource.com
Drilling Research Institute	www.drillers.com/pages/view/jobs
Bluewire Technologies	www.bluewire-technologies.com
Energy Careers	www.energycareers.com
Finishing.com	www.finishing.com
FM Link-Facilities Management	www.fmlink.com

HVACagent.com	www.hvacagent.com
iHireManufacturingEngineers.com	www.ihiremanufacturingengineers.com
JobsinManufacturing.com	www.jobsinmanufacturing.com
Inteletex	www.inteletex.com
Iron & Steel Society	www.issource.org
Jobwerx	www.jobwerx.com
MachinistJobSite.com	www.machinistjobsite.com
The Manufacturing Job	www.themanufacturingjob.com
ManufacturingJob.com	www.manufacturingjob.com
Manufacturing Job Store	www.manufacturingjobstore.com
ManufacturingJobs.com	www.manufacturingjobs.com
MaterialsJobs.com	www.materialsjobs.com
MDL CareerCenter	http://careercenter.devicelink.com
MiManufacturingJobs.com	www.mimanufacturingjobs.com
MoldingJobs.com	www.moldingjobs.com
National Association of Industrial Technology	http://atmae.org/
National Defense Industrial Association	http://ndia.monster.com
OilCareer.com	www.oilcareer.com
The Oil Directory	www.oildirectory.com
Petroleum Services Association of Canada Employment	www.psac.ca
Plant Maintenance Resource Center	www.plant-maintenance.com
Power Builder Journal	http://pbdj.sys-con.com/
Semicon	www.semicon.com
Semicon Bay	www.semiconbay.com
Sheet Metal and Air Conditioning Contractor's Association	www.smacna.org
SocialService.com	www.socialservice.com
Society of Petrologists & Well Log Analysts Job Opportunities	www.spwla.org
Subseaexplorer	www.subseaexplorer.com
SwissCNCJobs.com	www.swisscncjobs.com
Top Echelon Network	www.topechelon.com

USA Manufactuiring Jobs   www.usamanufacturingjobs.com

UtilityJobSearch.com [United Kingdom]   www.utilityjobsearch.com

Information Technology/Information Systems
(Software, Hardware, Middleware, Client server, Web specialists)

Information Technology-General

A1A Computer Jobs Mailing List   www.a1acomputerpros.net

A-Z Internet Jobs   www.a-zjobs.com

Ace thee Interview   www.acetheinterview.com

The Ada Project   http://women.cs.cmu.edu/ada

AD&A Software Jobs Home Page   http://softwarejobs.4jobs.com

The Advanced Computing Systems Association   http://usenix.org

Adviser Zone   www.adviserzone.com

AS400 Network   http://systeminetwork.com

Association for Computing Machinery Career   http://acpinternational.org
     Resource Center

Association for Educational Communications   www.aect.org
     and Technology Job Center

Association of Internet Professionals National   http://association.org
     Job Board

Asynchrony   www.asynchrony.com

Avatar Magazine   www.avatarmag.com

Beeline.com   www.beeline.com/workforce-solutions

Bluewire Technologies   www.bluewire-technologies.com

Brain Buzz   www.cramsession.com

Brain Power   www.brainpower.com

CanadaIT.com   www.canadait.com/cfm/index.cfm

CanadaJobs.com   www.canadajobs.com

CardBrowser.com   www.cardbrowser.com

CareerFile   www.careerfile.com

Career Magic   www.careermagic.com

Career Marketplace Network   www.careermarketplace.com

Career Shop	www.autohiresoftware.com
Cert Review	www.itspecialist.com/default.aspx
CIO	http://itjobs.cio.com/a/all-jobs/list?source= top_nav
CM Today (Configuration Management)	www.cmcrossroads.com
CNET's Ultimate ISP Guide	www.cnet.com
Cobol Jobs	www.coboljobs.com
Comforce	www.comforce.com
ComputerJobs.com	www.computerjobs.com/homepage.aspx
ComputerJobs.ie [Ireland]	www.computerjobs.ie
computerjobsbank.com	www.computerjobsbank.com
Computerwork.com	www.computerwork.com
Computing Research Association Job Announcements	www.cra.org/ads
Contract Employment Weekly	www.ceweekly.com
Contract Job Hunter	www.cjhunter.com
CREN	www.computingresources.com
CRN	www.crn.com/cwb/careers
Data Masters	www.datamasters.com
DevBistro.com	www.devbistro.com
Developers.Net	www.developers1.net
Devhead	www.zdnet.com/?tag=header;header-pri
DICE	www.dice.com
Discover Jobs	www.discover-jobs.com
Dr. Dobb's	www.drdobbs.com
eChannelLinecareers.com [Canada]	www.echannellinecareers.com
Eclectic [Netherlands]	www.eclectic.eu
eContent	www.ecmag.net
Educause	www.educause.edu
EE Times	www.eetimes.com
E-itsales.com [United Kingdom]	www.e-itsales.com
eLance	www.elance.com
Embedded.com	www.embedded.com

eMoonlighter	www.moonlighter.com
The Engineering Technology Site [United Kingdom]	www.engineers4engineers.co.uk
eWork Exchange	www.ework.com
15 Seconds Job Classifieds	www.15seconds.com
FutureGate [Great Britain]	www.futuregate.co.uk/internet.html
GetAFreelancer.com	www.getafreelancer.com
GisaJob.com [United Kingdom]	www.gisajob.com
Gurus.com.au [Australia]	http://gurus.com.au
GxPJobs.com [United Kingdom]	www.gxpjobs.com
H1B Sponsors	www.h1bsponsors.com
Hi-Tech Careers	www.careermarthi-tech.com
Hi-Tech Club	www.hitechclub.com
High Technology Careers	www.hightechcareers.com/hc3.asp
Hire Ability	www.hireability.com
Huntahead	www.huntahead.com/index.htm
Iitjobs.com	www.iitjobs.com
InfiNet	www.infi.net
InformationWeek Career	www.informationweek.com/career
In the Middle [United Kingdom]	www.inthemiddle.co.uk
Informix Jobs	www.premierjobs.com
Intega Online [United Kingdom]	www.compucaregroup.com
Inter City Oz	http://interoz.com
Internet.com	www.justtechjobs.com
iSmart People	www.ismartpeople.com
ITArchtectJobs.com	www.itarchitectjobs.com
ITcareers.com	http://itjobs.computerworld.com/a/all-jobs/list
IT Classifieds	www.itclassifieds.com/Main/Default.asp
IT Firms	www.itfirms.com
IT-JobBank [Denmark]	www.it-jobbank.dk
TheITJobBoard.com [United Kingdom]	www.theitjobboard.com
ITjobs.com	www.itjobs.com
ITjobs.ca [Canada]	www.itjob.ca

IT Jobs Online [United Kingdom]	www.itjobsonline.com
IT JobsPost [United Kingdom]	www.itjobspost.com
IT Jobs Vault	www.itjobsvault.co.uk
IT Talent	www.ittalent.com
ITVacancies.com [United Kingdom]	www.itvacancies.com
IT-webforum.com	www.it-webforum.com
JV Search	www.jvsearch.com
Job Ads	www.jobads.com
Job Authority	www.jobauthority.com
JobBoard.IT [United Kingdom]	www.jobboardit.com/CareerSite/jobboardit/index.htm
JobCircle.com	www.jobcircle.com
JobEngine	www.jobengine.com
The JobFactory	www.jobfactory.com
Job Island	www.jobisland.com
Jobit [United Kingdom]	www.jobit.co.uk
Job Net America	www.jobnetamerica.com
Job Serve	www.jobserve.us
Job Serve [United Kingdom]	www.jobserve.us/homepage.aspx
Job Warriors	http://jobwarriors.com
Job Webs	www.jobwebs.com
JobsDB	www.jobsdbusa.com
Jobs4IT.com	www.jobs4it.com
Jobs-net	www.jobs-net.com
JustIT [United Kingdom]	www.justit.co.uk
Just Tech Jobs	www.justtechjobs.com
KR Solutions [United Kingdom]	www.kr-solutions.co.uk
Lan Jobs	www.lanjobs.com
Latinos in Information Sciences and Technology Association	www.a-lista.org
Lotus Notes Jobs	http://lotusnotesjobs.com
Mojolin	www.mojolin.com
Neo Soft Corporation	www.neosoftware.com

Net Mechanic	www.netmechanic.com
Net-Temps	www.net-temps.com
OperationIT	www.operationIT.com
Oxygen [United Kingdom]	www.oxygenonline.co.uk
PC World	www.pcworld.com
PeopleSoft-Resources.com	www.peoplesoft-resources.com
The Perl Job Site	www.jobs.perl.org
PlanetRecruit [United Kingdom]	www.planetrecruit.com
Pracownicy.it [Poland]	www.pracownicy.it
PurelyIT.co.uk [United Kingdom]	www.purelyit.co.uk
Real-Time Engineering	www.realtime-engineering.com
Road Techs	www.roadtechs.com
SAS Institute	http://support.sas.com/usergroups/
Semiconductor Jobs	www.semiconductorjobs.com
Skills Village	https://support.oracle.com/CSP/ui/flash.html
Smarter Work	www.smarterwork.com
Society of Computer Professionals Online	www.comprof.com
SoftwareJobLink	http://softwarejoblink.com
Southern California Electronic Data Interchange Roundtable	www.scedir.org
staffITnow	www.staffitnow.com
Swift Jobs	www.swiftjobs.com
TechCareers	www.techcareers.com
.tech_centric	www.tech-centric.net
Tech-Engine	http://techengine.com
Tech Expo USA	www.techexpousa.com
TechEmployment.com	www.techemployment.com
Techie Gold	www.techiegold.com
Tech Job Bank	www.techjobbank.com
TechnoJobs [United Kingdom]	www.technojobs.co.uk
TechResults	www.techresults-nv.com
Tech Target	www.techtarget.com
TechWeb	www.techweb.com/home

Techs	www.techs.com
ThaiITJobs.com [Thailand]	www.thaiitjobs.com/en/index.asp
Top IT Consultant [United Kingdom]	www.topitconsultant.co.uk
VAR Business	www.crn.com/cwb/careers
Virtual Job Fair	http://careerexpo.jobing.com
Wireless Developers	www.wirelessdevnet.com
Work Exchange	www.workexchange.com
Element K Journals	www.elementkjournals.com

AS400

Just AS/400 Jobs	www.justas400jobs.com
News400.com	http://systeminetwork.com

Baan

BaanBoard.com	www.baanboard.com
Just BAAN Jobs	www.justbaanjobs.com

C++

C++ Jobs	www.cplusplusjobs.com
C++ Report	www.creport.com
C++ Users Group Job Links	www.hal9k.com/cug/jobs.htm
C Plus Plus Jobs	www.cplusplusjobs.com
Just C Jobs	www.justcjobs.com

Cobol

The Cobol Center	www.infogoal.com
CobolJobs.com	www.coboljobs.com
Just Cobol Jobs	www.justcoboljobs.com

Cold Fusion

Atlanta Cold Fusion User Group	www.acfug.org

Austin Cold Fusion Users Group	http://austincfug.wordpress.com/
CF Programmers	www.cfprogrammers.com
Chicago Central ColdFusion User Group	www.cccfug.org/cccfug/cccfug.cfm
ColdFusion Support Forums	www.adobe.com/cfusion/webforums/forum/index.
House of Fusion	cfm?forumid=1
	www.houseoffusion.com
Just Cold Fusion Jobs	www.justcoldfusionjobs.com

Database

Database Jobs	www.databasejobs.com
DataNewsJobs.com [Belgium]	http://datanews.rnews.be/datanews/nl/jobs
DBA Support	www.dbasupport.com
icrunchdata.com	www.icrunchdata.com
International DB2 Users Group	www.idug.org
Just DB2 Jobs	www.justdb2jobs.com
LazyDBA.com	www.lazydba.com
Learn ASP	www.learnasp.com/learnasp

Delphi

Delphi Jobs	www.delphijobs.com
Just Delphi Jobs	www.delphijobs.com

Electric Data Interchange

EDI Jobs Online	www.edijobsonline.com
EDI Coordinators & Consultants Clearinghouse	www.friend-edi.com
Just Exchange Jobs	www.justexchangejobs.com
Southern California Electronic Data Interchange Roundtable	www.scedir.org

ERP

ERP Central	www.erpcentral.com

ERP Fan Club	www.erpfans.com
ERP Jobs [Canada]	www.erp-jobs.com
ERP Knowledge Base	http://erp.ittoolbox.com
ERP People	www.erp-people.com
ERP Software	www.erpsos.com
The ERP Supersite	www.techra.com/mambo

Geographic Information Systems

Geo Community	www.geocomm.com
GeoJobs.org	www.geojobs.org
Get GIS Jobs	www.getgisjobs.com
GIScareers.com	www.giscareers.com
GIS Connection	www.gisconnection.com
GISjobs.com	www.gisjobs.com
GISjobs.org	www.gisjobs.org
GIS Jobs Clearinghouse	www.gjc.org
GISuser.com	www.gisuser.com

Java

All-Java-Jobs	www.all-java-jobs.com
Digital Cat	http://human.javaresource.com
Java Jobs	www.javajobs.com
Java World	www.javaworld.com
jGuru	www.jguru.com
Just Java Jobs	www.justjavajobs.com

Lotus Notes

Association of ex-Lotus Employees	www.axle.org
Just Notes Jobs	www.justnotesjobs.com
Lavatech	www.lotusnotes.com
Lotus Notes Jobs	http://lotusnotesjobs.com

MacIntosh

MacDirectory Job Opportunities	www.macdirectory.com
MacTalent.com	www.mactalent.com
The Mac Trading Post	www.mymac2u.com/themactradingpost

Network/LAN/WAN

iHireNetworkAdministrators.com	www.ihirenetworkadministrators.com
Just Netware Jobs	www.justnetwarejobs.com
Just Networking Jobs	www.justnetworkingjobs.com
LAN Jobs	www.lanjobs.com
The Network Engineer.com	www.thenetworkengineer.com
Network World Fusion	www.networkworld.com/careers

Oracle

Just Oracle Jobs	www.justoraclejobs.com
Orca—The Oracle Job Site	www.theoraclejobsite.com
Oracle Contractor Database	www.cois.com/houg/con.html
Oracle Fan Club	www.oraclefans.com
Oracle Fans	www.oraclefans.com
OraSearch.com	www.orasearch.com

PeopleSoft

Jobs for Programmers	www.prgjobs.com/Jobs.cfm/PeopleSoft
Just People Soft Jobs	www.justpeoplesoftjobs.com
People Soft Fans	www.peoplesoftfans.com
People Soft Links	www.itoolbox.com
PSoftPros.com	www.psoftpros.com

Power Builder

Just Power Builder Jobs	www.justpowerbuilderjobs.com
Power Builder Journal	http://pbdj.sys-con.com/

Programming

Code-Jobs.com	www.code-jobs.com
iDevjobs.com	www.idevjobs.com
iHireProgrammers.com	www.ihireprogrammers.com
Jobs for Programmers	www.prgjobs.com
Programmers Heaven	www.programmersheaven.com
Programming-Webmaster	www.programming.com
RentaCoder.com	www.vworker.com/RentACoder/DotNet/
Script Lance	default.aspx
	www.scriptlance.com
SoftwareJoblink.com	http://softwarejoblink.com
Superexpert	www.superexpert.com/blog/default.aspx

SAP

A1A Computer Jobs Mailing List	www.a1acomputerpros.net
Just SAP Jobs	www.justsapjobs.com
SAP Club	www.sapclub.com
The SAP Fan Club	www.sapfans.com
SAPInfo.net	www.sap.com/usa/index.epx
The SAP Job Board [Europe]	www.thesapjobboard.com
SAP Professional Organization	www.sapprofessionals.org
SAP Solutions	www.sap.com/usa/index.epx
The Spot 4 SAP	www.thespot4sap.com

Unix

Donohue's RS/6000 & UNIX Employment Site	www.s6000.com
Just UNIX Jobs	www.justunixjobs.com
Unix Guru Universe	www.ugu.com
UNIX admin search	www.unixadminsearch.com
Unix Review	www.networkcomputing.com
Unix World	www.networkcomputing.com

Visual Basic

Just VB Jobs	www.justvbjobs.com
V Basic Search	www.vbasicsearch.com
VB Code Guru	http://codeguru.com/vb
Visual Basic Jobs	www.visualbasicjobs.com

Web

All Web Jobs	www.allwebjobs.com
CGI Resource Index	http://cgi.resourceindex.com
DevBistro.com	www.devbistro.com
HTML Writers Guild HWG-Jobs	www.hwg.org/lists/hwg-jobs
I-Advertising	http://internetadvertising.org
Internet Job Store.com	www.internetjobstore.com
JobsInSearch.com	www.jobsinsearch.com
Just E-Commerce Jobs	www.juste-commercejobs.com
Just Web Jobs	www.justwebjobs.com
Search Hound	www.searchhound.com
SGML/XML Jobs	www.eccnet.com/xmlug
Site Experts	www.siteexperts.com
US Internet Industry	www.usiia.org
Web Programming Jobs	www.webprogrammingjobs.com
Web Site Builder	www.websitebuilder.com
XMLephant	www.xmlephant.com

Windows

Enterprise IT Planet	www.enterpriseitplanet.com
Information NT	www.informationnt.com
Just Tech Jobs	www.justtechjobs.com
Just Windows Jobs	www.justwindowsjobs.com
NTPRO	www.ntpro.org

Other Specialty

American Statistical Association Statistics Career Center	www.amstat.org/careers
Association for Women in Computing	www.awc-hq.org
Axaptajobs.com	www.axaptajobs.com
Black Data Processing Association Online	www.bdpa.org
Blackgeeks	www.blackgeeks.com
BroadbandCareers.com	www.broadband-careers.com
Carolina Computer Jobs	www.carolinacomputerjobs.com
Common Switzerland	www.common.ch
Controller Jobs	www.controllerjobs.com
CyberMediaDice.com [India]	www.cybermediadice.com
Donohue's RS/6000 & UNIX Employment Site	www.s6000.com
Ed Barlow's Sysbase Stuff	www.edbarlow.com
IrishDev.com [Ireland]	www.irishdev.com
IT Jobs in New York	www.it-jobs-in-new-york.com
Just Access Jobs	www.justaccessjobs.com
Just ASP Jobs	www.justaspjobs.com
Just Help Desk Jobs	www.justhelpdeskjobs.com
Just Informix Jobs	www.justinformixjobs.com
Just JD Edwards Jobs	www.justjdedwardsjobs.com
Just Mainframe Jobs	www.justmainframejobs.com
Just OLAP Jobs	www.justolapjobs.com
Just Perl Jobs	www.justperljobs.com
Just Progress Jobs	www.justprogressjobs.com
Just Project Manager Jobs	www.justprojectmanagerjobs.com
Just Q A Jobs	www.justqajobs.com
Just Security Jobs	www.justsecurityjobs.com
Just Siebel Jobs	www.justsiebeljobs.com
Just SQL Server Jobs	www.justsqlserverjobs.com
Just Sybase Jobs	www.justsybasejobs.com
Just Tech Sales Jobs	www.justtechsalesjobs.com
Just Telephony Jobs	www.justtelephonyjobs.com

Lapis Software	www.lapis.com
MinorityITJobs.com	www.minorityitjobs.com
MVShelp.com	www.mvshelp.com
NACCB	www.techservealliance.org/redirect.cfm
Project Manager	www.projectmanager.com
SAS-Jobs.com	www.sas-jobs.com
Software Contractor's Guild	www.scguild.com
Software Developer	www.softwaredeveloper.com
Software Engineer	http://softwareengineer.com
Software & IT Sales Employment Review	http://cardbrowser.com
Software QA and Testing Resource Center	www.softwareqatest.com
Sun Microsystems	www.oracle.com/index.html
Tech Writers	www.techwriters.com
Telecommuting Techies	www.telecommuting-techies.com
University of Maryland Computer Science Grads	www.cs.umd.edu/users
Texas A&M University Computer Science Grads	www.cs.tamu.edu
Women in Technology	www.womenintechnology.org
Women in Technology International (WITI) 4Hire	www.witi4hire.com

Insurance

Actuary.com	www.actuary.com
ActuaryJobs.com	www.actuaryjobs.com
Alliance of Merger and Acquisition Advisors	www.amaaonline.com
American Institute for Chartered Property Casualty Underwriters	www.aicpcu.org
Chartered Property Casualty Underwriters	www.cpcusociety.org
4 Insurance Jobs	www.4insurancejobs.com
Global Association of Risk Professionals Career Center	www.garp.com/careercenter/index.asp
Great Insurance Jobs	www.greatinsurancejobs.com
Great Insurance Recruiters	www.greatinsurancerecruiters.com
IFSjobs.com	www.ifsjobs.com

iHireInsurance.com	www.ihireinsurance.com
INSData	http://hanbiro.com/index.html
InsuranceClaimsWeb.com	www.insuranceclaimsweb.com
Insurance File	www.insfile.com
The Insurance Job Bank	www.iiin.com/iiinjobs.html
InsuranceJobs.com	www.insurancejobs.com
InsurancePathway.com	www.insurancepathway.com
InsuranceSalesJobs.com	www.insurancesalesjobs.com
InsuranceSalesWeb.com	www.insurancesalesweb.com
InsuranceUnderwritingWeb.com	www.insuranceunderwritingweb.com
InsuranceWorks.com [Canada]	www.insuranceworks.com/bins/index.asp
Jobs4Actuary	www.jobs4actuary.com
JobInsurance.ca [Canada]	www.jobassurance.ca
LIMRA International	www.limra.com
National Insurance Recruiters Association Online Job Database	www.nirassn.com
NationJob Network: Financial, Accounting and Insurance Jobs Page	www.nationjob.com/financial
Online Insurance Jobs [United Kingdom]	www.onlineinsurancejobs.co.uk
Property and Casualty	www.propertyandcasualty.com
Risk Info	www.riskinfo.com
Risk & Insurance Management Society Careers	www.rims.org
RiskManagementWeb.com	www.riskmanagementweb.com
Ultimate Insurance Jobs	www.ultimateinsurancejobs.com
UnderwritingJobs.com	www.underwritingjobs.com

International

International-General

AnyWorkAnywhere.com	www.anyworkanywhere.com
Campus Review	www.campusreview.com.au
CareerBridge	http://overview.careeredge.ca

CatererGlobal	www.catererglobal.com
Community Learning Network	www.cln.org
Danger Zone Jobs	www.dangerzonejobs.com
Empowered Network	http://empowerednetworks.com
Expat Exchange	www.expatexchange.com
ExpatHiring.com	www.expathiring.com
Expat Network	www.expatnetwork.com
Expatriates.com	www.expatriates.com
Escape Artist	www.escapeartist.com
Financial Job Network	www.financialjobnetwork.com
FT.com -Financial Times	www.ft.com
Global Workplace	www.qs.com/globalworkplace
International Jobs Center	www.internationaljobs.org
International Personnel Management Association	www.ipma-hr.org
International Society for Molecular Plant-Microbe Interactions	www.ismpminet.org/career
International Union of Food	www.iuf.org
JobsAbroad.com	www.jobsabroad.com
Jobs 4 All	www.jobs4all.com
Net Expat	www.netexpat.com
The Network	www.the-network.com
Oil Online	www.oilonline.com
OneWorld.net	http://us.oneworld.net/jobs
OverseasJobsExpress	www.overseasjobs.com
The Internet Pilot to Physics	http://physicsworld.com
Sales & Marketing Executives International Career Center	www.smei.org
Space Jobs	www.spacejobs.com
Top Jobs	www.topjobs.co.uk

Africa-General

AfricaJob.com	www.africajob.com

AfricaJobsSite.com	www.africajobsite.com
AfricaJobs.net	www.africajobs.net
FindaJobinAfrica.com	www.findajobinafrica.com
Job Searching for Africa	www.africa.upenn.edu
Kazinow.com	www.kazinow.com
NetServeAfrica	http://netserveafrica.com/jobs
WazobiaJobs.com	www.wazobiajobs.com

Argentina

Bumeran.com	www.bumeran.com
Buscares.com	www.buscares.com
Empleate.com	www2.empleate.com
Empleos.Clarin.com	www.empleos.clarin.com/Postulantes
Execuzone.com	www.execuzone.com
Jobrapido.ar	www.jobrapido.com.ar
Laborum.com	www.laborum.com/laborum_com/Default.htm
MineJobs.com	www.minejobs.com
TipTopJob.com	www.tiptopjob.com
Zeezo.com	www.zeezo.com
ZonaJobs.com.ar	www.zonajobs.com.ar

Asia-General

Asia Inc.	www.asia-inc.com
Asianet	www.asianetglobal.com
Asiaco Jobs Center	http://jobs.asiabot.com
Asianpro.com	http://asianpro.com
CareerJournal Asia	http://online.wsj.com/public/page/ news-career-jobs.html
Career Next	www.careernext.com
JobsDB	www.jobsdb.com
Job Street	www.jobstreet.com
Panda Career	www.pandacareer.com

Recruit.net   http://usa.recruit.net

Wang & Li Asia Resources Online   www.wang-li.com

Australia

Ambition	www.ambition.com.au
Artshub.com.au	www.artshub.com.au/au
The Australian Resume Server	www.herenow.com.au
TheBigChair.com.au	http://thebigchair.com.au
Campus Review	www.campusreview.com.au
CareerOne	www.careerone.com.au
Careers On Line	www.careersonline.com.au
Careers.vic.gov.au	www.careers.vic.gov.au
CG Society/society of Digital Artists [Australia]	www.gcsociety.org
Employment Opportunities In Australia	www.employment.com.au
Fairfax Market	http://classifieds.fairfax.com.au
GrapevineJobs.com.au	www.grapevinejobs.com/home.asp.au/home.asp
Gurus.com.au	http://gurus.com.au
Jobwire.com.au	www.jobwire.com.au/home.aspx
JobsDB	www.jobsdb.com
Jobsearch.gov.au	www.jobsearch.gov.au
JustEngineers.net	www.justengineers.net
LinkedMe	www.linkme.com.au
Manpower.com.au	www.manpower.com.au
MyCareer.com.au	http://mycareer.com.au/
MyMarketingJobs.com.au	http://mymarketingjobs.com.au/
Queensland Department of Primary Industries	www.dpi.qld.gov.au
RagTradeJobs	www.ragtradejobs.com
SEEK	www.seek.com.au
TotallyFinancial.com.au	www.totallyfinancial.com/australia
TotallyLegal.com.au	www.totallylegal.com/australia
TheWest.com.au	http://au.news.yahoo.com/thewest/
WorkingIn.com	www.workingin.com

Austria

Austria.at	www.austria.at
JobNews.at	www.jobnews.at
Jobrapido.at	www.jobrapido.at
Karriere.de	www.karriere.de
Kelzen.com	www.kelzen.com/en
Kununu.com	www.kununu.com
StepStone	www.stepstone.com
UniJobs.at	www.unijobs.at

Bahrain

Bayt	www.bayt.com

Baltics

CV Market	www.cvmarket.net

Bangladesh

JobsDB	www.jobsdb.com

Belarus

HeadHunter	http://hh.ru

Belgium

DataNewsJobs.com	http://datanews.rnews.be/datanews/nl/jobs/
JobsCareer.be	www.jobscareer.be
Organic Chemistry Jobs Worldwide	www.organicworldwide.net/jobs
StepStone	www.stepstone.com
ToplanguageJobs.be	www.toplanguagejobs.be
Vacature.com	www.vacature.com
Vlan.be	www.vlan.be

Bermuda

Bermuda Biological Station for Research, Inc.	www.bios.edu
BermudaJobs.com	www.bermudajobs.com

Brazil

Jobrapido.br	www.jobrapidobrasil.com
Zeezo	http://brazil.zeezo.com/jobs.htm

Bulgaria

Jobs.bg	www.jobs.bg

Canada

AbilityEdge	http://overview.careeredge.ca
ACREQ	www.cre.qc.ca
ActiJob	www.act1staff.com
AdminJob.ca	www.adminjob.ca
BaseJobs.com	www.basejobs.com
Battlefords Job Shop	http://regionalhelpwanted.com/home/279.htm
Calgary Job Shop	http://regionalhelpwanted.com/calgary-jobs
CallCenterJob.ca	www.callcenterjob.ca
CanadaIT.com	www.canadait.com/cfm/index.cfm
CanadaJobs.com	www.canadajobs.com
CanadaParttime.com	www.canadaparttime.com/content/flash
Canada's Fifty-Plus	www.fifty-plus.net
Canadian Association of Career Educators & Employers	www.cacee.com
Canadian Careers	www.canadiancareers.com
Canadian Relocation Systems	http://relocatecanada.com
Canadian Resume Centre	www.canres.com
Canadian Society of Biochemistry and Molecular and Cellular Biologists Experimental	www.medicine.mcgill.ca

Medicine Job Listing

Canadian Technical Recruiters Network	http://changethatsrightnow.com
Canjobs.com	www.canjobs.com
CanMed	www.canmed.com
CareerBridge	http://overview.careeredge.ca
CareerBuilder	www.careerbuilder.ca/CA/Default.aspx
CareerEdge	www.careeredge.ca
Career Internetworking	www.careerkey.com
Career Xchange	www.careerxchange.com
CASource	www.casource.com
Circuit Match	www.circuit-search.com/Esearch/applicant_ contact.asp
Diversity Careers	www.diversitycareers.ca
Eastern Ontario Job Shop	http://regionalhelpwanted.com/ eastern-ontario-jobs
eChannelLinecareers.com	www.echannellinecareers.com
Edmonton Job Shop	http://regionalhelpwanted.com/edmonton-jobs
Eluta.ca	www.eluta.ca
Globe and Mail	www.theglobeandmail.com
Grande Prairie Job Shop	http://regionalhelpwanted.com/home/307.htm
Hcareers	www.hcareers.ca
HeadHunt.com	www.thecounselnetwork.com
HRjob.ca	www.humanresourcesjobs.ca/default_en.html
Human Resource Professionals Association of Ontario	www.hrpa.ca/Pages/Default.aspx
InfoPresseJobs.com	www.infopressejobs.com
Institute of Chartered Accountants of Alberta	www.albertacas.ca
InsuranceWorks.com	www.insuranceworks.com/bins/index.asp
ITjob.ca	www.itjob.ca
Jobboom	www.jobboom.com
JobInsurance.ca	www.jobassurance.ca
JobLoft.com	www.jobloft.com
JobPostings.ca	www.jobpostings.ca

JobWings.com	www.jobwings.com
Jobs	www.jobs.ca
KW Job Shop	http://regionalhelpwanted.com/kitchener-waterloo-jobs
LegalJob.ca	www.legaljob.ca/default_en.html
Lethbridge Job Shop	http://regionalhelpwanted.com/lethbridge-jobs
Medicine Hat Job Shop	http://regionalhelpwanted.com/home/294.htm
Net @ccess	www.nac.net
New Brunswick Job Shop	http://regionalhelpwanted.com/new-brunswick-jobs
Newfoundland Labrador Job Shop	http://regionalhelpwanted.com/newfoundland-labrador-jobs
NiceJob.ca	www.nicejob.ca
Nova Scotia Job Shop	http://regionalhelpwanted.com/nova-scotia-jobs
Ottawa Area Computer Job Links Page	http://regionalhelpwanted.com/ottawa-jobs
Ottawa Job Shop	http://regionalhelpwanted.com/ottawa-jobs
Paralegaljob.ca	www.paralegaljob.ca
Payroll Jobs	www.payrolljobs.com
Petroleum Services Association of Canada	www.psac.ca
PMjob.ca	www.PMjob.ca
Prince Albert Job Shop	http://regionalhelpwanted.com/home/278.htm
Prince George Job Shop	http://regionalhelpwanted.com/home/309.htm
PubliPac.ca	www.publipac.ca
RecruitersCafe.com	www.recruiterscafe.com
Recrutech.ca	www.recrutech.ca
Red Deer Job Shop	http://regionalhelpwanted.com/home/285.htm
Regina Job Shop	http://regionalhelpwanted.com/regina-jobs
RetailJob.ca	www.retailjob.ca
SalesRep.ca	www.salesrep.ca
Saskatoon Job Shop	http://regionalhelpwanted.com/saskatoon-jobs
SCWIST Work Pathfinder	www.scwist.ca
SkilledWorkers.com	www.skilledworkers.com
Sympatico Work Place	www.sympatico.ca

Thompson Okanagan Job Shop	http://regionalhelpwanted.com/thompson-okanagan-jobs
Toronto Job Shop	http://regionalhelpwanted.com/toronto-jobs
Toronto Jobs	www.toronto.jobs.com
Toronto Society of Financial Analysts	www.tsfa.ca
Vancouver Job Shop	http://regionalhelpwanted.com/vancouver-jobs
Vancouver Jobs	www.vancouverjobs.com
Victoria Job Shop	http://regionalhelpwanted.com/victoria-jobs
Winnipeg Job Shop	http://regionalhelpwanted.com/winnipeg-jobs
Working.ca	www.working.ca
Workopolis	www.workopolis.com

Caribbean

CaribCareer.com	www.caribcareer.com
Caribbean JobFair	www.caribbeanjobfair.com
CaribbeanJobs.com	www.caribbeanjobs.com
CaribbeanJobsOnline.com	www.caribbeanjobsonline.com
Escape Artist	www.escapeartist.com
ResortJobs.com	www.resortjobs.com
TropicJobs.com	www.tropicjobs.com

Chile

Bumeran.com	www.bumeran.com
ChileTech.com	www.chiletech.com
Empleate.com	www2.empleate.com
Jobrapido.cl	www.jobrapido.cl
Laborum.com	www.laborum.com/laborum_com/Default.htm
TipTopJob.com	www.tiptopjob.com
Zeezo	http://chile.zeezo.com/jobs.htm

China

Asiaco Jobs Center	http://jobs.asiabot.com
CC-Jobs.com	www.cc-jobs.com
CJOL	www.cjol.com
ChinaHR.com	www.chinahr.com/index.htm
DragonSurf.biz	http://dragonsurf.biz
800HR	www.800hr.com
51job.com	www.51job.com
JobCN	www.jobcn.com
Job88.com	www.job88.com
Jobkoo	www.jobkoo.com
Job168.com	www.job168.com
JobSquare	www.jobsquare.com
JobsDB	www.jobsdb.com
Saongroup.cn	www.saongroup.cn
St 701	www.st701.com
Zaobao	www.zaobao.com
Zhaopin	www.zhaopin.com

Colombia

Bumeran.com	www.bumeran.com
Empleate.com	www2.empleate.com
Laborum.com	www.laborum.com/laborum_com/Default.htm
TipTopJob.com	www.tiptopjob.com

Croatia

MojPosao	www.moj-posao.net

Czech Republic

CV-Online	www.cvonline.cz
HotJobs.cz	www.hotjobs.cz

Jobs.cz	www.jobs.cz
Prace.cz	www.prace.cz
Sprace.cz	www.sprace.cz/index.fcgi

Denmark

IT-JobBank	www.it-jobbank.dk
Job-Index	www.jobindex.dk
+Jobs Danmark	www.denmark.plusjobs.com
StepStone	www.stepstone.com
TopLanguageJobs.dk	www.toplanguagejobs.dk

Egypt

Bayt	www.bayt.com

Estonia

CV Market	www.cvmarket.net
CV-Online	www.cvonline.cz

Europe-General

AuPair In Europe	www.planetaupair.com/aupaireng.htm
CareerJournal Europe	http://online.wsj.com/public/page/ news-career-jobs.html
CareersinAudit	www.careersinaudit.com/home/home.aspx
CVO Online	www.cvogroup.com
eFinancial Careers	www.efinancialcareers.com
Exposure Jobs	www.exposurejobs.com
EUjobzone.com	www.eujobzone.com
Euroleaders	www.euroleaders.com
Jobline International	www.jobline.net
The Network	www.the-network.com/
Russoft.org	www.russoft.org

The SAP Job Board	www.thesapjobboard.com
StepStone	www.stepstone.com
SupplyChainRecruit.com	www.supplychainrecruit.com
TipTopJob.com	www.tiptopjob.com
Top Language Jobs	www.toplanguagejobs.co.uk
Vault	www.vault.com/wps/portal/usa
Wideyes	www.wideyes.co.uk

Finland

StepStone	www.stepstone.com
Uranus	www.uranus.fi

France

AdenClassifieds	www.adenclassifieds.com
ANPE.fr	www.pole-emploi.fr/accueil
BlogEmploi	www.cadresonline.com/coaching/blog/index_ blog_emploi.php
Cadremploi.fr	www.cadremploi.fr
CadresOnline	www.cadresonline.com
CEGOS Worldwide	www.cegos.fr/Pages/default.aspx
CmonJob.fr	www.cmonjob.fr
Cooptin.com	www.cooptin.com
DialJob.com	www.dialjob.com
eFinancialCareers.fr	www.efinancialcareers.fr
eMailJob.com	www.emailjob.com
Jobrapido.fr	www.jobrapido.fr
KelJob.com	www.keljob.com
Les Echos	http://emploi.lesechos.fr
Mobiljob [France]	www.topannonces.fr
Monster.fr	www.monster.fr
ParisJob.com	www.parisjob.com
Purjob.com	www.purjob.com

| StepStone | www.stepstone.fr |
| TopLanguageJobs.fr | www.toplanguagejobs.fr |

Germany

All4Engineers.de	www.all4engineers.com
Arbeitlife.de	www.arbeitlife.de/arbeitlife_v2006/
Arbeitsagentur.de	www.arbeitsagentur.de
Association for Applied Human Pharmacology	www.agah.info
CallCenterProfi.de	www.callcenterprofi.de
City Jobs	www.cityjobs.com
EMBL Job Vacancies	www.embl.de/aboutus/jobs/index.php
FazJob.net	http://fazjob.net
Financial Times Deutschland	www.ftd.de
Germany-USA	www.germany-usa.com
Getjob.de	www.getjob.de
GrapevineJobs.de	www.mediajobs.de/home.asp
ICjobs	www.icjobs.de
JobBerlin.com	www.jobsinberlin.eu
Jobdoo.de	www.jobdoo.de
JobDumping.de	www.jobdumping.de
Jobline	www.jobline.de
JobPilot.de	www.jobpilot.de
Jobrapido.de	www.jobrapido.de
Jobs.de	www.jobs.de
JobScout 24	www.jobscout24.de
JobStairs.de	www.jobstairs.de
JobVoting.com	www.jobvoting.com
Jobware.de	www.jobware.de
Kimeta.de	www.kimeta.de
Meinestadt.de	www.meinestadt.de
Monster.de	www.monster.de
Pflegekarriere.de	www.pflegekarriere.de
Stellenanzeigen.de	www.stellenanzeigen.de

StepStone	www.stepstone.com
TopLanguageJobs.de	www.toplanguagejobs.de
Undertool.de	www.undertool.de
Virtueller Arbeitsmarkt	www.arbeitsagentur.de
WorkingOffice.de	www.workingoffice.de
Worldwide Jobs	www.worldwidejobs.de
Xing	www.xing.com
Yourcha.de	www.yourcha.com/de/employee/home/s

Greece

Kariera.gr	www.kariera.gr/GR/Default.aspx
Skywalker	www.skywalker.gr
StepStone	www.stepstone.com

Guam

Job Search in Guam	www.worldtenant.com/

Hong Kong

DragonSurf.biz	http://dragonsurf.biz
Hong Kong Jobs	www.hkjobs.com
Hong Kong Standard	www.thestandard.com.hk
JobsDB	www.jobsdb.com
Monster.com.hk	www.monster.com.hk

Hungary

CV-Online	www.cvonline.cz
CVO Online	www.cvogroup.com
GrapevineJobs.hu	www.grapevinejobs.hu/home/home.asp
Profession.hu	www.profession.hu
TopJob.hu	www.topjob.hu

India

AskNaukri.com	http://asknaukri.com
BPOJobSite.com	www.bpojobsite.com
CareerBuilderIndia.com	www.careerbuilder.co.in/IN/Default.aspx
Career India	http://jobs.oneindia.in/
Career Mosaic India	www.careermosaicindia.com
Cyber India Online	www.ciol.com
CyberMediaDice.com	www.cybermediadice.com
Icon Job	www.iconjob.com
Ikerala	www.ikerala.com
JobStreet.com	www.jobstreet.com
Jobs Ahead	www.jobsahead.com
JobsDB	www.jobsdb.com
MonsterIndia	www.monsterindia.com
Nasscom.in	www.nasscom.in
Naukri.com	www.naukri.com
RegisterJobs.com	www.registerjobs.com
TimesJobs.com	www.timesjobs.com

Indonesia

JobStreet.com	www.jobstreet.com.id

Iraq

All Iraq Jobs	www.alliraqjobs.com
Bayt	www.bayt.com

Ireland

AdminJobs.ie	www.adminjobs.ie
Antsjobs.ie	www.antsjobs.ie
ComputerJobs.ie	www.computerjobs.ie
Corporate Skills	www.irishjobs.com

Hcareers	www.hcareers.co.uk
IFSCjobs.com	www.ifscjobs.com
IrishDev.com	www.irishdev.com
Irishjobs	www.irishjobs.ie
The Irish Jobs Page	www.exp.ie
Jobrapido.ie	www.jobrapido.ie
JobSearchNI.com	www.jobsearchni.com
JobsinHealth.com	www.jobsinhealth.co.uk
JumptoJobs	www.jumptojobs.co.uk
Loadzajobs.co.uk	www.nijobfinder.co.uk
Northern Ireland Jobs	www.nijobs.com
RecruitIreland.com	www.recruitireland.com
SalesJobs.ie	www.salesjobs.ie/parodia/default.asp
ToplanguageJobs.ie	www.toplanguagejobs.ie
TotalJobs.com	www.totaljobs.com

Israel

AllJobs	www.alljobs.col.il
The Jerusalem Post	http://info.jpost.com/C005/IsraelJobs/
JobNet Israel	www.jobnet.co.il
Marksman	www.marksman.co.il
MyRecruiter.com	www.myrecruiter.com

Italy

Annunciveloci.it	www.infojobs.it
FaceCV	www.jobcrawler.it
Infojobs.it	www.jobonline.it
Jobcrawler.it	www.jobrapido.com
JobOnline.it	www.mediajobs.it
Jobrapido	www.monster.it
MediaJobs.it	www.stepstone.com
Monster.it	www.talentmanager.it

StepStone	www.toplanguagejobs.it
TalentManager	www.trovit.it
TopLanguageJobs.it	www.trovojobs.it
Trovit.it	

Jamaica

CarribeanJobs.com	www.carribeanjobs.com
SplashJamaica.com	www.splashjamaica.com

Japan

Career Forum	www.careerforum.net
Daijob.com	www.daijob.com
en-japan inc.	http://employment.en-japan.com
Japanese Jobs	www.japanesejobs.com
Job Easy	www.jobeasy.com
Mixi, Inc.	www.find-job.net
NAUKRI	www.naukri.com
O Hayo Sensei	www.ohayosensei.com
Tokyo Classified	http://classifieds.metropolis.co.jp/

Jordan

Akhtaboot	www.akhtaboot.com
Baytt	www.bayt.com

Kazakhstan

Headhunter	http://hh.ru

Korea

Asiaco Jobs Center	http://jobs.asiabot.com
Careerxiet	www.career.co.kr
Job Korea [not in English]	www.jobkorea.co.kr

Peoplenjob   www.peoplenjob.com/home

Kuwait

Bayt   www.bayt.com

Latin America

Asiaco Jobs Center   http://jobs.asiabot.com
Bumeran   www.bumeran.com
LatPro   www.latpro.com

Latvia

CV Market   www.cvmarket.net
CV-Online   www.cvonline.cz

Lebanon

Bayt   www.bayt.com

Libya

Bayt   www.bayt.com

Lithuania

CV Market   www.cvmarket.net
CV-Online   www.cvonline.cz

Luxembourg

Monster.lu   www.monster.lu
StepStone   www.stepstone.com

Malaysia

JobStreet.com	www.jobstreet.com.my
JobsDB	www.jobsdb.com
StarJobs Online	www.star-jobs.com

Mexico

ChambaMex.com	http://regionalhelpwanted.com/home/273.htm
Jobrapido.com.mx	www.jobrapido.com.mx
Laborum.com	www.laborum.com/laborum_com/Default.htm
OCCMundiall	www.occmundial.com

Middle East

Aljazeerajobs.com	www.aljazeerajobs.com
Arabia! Hot Jobs	www.arabiahotjobs.com
Bayt	www.bayt.com
Careerjunctionme.com	www.careerjunctionme.com
GulfJobSites.com	www.gulfjobsites.com
Gulftalent	www.gulftalent.com/home/index.php
MonsterGulf.com	www.monstergulf.com
My Middle East Jobs	www.mymiddleeastjobs.com
NaukriGulf.com	www.naukrigulf.com

Motenegro

Bestjobs.rs	www.bestjobs.rs

Morocco

Rekrute	www.rekrute.com

Netherlands

CareerBuilder.nl	www.careerbuilder.nl

City Jobs	www.cityjobs.com
CV Market	www.cvmarket.nl
EEGA	www.eega.nl
GrapevineJobs.nl	www.mediajobsonline.nl/home.asp
Hospitality Net Virtual Job Exchange	www.hospitalitynet.org/index.html
Jobrapido.nl	www.jobrapido.nl
Jobs Netherland	www.jobs.nl
JobTrack.nl	www.jobtrack.nl/jobtrack
MonsterBoard.nl	www.monsterboard.nl
NationaleVacaturebank.nl	www.nationalevacaturebank.nl
StepStone	www.stepstone.com
TopLanguageJobs.nl	www.toplanguagejobs.nl

New Zealand

Executive Taskforce	http://executivetaskforce.org/
Job.co.nz	www.job.co.nz
KiwiCareers	www.kiwicareers.govt.nz
RealContacts.com	http://jobs.realcontacts.com
SEEK	www.seek.co.nz
Trade Me	www.trademe.co.nz/Trade-me-jobs/index.htm
WineJobsOnline	www.winejobsonline.con
WorkingIn.com	www.workingin.com

Norway

CareerBuilder.no	www.careerbuilder.no
Finn.no	www.finn.no
Rubrikk.no	www.rubrikk.no
StepStone	www.stepstone.com
TopLanguageJobs.no	www.toplanguagejobs.no

Oman

Bayt	www.bayt.com

Pakistan

Bayt   www.bayt.com

Peru

Bumeran.com   www.bumeran.com
Empleate.com   www2.empleate.com
Laborum.com   www.laborum.com/laborum_com/Default.htm
TipTopJob.com   www.tiptopjob.com
Zeezo   http://peru.zeezo.com/jobs.htm

Philippines

JobStreet Philippines   www.jobstreet.com.ph
JobsDB   www.jobsdb.com
Jobs.NET   www.jobs.net
Philippines Jobs   www.philippinejobs.ph

Poland

CV-Online   www.cvonline.cz
Gazeta.pl   www.gazeta.pl/0,0.html
GazetaPraca.pl   http://gazetapraca.pl/gazetapraca/0,0.html
GrapevineJobs.pl   www.grapevinejobs.pl/glowna.asp
infoPraca.pl   www.infopraca.pl
JobPilot.pl   www.jobpilot.pl
Jobrapido.pl   www.jobrapido.pl
JobSpot.pl   www.jobspot.pl
MetroPlaca.pl   www.metroplaca.pl
MonsterPolska.pl   www.monsterpolska.pl
Pracownicy.it   http://pracownicy.it
Pracuj.pl   www.pracuj.pl
Targi24.pl   www.targi.pracuj.pl

Portugal

StepStone   www.stepstone.com
Super Emprego   http://emprego.sapo.pt

Qatar

Bayt   www.bayt.com

Romania

BestJobs   www.bestjobs.ro
CV-Online   www.cvonline.cz
JobsinRO.ro   www.jobsinro.ro
RomJob.ro   www.romjob.ro

Russia

Career.ru   www.career.ru
CV-Online   www.cvonline.cz
HeadHunter   http://hh.ru
Job.ru   www.job.ru
Joblist.ru   www.joblist.ru
100rabot.ru   www.100rabot.ru
Rabota.ru   www.rabota.ru
SuperJob.ru   www.superjob.ru

Saudi Arabia

All Saud Arabia Jobs   www.allsaudiarabiajobs.com
Bayt   www.bayt.com

Scotland

InternalAuditJobs.net   www.internalauditjobs.net
Jobsword   www.jobsword.co.uk/scotland.html

JobTonic.com	www.jobtonic.com
ScotCareers.co.uk	www.scotcareers.co.uk
Scot Ed Jobs	www.scotedjobs.com
ScotlandJobs.net	www.scotlandjobs.net
ScotRecruit.com	www.scotrecruit.com
ScottishHospitalityJobs.com	www.scottishhospitalityjobs.com
ScottishJobs.com	www.scottishjobs.com
ScottishLegalJobs.com	www.scottishlegaljobs.com
S1jobs.com	www.s1jobs.com
TechJobsScotland	www.techjobscotland.com
TotalJobs.com	www.totaljobs.com
WorkWithUs.org	www.workwithus.org/careers/Default.aspx

Serbia

BestJobs	www.bestjobs.rs
Infostud	http://jobs.infostud.com

Singapore

JobStreet.com	www.jobstreet.com.sg
Jobs Central.com.sg	http://jobscentral.com.sg
JobsDB	www.jobsdb.com
Singapore Jobs Directory	www.jobs.com.sg
SingaporeJobsOnline.com	www.singaporejobsonline.com
Singapore Press Holdings	www.st701.com

Slovakia

CV-Online	www.cvonline.cz
Profesia.sk	www.profesia.sk

Slovenia

Moje Delo	www.mojedelo.com

South Africa

Best Jobs South Africa	www.bestjobs.co.za
BioCareers.co.za	www.biocareers.co.za
CareerClassifieds South Africa	www.careerclassifieds.co.za
CareerJunction	www.careerjunction.co.za
Jobs.co.za	www.jobs.co.za

South Korea

Career	www.career.co.kr
Incruit.com	www.incruit.com

Spain

CareerBuilder.es	www.careerbuilder.es
InfoEmpleo.com	www.infoempleo.com
InfoJobs.net	www.infojobs.net
Jobrapido.es	www.jobrapido.es
Laboris.net	www.laboris.net
Miltrabajos.com	www.miltrabajos.com
Monster Espania	www.monster.es
Opcionempleo.com	www.opcionempleo.com
SmartCV.org	https://www.smartcv.org/smartcv2/Login.do
SmartEmployer.org	www.smartemployer.org
Spanish-Living.com	www.spanish-living.com/jobs_offers.php
TopLanguageJobs.es	www.toplanguagejobs.es
Trovit.es	www.trovit.es
Zeezo	http://spain.zeezo.com/jobs

Sweden

Dagens Industri	http://di.se
Jobb24.se	http://jobb24.se
Jobb.Eniro.se	http://jobb.eniro.se

Jobbguiden.se	www.careerbuilder.se
Jobbporten.se	http://jobbporten.se
JobSafari.se	www.jobbsafari.se
JobbSverige AB	www.jobbsverige.se
Jobrapido.se	www.jobrapido.se
Jobs.se	www.jobs.se
Lokus.se	http://lokus.se/Exp_SearchStart_all.asp?
Platsbanken	www.arbetsformedlingen.se/platsbanken
Shortcut	www.shortcut.nu
StepStone	www.stepstone.com
TopLanguageJobs.se	www.toplanguagejobs.se
Workey.se	www.workey.se
WorkShopping.com	www.workshopping.com

Switzerland

Common Switzerland	www.common.ch
JobPilot.ch	www.jobpilot.ch
Jobrapido.ch	www.jobrapido.ch
JobScout24.ch	www.jobscout24.ch
Jobs.ch	www.jobs.ch/en
LeTemps.ch	www.letemps.ch
Math-Jobs.ch	www.math-jobs.com
Monster.ch	www.monster.ch
StepStone	www.stepstone.com
TopJobs.ch	www.topjobs.ch

Tawain

DragonSurf.biz	http://dragonsurf.biz
JobsDB	www.jobsdb.com

Thailand

JobStreet.com Thailand	www.jobstreet.com.th

JobsDB	www.jobsdb.com
ThaiEngineeringJobs.com	www.thaiengineerjobs.com/en/index.asp
ThaiFinanceJobs.com	www.thaifinancejobs.com/en/index.asp
ThaiITJobs.com	www.thaiitjobs.com/en/index.asp

Turkey

Kariyer.net	www.kariyer.net

Ukraine

Rabota.ua	www.rabota.ua

United Arab Emirates

Bayt.com	www.bayt.com

United Kingdom

Access-Science Jobs	www.access-sciencejobs.co.uk
AccountancyAgeJobs.com	www.accountancyagejobs.com
AccountancyJobsboard	www.accountancyjobsboard.co.uk
AccountingWeb	www.accountingweb.co.uk
Activate.co.uk	www.activate.co.uk
Aeronautical Engineering Jobs	www.aeronauticalengineeringjobs.co.uk
Age Positive Jobs	www.agepositivejobs.com
Aged2Excel.co.uk	www.aged2excel.co.uk
AircraftEngineers.com [United Kingdom]	www.aircraftengineers.com
AllExecutiveJobs.com	www.allexecutivejobs.com
AllHospitality.co.uk	www.hospitalityonline.co.uk
AllHousingJobs.co.uk	www.allhousingjobs.co.uk
AllJobsUK.com	www.alljobsuk.com
Animal-Job.co.uk	www.animal-job.co.uk
Architecture Jobs	www.architecturejobs.co.uk
ArtsJobsOnline.com	www.artsjobsonline.com/home/home.asp

Association of Graduate Careers Advisory Service	www.agcas.org.uk
Association of Online Recruiters	www.rec.uk.com/home
Association of University Teachers	www.AUT4Jobs.com
Aston University	http://www1.aston.ac.uk/
Balfour Betty Rail UK	www.bbrailjobs.co.uk
Barzone	www.barzone.co.uk
Bconstructive	www.bconstructive.co.uk
Beachwood Recruit	www.beechwoodrecruit.com
Belperjobs	www.belperjobs.co.uk
BigBlueDog.com	www.bigbluedog.com
Billington UK.com	www.billingtonuk.com
BlowSearch.com	www.blowsearch.com
Blue Line Jobs	www.bluelinejobs.co.uk
BookaChef.co.uk	www.bookachef.co.uk
British Jobs	www.britishjobs.net
B7 Appointments	www.business7.co.uk/b7-appointments
BUBL Employment Bulletin Board	http://bubl.ac.uk
Building Services Jobs	www.buildingservicesjobs.co.uk
ButternutJobs.com	www.butternutjobs.com
Cactussearch.co.uk	www.cactussearch.co.uk
Call Centres	www.searchconsultancy.co.uk
Canary Wharf Careers.co.uk	www.canarywharfcareers.co.uk
CanaryWharfJobs.com	www.canarywharfjobs.com
CancerJobs.net	www.cancerjobs.net
Career-Ahead	www.career-ahead.co.uk
CareerBuilder.co.uk	www.careerbuilder.co.uk
Careers4a.com	www.careers4a.com
CareersinLogistics	www.careersinlogistics.co.uk
CareersinRacing.com	www.careersinracing.com
CareersInRecruitment.com	www.careersinrecruitment.com
Caterer.com	www.caterer.com
CatererGlobal.com	www.catererglobal.com

Changeboard	www.changeboard.com
CharityJob.co.uk	www.charityjob.co.uk
Check4Jobs	www.check4jobs.com
Chef Jobs	www.chefjobs.co.uk
ChemPeople.com	www.chempeople.com
Citifocus	www.citifocus.co.uk/home
City Careers	http://citycareers.com
CityJobs	www.citijobs.co.uk
ClearedJobs.co.uk	www.clearedjobs.co.uk
CollegeJobs.co.uk	www.collegejobs.co.uk
Confidential IT	www.confidentialit.com
Construction4Professional.co.uk	www.construction4professionals.co.uk
ConstructionJobSearch	www.constructionjobsearch.co.uk
ConstructionJobsNow.co.uk	www.constructionjobsnow.co.uk
Constructor	www.constructor.co.uk
ConsultantsBoard.com	www.consultantsboard.com
Consultants on the Net	www.consultantsonthenet.com
Consultants United	www.consultantsunited.com
Cronecorkill.co.uk	www.hirethinking.com/redirect/cc.aspx
The CV Index Directory	www.cvindex.com
CV-Library	www.cv-library.co.uk
CVServices.net	http://cv-masterclass.com/cv.html/
CVTrumpet.co.uk	www.cvtrumpet.co.uk
CWJobs.co.uk	www.cwjobs.co.uk
Datascope Recruitment	www.datascope.co.uk
Daxic.com	www.daxic.com
DERWeb	www.derweb.co.uk
DesignJobs.co.uk	www.designjobs.co.uk
DigitalMediaJobs.com	www.digitalmediajobs.com
DMjobs.co.uk	www.dmjobs.co.uk
Do-It	www.do-it.org.uk
dotJournalism	www.journalism.co.uk
DrapersOnline	www.drapersonline.com

Driving Jobs Board	www.drivingjobsboard.co.uk
Earthworks-Jobs	www.earthworks-jobs.com
EasyJobs.com	www.easyjobs.com
Edie's Environmental Job Centre	www.edie.net
Education-Jobs	www.education-jobs.co.uk
eFinancialCareers.com	www.efinancialcareers.com
EFL Web	www.eflweb.com
E-itsales.com	www.e-itsales.com
e-job	www.e-job.net
Emedcareers	www.emedcareers.com
ENDS	www.ends.co.uk/bs
The Engineer	www.theengineer.co.uk
Engineerboard.co.uk	www.engineerboard.co.uk
EngineeringJobs.co.uk	www.engineeringjobs.co.uk
EngineeringJobsnow.co.uk	www.engineeringjobsnow.co.uk
The Engineering Technology Site	www.engineers4engineers.co.uk
ERTonline.co.uk	www.ertonline.co.uk
Escape Artist	www.escapeartist.com
Eteach.com	www.eteach.com
Ethnicjobsite.co.uk	www.ethnicjobsite.co.uk
Euro London	www.eurolondon.com
Exec2Exec.com	www.exec2exec.com
TheExecutiveClub.com	www.theexecutiveclub.com
Executive-i.com	www.executive-i.com
ExecutiveOpenings.com	www.executiveopenings.com
ExecutivesOnline	www.executivesonline.co.uk
ExecutivesontheWeb.com	www.executivesontheweb.com
Experteer.co.uk	www.experteer.co.uk
FEcareers.co.uk	www.fecareers.co.uk
FEjobs.com	www.fejobs.com
50Connect.co.uk	www.50connect.co.uk
Findawork.co.uk	www.findawork.co.uk
First Choice Recruitment	www.first-choice-uk.co.uk

1st Job	www.1stjob.co.uk
1st 4 Jobs.com	www.1st4jobs.com
Fish4	http://www.fish4.co.uk/
Fledglings	www.fledglings.net
Focus-Management	www.focusmanagement.co.uk
Football-jobs.com	www.football-jobs.com
FootieJobs.com	www.footiejobs.com
4 Weeks	www.4weeks.com
Freeads.co.uk	http://uk.freeads.net/
FreeLancers Network	www.freelancers.net
Free-Recruitment.com	www.free-recruitment.com
Friday-Ad	www.friday-ad.co.uk
The Friday Pint	www.mediaweekjobs.co.uk
Front Recruitment	www.frontrecruitment.co.uk
Fss.co.uk	www.hirethinking.com
FuseJobs.co.uk	www.fusejobs.co.uk
FutureGate	www.futuregate.co.uk/internet.html
G2legal	www.g2legal.co.uk
GAAPWeb.com	www.gaapweb.com
GetMoreJobOffers.com	www.getmorejoboffers.com
GisaJob.com	www.gisajob.com
Glenrecruitment.co.uk	www.glenrecruitment.co.uk
GoJobSite	www.jobsite.co.uk
GoldJobs.com	www.goldjobs.com
Goldensquare.com	www.goldensquare.com
TheGraduate.co.uk	www.thegraduate.co.uk
Graduate-jobs.com	www.graduate-jobs.com
GraduatesYorkshire	www.graduatesyorkshire.co.uk
Grapevine Jobs	www.grapevinejobs.com/home.asp
GreenJobsOnline	www.greenjobsonline.co.uk
GrocerJobs.co.uk	http://jobs.thegrocer.co.uk
GTNews	www.gtnews.com
Guardian Jobs	www.guardianjobs.com

Guardian News and Media	http://jobs.guardian.co.uk
Gumtree.com	www.gumtree.com
GxPJobs.com	www.gxpjobs.com
Hcareers	www.hcareers.co.uk
HealthJobsUK.com	www.healthjobsuk.com/select_sector
Hedge Fund Intelligence LLC	www.hedgefundintelligence.com
HighTech Partners	www.hightechpartners.com
HospitalityRecruitment.co.uk	www.hospitalityrecruitment.co.uk
Hotcourses.com	www.givemeajob.co.uk
HotJobsandCareers	www.hotjobsandcareers.com
HotRecruit	www.hotrecruit.com
Hotel Jobs	www.hotel-jobs.co.uk
HR Staff	www.hrstaff.co.uk
Hy-phen	www.hy-phen.com
icNetwork.co.uk	www.icnetwork.co.uk
Ics Jobsboard	www.instituteofcustomerservicejobs.com
InAutomotive.com	www.inautomotive.com
In the Middle	www.inthemiddle.co.uk
Indeed.co.uk	www.indeed.co.uk
The Independent Consultants Network	www.inconet.com
Industry Appointments	www.industryappointments.com
InHR	www.inhr.co.uk
InRetail	www.inretail.co.uk
Intega Online	www.compucaregroup.com
InternalAuditJobs.net	www.internalauditjobs.net
ITCV	www.itcvrecruitment.co.uk/home.htm
TheITJobBoard.com	www.theitjobboard.com
ItJobs-online.com	www.itjobs-online.com
ITJobsPost.com	www.itjobspost.com
Itjobsvault.co.uk	www.itjobsvault.co.uk
ITVacancies.com	www.itvacancies.com
Jim Finder	www.jimfinder.com
Jobboard.IT	www.jobboardit.com

Jobcentre Plus	www.jobcentreplus.gov.uk
Jobcorner	www.jobcorner.com
JobChannel	www.jobchannel.cn
Job Finder	www.jobfinder.com
Job Force	www.jobforce.com
Job4me.com	www.job4me.com
Jobit	www.jobit.co.uk
Job Jobbed	www.jobjobbed.com
JobJourneyNorthWest.co.uk	http://northwest.jobjourney.co.uk/
JobLux	www.joblux.co.uk
Job Magic	www.jobmagic.net
Job Magnet	www.jobmagnet.co.uk
JobMax.co.uk	www.jobmax.co.uk
JobPlant.co.uk	www.jobplant.co.uk
Job-Quest	www.job-quest.net
Jobrapido.co.uk	www.jobrapido.co.uk
JobSafari	www.jobsafari.co.uk
Job Search UK	www.jobsearch.co.uk
JobseekersAdvice.com	www.jobseekersadvice.com
Job Serve	www.jobserve.us
Job Shop	www.workweb.co.uk
JobSite UK	www.jobsite.co.uk
Job Store	www.jobstore.co.uk
Job-surf.com	www.job-surf.com
JobTonic.com	www.jobtonic.com
JobTrack Online	http://jobs.mirror.co.uk/
Job Watch	www.jobwatch.org
Jobworld UK	www.computing.co.uk
Jobs.ac.uk	www.jobs.ac.uk
Jobs.brandrepublic.com	http://jobs.brandrepublic.com
Jobs.co.uk	www.jobs.co.uk
JobsCheshire.co.uk	www.jobscheshire.co.uk
JobsFinancial	www.jobsfinancial.com

Jobs4a.com	www.jobs4a.com
Jobsgopublic	www.jobsgopublic.com
JobsinCredit	www.jobsincredit.com
Jobsin.co.uk	www.jobsearch.co.uk
Jobs in Marketing	www.jobs-in-marketing.co.uk
JobsinCatering	www.jobsincatering.com
JobsinConstruction	www.jobsinconstruction.co.uk
JobsinContactCentres	www.jobsincontactcentres.com
JobsinEducation	www.jobsineducation.com
JobsinHealth	www.jobsinhealth.co.uk
JobsinHotels	www.jobsinhotels.com
JobsinLeisure	www.jobsinleisure.com
JobsinNHS	www.jobsinnhs.co.uk
JobsinPlymouth	www.jobsinplymouth.co.uk
JobsinPublicSector	www.jobsinpublicsector.co.uk
JobsinRetail	www.jobsinretail.com
JobsinRisk.com	www.jobsinrisk.com
JobsinSearch.com	www.jobsinsearch.com
JobsinSocialWork	www.jobsinsocialwork.com
JobsinSurveying	www.jobsinsurveying.co.uk
JobsinTravelandTourism	www.jobsintravelandtourism.com
JobsinWaste	www.jobsinwaste.co.uk
Jobs-Merseyside.co.uk	www.jobs-merseyside.co.uk
JobsMidlands.co.uk	www.jobsmidlands.co.uk
JobsNortheast.co.uk	www.jobsnortheast.co.uk
JobsNorthwest.co.uk	http://corporate.menmedia.co.uk/
Job Souk	www.jobsouk.com
Jobs-Southeast.co.uk	www.jobs-southeast.co.uk
Jobs.telegraph.co.uk	http://jobs.telegraph.co.uk
Jobs.ThirdSector.co.uk	http://jobs.thirdsector.co.uk/
Jobs2.com	www.jobs2.com
Jobs2seek.co.uk	www.jobsretail.co.uk
JobsWithBalls.com	www.jobswithballs.com

Johnston Vere	www.johnston-vere.co.uk
Journalism.co.uk	www.journalism.co.uk
JustClick.co.uk	www.justclick.co.uk
Just Construction	www.justconstruction.net
Just Engineers	www.justengineers.net
Just Go Contract!	www.gocontract.com
Just Graduates	www.justgraduates.net
JustIT	www.justit.co.uk
Just Rail	www.justrail.net
JustSalesandMarketing.net	www.justsalesandmarketing.net
JustTechnicalJobs	www.jobsgroup.net
KillerJobs.com	www.killerjobs.com
Labourstartjobs.org	www.labourstart.org
Laser Computer Recruitment	www.laserrec.co.uk
Law Gazette Jobs	www.lawgazettejobs.co.uk
Legal Jobs Board	www.legaljobsboard.co.uk
Legal Prospects	www.legalprospects.com
Leisure Jobs	www.leisurejobs.com
Leisure Jobs	www.leisurejobs.net
Leisure Jobs Now	www.leisurejobsnow.co.uk
Leisure Opportunities	www.leisureopportunities.co.uk
Leisure Recruit Ltd	www.thelrgroup.co.uk
LettingCareers	www.lettingcareers.com
Local Government Jobs	www.lgjobs.com
LocalJobSearch.co.uk	www.localjobsearch.co.uk
LocalRecruit.co.uk	www.localrecruit.co.uk
Locum Group Recruitment	www.locumgroup.co.uk//home.php
The London Biology Network	www.biolondon.org.uk
London Careers	www.londoncareers.net
London Jobs	www.londonjobs.co.uk
London Net	www.londonnet.co.uk
LondonOfficeJobs.co.uk	www.londonofficejobs.co.uk
TheLondonPaper.com	www.thelondonpaper.com

LondonSecretarialJobs.co.uk	www.londonsecretarialjobs.co.uk
LookTech.com	www.looktech.com
Mandy.com	www.mandy.com/1/filmtvjobs.cfm?jt=usa
Marine Recruitment Co.	www.marine-recruitment.co.uk
MarketingJobBoard.co.uk	www.marketingjobboard.co.uk
Maxim Recruitment	www.maximrecruitment.co.uk
MediaSalesJobs.co.uk	www.mediaweekjobs.co.uk
MedicSolve.com	www.medicsolve.com
Medjobsuk.com	www.medjobsuk.com
Milkround.com	www.milkround.com
Monster.com UK	www.monster.co.uk
MyAccountancyJobs	www.myaccountancyjobs.com
Mycvonline UK	www.mycv-online.com
MyHousingCareer	www.myhousingcareer.com
MyJobGroup.co.uk	www.myjobgroup.co.uk
My9to5.com	www.my9to5.com
My Oyster	www.myoyster.com
NannyJob.co.uk	www.nannyjob.co.uk
National Information Services and Systems	www.hero.ac.uk/uk/home/index.cfm
Net J	www.netjobs.co.uk
New Life Network	www.newlifenetwork.co.uk
NewMonday.co.uk	www.newmonday.co.uk
News International/The London Paper	www.thelondonpaper.com
NHS Jobs	www.jobs.nhs.uk
NHSjobs.com	www.nhsjobs.com/select_sector
Nixers.com	www.nixers.com
NMC4Jobs.com	www.nmc4jobs.com
Northwest Workplace	www.northwestworkplace.com
NurseryWorldJobs.co.uk	www.nurseryworldjobs.co.uk
Nurseserve	www.nurserve.co.uk
TheNursingJobSite.com	www.thenursingjobsite.com
Nursingnetuk	www.nursingnetuk.com/job_search/s1
Office Recruit	www.officerecruit.com

Offsite Jobs	www.offsitejobs.co.uk
Oil Careers	www.oilcareers.com/worldwide
1job.co.uk	www.1job.co.uk
Online Insurance Jobs	www.onlineinsurancejobs.co.uk
OnlineMarketingJobs.com	www.onlinemarketingjobs.com
OnrecJobs.com	www.onrecjobs.com
OutdoorStaff	www.outdoorstaff.co.uk
Oxygen	www.oxygenonline.co.uk
PersonnelTodayJobs.com	www.personneltoday.com
PFJobs	www.pfjobs.co.uk
Pharmacareers.co.uk	www.pharmacareers.co.uk
PharmaTalentPool.com	www.pharmatalentpool.com
Pharmiweb.com	www.pharmiweb.com
Phee Farrer Jones Consultancy	www.pfj.co.uk
PhoneAJob	www.phoneajob.com
PlanetAudit	www.planetaudit.net
PlanetRecruit	www.planetrecruit.com
PlatinumJobs.com	www.platinumjobs.com
Pr4a.com	www.pr4a.com
ProductionBase.co.uk	www.productionbase.co.uk
Prospects.ac.uk	www.prospects.ac.uk
PRWeek Jobs	www.prweekjobs.co.uk
The Publican	www.thepublican.com
PublicJobsDirect.com	www.publicjobsdirect.com
PurelyIT.co.uk	www.purelyit.co.uk
QUANTster.com	www.quantster.com
Qworx.com	www.qworx.com
Rail Job Search	www.railjobsearch.com/index.html
Ready People	www.readypeople.eu
Recruit Construction	wwww.recruitconstruction.com
RecruiterSite	www.recruitersite.co.uk
Recruitment	www.recruitment.com
Recruitmentcareers.co.uk	www.recruitmentcareers.co.uk

Recruitment Jobz	www.recruitmentjobz.com
Recruitment-Marketing	www.recruitment-marketing.co.uk
Recruit-TV.com	www.recruit-tv.com
Redadvertising	www.redadvertising.co.uk
Redgoldfish.co.uk	www.redgoldfish.co.uk
Reed.co.uk	www.reed.co.uk
RenewableEnergyJobs.com	www.renewableenergyjobs.com
Resourcing International Consulting	www.cyber-cv.com
Resortjobs.co.uk	www.resortjobs.co.uk
Resort Work	www.resortwork.co.uk
Restaurant Jobs	www.restaurantjobs.co.uk
RetailCareers.co.uk	www.retailcareers.co.uk
RetailChoice.com	www.retailchoice.com
RetailHomepage.co.uk	www.retailhomepage.co.uk
RetailJobsBoard.co.uk	www.retailjobsboard.co.uk
RetailMoves.com	www.retailmoves.com
RetailWeek.com	www.retailweek.com
Rugby-jobs	www.rugby-jobs.com
S1jobs.com	www.s1jobs.com
SalesTarget.co.uk	www.salestarget.co.uk
SalesVacancies.com	www.salesvacancies.com
SalesWise.co.uk	www.saleswise.co.uk
Sciencecareers.org	http://sciencecareers.sciencemag.org
ScientistWorld.com	www.scientistworld.com
Season Workers	www.seasonworkers.com
Seasonal-Jobs.com	www.seasonal-jobs.com
Secrecruit.co.uk	www.secrecruit.co.uk
SecretarialCareers.co.uk	www.secretarialcareers.co.uk
Secretarialjobsboard.co.uk	www.secretarialjobsboard.co.uk
Secsinthecity	www.secsinthecity.co.uk
SecurityClearedJobs.com	www.securityclearedjobs.com
SimplyHRJobs	www.simplyhrjobs.co.uk
SimplyITSalesJobs	www.simplyitsalesjobs.co.uk

SimplyLawJobs	www.simplylawjobs.com
SimplyMarketingJobs	www.simplymarketingjobs.co.uk
SimplyMediaSalesJobs	www.simplymediasalesjobs.co.uk
SimplyPRJobs	www.simplyprjobs.co.uk
SimplySalesJobs	www.simplysalesjobs.co.uk
SkillsArena.com	www.skillsarenacorporate.com
Smarter Work	www.smarterwork.com
SmugOne.com	www.smugone.com
Solar Jobs	www.solarjobs.com
SourceThatJob	www.sourcethatjob.com
SpaOpportunities	www.spaopportunities.com
StepStone	www.stepstone.com
SupplyChainOnline	www.supplychain.co.uk
SupplyChainRecruit.com	www.supplychainrecruit.com
Synergygroup.co.uk	www.synergygroup.co.uk
Teachnetwork.co.uk	www.teachnetwork.co.uk
Technojobs	www.technojobs.co.uk
Tefl-jobs.co.uk	www.tefl-jobs.co.uk
Temps Online	www.tempsonline.co.uk
TipTopJob.com	www.tiptopjob.com
Top-Consultant.com	www.top-consultant.com
Top Contracts	www.topcontacts.com
TopITconsultant	www.topitconsultant.co.uk
Top Jobs	www.topjobs.net
Top Jobs	www.topjobs.co.uk
Top Language Jobs	www.toplanguagejobs.co.uk
TotalJobs.com	www.totaljobs.com
Totally Legal	www.totallylegal.com
TrainingProviderJobs.co.uk	www.trainingproviderjobs.co.uk
TravelJobSearch.com	www.traveljobsearch.com
Trovit.co.uk	www.trovit.co.uk
247recruit.com	www.247recruit.com
UK Graduate Careers	www.gti.co.uk/home

UK Therapist.co.uk	www.uktherapist.co.uk
Utility Job Search	www.utilityjobsearch.com
Vault	www.vault.com/wps/portal/usa
Wirelessmobile-Jobsboard.com	www.wirelessmobile-jobsboard.com
Work4a.com	www.work4a.com
Workcircle.com	www.workcircle.com
Workhound.co.uk	www.workhound.co.uk
Workingmums.co.uk	www.workingmums.co.uk
WorksFM.com	www.worksfm.com
Workthing.co.uk	www.workthing.com
Worksfm.com	www.worksfm.com

Venezuela

Bumeran.com	www.bumeran.com
MeQuieroIr.com	www.mequieroir.com

Vietnam

JobStreet.com	www.jobstreet.com
JobsAbroad	www.jobsabroad.com/search/vietnam
VietnamWorks.com	www.vietnamworks.com

Wales

JobsinWales.com	www.jobsinwales.com
JobsWales.co.uk	www.jobswales.co.uk
WelshJobs.com	www.welshjobs.com

Investment/Brokerage

Advocis	www.advocis.ca
Annuitiesnet.com	www.annuitiesnet.com

Association for Investment Management
and Research

www.cfainstitute.org

Bond Buyer

www.bondbuyer.com

BrokerHunter.com

www.brokerhunter.com

CareerBank.com

www.careerbank.com

CommodityCareers

www.commoditycareers.com

efinancialCareers.com

www.efinancialcareers.com

International Association for Registered
Financial Planners

http://careers.iarfc.org

Investment Management and Trust Exchange

www.antaeans.com

National Association of Securities Professionals
Current Openings

www.nasphq.org/career.shtml

National Association of Securities Professionals
(Atlanta) Current Openings

www.naspatlanta.org

National Association of Securities Professionals
Railroad

www.nasp-ny.org   (New York) Underground

National Venture Capital Association

www.nvca.org

New York Society of Security Analysts Career
Resources

www.nyssa.org/AM/Template.
cfm?Section=career_development

Securities Industry Association Career
Resource Center

www.sifma.com/services/career_center/
career_center.html

Society of Actuaries

www.soa.org

Society of Risk Analysis Opportunities

www.sra.org/opportunities.php

-J-

Job Fairs Online

Job Dex

www.jobdex.com

NAACP Job Fair

www.naacpjobfair.com

OilCareerFair

www.oilcareerfair.com

TargetedJobFairs.com	www.targetedjobfairs.com
Targi24.pl [Poland]	www.targi.pracuj.PL

.

Journalism & Media (See also Graphic Arts)

Airwaves Job Services	www.airwaves.com
American Society of Journalists & Authors	www.freelancewritersearch.com
Animation Industry Database	www.aidb.com
Animation World Network	www.awn.com
Association of Electronic Journalists	www.rtnda.org
Association for Women in Communications	www.womcom.org
Association for Women in Communications WDC Chapter	www.awic-dc.org
Communications Roundtable	www.roundtable.org
Copy Editor Newsletter	http://jobs.copyeditor.com/home/index.cfm? site_id=502
Coroflot	www.coroflot.com
Creative Freelancers	www.freelancers.com
CyberJournalist.net	www.cyberjournalist.net
DigitalMediaJobs.com [United Kingdom]	www.digitalmediajobs.com
dotJournalism [United Kingdom]	www.journalism.co.uk
Editor & Publisher	www.editorandpublisher.com
eFront.com	www.efront.com
eLance.com	www.elance.com
FolioMag.com	www.foliomag.com
FreeLanceWriting.com	www.freelancewriting.com
The Friday Pint [United Kingdom]	www.mediaweekjobs.co.uk
GamesPress.com	www.gamespress.com
GrapevineJobs.com [United Kingdom]	www.grapevinejobs.com/home.asp
Grist.org	http://jobs.grist.org
Guru.com	www.guru.com
HTML Writers Guild HWG-Jobs	www.hwg.org/lists/hwg-jobs
I-Advertising	http://internetadvertising.org

International Association of Business Communicators Career Centre	www.iabc.com
The Internet Advertising Bureau Job Board	www.iab.net/jobs
JobLink for Journalists	http://newslink.org/newjoblinksearch.html
JobsinSearch.com	www.jobsinsearch.com
Journalism.co.uk [United Kingdom]	www.journalism.co.uk
JournalismJob.com	www.journalismjob.com
Journalism Jobs	www.journalismjobs.com
JournalismNext.com	www.journalismnext.com
Mandy.com	www.mandy.com/1/filmtvjobs.cfm?jt=usa
MassMediaJobs.com	www.massmediajobs.com
Mediabistro	www.mediabistro.com
Media Communications Association International Job Hotline	www.mca-i.org
Media Human Resource Association	http://jobs.com
Medialine	www.medialine.com
MediaRecruiter.com	www.mediarecruiter.com
National Alliance of State Broadcasters Associations CareerPage	www.careerpage.org
National Diversity Newspaper Job Bank	www.newsjobs.net
National Writers Union Job Hotline	https://nwu.org/
NationJob Advertising and Media Jobs Page	www.nationjob.com/media
News Jobs	www.newsjobs.net
Newspaper Association of America Newspaper CareerBank	www.naa.org/classified/index.html
OnlineMarketingJobs.com [United Kingdom]	www.onlinemarketingjobs.com
PaidContent.org	http://jobs.paidcontent.org
Print Jobs	www.printjobs.com
ProductionBase.co.uk [United Kingdom]	www.productionbase.co.uk
Silicon Alley Connections	www.salley.com
Society for Technical Communications	www.stc.org
SourceThatJob [United Kingdom]	www.sourcethatjob.com
StaffWriters Plus, Inc.	www.staffwriters.com

Sun Oasis	www.sunoasis.com
Telecommuting Jobs	www.tjobs.com
TV Jobs	www.tvjobs.com
Ultimate TV	www.ultimatetv.com
VFXWorld	www.vfxworld.com
VideoGameJournalismJobs.com	www.videogamejournalismjobs.com
Voice123	www.voice123.com
Webmonkey Jobs	www.webmonkey.com
Workinpr.com	www.workinpr.com
The Write Jobs for The Writers Write	www.writejobs.com
WritersWeekly.com	www.writersweekly.com

-L-

Law/Legal

Alliance of Merger and Acquisition Advisors	www.amaaonline.com
AlternativeLawyerJobs.com	www.alternativelawyerjobs.com
American Association of Law Libraries Job Placement Hotline	www.aallnet.org/hotline/hotline.asp
American Bankruptcy Institute Career Center	www.abiworld.org
American Bar Association	www.abanet.org
American Corporate Counsel Association	www.acc.com
American Immigration Lawyers Association	www.aila.org
Attorney Jobs	www.attorneyjobs.com
Attorney Pages	http://attorneypages.com
Barry University of Orlando	www.barry.edu/law/default.aspx
Bench & Bar	http://www2.mnbar.org/classifieds/ position-available.htm
Corporate Legal Times	www.insidecounsel.com./Pages/default.aspx
Counsel.net	www.counsel.net
Degree Hunter	http://degreehunter.net

eAttorney.com	www.martindale.com/Careers/Careers.aspx
Elite Consultants	www.eliteconsultants.com
Emplawyernet	www.emplawyernet.com
Find Law	http://careers.findlaw.com
FirmJobs.com	www.patentjobs.com
G2legal [United Kingdom]	www.g2legal.co.uk
HeadHunt.com [Canada]	www.thecounselnetwork.com
HG Legal Directories Legal Job Listings	www.hg.org/law-jobs.asp
Hieros Gamos Legal Employment Classified	www.hg.org/index.html
iHireLegal	www.ihirelegal.com
Intelproplaw	www.intelproplaw.com
International Association for Commercial and Contract Management	www.iaccm.com
The International Lawyers Network	www.iln.com
JobFox.com	www.jobfox.com
JobsLawInfo.com	http://jobs.lawinfo.com
TheLadders.com	www.theladders.com
Law.com	www.law.com/jsp/law/index.jsp
Law Bulletin	www.lawbulletin.com
LawCrossing	www.lawcrossing.com
Law Forum	www.lawforum.net
Law Gazette Jobs [United Kingdom]	www.lawgazettejobs.co.uk
Law Guru	www.lawguru.com
Law Info	www.lawinfo.com
Law Jobs	www.lawjobs.com
Law Match	www.lawmatch.com/
Law Office	http://lp.findlaw.com
Law Source	http://lawsource.com
Lawyers – About.com	http://legalcareers.about.com
Lawyers Weekly Jobs	http://classifieds.dolanmedia.com/LWJ01
The Legal Career Center Network	www.legalcareernetwork.com
The Legal Employment Search Site	www.legalemploy.com
Legal Gate	www.legalgate.com

Legal Hire	www.legalhire.com
LegalJob.ca [Canada]	www.legaljob.ca/default_en.html
Legal Job Store	www.legaljobstore.com
Legal Jobs Board [United Kingdom]	www.legaljobsboard.co.uk
Legal Jobs in New York	www.legal-jobs-in-new-york.com
Legal Prospects [United Kingdom]	www.legalprospects.com
Legal Report	www.legalreport.com
Legal Serve	www.legalserve.com
Legal Staff	www.legalstaff.com
National Association of Legal Assistants	www.nala.org
National Employment Lawyers Association	www.nela.org/NELA/
National Federation of Paralegal Associations	www.paralegals.org
National Paralegal	www.nationalparalegal.org
Nationwide Process Servers Association	www.processserversassociation.com
New Hampshire Legal Assistance	www.nhla.org
Paralegal City	www.paralegalcity.com
Paralegaljob.ca [Canada]	www.paralegaljob.ca
Paralegal Job Finder	www.paralegaljobfinder.com
Piper Pat	www.piperpat.co.nz
RegulatoryCareers.com	www.regulatorycareers.com
ScottishLegalJobs.com [Scotland]	www.scottishlegaljobs.com
SimplyLawJobs.com [United Kingdom]	www.simplylawjobs.com
Totally Legal [United Kingdom]	www.totallylegal.com
TotallyLegal.com.au [Australia]	www.totallylegal.com/australia
Trial Lawyers for Public Justice	www.tlpj.net

Law Enforcement & Fire Departments

American Society for Law Enforcement Training	www.aslet.org
Blue Line Jobs [United Kingdom]	www.bluelinejobs.co.uk
The Blue Line: Police Opportunity Monitor	www.theblueline.com
The Brass Key	www.thepoliceexecutive.com
DiscoverPolicing.org	www.discoverpolicing.org

EMSFireRescueJobs	www.emsfirerescuejobs.com
EMS World	www.emsresponder.com
FireandSecurityJobs.net	www.fireandsecurityjobs.net
FireJobs.com	www.firejobs.com
FireRecruit.com	www.firerecruit.com
FireRescue1	www.firerescue1.com
FireRescueJobs	www.firerescuejobs.com
FireServiceEmployment.com	www.fireserviceemployment.com
Firefighter Nation	www.firefighternation.com
Firehouse.com	www.firehouse.com
FiremenJobs	www.firemenjobs.com
GoLawEnforcement.com	www.golawenforcement.com
High Technology Crime Investigation Association	www.htcia.org
Hispanic American Police Command Officers Association	www.hapcoa.org
iHireLawEnforcement.com	www.ihirelawenforcement.com
JobCop	www.jobcop.com
LawEnforcementJobs.com	www.lawenforcementjobs.com
LawOfficer	www.lawofficer.com
National Black Police Association	www.blackpolice.org
National Organization of Black Law Enforcement Executives	www.noblenational.org
National Latino Peace Officers Association	www.nlpoa.org
911 Hot Jobs	www.911hotjobs.com
Officer.com	www.officer.com
Police Employment	www.policeemployment.com
Police Jobs	www.policejobs.com
Police Link	www.policelink.com
PoliceOne.com	www.policeone.com
Public Safety Jobs	www.publicsafetyjobs.com
Public Safety Recruitment	www.publicsafetyrecruitment.com
TechLawAdvisor.com Job Postings	http://techlawadvisor.com/jobs
Wild Fire Jobs	www.wildfirejobs.com

Women in Federal Law Enforcement   www.wifle.org

Library & Information Science

American Association of Law Libraries   www.aallnet.org/hotline/hotline.asp
    Job Placement Hotline

American Library Association   www.ala.org/ala/educationcareers/index.cfm

American Society for Information Science &   www.asis.org
    Technology

Art Libraries Society of North America JobNet   www.arlisna.org/jobnet.html

Association of Research Libraries   www.arl.org

BUBL Employment Bulletin Board [United   http://bubl.ac.uk
    Kingdom]

Inside Higher Ed   www.insidehighered.com

Libjobs.com   www.libjobs.com

LibraryJobPostings.org   www.libraryjobpostings.org

Library Journal   www.libraryjournal.com

LisJobs.com   www.lisjobs.com

LYRASIS   www.lyrasis.org

Media Central   http://mediacentral.net

Music Library Association Job Placement   www.musiclibraryassoc.org

New Mexico Library Association   www.nmla.org

Special Libraries Association   www.sla.org

Linguistics

Jobs in Linguistics   http://linguistlist.org/jobs/

Linguistic Enterprises   http://web.gc.cuny.edu/dept/lingu//

The Linguist List   http://linguistlist.org/jobs/index.cfm

Logistics & Maintenance

All Port Jobs	www.allportjobs.com
The Association for Operations Management	www.apicscareercenter.org
Blue Collar Jobs	www.bluecollarjobs.com
CareersinLogistics [United Kingdom]	www.careersinlogistics.co.uk
Energy Careers	www.energycareers.com
FM Link-Facilities Management	www.fmlink.com
HVAC Agent	www.hvacagent.com
iHIreLogistics	www.ihirelogistics.com
iHireMaintenanceandInstallation	www.ihiremaintenanceandinstallation.com
Jobstor.com	www.jobstor.com/cgi-bin/index.cgi
Jobs4Trucking.com	www.jobs4trucking.com
JobsinTrucks.com	www.jobsintrucks.com
JobsinLogistics.com	www.jobsinlogistics.com
LogisticsJobShop.com [United Kingdom]	www.logisticsjobshop.com
Logistics World	www.logisticsworld.com
LogJobs.com	www.logjobs.com
MaintenanceEmployment.com	www.maintenanceemployment.com
RoadTechs.com	www.roadtechs.com
SupplyChainBrain.com	www.supplychainbrain.com
SupplyChainJobs.com	www.supplychainjobs.com
SupplyChainOnline.co.uk [United Kingdom]	www.supplychainonline.co.uk
SupplyChainRecruit.com [Europe]	www.supplychainrecruit.com
Truckdriver.com	www.truckdriver.com
Virtual Logistics Directory	www.logisticsdirectory.com
WarehouseJobs.com	www.warehousejobs.com

-M-

Military Personnel Transitioning into the Private Sector

Army Career & Alumni Program	www.acap.army.mil
Blue-to-Gray	www.corporategray.com
CareerBuilder.com	www.careerbuilder.com
Center for Employment Management	https://www.cfainstitute.org/pages/index.aspx
ClearanceJobs.com	www.clearancejobs.com
Corporate Gray Online	www.corporategrayonline.com
The Defense Talent Network	www.defensetalent.com
Green-to-Gray	www.corporategray.com
HelmetstoHardhats.com	www.helmetstohardhats.com
Hire Quality	www.hire-quality.com
HireVetsFirst.gov	www.dol.gov/vets
Jobs4Vets.com	www.jobs4vets.com
Landmark Destiny Group	https://www2.recruitmilitary.com
Marine Executive Association	www.marineea.org
Military.com	www.military.com
Military Careers	www.todaysmilitary.com/careers
Military Connection	www.militaryconnection.com
Military Connections	www.militaryconnections.com
MilitaryHire.com	www.militaryhire.com
MilitaryExits	www.militaryexits.com
MilitaryJobWorld.com	www.militaryjobworld.com
Military JobZone	www.militaryjobzone.com
Military Spouse Corporate Career Network	www.msccn.org
Military Spouse Job Search	http://jobsearch.spouse.military.com
MilitaryStars.com	www.militarystars.com
My Future	www.myfuture.com
Operation Transition	www.dmdc.osd.mil/appj/dwp/index.jsp
RecruitAirForce.com	https://www2.recruitmilitary.com/
RecruitMarines.com	https://www2.recruitmilitary.com/

RecruitMilitary.com	https://www2.recruitmilitary.com/
RecruitNavy.com	https://www2.recruitmilitary.com/
Reserve Officers Association	www.roa.org/site/PageServer
Stripes.com	www.stripes.com
Transition Assistance Online	www.taonline.com
VeteranEmployment.com	www.veteranemployment.com
VeteranJobs.com	www.veteranjobs.com
VetJobs	www.vetjobs.com

Mining

Jobs4Mining	www.jobs4mining.com
MineJobs.com	www.minejobs.com
Petroleum & Mining Portal	www.pmjobs.net

Modeling

ModelService.com	www.modelservice.com
ModelService.com	www.modelservice.com
OneModelPlace.com	www.onemodelplace.com
Supermodel.com	www.supermodel.com

Music

FilmMusic.net	www.filmmusic.net
The Internet Music Pages	www.musicpages.com
Key Signature [United Kingdom]	www.keysignature.co.uk
MusiciansBuyLine.com	www.musiciansbuyline.com/music_ jobs_avail.html

-N-

Networking

Adholes.com	http://adholes.com
BusinessCard2.com	http://businesscard2.com
Eurekster	www.eurekster.com
Jobfox.com	www.jobfox.com
LinkedIn	www.linkedin.com
LinkedMe [Australia]	www.linkme.com.au
Monster Networking	www.monster.com
RealContacts	http://jobs.realcontacts.com
ReferYes.com	www.referyes.com
Rypple.com	www.rypple.com
Ryze Business Networking	www.ryze.com
Spoke	www.spoke.com
Wink.com	www.wink.com
Xing [Germany]	www.xing.com

Non-Profit

AllHousingJobs.co.uk [United Kingdom]	www.allhousingjobs.co.uk
American Society of Association Executives Career HQ	www.asaecenter.org
boardnetUSA	www.boardnetusa.org/public/home.asp
Bridgestar	www.bridgestar.org
Career Action Center	www.careeraction.org
CharityJob.co.uk [United Kingdom]	www.charityjob.co.uk
Chronicle of Philanthropy	http://philanthropy.com/section/Home/172
Community Career Center	www.nonprofitjobs.org
DotOrgJobs.com	www.dotorgjobs.com
ExecSearches	www.execsearches.com
The Foundation Center	http://foundationcenter.org

Fundraising Jobs	www.fundraisingjobs.com
Georgia Center for Nonprofits	www.gcn.org
Good Works	http://goodworksfirst.org//
Idealist	www.idealist.org
International Service Agencies	www.charity.org
JobsinPublicSector [United Kingdom]	www.jobsinpublicsector.co.uk
The National Assembly	www.nassembly.org
Non Profit Career Network	www.nonprofitcareer.com
Nonprofit Charitable Organizations	http://nonprofit.about.com
Non Profit Employment	www.nonprofitemployment.com
Non-Profit Marketing	www.cob.ohio-state.edu/fin/nonprofit.htm
Nonprofit Times	www.nptimes.com
NPO	www.npo.net
Opportunity Knocks	www.opportunityknocks.org
Philanthropy News Network Online	www.pnnonline.org/jobs
Social Service	www.socialservice.com
Tripod	www.tripod.lycos.com
VolunteerMatch	www.volunteermatch.org

-O-

Outdoors/Recreation/Sports

The Amateur Coaching Connection	www.tazsports.com
AnyWorkAnywhere.com [United Kingdom]	www.anyworkanywhere.com
Association for Environmental and Outdoor Education	www.aeoe.org
Camp Nurse Jobs	www.campnursejobs.com
CareersinRacing.com [United Kingdom]	www.careersinracing.com
C.O.A.C.H.	www.coachhelp.com
CoachingJobs.com	www.coachingjobs.com
Coaching Staff	www.coachingstaff.com

CoachingTalent.com	www.coachingtalent.com
Cool Works	www.coolworks.com
Cruise Job Link	www.cruisejoblink.com
Equimax	http://equ.equimax.com:8080/index.htm
FitnessJobs.com	www.fitnessjobs.com
Football-jobs.com [United Kingdom]	www.football-jobs.com
FootieJobs.com [United Kingdom]	www.footiejobs.com
Great Summer Jobs	www.petersons.com
Horticultural Jobs	www.horticulturaljobs.com
JobsinLeisure [United Kingdom]	www.jobsinleisure.com
Jobs In Sports	www.jobsinsports.com
JobsWithBalls.com [United Kingdom]	www.jobswithballs.com
Leisure Jobs [United Kingdom]	www.leisurejobs.com
Leisure Jobs [United Kingdom]	www.leisurejobs.net
Leisure Jobs Now [United Kingdom]	www.leisurejobsnow.co.uk
Leisure Recruit Ltd [United Kingdom]	www.thelrgroup.co.uk
Leisure Opportunities [United Kingdom]	www.leisureopportunities.co.uk
Lifeguarding Jobs	www.lifeguardingjobs.com
Motor Sports Employment	www.motorsportsemployment.com
National Sporting Goods Association	www.nsga.org
Online Sports Career Center	www.onlinesports.com/careercenter.html
Outdoor Ed	www.outdoored.com/jobs/oe/Default.aspx
OutdoorIndustryJobs.com	www.outdoorindustryjobs.com
The Outdoor Job	www.theoutdoorjob.com
OutdoorStaff [United Kingdom]	www.outdoorstaff.co.uk
Pet-Sitters.biz	www.pet-sitters.biz
PGA.com	www.pga.com/home
Resort Jobs	www.resortjobs.com
Resortjobs.co.uk [United Kingdom]	www.resortjobs.co.uk
Rugby-jobs [United Kingdom]	ww.rugby-jobs.com
SeasonalEmployment.com	www.seasonalemployment.com
Skiing the Net	www.skiingthenet.com
SportLink	www.sportlink.com

Sportscasting Jobs	www.sportscastingjobs.com
SummerJobs.com	www.summerjobs.com
TAZsport.com	www.tazsport.com
Teamwork Online	www.teamworkonline.com
Tennis Jobs	www.tennisjobs.com
WomenSportsJobs.com	www.womensportjobs.com
Women's Sport Services	www.wiscnetwork.com
WorkinSports.com	www.workinsports.com

-P-

Packaging for Food & Drug

Association of Industrial Metalizers, Coaters & Laminators	www.aimcal.org
Composite Can & Tube Institute	www.cctiwdc.org
CPGjobs.com	www.cpgjobs.com
Foodservice.com	http://foodservice.com
Institute of Food Science & Technology	www.ifst.org
Supermarket News	http://supermarketnews.com
Technical Association of the Pulp & Paper Industry Career Center	http://careers.tappi.org/

Pharmaceutical

Academy of Managed Care Pharmacy	www.amcp.org/home
American Academy of Pharmaceutical Physicians & Investigators	www.appinet.org
American Association of Pharmaceutical Sales Professionals	www.pharmaceuticalsales.org
American Association of Pharmaceutical Scientists	www.aapspharmaceutica.com/index.asp

American Chemical Society	http://portal.acs.org/portal/acs/corg/content
American College of Clinical Pharmacology	www.accp1.org
American College of Clinical Pharmacy	www.accp.com
American Pharmaceutical Association	www.pharmacist.com
American Society of Clinical Pharmacology and Therapeutics	www.ascpt.org
American Society of Health-System Pharmacists	www.ashp.org
American Society of Pharmacognosy	www.phcog.org
Association for Applied Human Pharmacology [Germany]	www.agah.info
The Biomedical Engineering Network	www.bmenet.org/BMEnet
BioSpace	www.biospace.com
Board of Pharmaceutical Specialties	www.bpsweb.org
CareerTopJobs	www.careertopjobs.com
Careers in Pharmaceutical	www.careersinpharmaceutical.com
ChemJobs.net	www.chemjobs.net/chemjobs.html
ChemPharma	www.chempharma.net
Drug Discovery Online	www.drugdiscoveryonline.com
Drug Information Association Employment Opportunities	www.diahome.org
Elite Pharmacy Jobs	www.elitepharmacyjobs.com
Georgia Pharmacy Association	www.gpha.org
HireLifeScience	www.hirelifescience.com
HireRX.com	www.hirerx.com
iHirePharmacy.com	www.ihirepharmacy.com
International Society for Pharmaceutical Engineering	www.ispe.org
Jobs in Chemistry	www//jobsinchemistry.com
Lifesciencejobs.com	www.lifesciencejobs.com
MedReps	www.medreps.com
Medzilla	www.medzilla.com
Missouri Pharmacy Association	www.morx.com
National Association of Boards of Pharmacy	www.nabp.net

National Association of Pharmaceutical Sales Representatives	www.napsronline.org
Pharmacareers.co.uk [United Kingdom]	www.pharmacareers.co.uk
PharmaceuticalJobsUSA.com	http://pharmaceuticaljobsusa.ning.com
Pharmaceutical Rep Jobs	http://pharmaceuticalrepjobs.org
PharmacyChoice.com	www.pharmacychoice.com
PharmacyWeek	www.pharmacyweek.com
PharmaDiversity	www.pharmadiversity.com
PharmaOpportunities	www.pharmaopportunites.com
Pharmasys	www.pharmweb.com
PharmaTalentPool.com [United Kingdom]	www.pharmatalentpool.com
Pharm-Chem.com	www.pharm-chem.com
RPh on the Go	www.rphonthego.com
RPhrecruiter.com	www.rphrecruiter.com
Rx Career Center	www.rxcareercenter.com
RxWebportal	www.rxwebportal.com

Physics

American Association of Physics Teachers	www.aapt.org
American Institute of Physics	www.aip.org
American Physical Society	www.aps.org
Board of Physics & Astronomy	http://www7.nationalacademies.org/careers/
Institute of Physics	www.iop.org
Optics.org	http://optics.org/cws/home
Physics & Astronomy Online	www.physlink.com
Physics Jobs Online	http://tiptop.iop.org/
PhysicsToday.org	www.physicstoday.org/jobs
Plasma Gate [Israel]	http://plasma-gate.weizmann.ac.il
The Science Jobs	www.thesciencejobs.com

Printing & Bookbinding

Digital Printing and Imaging Association Employment Exchange (with the Screenprinting & Graphic Imaging Association International)	www.sgia.org/employment
National Association for Printing Leadership	www.napl.org
Printing Impressions	www.piworld.com
Semper International	www.semperllc.com

Public Sector/Government

Blue Line Jobs [United Kingdom]	www.bluelinejobs.co.uk
The Blue Line: Police Opportunity Monitor	www.theblueline.com
Careers.vic.gov.au [Australia]	www.careers.vic.gov.au
Careers in Government	www.careersingovernment.com
Centers for Disease Control	www.cdc.gov
Civil Jobs	www.civiljobs.com
ClearedJobs.co.uk [United Kingdom]	www.clearedjobs.co.uk
Defense Jobs	http://ndia.monster.com
DEM Job	www.demjob.com
Fed World	www.fedworld.gov
FederalGovernmentJobs.us	www.federalgovernmentjobs.us
Federal Job Search	www.americajob.com/Default.asp
FederalJobs	www.federaljobs.net
Federal Jobs Digest	www.jobsfed.com
FRS	www.fedjobs.com
GetaGovJob.com	www.getagovjob.com
GOP Job	www.gopjob.com
Governmentjobs.com	www.governmentjobs.com
GovernmentSecurity.org	www.governmentsecurity.org/jobs.php
GovernmentSupportJobs.com	www.governmentsupportjobs.com
GovMedCareers.com	www.govmedcareers.com

Grist.org	http://jobs.grist.org
High Technology Crime Investigation Association	www.htcia.org
HRS Federal Job Search	www.hrsjobs.com
Intelligence Careers	www.intelligencecareers.com
Internet Job Source	http://statejobs.com
Jobsearch.gov.au [Australia]	www.jobsearch.gov.au
Jobsgopublic [United Kingdom]	www.jobsgopublic.com
Jobs In Government	www.jobsingovernment.com
JobsinNHS [United Kingdom]	www.jobsinnhs.co.uk
JobsinPublicSector [United Kingdom]	www.jobsinpublicsector.co.uk
Military.com	www.military.com
MilitaryJobWorld.com	www.militaryjobworld.com
NASA Jobs	www.nasajobs.nasa.gov
National Association of Hispanic Publications Online Career Center	www.nahp.org
NavyJobs.com	www.navy.com/navy/careers.html
NHS Jobs [United Kingdom]	www.jobs.nhs.uk
Opportunities in Public Affairs	www.opajobs.com
Poli Temps	www.politemps.com
Police Employment	www.policeemployment.com
Political Resources	http://politicalresources.com
PoliticalStaffing.com	http://politicalstaff.com
PublicJobsDirect.com [United Kingdom]	www.publicjobsdirect.com
Public Safety Jobs	www.publicsafetyjobs.com
Public Service Employees	www.pse-net.com
PWJobZone	www.publishersmarketplace.com
RegulatoryCareers.com	www.regulatorycareers.com
SecurityClearedJobs.com [United Kingdom]	www.securityclearedjobs.com
Security Job Zone	www.securityjobzone.com
Security Jobs Network	www.securityjobs.net
StudentJobs.gov	www.usajobs.gov/studentjobs
TenStepsforStudents.org	www.tenstepsforstudents.org
Transportation Security Administration	www.tsa.gov

United States Department of Labor	www.dol.gov
US Air Force Careers	www.af.mil/careers
USAJOBS/U.S. Office of Personnel Management	www.usajobs.opm.gov
U.S. Department of Defense	www.defense.gov

Publishing

Book Business	www.BookBusinessMag.com
Bookjobs.com	www.bookjobs.com
Council of Literary Magazines & Presses	www.clmp.org
Editorial Freelancers Association	www.the-efa.org
Fulfillment Management Association, Inc.	www.fmanational.org
National Writers Union Job Hotline	https://nwu.org/
PrintWorkers.com	www.printworkers.com
PrioritySearch.com	www.prioritysearch.com

Purchasing

BuyingJobs.com	www.buyingjobs.com
Institute for Supply Management Career Center	www.ism.ws
SupplyChainRecruit.com [Europe]	www.supplychainrecruit.com

-Q-

Quality/Quality Control

iHireQualityControl.com	www.ihirequalitycontrol.com
I Six Sigma	www.isixsigma.com
Just QA Jobs	www.justqajobs.com
QA Engineer Jobs	www.qaengineerjobs.com

QA-Jobs	www.qa-jobs.com
QCEmployMe.com	http://regionalhelpwanted.com/ quad-cities-il-ia-jobs
Quality America	www.qualityamerica.com
QualityEngineerJobs.com	www.qualityengineerjobs.com
Software QA and Testing Resource Center	www.softwareqatest.com

-R-

Real Estate

American Real Estate Society	www.aresnet.org/Jobs.phtml
Apartment Association of Greater Dallas	www.aagdallas.org
Apartment Association of Tarrant County	www.aatcnet.org/subsite/CareerCenter/ careercenterindex.htm
ApartmentCareerHQ.org	www.apartmentcareerHQ.org
Apartment Careers	www.apartmentcareers.com
BuilderJobs	www.builderjobs.com
California Mortgage Brokers Association Career Center	www.cambweb.org
Escrowboard.net	www.escrowboard.net
FacilitiesJobs.com	www.facilitiesjobs.com
iHireRealEstate.com	www.ihirerealestate.com
Institute of Real Estate Management Job Bulletin	www.irem.org
Job Directories	http://inrealty.com
Jobsite.co.uk [United Kingdom]	www.jobsite.co.uk
Leasing Jobs	www.leasingjobs.com
LettingCareers [United Kingdom]	www.lettingcareers.com
Loan Closer Jobs	www.loancloserjobs.com
Loan Originator Jobs	www.loanoriginatorjobs.com
Loop Net	www.loopnet.com
MortgageBoard.com	www.mortgageboard.com

Mortgage Job Market	www.jobmag.com
Mortgage Jobstore	www.mortgagejobstore.com
MyHousingCareer [United Kingdom]	www.myhousingcareer.com
NACORE International	www.nacore.com
National Apartment Association	www.naahq.org/Pages/welcome.aspx
NewHomeSalesJobs.com	www.newhomesalesjobs.com
Pike Net	www.pikenet.com
Real Estate Best Jobs	www.realestatebestjobs.com
Real Estate Careers	www.realestateexpress.com
Real Estate Finance Jobs	www.realestatefinancejobs.com
Real Estate Job Store	www.realestatejobstore.com
Real Estate Lenders Association	www.rela.org
Real Jobs	www.real-jobs.com
Rebuz	www.rebuz.com
SelectLeaders.com	www.selectleaders.com
Texas Apartment Association	www.taa.org/sitemap
Titleboard.net	www.titleboard.net
TopBuildingJobs.com	www.topbuildingjobs.com
Washington Multi-Family Housing Association	http://careers.wmfha.org

Recruiters Resources

Abso	http://abso.com
Academy of Healthcare Recruiters	www.academyofhealthcarerecruiters.com
AIRS Directory	www.airsdirectory.com
Alliance of Medical Recruiters	www.physicianrecruiters.com
American Staffing Association	www.staffingtoday.net
Arbita	www.arbita.net
Arizona Technical Recruiters Association	www.atraaz.org
Association of Executive Search Consultants	www.aesc.org/eweb
Association of Financial Search Consultants	www.afsc-jobs.com
Association of Staff Physician Recruiters	www.aspr.org
BackgroundBureau.com	www.backgroundbureau.com

BrainHunter	www.brainhunter.com
The Breckenridge Group, Inc.	www.breckenridgegroup.com
California Staffing Professionals	www.catss.org
Canadian Technical Recruiters Network	www.ctrn.org
Career MetaSearch	www.careermetasearch.com
CareersinRecruitment [United Kingdom]	www.careersinrecruitment.com
Changeboard [United Kingdom]	www.changeboard.com
Cheezhead.com	www.jobing.com
Colorado Technical Recruiters Network	www.ctrn.org
CyberEdit	www.cyberedit.com
DataFrenzy.com	www.datafrenzy.com
DBM Career Services	https://www.dbmcareerservices.com
Defense Outplacement Referral System	https://www.dmdc.osd.mil/appj/dwp/index.jsp
Delaware Valley Technical Recruiters Network	www.dvtrn.org
Employment Management Association	www.shrm.org
ERE.net	www.ere.net
eQuest	www.joblauncher.com
ExecutiveResumes.com	www.executiveresumes.com
Free-For-Recruiters	www.free-for-recruiters.com
FreeResumeSites.com	www.freeresumesites.com
Global Media	www.globalmediarecruitment.com
GotResumes.com	www.gotresumes.com
H3.com	www.h3.com
Houston High Tech Recruiters Network	www.hhtrn.org
Human Resource Management Association of Western New England	www.hrmawne.org
Human Resource Management Center	www.hrmc.com
Illinois Association of Personnel Services	www.searchfirm.com
Interbiznet.com	www.interbiznet.com/hrstart.html
International Association of Corporate and Professional Recruitment	www.iacpr.org
Investment Positions	www.investmentpositions.com
Job Rooster	www.jobrooster.com

Jobster.com	www.jobster.com
Jobvite	www.jobvite.com
KarmaOne	www.karmaone.com
Lead411.com	www.lead411.com
Lee Hecht Harrison	www.lhh.com/Pages/default.aspx
Minnesota Technical Recruiters Network	www.mntrn.com
MovingCenter.com	www.movingcenter.com
Nasscom.org	www.nasscom.in
National Association of Executive Recruiters	www.naer.org
National Association for Health Care Recruitment	www.nahcr.com
National Association of Legal Search Consultants	www.nalsc.org
National Association of Personnel Services	www.napsweb.org
National Association of Physician Recruiters	www.napr.org
National Insurance Recruiters Association Online Job Database	www.nirassn.com
New Jersey Metro Employment Management Association	www.njmetroema.org
New Jersey Staffing Association	www.njsa.com
New Jersey Technical Recruiters Alliance	www.njtra.org
Northeast Human Resource Association	www.nehra.com
Northwest Recruiters Association	www.nwrecruit.org/nwra
NowHiring.com	www.nowhiring.com
The Portland Human Resource Management Assn	www.pbcs.jp
Project S.A.M.E.	www.staffingadvisors.com
Project S.A.V.E.	www.cluffassociates.com/projectsave.htm
PubliPac.ca [Canada]	www.publipac.ca
RecruitUSA	www.recruitusa.com
Recruiters Alliance	www.recruitersalliance.com
Recruiters Café	www.recruiterscafe.com
Recruiters for Christ	www.edmondspersonnel.com
Recruiters Network	www.recruitersnetwork.com
Recruiters Online Network	www.recruitersonline.com

Recruiting.com	www.recruiting.com
RecruitingJobs.com	www.recruitingjobs.com
RecruitingMastery.com	www.greatrecruitertraining.com
Recruitment-Marketing [United Kingdom]	www.recruitment-marketing.co.uk
ReferYes.com	www.referyes.com
The Regional Technical Recruiter's Association	www.rtra.com
ResumeBlaster	www.resumeblaster.com
ResumeXPRESS	www.resumexpress.com
Resume-Link	http://resume-link.com
Resume Network	www.resume-network.com
ResumeRabbit.com	www.resumerabbit.com
Resumes on the Web	www.resweb.com
Resume Workz	www.resumeworkz.com
Russsoft.org	www.russoft.org
Sacramento Area Human Resources Association	www.sahra.org
San Francisco Bay Area ASA	www.sfasa.org/joblist.htm
Semco	www.semcoenterprises.com
SHRM Atlanta	www.shrmatlanta.org
SHRM Jacksonville	www.shrmjax.org
SkillsArena.com [United Kingdom]	www.skillsarenacorporate.com
The Smart POST Network	www.smartpost.com/home/index.asp
Society for Human Resource Management **HRJobs**	http://jobs/shrm.org
Southeast Employment Network Inc.	www.nonprofitdata.com
SplitIt.com	www.splitit.com
Taleo (iLogos)	http://new.taleo.com
Technical Recruiters Network	www.trnchicago.org
Texas Association of Staffing	www.texasstaffing.org
Top Echelon Recruiters	www.topechelon.com
UpSeek	www.upseek.com
VacancyFinder.co.uk [United Kingdom]	www.vacancyfinder.info/login.php
Virtual-Edge	https://www.virtual-edge.net/login/index.cfm
WebHire Network	www.webhire.com

WEDDLE's Research & Publications   www.weddles.com

You Achieve   www.youachieve.com

ZillionResumes.com   www.zillionresumes.com

Recruitment Advertising-Non-Newspaper/Print & Online

Advertising Age's Online Job Bank   http://adage.com

American Medical Association Journal   www.ama-assn.org
of the AMA (JAMA) Physician
Recruitment Ads

American Psychological Association   www.apa.org/careers/psyccareers

Association for Computing Machinery Career   http://acpinternational.org
Resource Center

Bernard Hodes Group   www.hodes.com

Book Business   www.bookbusinessmag.com

BuilderJobs   www.builderjobs.com

Career MetaSearch   www.careermetasearch.com

Cell Press Online   www.cell.com/cellpress

The Chronicle of Higher Education   http://chronicle.com/section/Jobs/61/

Chronicle of Philanthropy   http://philanthropy.com/section/Home/172/

CMPnet   www.ubmtechnology.com

Contract Employment Weekly Jobs Online   www.ceweekly.com

Daxic.com [United Kingdom]   www.daxic.com

eCareer Connections   www.ecareerconnections.com

eMarketing & Commerce's Job Connection   http://jobs.emarketingandcommerce.com

Engineering News Record   www.enrconstruction.com

The ePages Classifieds   www.ep.com

ERTOnline.co.uk [United Kingdom]   www.ertonline.co.uk

FolioMag.com   www.foliomag.com

FSS.co.uk [United Kingdom]   www.hirethinking.com

Heart Advertising   www.career.com

InformationWeek Career   www.informationweek.com/career

ITWorld.com's IT Careers   http://itjobs.computerworld.com/a/all-jobs/list

E&P Classifieds	www.editorandpublisher.com/Jobs.aspx
Louisville Internet Business Directory	www.beyondbis.com/lsvdir.html
Main Street On-Line Classifieds Service	http://classifieds.maine.com/Catalog/
	classifieds.cgi/index.html
MEDopportunities.com	www.medopportunities.com
NAS Recruitment Communications	www.nasrecruitment.com
Oil Online	www.oilonline.com
Online Help Wanted	www.ohw.com
Prospect City	www.prospectcity.com
PRWeekjobs.com	www.prweekus.com/Jobs/section/257
Shaker Advertising	www.shaker.com
Star Recruiting	www.bjonesassociates.com
TMP Worldwide	www.tmp.com/home.aspx/home.aspx

Regional-USA

Alabama

AlabamaJobs.com	www.alabamajobs.com
Alabama's Job Bank	http://dir.alabama.gov
Al.com	www.al.com
AuburnOpelikaHelpWanted.com	http://regionalhelpwanted.com/
	auburn-opelika-jobs
BestMobileJobs.com	www.bestmobilejobs.com
BetterAuburnJobs.com	www.betterauburnjobs.com
BetterMontgomeryJobs.com	www.bettermontgomeryjobs.com
Biotechnology Association of Alabama	www.bioalabama.com
BirminghamHelpWanted.com	http://regionalhelpwanted.com/birmingham-jobs
Birmingham News	www.bhamnews.com
DothanHelpWanted.com	http://regionalhelpwanted.com/dothan-jobs
HuntsvilleHelpWanted.com	http://regionalhelpwanted.com/huntsville-jobs
Huntsville Times	www.htimes.com
MobileHelpWanted.com	http://regionalhelpwanted.com/mobile-jobs

Mobile Register Online	www.mobileregister.com
Montgomery Advertiser	www.montgomeryadvertiser.com
MontgomeryAreaHelpWanted.com	http://regionalhelpwanted.com/montgomery-jobs
MyLakeAreaJobs.com	www.mylakeareajobs.com
The Tuscaloosa News	www.tuscaloosanews.com

Alaska

Anchorage Daily News	www.adn.com
Anchorage Diversity	www.anchoragediversity.com
Alaska Fishing Jobs	www.fishingjobs.com
AlaskaJobs.com	www.alaskajobs.com
Alaska's Job Bank	http://jobs.alaska.gov
AlaskaJobFinder.com	www.alaskajobfinder.com
Anchorage Daily News	www.adn.com
AnchorageHelpWanted.com	http://regionalhelpwanted.com/anchorage-jobs
Fairbanks Daily News	http://fairbanks.abracat.com
FairbanksHelpWanted.com	http://regionalhelpwanted.com/fairbanks-jobs
Frontiersman	www.frontiersman.com
HelpWantedAlaska.com	www.helpwantedalaska.com
I Love Alaska	http://ilovealaska.com/taxonomy/term/11
Juneau Empire	www.juneauempire.com
KodiakHelpWanted.com	http://regionalhelpwanted.com/kodiak-island-jobs
Nome Nugget	www.nomenugget.com

Arizona

Arizona Daily Sun (Flagstaff)	www.azdailysun.com
AZFamily.com	www.azfamily.com
Arizona Hospital and Healthcare Association AZHealthJobs	www.azhha.org
ArizonaJobs.com	www.arizonajobs.com
AZ-Jobs	www.az-jobs.com

BetterPrescottJobs.com	www.betterprescottjobs.com
The Daily Courier (Prescott)	www.dcourier.com
East Valley Tribune (Mesa)	www.eastvalleytribune.com
Geebo	www.geebo.com
HelpWantedPhoenix.com	http://regionalhelpwanted.com/phoenix-jobs
JobDig	www.jobdig.com
Jobing.com	www.jobing.com
LocalCareers.com	www.localcareers.com
Phoenix Employment	http://phoenix.jobing.com/
Phoenix Jobs	www.phoenixjobs.com
Phoenix News Times	www.phoenixnewtimes.com
Phoenix One Stop Career Center	www.ci.phoenix.az.us
SierraVistaHelpWanted.com	http://regionalhelpwanted.com/sierra-vista-jobs
Today's News-Herald (Lake Havasu City)	www.havasunews.com
TucsonHelpWanted.com	http://regionalhelpwanted.com/tucson-jobs

Arkansas

ARHelpWanted.com	http://regionalhelpwanted.com/arkansas-jobs
Arkansas Human Resources Association	www.ahra.org
ArkansasJobs.com	www.arkansasjobs.com
Arkansas Jobs	www.arkansasjobs.com
Arkansas Online	www.arkansasonline.com
Benton Courier	www.bentoncourier.com
HotSpringsHelpWanted.com	http://regionalhelpwanted.com/hot-springs-jobs
Jobdig	www.jobdig.com
JonesboroHelpWanted.com	http://regionalhelpwanted.com/jonesboro-jobs
Jonesboro Sun	www.jonesborosun.com
LittleRockHelpWanted.com	http://regionalhelpwanted.com/little-rock-jobs
RiverValleyHelpWanted.com	http://regionalhelpwanted.com/river-valley-jobs
The Sentinel-Record (Hot Springs)	www.hotsr.com
TexarkanaHelpWanted.com	http://regionalhelpwanted.com/texarkana-jobs
University of Arkansas	www.uark.edu/home
What A Job	www.whatajob.com

California

680 Careers.com	www.680careers.com/index.php
Abag	www.abag.ca.gov
Association for Environmental and Outdoor Education	www.aeoe.org
BAJobs	www.bajobs.com
BakersfieldHelpWanted.com	http://regionalhelpwanted.com/bakersfield-jobs
Bay Area Careers	www.bayareacareers.com/bay_area.php
Bay Bio	www.baybio.org
BayAreaClassifieds.com	www.bayareaclassifieds.com
BayAreaHelpWanted.com	http://regionalhelpwanted.com/bay-area-jobs
BayAreaJobFinder.com	www.bayareajobfinder.com
California Academy of Family Physicians	www.fpjobsonline.org
California Agricultural Technical Institute ATI-Net AgJobs	www.atinet.org/jobs.asp
CaliforniaCoastHelpWanted.com	http://regionalhelpwanted.com/ california-coast-jobs
California Dental Hygienists' Association Employment Opportunities	www.cdha.org/employment/index.html
CaliforniaJobs.com	www.californiajobs.com
California Mortgage Brokers Association Career Center	www.cambweb.org
California Separation Science Society	www.casss.org
California State University - Chico	www.csuchico.edu/careers
CentralCaliforniaHelpWanted.com	http://regionalhelpwanted.com/ central-california-jobs/
CentralCoastHelpWanted.com	http://regionalhelpwanted.com/ central-coast-ca-jobs
CentralValleyHelpWanted.com	http://regionalhelpwanted.com/ central-valley-ca-jobs
ChicoHelpWanted.com	http://regionalhelpwanted.com/chico-jobs
ChicoJobs.com	www.chicojobs.com
Coastline	www.ventura.com
ContraCostaJobs.com	www.contracostajobs.com

craigslist	www.craigslist.org
DesertHelpWanted.com	http://regionalhelpwanted.com/desert-ca-jobs
FinancialJobs.com	www.financialjobs.com
Foothill-De Anza Community College	www.fhda.edu/jobs
Forty Plus	www.fortyplus.org
Geebo	www.geebo.com
Go Job Zone	www.gojobzone.com
HelpWantedSanDiego.com	http://regionalhelpwanted.com/san-diego-jobs
HighDesertHelpWanted.com	http://regionalhelpwanted.com/high-desert-jobs
Hispanic-Jobs.com	www.hispanic-jobs.com
HireDiversity.com	www.hirediversity.com
Human Resource Independent Consultants (HRIC) On-Line Job Leads	www.hric.org
InlandEmpireHelpWanted.com	http://regionalhelpwanted.com/ inland-empire-ca-jobs
JobConnect.org	www.jobconnections.org
Job Meister	www.jobmeister.com
LA Working World	www.workingworld.com
LocalCareers.com	www.localcareers.com
LosAngelesHelpWanted.com	http://regionalhelpwanted.com/los-angeles-jobs
Los Angeles Times	www.latimes.com
MercedHelpWanted.com	http://regionalhelpwanted.com/merced-jobs
Mercury Center	www.mercurynews.com
Mercury News (San Jose)	www.bayarea.com
ModestoJobFinder.com	www.modestojobfinder.com
MontereyBayHelpWanted.com	http://regionalhelpwanted.com/monterey-bay-jobs
MontereyBayJobs.com	www.montereybayjobs.com
NorthBayCareers.com	www.northbaycareers.com/index.php
NorthBayHelpWanted.com	http://regionalhelpwanted.com/north-bay-jobs
Orange County Register	www.ocregister.com
Palo Alto Weekly	www.paloaltoonline.com
Presidio Jobs	www.presidio.gov/trust/jobs
ReddingHelpWanted.com	http://regionalhelpwanted.com/redding-jobs

ReddingJobs.com	www.reddingjobs.com
Sacramento Bee	www.sacbee.com
SacramentoHelpWanted.com	http://regionalhelpwanted.com/sacramento-jobs
SacramentoJobFinder.com	www.sacramentojobfinder.com
Sacramento Recruiter	www.sacramentorecruiter.com
San Diego Careers	www.sandiegocareers.com/index.php
San Diego Jobs	www.sandiegojobs.com
San Diego Software Industry Council	www.sdsic.org
San Francisco Chronicle	www.sfgate.com
San Francisco Bay Area ASA	www.sfasa.org/joblist.htm
San Francisco Bay Area Job Hub	www.jobhub.com
San Francisco State University Instructional Technologies	www.itec.sfsu.edu
SantaBarbaraJobs.net	www.santabarbarajobs.net
SantaCruzJobs.com	www.santacruzjobs.com
SantaMariaJobAlert.com	www.santamariajobalert.com
SantaRosaJobs.com	www.santarosajobs.com
SLOJobs.com	www.slojobs.com
Sonic Net	www.sonic.net/jobs/ent
SonomaCountyHelpWanted.com	http://regionalhelpwanted.com/sonoma-county-jobs
SouthBayHelpWanted.com	http://regionalhelpwanted.com/south-bay-jobs
Southern California Electronic Data Interchange Roundtable	www.scedir.org
StocktonJobFinder.com	www.stocktonjobfinder.com
SutterButtesHelpWanted.com	http://regionalhelpwanted.com/sutter-buttes-jobs
University of California- Berkeley Work-Study Programs	http://workstudy.berkeley.edu
The Valley Exchange	www.thevalleyexchange.com
Jobs.WestsideRentals.com	www.westsiderentals.com/jobs

Colorado

Aspen Daily News	www.aspendailynews.com
BetterColoradoSpringsJobs.com	www.bettercoloradospringsjobs.com
BetterPuebloJobs.com	www.betterpueblojobs.com
Colorado Academy of Family Physicians	www.fpjobsonline.org
Colorado Computerwork	http://colorado.computerwork.com
Colorado Health and Hospital Association	www.cha.com
Colorado Human Resource Association Online	www.chra.org
Colorado Jobs	http://colorado.jobing.com/
ColoradoJobs.net	www.coloradojobs.net
Colorado Online Job Connection	www.peakweb.com
ColoradoSpringsHelpWanted.com	http://regionalhelpwanted.com/ colorado-springs-jobs
Colorado Springs Independent	www.csindy.com
Colorado Springs Society for Human Resource Management	www.csshrm.org
Colorado Technical Recruiters Network	www.ctrn.org
The Daily Sentinel (Grand Junction)	www.gjsentinel.com
Denver Post	www.denverpost.com
Durango Herald	www.durangoherald.com
HighCountryHelpWanted.com	http://regionalhelpwanted.com/ high-country-co-jobs
NorthernColoradoHelpWanted.com	http://regionalhelpwanted.com/ northern-colorado-jobs
RockyMountainHelpWanted.com	http://regionalhelpwanted.com/ rocky-mountain-co-jobs
Rocky Mountain News	www.rockymountainnews.com/jobs
State of Colorado	www.state.co.us
WesternSlopeHelpWanted.com	http://regionalhelpwanted.com/ western-slope-co-jobs

Connecticut

The Advocate (Stamford)	www.stamfordadvocate.com
AllCountyJobs.com	www.allcountyjobs.com
Connecticut's BioScience Cluster	www.curenet.org
Connecticut Hospital Association	www.chime.org
ConnecticutJobs.com	www.connecticutjobs.com
CT High Tech	www.cthightech.com
CT Jobs	www.ctjobs.com
Danbury News-Times	www.newstimes.com
EasternCTHelpWanted.com	http://regionalhelpwanted.com/ eastern-connecticut-jobs
Fairfield, CT Jewish Jobs	www.jewishjobs.com
FairfieldCountyHelpWanted.com	http://regionalhelpwanted.com/ fairfield-county-jobs
FairfieldCountyJobs.com	www.fairfieldcountyjobs.com
GetCTJobs.com	www.getctjobs.com
HartfordCountyJobs.com	www.hartfordcountyjobs.com
Hartford Courant	www.courant.com
HartfordHelpWanted.com	http://regionalhelpwanted.com/hartford-jobs
New England Higher Education Recruitment Consortium	www.newenglandherc.org
New England Job	www.jobct.com
NewHavenCountyJobs.com	www.newhavencountyjobs.com
NewHavenHelpWanted.com	http://regionalhelpwanted.com/new-haven-jobs
New Haven Register	www.newhavenregister.com
NewLondonCountyJobs.com	www.newlondoncountyjobs.com
Tri-StateJobs.com	www.tristatejobs.com
Waterbury Republican American	www.rep-am.com

Delaware

DelawareJobs.com	www.delawarejobs.com
Delaware Online	www.delawareonline.com

Delaware Valley Technical Recruiters Network	www.dvtrn.org
Delaware's Employment	www.delmarweb.com
Delaware JobLink	https://joblink.delaware.gov/ada
Dover Post	www.doverpost.com
HelpWantedDelaware.com	http://regionalhelpwanted.com/delaware-jobs/
JobCircle.com	www.jobcircle.com
JobNet	http://jobcircle.com/jobnet
ServiceSource Network	www.ourpeoplework.org
Tri-State Human Resource Management Assn	http://wss3.tristatehr.org/default.aspx

District of Columbia

AllCountyJobs.com	www.allcountyjobs.com
Capital Communicator	www.capitalcommunicator.com
The Catholic University of America Career Services Office	http://careers.cua.edu
dcaccountingjobs.com	www.dcaccountingjobs.com
DC Job Source	http://dcjobsource.com
DC Registry	www.dcregistry.com
DCWebWomen	www.dcwebwomen.org
DistrictofColumbiaJobs.com	www.districtofcolumbiajobs.com
Geebo	www.geebo.com
HelpWantedDC.com	http://regionalhelpwanted.com/ washington-dc-jobs
Human Resource Association of the National Capital Area Job Bank Listing	http://hra-nca.org/job_list.asp
JobFetch.com	www.jobfetch.com
WashingtonJobs.com	www.washingtonpost.com
The Washington Post	www.washingtonpost.com
Washington Times	www.washingtontimes.com

East Coast

East Bay Works	www.eastbayworks.org

East Coast Jobs	www.eastcoastjobs.net
Planet Tech	www.planet-tech.si

Florida

BioFlorida	www.bioflorida.com
Central Florida Human Resource Association	www.cfhra.org
CoastalHelpWanted.com	http://regionalhelpwanted.com/coastal-fl-jobs
DaytonaHelpWanted.com	http://regionalhelpwanted.com/daytona-jobs
EmeraldCoastHelpWanted.com	http://regionalhelpwanted.com/emerald-coast-jobs
EmeraldCoastJobAlert.com	www.emeraldcoastjobalert.com
Florida Academy of Family Physicians	www.fpjobsonline.org
Florida Banking Jobs Online	www.bankjobsflorida.com
Florida CareerLINK	http://regionalhelpwanted.com/florida-jobs
FloridaCareers.com	www.FloridaCareers.com
Florida Jobs	www.floridajobs.com
Florida Jobs Online!	www.florida-jobs-online.com
Florida Times Union (Jacksonville)	http://jacksonville.com
FloridianJobs.com	www.floridianjobs.com
GainesvilleOcalaHelpWanted.com	http://regionalhelpwanted.com/gainesville-ocala-jobs
Geebo	www.geebo.com
GulfCoastJobAlert.com	www.gulfcoastjobalert.com
Human Resource Association of Broward County	www.hrabc.org
JacksonvilleHelpWanted.com	http://regionalhelpwanted.com/jacksonville-recruitment
JobCrank.com	www.jobcrank.com
Miami Herald	www.miami.com
Miami Jobs	www.miami-jobs.net
NorthFloridaHelpWanted.com	http://regionalhelpwanted.com/north-florida-jobs
Nova Southeastern University	www.nova.edu
OrlandoHelpWanted.com	http://regionalhelpwanted.com/orlando-jobs
Orlando Jobs	www.orlando-jobs.com

Orlando Sentinel	www.orlandosentinel.com
PanamaCityHelpWanted.com	http://regionalhelpwanted.com/panama-city-jobs
PensacolaHelpWanted.com	http://regionalhelpwanted.com/pensacola-jobs
Pensacola News Journal	www.pnj.com
RhinoMite	www.jobing.com/?chang=local&welcome=rhinomite
SarasotaHelpWanted.com	http://regionalhelpwanted.com/sarasota-jobs
St. Petersburg Times	www.sptimes.com
SHRM Jacksonville	www.shrmjax.org
SouthFloridaHelpWanted.com	http://regionalhelpwanted.com/south-florida-jobs
SouthwestFloridaHelpWanted.com	http://regionalhelpwanted.com/southwest-florida-jobs
SpaceCoastHelpWanted.com	http://regionalhelpwanted.com/space-coast-fl-jobs
Sun-Sentinel Career Path	www.sun-sentinel.com/classified/jobs
TallahasseeHelpWanted.com	http://regionalhelpwanted.com/tallahassee-jobs
Tampa Bay Employment	www.tampabaywired.com
Tampa Jobs.com	www.tampa-jobs.com
WestPalmBeachBocaHelpWanted.com	http://regionalhelpwanted.com/west-palm-beach-boca-raton-jobs

Georgia

The Albany Herald	www.albanyherald.net/classbrowse.htm
AtlantaHelpWanted.com	http://regionalhelpwanted.com/atlanta-jobs
Atlanta Job Resource Center	www.ajrc.com
Atlanta JobZone	http://atlanta.jobing.com
Atlanta-Jobs	www.atlanta-jobs.com
Atlanta Journal and Constitution	www.ajc.com
Augusta Chronicle	http://chronicle.augusta.com
AugustaHelpWanted.com	http://regionalhelpwanted.com/augusta-jobs
ChattahoocheeHelpWanted.com	http://regionalhelpwanted.com/chattahoochee-jobs
Emory University Rollins School of Public Health	www.sph.emory.edu

Georgia Academy of Family Physicians	www.fpjobsonline.org
Georgia Association of Personnel Services	http://70.85.148.53:5574/JobBoard/tabid/53/ Default.aspx
GeorgiaCareers.com	www.georgiacareers.com
Georgia Center for Nonprofits	www.gcn.org
Georgia Department of Human Resources	www.dhrjobs.com
Georgia Pharmacy Association	www.gpha.org
Georgia State University Career Services	www.gsu.edu/career
Georgia Tech Career Services Office	www.career.gatech.edu
GreatColumbusJobs.com	www.greatcolumbusjobs.com
Job Net	www.westga.edu
Macon Telegraph	www.macon.com
MidGeorgiaHelpWanted.com	http://regionalhelpwanted.com/mid-georgia-jobs
MyMiddleGeorgiaJobs.com	www.mymiddlegeorgiajobs.com
National Association of Securities Professionals (Atlanta) Current Openings	www.naspatlanta.org
NW Georgia Careers	www.careerdepot.org
SavannahHelpWanted.com	http://regionalhelpwanted.com/savannah-jobs
SavannahJobs.com	www.savannahjobs.com
Savannah Morning News	www.savannahnow.com
SHRM Atlanta	www.shrmatlanta.org
SoutheastGeorgiaHelpWanted.com	http://regionalhelpwanted.com/ southeast-georgia-jobs
Southeast Employment Network Inc.	www.nonprofitdata.com/
SouthwestGeorgiaHelpWanted.com	http://regionalhelpwanted.com/ southwest-georgia-jobs
SouthGeorgiaHelpWanted.com	http://regionalhelpwanted.com/south-georgia-jobs

Hawaii

HawaiiJobs.net	www.hawaiijobs.net
HawaiiJobsOnDemand.com	www.hawaiijobsondemand.com
Hawaii Tribune-Herald (Hilo)	www.hawaiitribune-herald.com/index.html
Honolulu Advertiser	www.honoluluadvertiser.com

HonoluluHelpWanted.com	http://regionalhelpwanted.com/honolulu-jobs
Honolulu Star-Bulletin	www.starbulletin.com
JobsOnKauai.com	http://regionalhelpwanted.com/kauai-jobs
KamaainaJobs.com	www.kamaainajobs.com
Maui.net	www.maui.net
Maui News	www.mauinews.com
Starbulletin	www.starbulletin.com
West Hawaii Today (Kailua)	www.westhawaiitoday.com

Idaho

BetterIdahoFallsJobs.com	www.betteridahofallsjobs.com
BetterPocatelloJobs.com	www.betterpocatellojobs.com
BetterTwinFallsJobs.com	www.bettertwinfallsjobs.com
BoiseHelpWanted.com	http://regionalhelpwanted.com/boise-jobs
BoiseIdahoJobs.com	www.boiseidahojobs.com
Cedar Rapids Gazette	www.gazetteonline.com
The Daily Nonpareil (Council Bluffs)	http://southwestiowanews.com/ council_bluffs/front/
Des Moines Register	www.desmoinesregister.com
Idaho Department of Labor	http://labor.idaho.gov/dnn/Default. aspx?alias=labor.idaho.gov/dnn/idl
IdahoJobs.com	http://idaho.jobing.com
NorthIdahoHelpWanted.com	http://regionalhelpwanted.com/north-idaho-jobs
Quad City Times (Davenport)	http://qctimes.com
Sioux City Journal	www.siouxcityjournal.com
SouthernIdahoHelpWanted.com	http://regionalhelpwanted.com/ southern-idaho-jobs

Illinois

Accountant Jobs Chicago	www.accountantjobschicago.com
Audit Jobs Chicago	www.auditjobschicago.com
BloomingtonHelpWanted.com	http://regionalhelpwanted.com/bloomington-jobs

CentralIllinoisHelpWanted.com	http://regionalhelpwanted.com/central-illinois-jobs
Chicago AMA	http://chicagoama.org
ChicagoJobs.com	www.chicagojobs.com
ChicagoJobs.org	www.chicagojobs.org
Chicago Medical Society	www.cmsdocs.org
Chicago Software Newspaper	www.chisoft.com
Chicago Tribune	www.chicagotribune.com
Chicagoland's Virtual Job Resource	www.chicagojobresource.com
FetchMeAJob.com	www.fetchmeajob.com
Geebo	www.geebo.com
HelpWantedSpringfield.com	http://regionalhelpwanted.com/springfield-illinois-jobs
Herald & Review (Decatur)	www.herald-review.com
Human Resource Association of Greater Oak Brook	www.hraoakbrook.org
ILJobs.com	www.iljobs.com
IllianaHelpWanted.com	http://regionalhelpwanted.com/illiana-jobs
IlliniHelpWanted.com	http://regionalhelpwanted.com/illini-jobs
Illinois Academy of Family Physicians	www.fpjobsonline.org
IllinoisCareers.com	www.illinoiscareers.com
Illinois CPA Society Career Center	www.icpas.org
IllinoisJobs.com	www.illinoisjobs.com
IllinoisJobs.net	www.illinoisjobs.net
Illinois Recruiters Association	http://illinoisrecruiter.ning.com
Job Force Network	www.jobforce.net
Jobs in Chicago	www.jobsinchicago.com
Loyola College	www.loyola.edu/thecareercenter/index.html
The News-Gazette (Champaigne)	www.news-gazette.com
NPO	www.npo.net
PeoriaHelpWanted.com	http://regionalhelpwanted.com/peoria-recruitment
The Regional Technical Recruiter's Association	www.rtra.com
Register-News (Mount Vernon)	http://register-news.com
The State Journal Register (Springfield)	www.sj-r.com

SuburbanChicagoHelpWanted.com   http://regionalhelpwanted.com/chicago-area-jobs

Tax Jobs Chicago   www.taxjobschicago.com

University of Chicago   www.uchicago.edu/alumni

Indiana

BloomingtonHelpWanted.com   http://regionalhelpwanted.com/bloomington-jobs

CentralIndianaHelpWanted.com   http://regionalhelpwanted.com/
central-indiana-jobs

The Evansville Courier   http://ads.evansville.net/employment

FetchMeAJob.com   www.fetchmeajob.com

FortWayneHelpWanted.com   http://regionalhelpwanted.com/fort-wayne-jobs

The Herald-Times (Bloomington)   www.heraldtimesonline.com

IndianaJobs.com   www.indianajobs.com

IndianapolisHelpWanted.com   http://regionalhelpwanted.com/indianapolis-jobs

Indianapolis Star News   www.indystar.com

Indy Mall   www.indymall.com

LafayetteHelpWanted.com   http://regionalhelpwanted.com/
lafayette-recruitment

The News-Sentinel (Fort Wayne)   www.fortwayne.com

Online Jobs Indiana   http://www2.indystar.com/webcat/classified

Purdue University Management   www.krannert.purdue.edu/departments/gcs
    Placement Office

Post-Tribune (Gary)   www.post-trib.com/index.html

SouthBendHelpWanted.com   http://regionalhelpwanted.com/south-bend-jobs

South Bend Tribune   www.sbinfo.com

TerreHauteHelpWanted.com   http://regionalhelpwanted.com/terre-haute-jobs

TriStateHelpWanted.com   http://regionalhelpwanted.com/tri-state-jobs

Iowa

Access Dubuque   http://jobs.accessdubuque.com

AGC Iowa Careers   www.agciajobs.com

BetterHawkeyeJobs.com   www.betterhawkeyejobs.com

BetterQCJobs.com	www.betterqcjobs.com
BetterSiouxlandJobs.com	www.bettersiouxlandjobs.com
CedarRapidsIowaCityHelpWanted.com	http://regionalhelpwanted.com/ cedar-rapids-iowa-city-jobs
CentralIowaHelpWanted.com	http://regionalhelpwanted.com/central-iowa-jobs
Corridor Careers	www.corridorcareers.com
DesMoinesHelpWanted.com	http://regionalhelpwanted.com/des-moines-jobs
Des Moines Register	www.desmoinesregister.com
Drake University	www.drake.edu
DubuqueHelpWanted.com	http://regionalhelpwanted.com/dubuque-jobs
FortDodgeHelpWanted.com	http://regionalhelpwanted.com/ fort-dodge-recruitment
Iowa Biotechnology Association	www.iowabiotech.org
Iowa Jobs	www.iowajobs.org
IowaJobs.net	www.iowajobs.net
NorthernIowaHelpWanted.com	http://regionalhelpwanted.com/northern-iowa-jobs
SiouxLandHelpWanted.com	http://regionalhelpwanted.com/sioux-land-jobs
SouthernIowaHelpWanted.com	http://regionalhelpwanted.com/ southern-iowa-jobs

Kansas

Daily Union (Junction City)	www.thedailyunion.net
Kansas City Kansan	www.kansascitykansan.com
KansasJobs.net	www.kansasjobs.net
Kansas Works	www.kansasworks.com
My Kansas	www.kansas.gov/index.php
Salina Journal	www.saljournal.com
The Topeka Capital Journal	www.cjonline.com
TopekaHelpWanted.com	http://regionalhelpwanted.com/topeka-jobs
Wichita Eagle	www.kansas.com
WichitaHelpWanted.com	http://regionalhelpwanted.com/wichita-jobs

Kentucky

BluegrassHelpWanted.com	http://regionalhelpwanted.com/bluegrass-ky-jobs
The Courier-Journal (Louisville)	www.courier-journal.com
The Daily News (Bowling Green)	www.bgdailynews.com
Grayson County News-Gazette (Leitchfield)	www.gcnewsgazette.com
HelpWantedLexington.com	http://regionalhelpwanted.com/lexington-jobs
HuntingtonAshlandHelpWanted.com	http://regionalhelpwanted.com/huntington-ashland-jobs
KentuckyJobs.com	www.kentuckyjobs.com
Lexington Herald Leader	www.kentucky.com
LouisvilleHelpWanted.com	http://regionalhelpwanted.com/louisville-jobs
Louisville Internet Business Directory	www.beyondbis.com/lsvdir.html
Sentinel News (Shelbyville)	www.sentinelnews.com

Louisiana

AcadianaHelpWanted.com	http://regionalhelpwanted.com/acadiana-jobs
The Advocate (Baton Rouge)	www.advocate.com
BatonRougeHelpWanted.com	http://regionalhelpwanted.com/baton-rouge-jobs
BetterAcadianaJobs.com	www.betteracadianajobs.com
BetterBatonRougeJobs.com	www.betterbatonrougejobs.com
BetterHammondJobs.com	www.betterhammondjobs.com
BetterNorthshoreJobs.com	www.betternorthshorejobs.com
CenLAHelpWanted.com	http://regionalhelpwanted.com/central-louisiana-jobs
Info Louisiana	www.state.la.us
LouisianaJobs.com	www.louisianajobs.com
Med Job Louisiana	www.medjoblouisiana.com
MonroeHelpWanted.com	http://regionalhelpwanted.com/monroe-recruitment
NewOrleansHelpWanted.com	http://regionalhelpwanted.com/new-orleans-jobs
Orleans Parish Medical Society	www.opms.org

ShreveportHelpWanted.com http://regionalhelpwanted.com/shreveport-jobs

The Times (Shreveport) www.shreveporttimes.com

The Times-Picayune (New Orleans) www.nola.com

Maine

Bangor Daily News www.bangordailynews.com

Biotechnology Association of Maine www.mainebiotech.org

CentralMaineHelpWanted.com http://regionalhelpwanted.com/central-maine-jobs

EasternMaineHelpWanted.com http://regionalhelpwanted.com/
eastern-maine-recruitment

Employment Times Online www.myjobwave.com

JobsinME.com www.jobsinme.com

Kennebec Journal (Augusta) www.kjonline.com

Lewiston Sun Journal www.sunjournal.com

Maine-Job.com www.maine-job.com

MaineJobs.net www.mainejobs.net

Maine Street On-Line Classifieds Service http://classifieds.maine.com

New England Higher Education Recruitment www.newenglandherc.org
Consortium

Portland Press Herald www.portland.com

SouthernMaineHelpWanted.com http://regionalhelpwanted.com/
southern-maine-jobs

The Times Record (Brunswick) www.timesrecord.com

Maryland

AllCountyJobs.com www.allcountyjobs.com

BaltimoreHelpWanted.com http://regionalhelpwanted.com/baltimore-jobs

Baltimore Sun www.baltimoresun.com

The Capital (Annapolis) www.hometownannapolis.com

Chesapeake Human Resource Association www.chra.com

EasternShoreHelpWanted.com http://regionalhelpwanted.com/
eastern-shore-de-md-jobs

FrederickHelpWanted.com	http://regionalhelpwanted.com/frederick-jobs
The Herald-Mail (Hagerstown)	www.herald-mail.com
Howard County Human Resources Society	www.hocohrs.org
Human Resource Association of the National Capital Area Job Bank Listing	http://hra-nca.org/job_list.asp
JobFetch.com	www.jobfetch.com
Maryland Association of CPAs Job Connect	www.macpa.org
MarylandJobs.com	www.marylandjobs.com
MdBio, Inc. (Maryland Bioscience)	http://techcouncilmd.com/mdbio
Sailor	www.sailor.lib.md.us
The Star Democrat (Easton)	www.stardem.com
WashingtonJobs.com	www.washingtonpost.com

Massachusetts

AllCountyJobs.com	www.allcountyjobs.com
The Boston Globe	www.boston.com/bostonglobe
Boston.com	www.boston.com/jobs
Boston Hire	www.bostonhireonline.com
Boston Job Bank	www.bostonjobs.com
BostonJobs.com	www.bostonjobs.com
Boston JobZone	www.bostonjobzone.com
BostonSearch.com	www.bostonsearch.com
CapeAndIslandsHelpWanted.com	http://regionalhelpwanted.com/cape-and-islands-jobs
The Eagle-Tribune (Lawrence)	www.eagletribune.com
Geebo	www.geebo.com
HelpWantedBoston.com	http://regionalhelpwanted.com/boston-jobs
HireCulture	www.hireculture.org
JobsinMA.com	www.jobsinma.com
JVS Career Moves	www.jvs-boston.org
Massachusetts Biotechnology Council	www.massbio.org
Massachusetts Environmental Education Society	www.massmees.org

Massachusetts Healthcare Human Resources Association	www.mhhra.org
MassachusettsJobs.com	www.massachusettsjobs.com
New England Higher Education Recruitment Consortium	www.newenglandherc.org
Personnel Management Association of Western New England	http://hrmawne.shrm.org/webmodules/webarticlesnet/templates/?a=1&z=1
SpringfieldHelpWanted.com	http://regionalhelpwanted.com/springfield-jobs
The Sun (Lowell)	www.lowellsun.com
The Salem News	www.salemnews.com
Union-News & Sunday Republican (Springfield)	www.masslive.com
WesternMassWorks.com	www.westernmassworks.com
Wicked Local	www.wickedlocal.com
Worchester Polytechnic Institute	www.wpi.edu

Michigan

Ann Arbor News	www.mlive.com/annarbornews
BetterMichiganJobs.com	www.bettermichiganjobs.com
Detroit Free Press	www.freep.com
FetchMeAJob.com	www.fetchmeajob.com
FlintHelpWanted.com	http://regionalhelpwanted.com/flint-recruitment
Flint Journal	www.mlive.com/flintjournal
GrandRapidsHelpWanted.com	http://regionalhelpwanted.com/grand-rapids-jobs
Grand Rapids Press	www.mlive.com/grpress
Human Resource Management Association of Mid Michigan Job Postings	www.hrmamm.com/jobpostings/index.php
HudsonValleyHelp Wanted.com	http://regionalhelpwanted.com/hudson-valley-jobs
KalamazooHelpWanted.com	http://regionalhelpwanted.com/kalamazoo-jobs
Lansing State Journal	www.lansingstatejournal.com
MichBIO	www.michbio.org
Michigan CareerSite	www.themedc.org/jobs
MichiganJobs.com	www.michiganjobs.com
Michigan-Online	www.michigan-online.com

Michigan Web	www.michiganweb.com/site.html
MidMichiganHelpWanted.com	http://regionalhelpwanted.com/mid-michigan-jobs
MotorCityHelpWanted.com	http://regionalhelpwanted.com/motor-city-jobs
MuskegonHelpWanted.com	http://regionalhelpwanted.com/muskegon-jobs
MyTriCityJobs.com	www.mytricityjobs.com
Oakland University	www.oakland.edu/careerservices
Pride Source	www.pridesource.com
SouthwestMichiganJobs.com	http://regionalhelpwanted.com/ southwest-michigan-jobs
HudsonValleyHelp Wanted.com	http://regionalhelpwanted.com/hudson-valley-jobs

Midwest

JobsintheMidwest.com	www.jobsinthemidwest.com
MidWest Career Matrix	www.careermatrix.com

Minnesota

Duluth News-Tribune	www.duluthnewstribune.com
Elk River Star News	www.erstarnews.com
The Journal (New Ulm)	www.oweb.com
HelpWantedRochester.com	http://regionalhelpwanted.com/rochester-mn-jobs
Hennepin County Job Openings	www.co.hennepin.mn.us
MinJobs.com	www.minjobs.com
Minneapolis Jobs	www.minneapolis-jobs.com
Minneapolis Star Tribune	www.startribune.com
MinnesotaDiversity.com	www.minnesotadiversity.com
MinnesotaJobs.com	www.minnesotajobs.com
NorthlandHelpWanted.com	http://regionalhelpwanted.com/northland-jobs/
SouthernMinnesotaHelpWanted.com	http://regionalhelpwanted.com/ southern-minnesota-jobs
StCloudHelpWanted.com	http://regionalhelpwanted.com/st-cloud-jobs
Saint Paul Pioneer Press	www.twincities.com
TwinCitiesHelpWanted.com	http://regionalhelpwanted.com/twin-cities-jobs

Mississippi

BetterGulfCoastJobs.com	www.bettergulfcoastjobs.com
CentralMississippiHelpWanted.com	http://regionalhelpwanted.com/ central-mississippi-jobs
The Clarion Ledger (Jackson)	www.clarionledger.com
GulfCoastHelpWanted.com	http://regionalhelpwanted.com/gulf-coast-jobs
MeridianHelpWanted.com	http://regionalhelpwanted.com/meridian-jobs
Meridian Star	www.meridianstar.com
MississippiJobs.net	www.mississippijobs.net
The Natchez Democrat	www.natchezdemocrat.com
The Sun Herald (Biloxi)	www.sunherald.com
TupeloHelpWanted.com	http://regionalhelpwanted.com/tupelo-jobs
The Vicksburg Post	www.vicksburgpost.com

Missouri

BetterBransonJobs.com	www.betterbransonjobs.com
BetterSpringfieldJobs.com	www.betterspringfieldjobs.com
The Examiner (Independence)	www.examiner.net
Hannibal Courier-Post	www.hannibal.net
HeartlandJobs.com	http://regionalhelpwanted.com/heartland-mo-jobs
Human Resource Management Association of Greater Kansas City	http://hrma-kc.org
Jefferson City News Tribune	www.newstribune.com
Joplin Globe	www.joplinglobe.com
JoplinHelpWanted.com	http://regionalhelpwanted.com/joplin-jobs
Kansas City.com	www.kansascity.com
KansasCityHelpWanted.com	http://regionalhelpwanted.com/kansas-city-jobs
KCJobs.com	www.kcjobs.com
MidMissouriHelpWanted.com	http://regionalhelpwanted.com/mid-missouri-jobs
Missouri Academy of Family Physicians	www.fpjobsonline.org
Missouri Association of Personnel Services	www.moaps.com
MissouriJobs.com	www.missourijobs.com

Missouri Pharmacy Association	www.morx.com
Missouri State Government	www.mo.gov/working-in-missouri/ job-seekers-employers/
Online Columbia	www.onlinecolumbia.com/jobsearch.asp
OzarksHelpWanted.com	http://regionalhelpwanted.com/ozarks-jobs
Riverfront Times Virtual Career Fair	www.riverfronttimes.com
Springfield News-Leader	www.news-leader.com
StLouisHelpWanted.com	http://regionalhelpwanted.com/st-louis-jobs
St. Louis Jobs	http://st.louis.jobs.com
SouthCentralMOHelpWanted.com	http://regionalhelpwanted.com/ south-central-missouri-jobs

Montana

Billings Gazette	http://billingsgazette.com
BillingsHelpWanted.com	http://regionalhelpwanted.com/billings-jobs
Bozeman Daily Chronicle	http://www.bozemandailychronicle.com/
Helena Independent Record	www.helenair.com
Missoulian	www.missoulian.com
MontanaHelpWanted.com	http://regionalhelpwanted.com/montana-jobs
Montana Job Service	http://wsd.dli.mt.gov
MontanaJobs.com	www.montanajobs.com
The Montana Standard (Butte)	www.mtstandard.com
SouthwestMontanaHelpWanted.com	http://regionalhelpwanted.com/ southwest-montana-jobs
WesternMontanaHelpWanted.com	http://regionalhelpwanted.com/ western-montana-jobs

Nebraska

Columbus Telegram	www.columbustelegram.com
CornhuskerHelpWanted.com	http://regionalhelpwanted.com/cornhusker-jobs
Greater Omaha Economic Development Partnership	www.selectgreateromaha.com

Lincoln Journal Star	www.journalstar.com
NebraskaJobs.com	www.nebraskajobs.com
North Platte Telegraph	www.nptelegraph.com
OmahaHelpWanted.com	http://regionalhelpwanted.com/omaha-jobs
Omaha World-Herald	www.omaha.com
Scotts Bluff Star-Herald	www.starherald.com

Nevada

CarsonValleyJobs.com	www.carsonvalleyjobs.com
Elko Daily Free Press	http://elkodaily.com
LasVegasHelpWanted.com	http://regionalhelpwanted.com/las-vegas-jobs
Las Vegas Review-Journal	www.lvrj.com
Las Vegas Sun	www.lasvegassun.com
Nevada Appeal (Carson City)	www.nevadaappeal.com
NevadaJobs.com	www.nevadajobs.com
Nevada Mining	www.nevadamining.org
NVNurses.com	www.nvnurses.com
NVPublicJobs.com	www.nvpublicjobs.com
NVTeacherJobs.com	www.nvteacherjobs.com
NVMedicalJobs.com	www.nvmedicaljobs.com
NVAccountingJobs.com	www.nvaccountingjobs.com
NVTechnologyJobs.com	www.nvtechnologyjobs.com
RenoHelpWanted.com	http://regionalhelpwanted.com/reno-jobs
Reno Gazette Journal	www.rgj.com
RenoTahoeJobs.com	www.renotahoejobs.com
Vegas.com	www.vegas.com
WorkReno	http://reno.jobing.com

New England

Jobfind.com	www.bostonherald.com/jobfind
New England Job	www.newenglandjob.com
New England Careers	www.newenglandcareers.com

Northeast Human Resource Association	www.nehra.com
New England Higher Education Recruitment Consortium	www.newenglandherc.org
New England Journal of Medicine Career Center	http://content.nejm.org
OceanStateHelpWanted.com	http://regionalhelpwanted.com/ocean-state-jobs
Opportunity Knocks	www.opportunityknocks.org

New Hampshire

AllCountyJobs.com	www.allcountyjobs.com
Across New Hampshire	www.across-nh.com
Concord Monitor	www.concordmonitor.com
Employment Times Online	www.myjobwave.com
JobsinNH.com	www.jobsinnh.com
Keene Sentinel	www.keenesentinel.com
New England Higher Education Recruitment Consortium	www.newenglandherc.org
NewHampshireHelpWanted.com	http://regionalhelpwanted.com/ new-hampshire-jobs
NewHampshireJobs.net	www.newhampshirejobs.net
New Hampshire Legal Assistance	www.nhla.org
NH.com	www.nh.com
nhjobs.com	www.nhjobs.com
Portsmouth Herald	www.seacoastonline.com
The Telegraph (Nashua)	www.nashuatelegraph.com
The Union Leader (Manchester)	www.theunionleader.com

New Jersey

ACHelpWanted.com	http://regionalhelpwanted.com/atlantic-city-jobs
App.com	www.app.com
AllCountyJobs.com	www.allcountyjobs.com
Atlantic City Jobs	www.acjobs.com
Asbury Park Press	www.app.com

Biotechnology Council of New Jersey	www.newjerseybiotech.org
CareerLocal.net	www.careerlocal.net
Courier-Post (Cherry Hill)	www.courierpostonline.com
Employment Channel	www.employ.com
JobCircle.com	www.jobcircle.com
JobNet	http://jobcircle.com/jobnet
MonmouthOceanHelpWanted.com	http://regionalhelpwanted.com/ monmouth-ocean-recruitment
The Montclair Times	www.northjersey.com/towns/Montclair.html
NewJerseyHelpWanted.com	http://regionalhelpwanted.com/new-jersey-jobs
The New Jersey Higher Education Recruitment Consortium	www.njepadeherc.org
New Jersey Human Resource Planning Group	www.njhrpg.org
NewJerseyJobs.com	www.newjerseyjobs.com
New Jersey Metro Employment Management Association	www.njmetroema.org
New Jersey Net Connections	www.netconnections.net/nj/nj.html
New Jersey Online	www.nj.com
New Jersey Staffing Association	www.njsa.com
New Jersey Technical Recruiters Alliance	www.njtra.org
New Jersey Technology Council	www.njtc.org
NJ Careers	http://hus.parkingspa.com/hc3.asp
NJ Jobs	www.njjobs.com
NJPAHelpWanted.com	http://regionalhelpwanted.com/ edison-trenton-allentown-nj-pa-jobs
NorthJerseyHelpWanted.com	http://regionalhelpwanted.com/north-jersey-jobs
Princeton Info	www.princetoninfo.com
The Star Ledger (Newark)	www.nj.com
The Trentonian	www.trentonian.com
Tri-StateJobs.com	www.tristatejobs.com

New Mexico

Albuquerque Journal	www.abqjournal.com

The Gallup Independent	www.gallupindependent.com
HelpWantedNewMexico.com	http://regionalhelpwanted.com/new-mexico-jobs
HighPlainsHelpWanted.com	http://regionalhelpwanted.com/
	high-plains-nm-tx-jobs
Los Alamos Monitor	www.lamonitor.com
New Mexico High Tech Job Forum	www.nmtechjobs.com
NewMexicoJobs.net	www.newmexicojobs.netbs.net
New Mexico Library Association	www.nmla.org
Santa Fe New Mexican	www.santafenewmexican.com
The Silver City Daily Press	www.scdailypress.com

New York

Accounting Jobs in New York	www.accounting-jobs-in-new-york.com
AdirondackHelpWanted.com	http://regionalhelpwanted.com/adirondack-jobs
Albany Democrat Herald	http://democratherald.com
AllCountyJobs.com	www.allcountyjobs.com
BigAppleHelpWanted.com	http://regionalhelpwanted.com/tri-state-ny-nj-jobs
BinghamtonHelpWanted.com	http://regionalhelpwanted.com/binghamton-jobs
BuffaloHelpWanted.com	http://regionalhelpwanted.com/buffalo-jobs
CapitalAreaHelpWanted.com	http://regionalhelpwanted.com/capital-area-jobs
CentralNewYorkHelpWanted.com	http://regionalhelpwanted.com/
	central-new-york-jobs
ColumbiaCountyJobs.com	www.columbiacountyjobs.com
ColumbiaGreeneHelpWanted.com	http://regionalhelpwanted.com/
	columbia-greene-jobs
Employment Weekly	www.employment-weekly.com
FingerLakesHelpWanted.com	http://regionalhelpwanted.com/finger-lakes-jobs
411 NYC Jobs	http://allnewyorkcityjobs.com/
Geebo	www.geebo.com
HelpWantedLongIsland.com	http://regionalhelpwanted.com/long-island-jobs
HudsonValleyHelpWanted.com	http://regionalhelpwanted.com/hudson-valley-jobs
Human Resource Association of New York	www.nyshrm.org

IthacaCortlandHelpWanted.com	http://regionalhelpwanted.com/ ithaca-cortland-jobs
Ithaca Times	www.zwire.com/site/news. cfm?brd=1395&nr=1&nostat=1
JobCircle.com	www.jobcircle.com
TheJobWire.com	www.thejobwire.com
LI Jobs	www.lijobs.com
LocalCareers.com	www.localcareers.com
National Association of Securities Professionals (New York) Underground Railroad	www.nasp-ny.org
New York American Marketing Association	www.nyama.org
The New York Biotechnology Association	www.nyba.org
New York Department of Labor	www.labor.ny.gov/home
New York Foundation for the Arts	www.nyfa.org
NewYorkJobs.com	www.newyorkjobs.com
New York Post	www.nypost.com
New York Society of Association Executives Career Center	www.nysaenet.org
New York Society of Security Analysts Career Resources	www.nyssa.org/AM/Template. cfm?Section=career_development
New York State Academy of Family Physicians	www.fpjobsonline.org
New York State Society of CPAs	www.nysscpa.org/classified/main.cfm
The New York Times	www.nytimes.com
New York's Preferred Jobs	www.nycityjobs.com
NYCareers.com	www.nycareers.com
NY Job Source	www.nyjobsource.com
NY Preferred Jobs	http://newyork.preferredjobs.com
NYC Job Bank	www.nycjobbank.com
NYPAHelpWanted.com	http://regionalhelpwanted.com/ erie-warren-bradford-buffalo-ny-pa-jobs
OleanHelpWanted.com	http://regionalhelpwanted.com/olean-jobs
Rensselaer Polytechnic Institute Career Development Center	www.rpi.edu/dept/cdc

RochesterHelpWanted.com	http://regionalhelpwanted.com/rochester-jobs
Rochester, NY Careers	www.rochestercareers.com
SeawayHelpWanted.com	http://regionalhelpwanted.com/seaway-jobs
Silicon Alley Insider	http://jobs.businessinsider.com/
SyracuseHelpWanted.com	http://regionalhelpwanted.com/syracuse-jobs
Syracuse New Times	www.newtimes.com
Syracuse Online	www.syracuse.com
1000IslandsHelpWanted.com	http://regionalhelpwanted.com/1000-islands-jobs
Tri-StateJobs.com	www.tristatejobs.com
TwinTiersHelpWanted.com	http://regionalhelpwanted.com/twin-tiers-jobs
WestchesterCountyJobs.com	www.westchestercountyjobs.com
Westchester Jobs	www.westchesterjobs.com
Western NY JOBS	www.wnyjobs.com

North Carolina

AshevilleHelpWanted.com	http://regionalhelpwanted.com/asheville-jobs
BetterGreenvilleJobs.com	www.bettergreenvillejobs.com
Career Women	www.careerwomen.com
Carolina Computer Jobs	www.carolinacomputerjobs.com
CharlotteHelpWanted.com	http://regionalhelpwanted.com/charlotte-jobs
Charlotte Observer	www.charlotteobserver.com
Duke University Job Resources	http://career.studentaffairs.duke.edu
EastCarolinaHelpWanted.com	http://regionalhelpwanted.com/east-carolina-jobs
Employment Security Commission Home Page	www.ncesc.com/default.aspx
FayettevilleHelpWanted.com	http://regionalhelpwanted.com/fayetteville-jobs
Greensboro News-Record	www.news-record.com
News & Observer (Raleigh)	www.newsobserver.com
North Carolina Biotechnology Center	www.ncbiotech.org
North Carolina Genomics & Bioinformatics Consortium	www.ncgbc.org
North Carolina JobLink Career Center	www.nccommerce.com
NorthCarolinaJobs.net	www.northcarolinajobs.net
The North Carolina Office of State Personnel	www.osp.state.nc.us

PiedmontHelpWanted.com	http://regionalhelpwanted.com/piedmont-jobs
StarNewsOnline.com	www.starnewsonline.com
TriangleHelpWanted.com	http://regionalhelpwanted.com/triangle-nc-jobs
Welcome to North Carolina	www.ncgov.com
WilmingtonHelpWanted.com	http://regionalhelpwanted.com/wilmington-jobs
Winston-Salem Journal	http://www2.journalnow.com/home

North Dakota

BismarckMandanHelpWanted.com	http://regionalhelpwanted.com/ bismarck-mandan-jobs
Bismarck Tribune	www.bismarcktribune.com
FargoJobs.com	http://regionalhelpwanted.com/fargo-jobs
Grand Forks Herald	www.grandforks.com
The Jamestown Sun	www.jamestownsun.com
Minot Daily News	www.minotdailynews.com
NorthDakotaJobs.com	www.northdakotajobs.com
NorthernPlainsHelpWanted.com	http://regionalhelpwanted.com/ northern-plains-md-jobs

Ohio

BetterTriStateJobs.com	www.bettertristatejobs.com
CareerBoard	www.careerboard.com
Case Western Reserve University	www.cwru.edu
Cincinnati Enquirer	www.enquirer.com
Cincinnati/Jobs	http://careerfinder.cincinnati.com
Cleveland Careers	www.cleveland.com
ClevelandHelpWanted.com	http://regionalhelpwanted.com/cleveland-jobs
The Cleveland Nation	www.clnation.com
Columbus Dispatch	www.dispatch.com
ColumbusHelpWanted.com	http://regionalhelpwanted.com/columbus-jobs
Dayton Daily News	www.daytondailynews.com
DaytonHelpWanted.com	http://regionalhelpwanted.com/dayton-jobs

FetchMeAJob.com	www.fetchmeajob.com
HelpWantedCincinnati.com	http://regionalhelpwanted.com/cincinnati-jobs
LimalandHelpWanted.com	http://regionalhelpwanted.com/limaland-jobs
MahoningValleyHelpWanted.com	http://regionalhelpwanted.com/mahoning-valley-jobs
MansfieldAreaHelpWanted.com	http://regionalhelpwanted.com/mansfield-area-jobs
MidOhioValleyJobs.com	www.midohiovalleyjobs.com
Ohio Careers Resource Center	www.ohiocareers.com
Ohio Job Prospector	www.jobprospector.com
OhioJobs.com	www.ohiojobs.com
Ohio State Council	www.ohioshrm.org
SanduskyHelpWanted.com	http://regionalhelpwanted.com/sandusky-jobs
SoutheasternOhioHelpWanted.com	http://regionalhelpwanted.com/southeastern-ohio-jobs
Springfield News Sun	www.springfieldnewssun.com
ToledoHelpWanted.com	http://regionalhelpwanted.com/toledo-jobs

Oklahoma

Altus Times	www.altustimes.com
Lawton Constitution	www.lawton-constitution.com
OKC.gov	www.okc.gov
OklahomaCityHelpWanted.com	http://regionalhelpwanted.com/oklahoma-city-jobs
OklahomaJobs.com	www.oklahomajobs.com
Oklahoma State Medical Association	www.osmaonline.org
The Oklahoman (Oklahoma City)	www.newsok.com
Ponca City News	www.poncacitynews.com
Tulsa Area Human Resources Association	www.tahra.org
TulsaHelpWanted.com	http://regionalhelpwanted.com/tulsa-jobs
Tulsa World	www.tulsaworld.com

Oregon

AshlandJobAlert.com	www.ashlandjobalert.com
CentralOregonJobs.com	http://regionalhelpwanted.com/ central-oregon-jobs
Columbia-Willamette Compensation Group	
East Oregonian (Pendleton)	www.cwcg.org
EugeneHelpWanted.com	http://eastoregonian.com/index.asp
EugeneJobs.net	http://regionalhelpwanted.com/eugene-jobs
JobDango.com	www.eugenejobs.net
KlamathJobs.net	www.jobdango.com
Oregon Bioscience Association	www.klamathjobs.net
Oregon Education Jobs	www.oregon-bioscience.com
Oregon Employment Department	www.cosa.k12.or.us
OregonJobs.com	www.employment.oregon.gov
The Oregonian (Portland)	http://oregon.jobing.com
PortlandHelpWanted.com	www.oregonian.com
The Portland Human Resource Management Assn	http://regionalhelpwanted.com/portland-jobs
	www.pbcs.jp
PortlandJobFinder.com	www.portlandjobfinder.com
The Register-Guard (Eugene)	www.registerguard.com
RogueValleyJobs.net	www.roguevalleyjobs.net
SalemJobFinder.com	www.salemjobfinder.com
SouthernOregonHelpWanted.com	http://regionalhelpwanted.com/ southern-oregon-jobs
SouthernOregonJobs.com	www.southernoregonjobs.com
Springfield News	www.hometownnews.com
Statesman Journal (Salem)	www.statesmanjournal.com

Pennsylvania

AllCountyJobs.com	www.allcountyjobs.com
Allegheny County Medical Society	www.acms.org
CentreCountyHelpWanted.com	http://regionalhelpwanted.com/centre-county-jobs

ClearfieldJeffersonHelpWanted.com	http://regionalhelpwanted.com/ clearfield-jefferson-jobs
Drexel University	www.drexel.edu
Erie Daily Times-News	www.goerie.com
ErieHelpWanted.com	http://regionalhelpwanted.com/erie-jobs
Geebo	www.geebo.com
HarrisburgHelpWanted.com	http://regionalhelpwanted.com/harrisburg-jobs
HelpWantedCentralPA.com	http://regionalhelpwanted.com/ central-pennsylvania-jobs
TriStateHelpWanted.com	http://regionalhelpwanted.com/tri-state-jobs
JobCircle.com	www.jobcircle.com
JobNet	http://jobcircle.com/jobnet
JohnstownHelpWanted.com	http://regionalhelpwanted.com/johnstown-jobs
KeystoneHelpWanted.com	http://regionalhelpwanted.com/keystone-jobs
LehighValleyHelpWanted.com	http://regionalhelpwanted.com/lehigh-valley-jobs
NEPAHelpWanted.com	http://regionalhelpwanted.com/ northeast-pennsylvania-jobs
PAJobMatch.com	http://jobs.triblive.com/
Pennsylvania Academy of Family Physicians	www.fpjobsonline.org
PennsylvaniaJobs.com	www.pennsylvaniajobs.com
PennsylvaniaJobs.net	www.pennsylvaniajobs.net
PhiladelphiaHelpWanted.com	http://regionalhelpwanted.com/philadelphia-jobs
The Philadelphia Inquirer	www.philly.com
Philadelphia-Jobs	http://philadelphia.jobs.com
Philly.com	www.philly.com
PhillyWorks	www.phillyworks.com
PittsburghHelpWanted.com	http://regionalhelpwanted.com/pittsburgh-jobs
PittsburghJobs.com	www.pittsburghjobs.com
Pittsburg Post-Gazette	www.post-gazette.com
Scranton Times Tribune	http://thetimes-tribune.com
Three Rivers	http://trfn.clpgh.org
The Times Leader (Wilkes-Barre)	www.timesleader.com

Tri-StateJobs.com	www.tristatejobs.com
WesternPAHelpWanted.com	http://regionalhelpwanted.com/ western-pennsylvania-jobs
WilliamsportHelpWanted.com	http://regionalhelpwanted.com/williamsport-jobs

Rhode Island

AllCountyJobs.com	www.allcountyjobs.com
JobsinRI.com	www.jobsinri.com
The Narragansett Times (Wakefield)	www.narragansetttimes.com
OceanStateHelpWanted.com	http://regionalhelpwanted.com/ocean-state-jobs
Networkri.org	www.networkri.org
The Pawtucket Times	www.pawtuckettimes.com
Providence Journal Bulletin	www.projo.com
Rhode Island Department of Labor and Training	www.dlt.state.ri.us
RhodeIsland Jobs.com	www.rhodeislandjobs.com
Sakonnet Times (Portsmouth)	www.eastbayri.com

South Carolina

Camden Chronicle Independent	www.chronicle-independent.com
Career Women	www.careerwomen.com
Carolina Computer Jobs	www.carolinacomputerjobs.com
Clemson University	www.clemson.edu
ColumbiaHelpWanted.com	http://regionalhelpwanted.com/columbia-jobs
Free Times (Columbia)	www.free-times.com
The Greenville News	www.greenvilleonline.com
LowCountryHelpWanted.com	http://regionalhelpwanted.com/ low-country-sc-jobs
MyrtleBeachHelpWanted.com	http://regionalhelpwanted.com/myrtle-beach-jobs
OrangeburgHelpWanted.com	http://regionalhelpwanted.com/orangeburg-jobs
PeeDeeHelpWanted.com	http://regionalhelpwanted.com/pee-dee-jobs
The Post and Courier (Charleston)	www.postandcourier.com
SouthCarolinaJobs.net	www.southcarolinajobs.net

South Carolina State Jobs	www.ohr.sc.gov
SumterHelpWanted.com	http://regionalhelpwanted.com/sumter-jobs
The Sun Times (Myrtle Beach)	www.thesunnews.com/myrtlebeachonline
UpstateHelpWanted.com	http://regionalhelpwanted.com/upstate-sc-jobs

South Dakota

Argus Leader (Sioux Falls)	www.argusleader.com
BlackHillsHelpWanted.com	http://regionalhelpwanted.com/black-hills-sd-jobs
Brookings Daily Register	www.brookingsregister.com
The Capital Journal (Pierre)	www.capjournal.com
The Freeman Courier	www.freemansd.com
Huron Plainsman	www.plainsman.com
SiouxFallsHelpWanted.com	http://regionalhelpwanted.com/sioux-falls-jobs
SouthDakotaJobs.com	www.southdakotajobs.com

Southeast

MyGA.net	www.myga.net
Thinkjobs	www.thinkjobs.com

Tennessee

BetterChattanoogaJobs.com	www.betterchattanoogajobs.com
BetterJacksonJobs.com	www.betterjacksonjobs.com
BetterKnoxvilleJobs.com	www.betterknoxvillejobs.com
BetterTCJobs.com	www.bettertcjobs.com
ChattanoogaHelpWanted.com	http://regionalhelpwanted.com/chattanooga-jobs
Chattanooga Times Free Press	www.timesfreepress.com
ClarksvilleHelpWanted.com	http://regionalhelpwanted.com/clarksville-jobs
CookevilleHelpWanted.com	http://regionalhelpwanted.com/cookeville-jobs
Daily Post-Athenian	www.dpa.xtn.net
JobDig	www.jobdig.com
KnoxvilleHelpWanted.com	http://regionalhelpwanted.com/knoxville-jobs
Knoxville News Sentinel	www.knoxnews.com

Memphis Flyer	www.memphisflyer.com
MemphisHelpWanted.com	http://regionalhelpwanted.com/memphis-jobs
Memphis Jobs Today	www.memphisjobstoday.com
MiddleTennesseeHelpWanted.com	http://regionalhelpwanted.com/ middle-tennessee-jobs
Middle Tennessee-SHRM Central	www.mtshrm.org
NashvilleHelpWanted.com	http://regionalhelpwanted.com/nashville-jobs
Nashvillejobslink.com	www.nashvillechamber.com
TennesseeJobs.com	www.tennesseejobs.com
Tennessee Society of CPA's	www.tscpa.com
The Tennessean (Nashville)	www.tennessean.com
WestTennesseeHelpWanted.com	http://regionalhelpwanted.com/ west-tennessee-jobs

Texas

AmarilloHelpWanted.com	http://regionalhelpwanted.com/amarillo-jobs
Apartment Association of Greater Dallas	www.aagdallas.org
Apartment Association of Tarrant County	www.aatcnet.org/subsite/CareerCenter/ careercenterindex.htm
Austin American-Statesman	www.austin360.com
AustinHelpWanted.com	http://regionalhelpwanted.com/austin-jobs
Austin Jobs	www.austin-jobs.com
Austin@Work	www.catf-austin.org
Austin Texas Jobs	www.search-beat.com/austinjobs.htm
Austin-City Jobs	www.ci.Austin.tx.us
BetterTexarkanaJobs.com	www.bettertexarkanajobs.com
BetterTexomaJobs.com	www.bettertexomajobs.com
BrownwoodHelpWanted.com	http://regionalhelpwanted.com/brownwood-jobs
CareersinHouston.com	www.careersinhouston.com
CoastalBendHelpWanted.com	http://regionalhelpwanted.com/ coastal-bend-tx-jobs

Dallas Human Resource Management Association	www.dallashr.org
Dallas Jobs	http://dallas.jobs.net
Dallas Morning News	www.dallasnews.com
Dallas News	www.dallasnews.com/classifieds/jobcenter
DFWHelpWanted.com	http://regionalhelpwanted.com/ dallas-fort-worth-jobs
EastTexasHelpWanted.com	http://regionalhelpwanted.com/east-texas-jobs
ElPasoHelpWanted.com	http://regionalhelpwanted.com/el-paso-jobs
El Paso Times	www.elpasotimes.com
FortBendJobs.com	www.fortbendjobs.com
Geebo	www.geebo.com
Harris County Medical Society	www.hcms.org
Houston Chronicle	www.chron.com
Houston Human Resource Management Association	www.hrhouston.org
Houston Jobs	www.houstonjobs.com
Institute for Sustainable Charities	www.iscvt.org/who_we_are/jobs
JobDig	www.jobdig.com
Jobing.com	http://houston.jobing.com
LocalCareers.com	www.localcareers.com
LubbockHelpWanted.com	http://regionalhelpwanted.com/lubbock-jobs
Metroplex Association of Personnel Consultants	www.recruitingfirms.com
NACCB	www.techservealliance.org
National Association of Hispanic Nurses Houston Chapter	www.nahnhouston.org
North Central Texas Workforce Solutions	www.dfwjobs.com
San Antonio Express News	www.mysanantonio.com
SanAntonioHelpWanted.com	http://regionalhelpwanted.com/san-antonio-jobs
SoutheastTexasHelpWanted.com	http://regionalhelpwanted.com/ southeast-texas-jobs
SouthTexasHelpWanted.com	http://regionalhelpwanted.com/south-texas-jobs
StephenvilleHelpWanted.com	http://regionalhelpwanted.com/stephenville-jobs

Texas Apartment Association	www.taa.org
Texas Association of Staffing	www.texasstaffing.org
Texas Healthcare & Bioscience Institute	www.thbi.org
TxJobs.com	www.txjobs.com
TexasJobs.com	www.texasjobs.com
Texas Marketplace	www.texas-one.org
Texas Medical Association	www.texmed.org
Texas Workforce Commission	www.twc.state.tx.us
TexomaHelpWanted.com	http://regionalhelpwanted.com/texoma-jobs
ValleyHelpWanted.com	http://regionalhelpwanted.com/valley-tx-jobs
WichitaFallsHelpWanted.com	http://regionalhelpwanted.com/wichita-falls-jobs
WorkAustin	http://austin.jobing.com
WT.Net	www.wt.net

Utah

The Daily Herald (Provo)	www.heraldextra.com
Herald Journal (Logan)	www.hjnews.com
JobDig	www.jobdig.com
SaltLakeCityHelpWanted.com	http://regionalhelpwanted.com/salt-lake-city-jobs
Salt Lake Tribune	www.sltrib.com
SouthernUtahHelpWanted.com	http://regionalhelpwanted.com/southern-utah-jobs
Standard-Examiner (Ogden)	www.standard.net
Utah Job Store	www.utahjobstore.com
UtahJobs.net	http://utah.jobing.com
Utah Life Sciences Association	www.utahlifescience.com

Vermont

Addison County Independent (Middlebury)	www.addisonindependent.com
AllCountyJobs.com	www.allcountyjobs.com
Burlington Free Press	www.burlingtonfreepress.com
Deerfield Valley News (West Dover)	www.dvalnews.com
JobsinVT.com	www.jobsinvt.com

New England Higher Education Recruitment Consortium	www.newenglandherc.org
NorthCountryHelpWanted.com	http://regionalhelpwanted.com/north-country-jobs
Stowe Reporter	www.stowetoday.com
Valley News (White River Junction)	www.vnews.com
VermontJobs.net	www.vermontjobs.net

Virginia

BlueRidgeHelpWanted.com	http://regionalhelpwanted.com/blue-ridge-jobs
Career Pro	www.career-pro.com
CharlottesvilleHelpWanted.com	http://regionalhelpwanted.com/charlottesville-jobs
The Daily Progress (Charlottesville)	http://www2.dailyprogress.com
Danville Register Bee	http://www2.godanriver.com
HamptonRoadsHelpWanted.com	http://regionalhelpwanted.com/ hampton-roads-jobs
HarrisonburgHelpWanted.com	http://regionalhelpwanted.com/harrisonburg-jobs
HighlandsHelpWanted.com	http://regionalhelpwanted.com/ highlands-virginia-jobs
Human Resource Association of the National Capital Area Job Bank Listing	www.hra-nca.org
JobFetch.com	www.jobfetch.com
LocalVirginiaJobs.com	www.localvirginiajobs.com
The News-Advance (Lynchburg)	http://www2.newsadvance.com
North Virginia Job Openings	www.northern-viriginia.jobopenings.net
NRVHelpWanted.com	http://regionalhelpwanted.com/ new-river-valley-va-jobs
Pilot Online	http://pilotonline.com
RichmondHelpWanted.com	http://regionalhelpwanted.com/richmond-jobs
Richmond Preferred Jobs	http://richmond.preferredjobs.com
Richmond Times-Dispatch	http://www2.timesdispatch.com
Roanoke.com	www.roanoke.com
RoanokeValleyJobs.com	www.roanokevalleyjobs.com

ShenandoahValleyHelpWanted.com	http://regionalhelpwanted.com/ shenandoah-valley-jobs
TriCitiesHelpWanted.com	http://regionalhelpwanted.com/tri-cities-jobs
University of Virginia Career Planning and Placement	www.hrs.virginia.edu
Virginia Biotechnology Association	http://vabio.org/
Virginia-Jobs	www.virginia-jobs.com
Virginia Working 925	www.working925.com
Virginian-Pilot (Norfolk)	http://pilotonline.com
WashingtonJobs.com	www.washingtonpost.com
Washington and Lee University	www.wlu.edu

Washington

BetterTriCityJobs.com	www.bettertricityjobs.com
The Columbian (Vancouver)	www.columbian.com
Communicators & Marketers Jobline (Seattle & Puget Sound)	http://cmjobline.org
Geebo	www.geebo.com
JobDango.com	www.jobdango.com
LocalWashingtonJobs.com	http://washington.jobing.com
Navigator Online	www.lwhra.org
The News Tribune (Tacoma)	www.thenewstribune.com
NorthwestWashingtronHelpWanted.com	http://regionalhelpwanted.com/ northwest-washington-jobs
The Olympian (Olympia)	www.theolympian.com
PugetSoundHelpWanted.com	http://regionalhelpwanted.com/puget-sound-jobs
SeattleJobs	www.seattlejobs.com
Seattle Post-Intelligencer	www.seattlepi.com
SeattleTacomaJobs.com	www.seattletacomajobs.com
Seattle Times	www.nwjobs.com
SoutheasternWashingtonHelpWanted.com	http://regionalhelpwanted.com/ southeastern-washington-jobs
SpokaneHasJobs.com	http://spokane.careerlink.com

SpokaneHelpWanted.com	http://regionalhelpwanted.com/spokane-jobs
SpokaneJobFinder.com	www.spokanejobfinder.com
The Spokesman-Review (Spokane)	www.spokane.net
University of Washington	www.washington.edu
Washington Biotechnology & Biomedical Association	www.wabio.com
Washington Multi-Family Housing Association	http://careers.wmfha.org
Washington Workforce	http://access.wa.gov/employment/index.aspx
WesternWashingtonHelpWanted.com	http://regionalhelpwanted.com/ western-washington-jobs
YakimaHelpWanted.com	http://regionalhelpwanted.com/yakima-jobs
YakimaValleyJobs.com	www.yakimavalleyjobs.com

West Virginia

BetterCharlestonJobs.com	www.bettercharlestonjobs.com
BluefieldHelpWanted.com	http://regionalhelpwanted.com/bluefield-jobs
Charlestown Daily Mail	www.dailymail.com
CharlestonHelpWanted.com	http://regionalhelpwanted.com/ charleston-jobs
Clarksburg Exponent Telegram	www.cpubco.com
The Dominion Post (Morgantown)	www.dominionpost.com
GreenBrierValleyHelpWanted.com	http://regionalhelpwanted.com/ green-brier-valley-jobs
HuntingtonAshlandHelpWanted.com	http://regionalhelpwanted.com/ huntington-ashland-jobs
OhioValleyHelpWanted.com	http://regionalhelpwanted.com/ohio-valley-jobs
SouthernWestVirginiaJobs.com	www.southernwestvirginiajobs.com
Times West Virginian (Fairmont)	http://timeswv.com
WestVaHelpWanted.com	http://regionalhelpwanted.com/west-virginia-jobs
WestVirginiaJobs.com	www.westvirginiajobs.com
Wheeling News-Register	www.news-register.com

Wisconsin

CareerBoard.com	www.careerboard.com
ChippewaValleyHelpWanted.com	http://regionalhelpwanted.com/ chippewa-valley-jobs
FetchMeAJob.com	www.fetchmeajob.com
Green Bay Press Gazette	www.greenbaypressgazette.com
HelpWantedMadison.com	http://regionalhelpwanted.com/madison-jobs
HelpWantedMilwaukee.com	http://regionalhelpwanted.com/milwaukee-jobs
HelpWantedWisconsin.com	http://regionalhelpwanted.com/wisconsin-jobs
Jobing.com	http://wisconsin.jobing.com
The Journal Times (Racine)	www.journaltimes.com
La Crosse Tribune	www.lacrossetribune.com
LocalCareers.com	www.localcareers.com
Milwaukee Journal Sentinel	www.jsonline.com
NEWHelpWanted.com	http://regionalhelpwanted.com/ northeast-wisconsin-jobs
SouthValleyHelpWanted.com	http://regionalhelpwanted.com/ south-valley-wi-jobs
University of Wisconsin-Madison School of Business Career Center	www.bus.wisc.educ/areer
Wisconsin.gov	www.wisconsin.gov/state
Wisconsin Academy of Family Physicians	www.fpjobsonline.org
Wisconsin Biotechnology Association	www.wisconsinbiotech.org
Wisconsin Department of Workforce Development	www.dwd.state.wi.us
WisconsinJobNetwork.com	www.wisconsinjobnetwork.com
Wisconsin Medical Society	www.wisconsinmedicalsociety.org
Wisconsin State Journal (Madison)	http://host.madison.com

Wyoming

Douglas Budget	www.douglas-budget.com
WyomingatWork.com	https://www.wyomingatwork.com

WyomingHelpWanted.com	http://regionalhelpwanted.com/wyoming-jobs
WyomingJobs.com	www.wyomingjobs.com
Wyoming News.com	www.wyomingnews.com
Wyoming Tribune-Eagle	www.wyomingnews.com

Religion

BaptistLife	www.baptistlife.com
CatholicJobs.com	www.catholicjobs.com
CatholicSource	www.catholicsource.org
Catho Online [Brazil]	www.catho.com.br
ChristiaNet	www.christianet.com
Christian Help	www.christianhelp.org
ChurchEmployment.com	www.churchemployment.com
ChurchJobs.net	www.churchjobs.net
Church Jobs Online	www.churchjobsonline.com
Church Music Jobs	www.churchmusicjobs.com
ChurchStaffing.com	www.churchstaffing.com
Crosswalk.com	www.crosswalk.com
Gospel Communications Network	www.gospel.com
Jewish Community Center	www.jccworks.com
JewishJobs.com	www.jewishjobs.com
Jewish Vocational Service Career Moves	www.jvs-boston.org
Ministry Connect	http://ministryconnect.org
MinistryJobs.com	www.ministryjobs.com
MinistryEmployment.com	www.ministryemployment.com
MinistrySearch.com	www.ministrysearch.com
PastorFinder.com	www.pastorfinder.com

Retail

| AllRetailJobs.com | www.allretailjobs.com |

Be The 1	www.bethe1.com
Careers in Grocery	www.careersingrocery.com
ERTOnline.co.uk [United Kingdom]	www.ertonline.co.uk
RetailChoice.com [United Kingdom]	www.retailchoice.com
EmploymentGuide.com	www.employmentguide.com
GroceryHire	www.groceryhire.com
Grocer Jobs [United Kingdom]	http://jobs.thegrocer.co.uk
iHireRetail.com	www.ihireretail.com
Inc.com	www.inc.com
In Retail [United Kingdom]	www.inretail.co.uk
JobLoft.com [Canada]	www.jobloft.com
Jobs Retail	www.nowjob.com
JobsinRetail [United Kingdom]	www.jobsinretail.com
RetailCareers.co.uk [United Kingdom]	www.retailcareers.co.uk
RetailCareersNow	www.retailcareersnow.com
RetailJobs.ca [Canada]	www.retailjobs.ca
RetailingJobs.com	www.retailingjobs.com
RetailMoves.com [United Kingdom]	www.retailmoves.com

-S-

Sales and Marketing

Sales & Marketing-General

Adholes.com	http://adholes.com
BizJobs	www.bizjobs.com
Career Marketplace.com	www.careermarketplace.com
eChannelLinecareers.com [Canada]	www.echannellinecareers.com
eMarketing & Commerce's Job Connection	http://jobs.emarketingandcommerce.com
FINS from The Wall Street Journal	www.fins.com
Grist.org	http://jobs.grist.org
The Internet Advertising Bureau Job Board	www.iab.net/jobs

Just Sales and Marketing [United Kingdom]	www.justsalesandmarketing.net
TheLadders.com	www.theladders.com
NationJob Network: Marketing and Sales Job Page	www.nationjob.com/marketing
Sales & Marketing Executives International Career Center	www.smei.org

Sales-Specific

ACareerinSales.com	www.acareerinsales.com
CareerinSales.com	www.careerinsales.com
HotSalesJobs.com	www.hotsalesjobs.com
iHireSalesPeople.com	www.ihiresalespeople.com
Jobs4Sales.com	www.jobs4sales.com
National Association of Sales Professionals Career Center	www.nasp.com
SalesAnimals.com	www.salesanimals.com
SalesCareersOnline.com	www.salescareersonline.com
Sales Classifieds	www.salesclassifieds.com
SalesEngineer.com	www.SalesEngineer.com
SalesGravy.com	www.salesgravy.com
SalesJob.com	www.salesjob.com
SalesJobs.com	www.salesjobs.com
SalesJobs.ie [Ireland]	www.salesjobs.ie
SalesRecruits.com	http://cardbrowser.com
SalesRep.ca [Canada]	www.salesrep.ca
SalesTarget.co.uk [United Kingdom]	www.salestarget.co.uk
Sales Trax	www.salestrax.com
SalesWise.co.uk [United Kingdom]	www.saleswise.co.uk
SellingJobs.com/BrandingJobs.com	www.sellingjobs.com
Tigerjobs.com, Inc.	www.tigerjobs.com
Top Sales Positions	www.topsalespositions.com

Marketing-Specific

American Marketing Association Career Center	www.marketingpower.com
eMarketing Silo	www.emarketingsilo.com
iHireMarketing.com	www.ihiremarketing.com
Jobs In Marketing [United Kingdom]	www.jobs-in-marketing.co.uk
Marketing Career Network	www.marketingcareernetwork.com
MarketingHire.com	www.marketinghire.com
MarketingJobs.com	www.marketingjobs.com
MarketingProfs	www.marketingprofs.com
Marketing Sherpa	www.marketingsherpa.com
MyMarketingJobs.com.au [Australia]	http://mymarketingjobs.com.au
New York American Markerting Association	www.nyama.org
Promotion Marketing Association Job Bank	www.pmalink.org/?jobbank

Industry-Specific

Advertising Age's Online Job Bank	http://adage.com
Aeroindustryjobs	www.aeroindustryjobs.com
AllRetailJobs.com	www.allretailjobs.com
American Association of Pharmaceutical Sales Professionals	www.pharmaceuticalsales.org
Autojobs.com, Inc.	www.autojobs.com
BrokerHunter.com	www.brokerhunter.com
CallCenterCareers.com	www.callcentercareers.com
CallCenterJobs.com	www.callcenterjobs.com
CRN	www.crn.com/cwb/careers
Direct Marketing Association	www.the-dma.org/careercenter
DMjobs.co.uk [United Kingdom]	www.dmjobs.co.uk
GxPJobs.com [United Kingdom]	www.gxpjobs.com
iHireRetail.com	www.ihireretail.com
Industry Sales Pros	www.industrysalespros.com
InfoPresseJobs.com [Canada]	www.infopressejobs.com
In Retail [United Kingdom]	www.inretail.co.uk

InsuranceSalesJobs.com	www.insurancesalesjobs.com
InsuranceSalesWeb.com	www.insurancesalesweb.com
Job.com Retail JobNet	www.job.com
Just Tech Sales Jobs	www.justtechsalesjobs.com
Medical Marketing Association	www.mmanet.org
MedicalReps.com	www.medicalreps.com
MedicalSalesJobs.com	www.mymedicalsalesjobs.com
MedReps.com	www.medreps.com
Motorstaff.com	www.motorstaff.com
MyMedicalSalesJobs.com	www.mymedicalsalesjobs.com
National Association of Pharmaceutical Sales Representatives	www.napsronline.org
National Field Selling Association	www.nfsa.com
OnlineMarketingJobs.com [United Kingdom]	www.onlinemarketingjobs.com
NewHomeSalesJobs.com	www.newhomesalesjobs.com
Pharmacareers.co.uk [United Kingdom]	www.pharmacareers.co.uk
Pharmaceuticalrepjobs.com	http://pharmaceuticalrepjobs.org/
Retail-Recruiter	www.retail-recruiter.com
RetailingJobs.com	www.retailingjobs.com
Software & IT Sales Employment Review	http://cardbrowser.com
SoftwareSalesJobs.com	www.softwaresalesjobs.com
Television Bureau of Advertising	www.tvb.org/nav/build_frameset.aspx

Science/Scientists

Access-Science Jobs [United Kingdom]	www.access-sciencejobs.co.uk
American Association for the Advancement of Science	http://aas.org/career
American Association of Brewing Chemists	www.asbcnet.org
American Association of Cereal Chemists	www.aaccnet.org
American Association of Pharmaceutical Scientists	www.aapspharmaceutica.com

American Association of Physics Teachers	www.aapt.org
American Chemical Society	http://portal.acs.org/portal/acs/corg/content
American Institute of Biological Sciences	www.aibs.org
American Institute of Physics	www.physicstoday.org/jobs
PhysicsToday Jobs	
American Meteorological Society Employment Announcements	www.ametsoc.org
American Psychological Society	www.psychologicalscience.org/jobs
American Society of Agronomy	www.agronomy.org
American Society of Animal Science	www.fass.org/job.asp
American Society for Cell Biology	www.ascb.org
American Society for Clinical Laboratory Science	www.ascls.org
American Society for Clinical Pathology	www.ascp.org
American Society of Clinical Pharmacology and Therapeutics	www.ascpt.org
American Society for Microbiology	www.asm.org
American Society for Gravitational and Space Biology	http://asgsb.org/index.php
American Society of Horticultural Science HortOpportunities	www.ashs.org/db/hortopportunities/ assist_listing.lasso
American Society of Plant Biologists	www.aspb.org
American Water Works Association Career Center (Water Jobs)	www.awwa.org
Animal-job.co.uk [United Kingdom]	www.animal-job.co.uk
Association for Applied Human Pharmacology [Germany]	www.agah.info
Bay Bio	www.baybio.org
Bermuda Institute of Ocean Sciences	www.bios.edu
BioCareers.co.za [South Africa]	www.biocareers.co.za
Biofind	www.biofind.com
Bio Research Online	www.bioresearchonline.com
BioSource Technical Service	http://manpowerprofessional.com/us/ en/default.jsp

BioSpace — www.biospace.com

Biotechnology Calendar, Inc. — www.biotech-calendar.com

Bioview — www.bioview.co.il

Board of Physics and Astronomy — http://www7.nationalacademies.org/careers/

California Agricultural Technical Institute ATI-Net — www.atinet.org

California Separation Science Society — www.casss.org

Cell Press Online — www.cell.com/cellpress

Center for Biological Computing — http://papa.indstate.edu

Chemistry & Industry — www.soci.org

ChemJobs.net — www.chemjobs.net

Citysearch.com-Biotech — www.biofind.com

Controlled Release Society — www.controlledrelease.org

Earth Works — www.earthworks-jobs.com

Environmental Careers World — www.environmentaljobs.com

Environmental Careers Bulletin Online — www.eceajobs.com

Environmental Jobs & Careers — www.ejobs.org

Environmental Careers Organization — www.eco.org

FASEB Career Resources — www.faseb.org

GeoWebServices-RocketHire — www.geowebservices.com

GIS Jobs Clearinghouse — www.gjc.org

GxPJobs.com [United Kingdom] — www.gxpjobs.com

History of Science Society — www.hssonline.org

HUM-MOLGEN [Germany] — http://hum-molgen.org/positions

iHireChemists.com — www.ihirechemists.com

Institute of Physics — www.iop.org

International Society for Molecular Plant-Microbe Interactions — www.ismpminet.org/career

The Internet Pilot to Physics — http://physicsworld.com

Jobscience Network — http://jobs.jobscience.com

Jobs.ac.uk [United Kingdom] — www.jobs.ac.uk

Jobs in Chemistry — www.jobsinchemistry.com

LaboratoryNetwork.com — www.laboratorynetwork.com

The London Biology Network [United Kingdom] — www.biolondon.org.uk

MeteorologyJobs	www.meteorologyjobs.com
National Organization of Black Chemists and Chemical Engineers	www.engin.umich.edu/societies/nobcche
National Society of Black Physicists	www.nsbp.org
National Weather Association Job Corner	www.nwas.org
Naturejobs	www.nature.com
New Scientist	www.newscientist.com
NukeWorker.com	www.nukeworker.com
Oceanography Society	www.tos.org
OSU: College of Food, Agricultural and Environmental Sciences	http://cfaes.osu.edu/current-students/launch-your-career/
Optics.org	http://optics.org/cws/home
Organic Chemistry Jobs Worldwide [Belgium]	www.organicworldwide.net/jobs
PhysicsToday.org	www.physicstoday.org
Plant Pathology Online APSnet	www.scisoc.org
Plasma Gate [Israel]	http://plasma-gate.weizmann.ac.il
Poly Sort	www.polysort.com
Royal Society of Chemistry	http://jobs.rsc.org/careers/jobsearch
RPh on the Go	www.rphonthego.com
RPhrecruiter.com	www.rphrecruiter.com
Sci Central	www.scicentral.com
Science Careers	http://sciencecareers.sciencemag.org
ScienceCareers.org [United Kingdom]	http://sciencecareers.sciencemag.org/
Sciencejobs.com	www.newscientistjobs.com
The Science Jobs	www.thesciencejobs.com
Science Online	www.scienceonline.org
Science Professional Network	http://sciencecareers.sciencemag.org/
ScientistWorld.com [United Kingdom]	www.scientistworld.com
Scijobs.org	http://sciencecareers.sciencemag.org/
Society of Mexican American Engineers and Scientists	www.maes-natl.org
Space Jobs	www.spacejobs.com
SPIE Web-International Society for Optical Engineering	http://spie.org/app/buyersguide/index.aspx

Student Conservation Association	www.thesca.org
Texas A&M Poultry Science Department	http://gallus.tamu.edu/
Texas Healthcare & Bioscience Institute	www.thbi.org
Utah Life Sciences Association	www.utahlifescience.com
Weed Science Society of America WeedJobs: Positions in Weed Science	www.wssa.net

Search Engines-Employment

Beyond	www.beyond.com
CareerJet	www.careerjet.com
Check4Jobs [United Kingdom]	www.check4jobs.com
Employment Crossing	www.employmentcrossing.com
Finn.no [Norway]	www.finn.no
FlipDog	www.flipdog.com
Fusejobs.co.uk [United Kingdom]	www.fusejobs.co.uk
Gad Ball	www.gadball.com
Getjob.de [Germany]	www.getjob.de
GetTheJob.com	www.getthejob.com
Google Base	www.google.com/base/
Hound	www.hound.com
ICjobs.de [Germany]	www.icjobs.de
Indeed	www.indeed.com
Indeed.co.uk [United Kingdom]	www.indeed.co.uk
JobAhoy [United Kingdom]	www.jobahoy.com
Jobalot.com	www.jobalot.con
Jobbi	www.jobbi.com
Jobbporten.se [Sweden]	http://jobbporten.se
JobCentral.com	www.jobcentral.com
JobCrawler.it [Italy]	www.jobcrawler.it
JobIndex.dk [Denmark]	www.jobindex.dk
Jobrapido [Italy]	www.jobrapido.it
Jobrapido.es [Spain]	www.jobrapido.es

JobSafari.se [Sweden]	www.jobbsafari.se
JobsCareers24	www.jobscareers24.com
JobsOnline	www.jobsonline.com
Jobster	www.jobster.com
JobsTodayNetwork.com	www.jobstodaynetwork.com
Juju	www.juju.com
JumpToJobs [Ireland]	www.jumptojobs.co.uk
Keljob.com [France]	www.keljob.com
Kimeta.de [Germany]	www.kimeta.de
Lokus.se [Sweden]	http://lokus.se/Exp_SearchStart_all.asp?
Miltrabajos.com [Spain]	www.miltrabajos.com
NiceJob.ca [Canada]	www.nicejob.ca
1Job.co.uk [United Kingdom]	www.1job.co.uk
Oodle.com	www.oodle.com
Opcionempleo.com [Spain]	www.opcionempleo.com
Purjob.com [France]	www.purjob.com
Rubrikk.no [Norway]	www.rubrikk.no
SearchforJobs.com	www.searchforjobs.com
Second Life Jobfinder	www.SLJobFinder.com
SimplyHired	www.simplyhired.com
Srchnkd.com	www.srchnkd.com
TipTopJob	www.tiptopjob.com
TopUSAJob	www.topusajob.com
Trovit.it [Italy]	www.trovit.it
Trovit.co.uk [United Kingdom]	www.trovit.co.uk
Trovit.es [Spain]	www.trovit.es
Wink.com	www.wink.com
Workey.se [Sweden]	www.workey.se
Workhound.co.uk [United Kingdom]	www.workhound.co.uk
WorkShopping.com [Sweden]	www.workshopping.com
WorkTree.com	www.worktree.com
Worldcircle.com [United Kingdom]	www.worldcircle.com

Search Firms/Staffing Agencies/Recruiters

Accounting Position	www.taftsearch.com
AD&A Software Jobs Home Page	http://softwarejobs.4jobs.com
Adecco	www.adecco.com
All Advantage	www.alladvantage.com
Alpha Systems	www.jobbs.com
American Staffing Association	www.staffingtoday.net
Aquent Partners	http://aquent.us
Association of Executive Search Consultants	www.bluesteps.com
The Beardsley Group	www.beardsleygroup.com
Best Internet Recruiter	www.bestrecruit.com
J. Boragine & Associates	www.jboragine.com
BountyJobs.com	www.bountyjobs.com
Buck Systems Inc.	www.bisinc.com
The Caradyne Group	www.pcsjobs.com/jobs.htm
Career Image Associates	www.career-image.com
Champion Personnel System	www.championjobs.com
Chancellor & Chancellor's	www.chancellor.com
Comforce	www.comforce.com
Corporate Staffing Group, Inc.	www.corporatestaffing.com
Creative Focus	www.focusstaff.com
Daley Consulting & Search/Daley Technical Search	www.dpsearch.com.sg
Darwin Partners	www.seek-consulting.com
Datalake-IT.com	www.datalake-IT.com
Dawson & Dawson Consultants, Inc.	www.dawson-dawson.com
EPCglobal.com	www.epcglobal.com
Erickson & Associates, Inc.	www.nursesearch.com
Executive Placement Services	www.execplacement.com
Fogarty and Associates, Inc.	www.fogarty.com
Gables	www.gablessearch.com
Global Careers	www.globalcareers.com

Hamilton, Jones & Koller [Australia]	www.hjk.com.au
Headhunters 4u	www.headhunters.com
Healthcare Recruiters	www.hcrnetwork.com
The HEC Group	http://hec-group.com
HireMeNow.com	www.hiremenow.com
Hire Quality	www.hire-quality.com
HR Connections	www.hrconnections.com
Hyman Associates	www.hymanassociatesconsulting.com
Ian Martin Limited	www.iml.com
Insurance National Search, Inc.	www.insurancerecruiters.com
Insurance Overload Systems	www.iosstaffing.com
Inter-City Personnel Associates	www.ipaservices.com
Int-Exec.com	www.int-exec.com
Laser Computer Recruitment [United Kingdom]	www.laserrec.co.uk
Life Work, Inc.'s Military Recruiting Group	www.lifeworkinc.com
The Little Group	www.littlegroup.com
Made-In-China.com	www.made-in-china.com
Manpower	www.manpower.com
Manpower.com.au [Australia]	www.manpower.com.au
MarketPro	www.marketproinc.com
McGregor Boyall [United Kingdom]	www.mcgregor-boyall.com
Medical Sales Associates	www.msajobs.com
Metroplex Association of Personnel Consultants	www.recruitingfirms.com
Mindsource Software	www.mindsrc.com
National Banking Network	www.banking-financialjobs.com
On-Campus Resources, Inc.	www.on-campus.com
1to1media.com	www.1to1media.com
Pacific Coast Recruiting	www.pacificcoastrecruiting.com
People Connect Staffing	www.peopleconnectstaffing.com
Power Brokers	www.powerbrokersllc.com
Premier Staffing, Inc.	www.premier-staff.com
Priority Search.com	www.prioritysearch.com
Pro Match of Silicon Valley	www.promatch.org

ProQwest, Inc.	www.proqwest.com
Provident Search Group	www.dpjobs.com
RAI	www.raijobs.com
Recruit Employment Services	www.recruitemployment.co.uk
Recruiter Networks	www.recruiternetworks.com
Recruiters for Christ	www.edmondspersonnel.com
RecruitingOptions	www.recruitingoptions.net
Robert Half	www.roberthalffinance.com
Rollins Search Group	www.rollinssearch.com
Romac International	www.romacintl.com
Roz Goldfarb Associates	www.rgarecruiting.com
Sanford Rose Associates	www.sanfordrose.com
Self Opportunity	www.selfopportunity.com
Semper International	www.semperllc.com
Silverman McGovern Staffing	www.silvermanmcgovern.com
SnagAJob	www.snagajob.com
Solomon Page Executive Search	www.spges.com
Sonasearch	www.sonasearch.com
Spherion Corporation	www.spherion.com
Stanley, Barber & Associates	http://stanleyb.net
Student Search System, Inc.	www.studentsearch.com
TechNix Inc. [Canada]	www.technix.ca
TMP Worldwide	www.tmp.com
Volt Information Sciences	www.volt.com
Winter, Wyman & Co.	www.winterwyman.com
The Virtual Coach	www.virtual-coach.com
Yoh Company	www.yoh.com
Amy Zimmerman & Associates, Inc.	www.weemployyou.net

Security/Building & Business

Fire and Security Jobs	www.fireandsecurityjobs.net
iHireSecurity.com	www.ihiresecurity.com

Insecure.org	http://seclists.org
Just Security Jobs	www.justsecurityjobs.com
Maritime Security Jobs	www.maritimesecurityjobs.com
Private Security Jobs	www.privatesecurityjobs.com
Public Safety Jobs	www.publicsafetyjobs.com
SecurityFocus.com	www.securityfocus.com
SecurityJobs.com	www.securityjobs.com
Security Jobs Network	www.securityjobs.net
SecurityJobsToday.com	www.securityjobstoday.com
Transportation Security Administration	www.tsa.gov

Senior Workers/Mature Workers/"Retired" Workers

AARP	www.aarp.org/work
BoomerCareer.com	www.boomercareer.com
50Connect.co.uk [United Kingdom]	www.50connect.co.uk
GeezerJobs.com	www.geezerjobs.com
PrimeCB.com	www.primecb.com
RetiredBrains	www.retiredbrains.com
TheRetiredWorker.com	www.theretiredworker.com
RetirementJobs.com	www.retirementjobs.com
SeniorJobBank.com	www.seniorjobbank.com
Seniors4Hire.org	www.seniors4hire.org
SeniorsforJobs.com	www.seniorsforjobs.com

Social Service/Human Service

ExOffenderReentry.com	www.exoffenderreentry.com
Georgia Department of Human Resources	www.dhrjobs.com
HSCareers.com	www.hscareers.com
iHireSocialServices.com	www.ihiresocialservices.com
Human Services Career Network	www.hscareers.com

JobsinSocialWork [United Kingdom]   www.jobsinsocialwork.com

Jobs.ThirdSector.co.uk [United Kingdom]   http://jobs.thirdsector.co.uk/

National Association of Social Workers Joblink   www.socialworkers.org

The New Social Worker's Online Career Center   www.socialworker.com

SocialService.com   www.socialservice.com

socialservicenetwork.com   www.socialservicenetwork.com

SocialWorkJobBank.com   www.socialworkjobbank.com

Tripod   www.tripod.lycos.com

Worklife Solutions   www.worklifesolutions.com

Statistical

American Statistical Association Statistics Career Center   www.amstat.org/careers

icrunchdata.com   www.icrunchdata.com

Mathematical Association of America   www.mathclassifieds.com

Math-Jobs.com   www.math-jobs.com

MathJobs.org   www.mathjobs.org

Phds.org   www.phds.org

San Francisco Bay Area ASA   www.sfasa.org/joblist.htm

StatisticsJobs.com   www.statisticsjobs.com

Statistics Jobs in Australia & New Zealand   www.statsci.org/jobs/

StatsCareers   www.statscareers.com

-T-

Telecommunications

Active Wireless   www.activewireless.com

Alden Systems   www.telcorock.com

Anywhere You Go   www.anywhereyougo.com

BroadbandCareers.com   www.broadband-careers.com

Cellular-News.com	www.cellular-news.com
CTIA	www.ctia.org
Fierce Wireless	www.fiercewireless.com
MobileWirelessJobs.com	www.mobilewirelessjobs.com
PlanetRecruit [United Kingdom]	www.planetrecruit.com
RF Job Network	www.rfjn.com
Telecom Careers	www.telecomcareers.net
Telecom Jobs	www.telecomcareers.net
Telecom Jobsite	www.telecomjobsite.com
Telecommunication Industry Association Online	www.tiaonline.org
Telepeople	www.telepeople.net
Teletron	www.telecomcareers.com
Utility Jobs Online	www.utilityjobsonline.com
Wirelessmobile-Jobsboard.com [United Kingdom]	www.wirelessmobile-jobsboard.com
Workaholics4Hire.com	www.workaholics4hire.com

Telecommuting

GenerationMom.com	www.generationmom.com
MommysPlace.net	www.mommysplace.net
Telecommuting Jobs	www.tjobs.com
Telecommuting Techies	www.telecommuting-techies.com
TeleworkRecruiting.com	www.teleworkrecruiting.com
VirtualAssistants.com	www.virtualassistants.com
VirtualVocations	www.virtualvocations.com
WhyDoWork	www.whydowork.com

Trade Organizations

American Industrial Hygiene Association	www.aiha.org
Biotechnology Industry Organization	www.bio.org

Building Industry Exchange	www.building.org
Drilling Research Institute	www.drillers.com
Drug Information Association Employment Opportunities	www.diahome.org
Equipment Leasing and Finance Association	www.elfaonline.org
Financial Executives Institute Career Center	www.financialexecutives.org
GamesIndustry.biz	www.gamesindustry.biz
Institute of Food Science & Technology	www.ifst.org
Institute of Real Estate Management Jobs Bulletin	www.irem.org
International Association of Conference Centers Online	www.iacconline.org
International Association of Employment Web Sites	www.employmentwebsites.org
International Map Trade Association	www.maptrade.org
Media Communications Association International Job Hotline	www.mca-i.org
National Association for Printing Leadership	www.napl.org
National Contract Management Association	www.ncmahq.org
National Federation of Paralegal Associations Career Center	www.paralegals.org
National Field Selling Association	www.nfsa.com
National Fire Prevention Association Online Career Center	www.nfpa.org
National Weather Association	www.nwas.org
Petroleum Services Association of Canada Employment	www.psac.ca
Risk & Insurance Management Society Careers	www.rims.org
Securities Industry Association Career Resource Center	www.sifma.com
Sheet Metal and Air Conditioning Contractor's Association	www.smacna.org
Society of Automotive Engineers Job Board	http://careercenter.sae.org

Society of Risk Analysis Opportunities	www.sra.org/opportunities.php
SteelontheNet.com	www.steelonthenet.com
Technical Association of the Pulp & Paper Industry Career Center	http://careers.tappi.org
Telecommunication Industry Association Online	www.tiaonline.org

Training

American Society for Law Enforcement Training	www.aslet.org
American Society for Training & Development	http://jobs.astd.org Job Bank
Instructional Systems Technology Jobs	www.indiana.edu
International Society for Performance Improvement Job Bank	www.ispi.org
OD Network	www.odnetwork.org
Saba	www.saba.com
San Francisco State University Instructional Technologies	www.itec.sfsu.edu
TrainingConsortium.com	www.trainingconsortium.com
Training Forum	www.trainingforum.com
Trainingjob.com	www.trainingjob.com

Transportation, Land & Maritime

The Airline Employment Assistance Corps	www.avjobs.com
All Port Jobs	www.allportjobs.com
All-Trucking-Jobs.com	www.all-trucking-jobs.com
AviaNation.com	www.avianation.com
Aviation Employee Placement Service	www.aeps.com
Aviation Employment.com	www.aviationemployment.com
BigRigJobs	www.bigrigjobs.com
Careers in Gear	www.careersingear.com
CDLjobs.com	www.cdljobs.com

Classatransport.com	www.classatransport.com
Climbto350.com	www.climbto350.com
DrivingJobsBoard.co.uk [United Kingdom]	www.drivingjobsboard.co.uk
FastLaneHIres	www.fastlanehires.com
Find a Pilot	www.findapilot.com
FindaTruckingJob.com	www.findatruckingjob.com
Get Maritime Jobs	www.getmaritimejobs.com
Get Taxi Limo Jobs	www.gettaxilimojobs.com
HotCDLJobs.com	www.hotcdljobs.com
International Seafarers Exchange JobXchange	www.jobxchange.com
Jobs4Trucking.com	www.jobs4trucking.com
JobsinLogistics.com	www.jobsinlogistics.com
JobsinTrucks.com	www.jobsintrucks.com
Just Rail [United Kingdom]	www.justrail.net
Layover.com	www.layover.com
Maritime Career	www.maritimecareer.com
Maritime Employment	www.maritimeemployment.com
Maritime Job Search	www.maritimejobsearch.com
MaritimeJobs.com	www.maritimejobs.com
Maritime Security Jobs	www.maritimesecurityjobs.com
National Parking Association	http://careers.npapark.org
Oil Offshore Marine	www.oil-offshore-marine.com
RailJobSearch.com [United Kingdom]	www.railjobsearch.com
RoadTechs.com	www.roadtechs.com
TransportationJobStore.com	www.transportationjobstore.com
TruckDriver.com	www.truckdriver.com
TruckerJobSearch.com	www.truckerjobsearch.com
Truck Net	www.truck.net
TruckingJobs	www.truckingjobs.com
TruckinJobs	www.truckinjobs.com

Travel & Tourism

Adventure Travel Trade Association	www.adventuretravel.biz
Hcareers	www.hcareers.com
Job.com	www.job.com
JobDango.com	www.jobdango.com
JobsinCatering [United Kingdom]	www.jobsincatering.com
Season Workers [United Kingdom]	www.seasonworkers.com
SeasonalEmployment.com	www.seasonalemployment.com
Seasonal-Jobs.com [United Kingdom]	www.seasonal-jobs.com
TravelJobSearch.com [United Kingdom]	www.traveljobsearch.com
Vault	www.vault.com
WomensJobList.com	www.womensjoblist.com

-V-

Video - Resume & Interview

HireVue	www.hirevue.com
JobPlant.co.uk [United Kingdom]	www.jobplant.co.uk
MyPersonalBroadcast	www.mypersonalbroadcast.com
VideoJobShop	www.videojobshop.com
Workblast	www.workblast.com

Volunteer Positions

Do-It [United Kingdom]	www.do-it.org.uk
GlobalCrossroad.com	www.globalcrossroad.com
Jobs.ThirdSector.co.uk [United Kingdom]	http://jobs.thirdsector.co.uk/
Monster.com	www.monster.com
Volunteer Match	www.volunteermatch.org
VSO Worldwide Vacancies [United Kingdom]	www.vso.org.uk

-Y-

Young Adult/Teen Positions

CanadaParttime.com	www.canadaparttime.com
CoolWorks.com	www.coolworks.com
GrooveJob.com	www.groovejob.com
HotRecruit [United Kingdom]	www.hotrecruit.com
InternsWanted	www.campusinternships.com
TheJobBox.com	www.thejobbox.com
JobDoggy.com	www.jobdoggy.com
MySpace	www.myspace.com/careers
Part-Time Jobs	www.gotajob.com
SnagaJob	www.snagajob.com
StudentJobs.gov	www.usajobs.gov/studentjobs/
Summerjobs.com	www.summerjobs.com
Teens4Hire	www.teens4hire.org
TeenJobSection.com	www.teenjobsection.com